American Literature

by Molly Harrington Dugan

AGS®

American Guidance Service, Inc.
Circle Pines, Minnesota 55014-1796
800-328-2560

About the Author

Molly Harrington Dugan received her Bachelor of Arts from the University of Baltimore and her Master of Education in American Literature from Loyola College, both in Maryland. She has taught English in junior and senior high schools for several years. Ms. Dugan also spent fourteen years as an educational consultant for *The Baltimore Sun*. In this capacity she developed newspaper education courses, curricula, and student workbooks, including *Getting Along* and *Maryland, Our Maryland*.

She has also been an instructor and assistant professor in journalism and in education at various colleges, including Towson University, Western Maryland College, Morgan State University, and Loyola College. In addition, she is the author of *Famous Physical Scientists*, a book on reading in the content area.

Literature Consultant

Jack Cassidy, Ph.D.
Texas A&M University
Corpus Christi, Texas

Original cover art: Connie Hayes

Printed in the United States of America

ISBN 0-7854-1879-2

Product Number 93000

A 0 9 8 7 6 5 4 3 2 1

Contents

Unit 7 Contemporary American Literature: 1971–Present 413

How to Use This Book

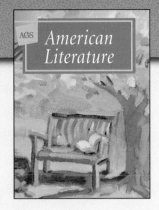

This book is an anthology of American Literature. An anthology is a collection of literature written by different authors. The literature can be poems, plays, short stories, essays, parts of novels, folktales, legends, or myths. Sometimes, an anthology is organized around selections from a certain country or continent. For example, you might also have an anthology with great literature from America. The first section of an American literature anthology might include a section with early American Indian poetry or Puritan diaries. Sometimes, anthologies are organized around different types of literature (genre). Then, you might have sections on poems, short stories, plays, essays, or folktales.

Why is a literature anthology important?

This anthology contains much enjoyable literature. An anthology helps you understand yourself and other people. Sometimes, you will read about people from other countries. Sometimes, you will read about people who lived in the past. Try to relate what the author is saying to your own life. Have I ever felt this way? Have I known anyone like this person? Have I seen anything like this?

A literature anthology can also help you appreciate the beauty of language. As you read, find phrases or sentences that you particularly like. You may want to start a notebook of these. You could also include words that are difficult.

This anthology is also important because it introduces you to great works of literature. Many times, you will find references to these works in everyday life. Sometimes, you will hear a quotation on TV or read it in the newspaper. Reading great literature helps you to become more literate. Generally, literate people are more likely to get better paying jobs.

What is in this book?

This book is filled with interesting works of literature. Great literature can come in many forms. On the next page are definitions of some kinds of literature genres in an anthology.

Genre Definitions

autobiography The story of a person's life written by that person.

biography The story of a person's life written by someone else. You will find many biographies of famous authors in this book.

diary A record of personal events, thoughts, or private feelings. Usually people write in a diary every day or weekly. Mostly, people write diaries for themselves. Sometimes authors will create a fictional diary.

drama A play that often involves intense emotional conflict. Usually, a drama is serious.

essay A written work that shows a writer's opinions on some basic or current issue.

fable A short story or poem with a moral, often with animals who act like humans. Aesop was a famous author of fables.

fiction Writing that is made up and usually intended to entertain. Fiction is usually in prose form. Short stories, novels, folktales, myths, legends, and most plays are works of fiction.

folktale A story that has been handed down from one generation to another. The characters are usually either good or bad. Folktales make use of rhyme and repetitive phrases. Sometimes, they are called tall tales, particularly if they are humorous and exaggerated. They are also called folklore.

journal Writing that expresses an author's feelings or first impressions about a subject. A journal is like a diary, but it expresses more of the author's feelings. Sometimes, students keep journals that give their feelings about what they have read.

legend A traditional story that at one time was told orally and was handed down from one generation to another. Legends are like myths, but they do not have as many supernatural forces. Usually, they have some historical base.

myth A story designed to explain the mysteries of life. A myth explains natural events, such as the change of seasons. Like fables and folktales, myths were first oral stories. Most early cultures have myths.

nonfiction Writing about real people and events. Nonfiction is usually designed to explain, argue, or describe. Essays, speeches, diaries, journals, autobiographies, and biographies are all usually nonfiction.

novel Fiction that is book-length and has more plot and character details than a short story.

poem A short piece of literature that usually has rhythm and paints powerful or beautiful impressions with words. Often, poems have sound patterns such as rhyme. Songs are poetry set to music. Prose is the opposite of poetry.

prose Written language that is not verse. Short stories, novels, autobiographies, biographies, diaries, journals, and essays are examples of prose.

science fiction A type of literature that deals with people, places, and events that could not happen in our reality. However, science fiction is sometimes based on projected scientific developments. Most stories are set in the future. Stories about space are examples of science fiction. Jules Verne was one of the first science fiction authors.

short story A brief prose narrative. Short stories are designed to create unified impressions forcefully. Edgar Allan Poe was a great writer of short stories.

What is a literary term?

Literary terms are words or phrases that we use to study and discuss works of literature. These terms describe the devices that an author uses to make us enjoy and understand what we are reading. Some of the terms also describe a genre. In this anthology, you will see shaded boxes on the side of the Introducing the Selection pages that define some literary terms. These terms are important in understanding and discussing the selection being read. By understanding these literary terms, we can appreciate the author's craft.

Below are literary terms that apply to all works of literature. You should be familiar with these terms as you read this anthology. All of the literary terms used in this book can be found in the Handbook of Literary Terms on page 460.

Literary Terms

autobiography a story about a person's life written by that person

setting the place and time in a story

Key Literary Term Definitions

characterization The devices authors use to reveal characters. Characters are revealed by their actions, speech, appearance, others' comments, or the author's comments.

conflict The struggle the main character of a story faces. Conflict is an important part of the plot of a short story or novel. Main characters can struggle against themselves, other people, society, or nature. The four types of conflict are defined as person-against-person, person-against-self, person-against-society, and person-against-nature.

plot The series of events in a story. The plot shows what happens to the characters. Plots have conflict and resolutions to that conflict. Plots are very important in stories. Plots should have rising action, foreshadowing, a climax, and falling action.

setting The time and place in a story. Sometimes authors describe the setting in detail. Sometimes, the setting is left unclear so the reader can imagine it. A setting can even be a person's mind.

theme The idea that holds the whole piece of literature together. A theme is a generalization about humankind that the author wants to make. Themes are underlying statements about a topic. A theme is the topic of a piece of literature and the author's opinion about that topic.

How do I read this book?

Different works of literature should be read in different ways. However, there are some strategies that you should use with all works of literature.

Before beginning a unit:
- Read the unit title and selection titles.
- Read any introductory paragraphs about the unit.
- Look at the pictures and other graphics in the unit. There may be timelines or maps to help you.
- Think about the unit's main topic.
- Think about what you want to learn about this topic.
- Think about what you already know about the unit.
- Develop questions in your mind that you think will be answered in this unit.

Before beginning the reading of a selection:
- Read the selection's title.
- Look at the pictures and other visuals.
- Read the background material included in About the Author and About the Selection.
- Predict what you think the selection is going to be about.
- Ask yourself questions about the material.

As you read the selections:
- Think about the predictions that you made before reading. Were they right?
- Make new predictions as you read.
- Read the notes in the side columns. These will help you understand and think about the main concepts.
- Think of people or events in your own life that are similar to those described.
- Reread sentences or paragraphs that you do not understand.
- Refer to the definitions at the bottom of the page for words that you do not know.
- In a notebook or on note cards, record words that you do not know. Also, record words defined in the text that you find interesting or unusual.

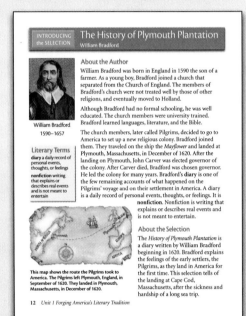

| affirm to state positively | miseries things that cause one to suffer | tedious tiresome; boring |

REVIEWING the SELECTION

The History of Plymouth Plantation
William Bradford

Directions Write the answers to these questions using complete sentences.

Comprehension: Identifying Facts

1. What did the people do when they reached land?

2. Which season of the year did the settlers face when they first arrived?

3. What separated the settlers from the "civil parts of the world"?

Comprehension: Understanding Main Ideas

4. What is the mood of Bradford's writing?

5. What things did the settlers fear in the new land?

6. How does the last paragraph seem more positive than others?

Understanding Literature: Diary
The History of Plymouth Plantation is a chronicle, or diary. This type of writing means that the story is a true account of the events told in the order in which they happened. A diary is usually a personal account; however, sometimes a diary is written for others to read. In this case, Bradford's diary is one of the very few records we have of life in 1620–1621 at Plymouth Plantation.

7. Does Bradford's diary give you a good idea about life at Plymouth? Why or why not?

8. In what ways does this diary seem like it was meant to be read by others?

Critical Thinking

9. What part of this story did you like best? Why?

10. Do you think you would have liked to be a Pilgrim? Why or why not?

 Writing on Your Own Use your imagination to write a diary entry as if you are a colonist seeing America in the 1600s for the first time. Use what you have learned about a diary and about America in the 1600s to do one of the following: describe what you see, explain your fears, or tell what you have done recently.

Forging America's Literary Tradition Unit 1 **15**

After reading the selections:

■ Think about the questions that you asked yourself before you read. Were your answers to these questions right?

■ Reread interesting or difficult parts of the selection.

■ Reflect on what you have learned.

■ Write the answers to the review questions in the Reviewing the Selection.

■ Use graphic organizers to help you organize and remember information. (See "What is a graphic organizer?" on page 5 to get some ideas.)

How do I read specific types of literature?

The strategies already described will work for all kinds of literature, but some types of literature need specific strategies.

When reading poetry:

■ Read the poem aloud.

■ Listen to the sounds of the words.

■ Picture the images the author is describing.

■ Reread poems over and over again to appreciate the author's use of language.

When reading essays:

■ Review the questions in the Reviewing the Selection before you begin reading.

■ Use the questions to help you make your own predictions before reading.

■ Remember that essays usually express an author's opinions. Try to understand how the author arrived at these opinions.

When reading plays:

■ Picture the setting of the play. Usually, you do not have much description. Try to relate it to what you have seen before.

■ Pay attention to the dialogue. How does the dialogue reveal the character's personality? Have you ever known anyone like this? Are you like this?

What is a graphic organizer?

A graphic organizer is visual representation of information. It can help you see how ideas are related to each other. A graphic organizer can help you study for a test or organize information before writing an essay. Following are some examples.

Character Analysis Guide

The graphic organizer below can help you better understand characters in a story or real people in a biography or autobiography. Fill in the character trait on the ray and then list events in the story or in the person's life that demonstrate that character trait.

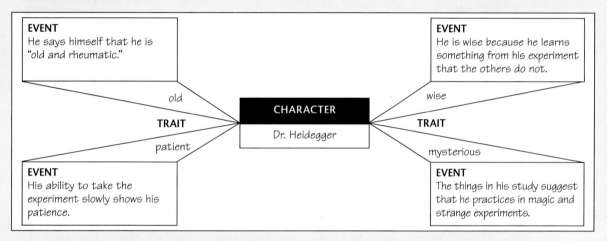

EVENT
He says himself that he is "old and rheumatic."

EVENT
He is wise because he learns something from his experiment that the others do not.

old

wise

TRAIT

CHARACTER
Dr. Heidegger

TRAIT

patient

mysterious

EVENT
His ability to take the experiment slowly shows his patience.

EVENT
The things in his study suggest that he practices in magic and strange experiments.

Venn Diagram

The Venn Diagram below and to the right can help you compare and contrast two characters, two authors, or two pieces of literature. List the similarities on the overlap between the circles. List the differences on the parts of the circles that do not overlap.

Remember that all graphic organizers can be used in various ways. They can be used to help you organize your writing. They can be used to help you analyze your thoughts, and they can be used to help you study for a test. You can even create your own graphic organizer.

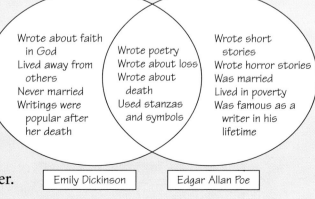

Wrote about faith in God
Lived away from others
Never married
Writings were popular after her death

Wrote poetry
Wrote about loss
Wrote about death
Used stanzas and symbols

Wrote short stories
Wrote horror stories
Was married
Lived in poverty
Was famous as a writer in his lifetime

Emily Dickinson

Edgar Allan Poe

What strategies should I use when I encounter a word that I don't know?

■ If the word is boldface, look for the definition of the word at the bottom of the page.
■ If the word is not boldface, read to the end of the sentence and maybe the next sentence. Can you determine the unknown word now?
■ If your teacher has given you a Selection Glossary, use it to look up additional terms that are not boldface.
■ Look at the beginning sound of the unknown word.
■ Ask yourself, "What word would make sense here that begins with this sound"?
■ Sound out the syllables of the word.
■ If you still cannot determine the unknown word, see if you know any parts of the word: prefixes, suffixes, or roots.
■ If this does not work, write the word on a note card or in a vocabulary notebook and look it up in the dictionary after you have finished reading the selection.
■ If the word is necessary to understand the passage, look it up in a dictionary or glossary immediately.

Word Study Tip

■ Start a vocabulary file with note cards to use for review.
■ Write one word on the front of each card. Write the unit number, selection title, and the definition on the back.
■ You can use these cards as flash cards by yourself or with a study partner to test your knowledge.

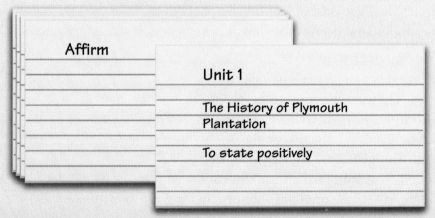

Affirm

Unit 1

The History of Plymouth Plantation

To state positively

What should I know about taking a literature test?

Before the test day:

- Read all the works assigned.
- Review your class notes, the Unit Summary, and the Unit Review.
- Ask your teacher what kinds of questions will be on the test.
- Review any notes that you have taken or graphic organizers developed.
- Try to predict what questions will be asked and develop answers to those questions.
- Review the Test-Taking Tips at the bottom of the Unit Review pages in this book.

UNIT 1 SUMMARY

Unit 1 covers 1620 to 1849. The development of new colonies, the struggle between Europeans and American Indians, and the American Revolution took place during this time.

Four styles of literature—native, colonial, revolutionary, and early national—represent early America. Native literature in this unit includes American Indian poems and a myth that had been passed down orally. Colonial literature in this unit includes the works of William Bradford, Anne Dudley Bradstreet, and Benjamin Franklin. These writings copied European styles. The revolutionary literature in this unit is by Thomas Paine, a writer during the American Revolution. Early national literature came about in the 1800s. Two professional writers, Washington Irving and Edgar Allan Poe, were part of this movement. They studied the inner workings of people and society. Early national literature began to replace letters, essays, and speeches that were popular in the past.

- "To My Dear and Loving Husband" by Anne Dudley Bradstreet is a love poem from a wife to her husband.
- The selection from *Poor Richard's Almanac* by Benjamin Franklin is a list of aphorisms, or clever sayings.
- *The American Crisis, Number 1* by Thomas Paine is a pamphlet that expresses the desire for freedom and urges Americans to continue their struggle against England.
- "Wouter Van Twiller" by Washington Irving is a sketch that uses satire and exaggeration to poke fun at a man's undeserved fame.
- Three American Indian poems by the Omaha, Sioux, and Chippewa express American Indian attitudes toward death and love for the land.
- "The Origin of Plumage" is an Iroquois myth, or story that explains how something in the natural world came to be. This myth explains how all birds got their feathers.
- "The Black Cat" by Edgar Allan Poe is a horror short story about one man's madness and his cat.
- "Annabel Lee" by Edgar Allan Poe is a poem about the grief caused by the death of a lover.

UNIT 1 REVIEW

Directions Write the answers to these questions using complete sentences.

Comprehension: Identifying Facts

1. Why did the Puritans and Pilgrims leave England?
2. What was established in the South?
3. Who were three political leaders of the 1700s?
4. Which two authors in this unit represent the time after the American Revolution?
5. Who were the very first people to live in America?

Comprehension: Understanding Main Ideas

6. What similarities and differences can you see in the works of Washington Irving and Edgar Allan Poe? How did each writer's background affect his works?
7. Describe the similarities and differences found in the poetry of Anne Dudley Bradstreet and Edgar Allan Poe.

8. How does Benjamin Franklin's writing differ from William Bradford's? Are their writings similar in any way? Explain your answer.
9. In what ways are the American Indian poems in this unit similar to and different from the other poetry in this unit?
10. What are three common themes of the selections in this unit?

Understanding Literature: Fiction and Nonfiction

Most early American literature is nonfiction and based on writing styles used in Europe. Nonfiction describes actual people and real events. Toward the middle of the nineteenth century, fiction was introduced. Fiction describes imaginary characters and made-up events. An American style of writing also developed.

11. Identify each selection in Unit 1 by genre (poem, short story, essay, etc.). If the work is not a poem, tell whether the selection is fiction or nonfiction.
12. Choose two works from Unit 1. How are these two works different? Compare these two selections for language, style, content, and characters.

13. Write the name of the selection from Unit 1 that surprised you the most. Explain the reasons for your choice.
14. Which selection from this unit describes life in America best? Why?
15. Is it important for a nation to have its own style of writing? Explain.

Critical Thinking

16. Anne Dudley Bradstreet is the only woman represented in this unit. Do you think she would be admired today? Explain your answer.
17. Do you like the early American literature from this unit? Why or why not?
18. Explain what you think is most important about early American literature.
19. Which author from this unit did you like best? Why?
20. Which poem from this unit did you like best? Why?

Speak and Listen

Think how society has changed since the 1800s. What are some ways in which modern life is different from the life of a young person who lived 150 to 200 years ago? What is the one thing that you would miss most if you were to go back

in time to the 1800s? For your class, prepare a brief speech that answers these questions. Think about what you will say. Make a few notes to help you remember what to say. Practice by giving your speech to a partner. Listen to your partner's speech and give each other suggestions. Then you are ready to give your speech to the class.

Beyond Words

Review the selections included in Unit 1. Think about how you might illustrate one poem or story. Draw a picture or poster that illustrates some selection in this unit.

Writing on Your Own Write an essay describing your favorite selection from Unit 1. Explain why you liked the selection, how it made you feel, and what you learned by reading it. Include an introductory sentence, a body, and a conclusion.

Test-Taking Tip Avoid waiting until the night before a test to study. Plan your time so that you can get a good night's sleep the night before a test.

During the test:

- Come to the test with a positive attitude.
- Preview the test and read the directions carefully.
- Plan your time.
- Answer the essay questions and the questions that you know first.
- Go back and answer the more difficult questions.
- Allow time to reread all of the questions and your answers.
- Put your name on the paper.

"These lands are ours. No one has a right to remove us, because we were the first owners. The Great Spirit above has appointed this place for us, on which to light our fires, and here we will remain."

—Tecumseh, Chief of the Shawnees, to Joseph Barron, messenger of President James Madison, 1810

"Our fathers were Englishmen which came over this great ocean, and were ready to perish in this wilderness."

—William Bradford, *The History of Plymouth Plantation*, 1620

UNIT 1 *Forging America's Literary Tradition: 1620–1849*

Think about what life would have been like 400 years ago. American Indians lived across a vast stretch of land. There was a time when American Indians had never seen a European. But in 1620, all that changed. Colonists from Europe came to the "new land" to live. For the next 200 years, this part of the world went through extreme changes. Many chose to express themselves with writing. This was the beginning of American literature.

In this unit, you will learn the historical beginnings of America and study some of the first American literature.

The seventeenth century (also called the 1600s) was a time of promise for European colonists living in what later would be called America. Colonies grew as men and women came from Europe to look for religious freedom, riches, and opportunities. There they joined the American Indians who had lived on the land for hundreds of years. It marked the beginning of the long struggle between native peoples in America and colonists who took over American Indian lands.

The European settlers found opportunities and hardships in this new land. Staying alive was very difficult work, at first. The Pilgrims and the Puritans were two of the first groups to come to America. They came to seek religious freedom. Other colonists started plantations in the South. These plantations were large farms that used slave labor to grow crops. Enslaved Africans were brought against their will to America to work for colonists. Many enslaved Africans ended up working on plantations.

Conflict, both religious and political, existed between the colonists and England. This conflict would later cause the American Revolution. This was the struggle between the colonies and England over independence during the 1770s and 1780s. Thomas Jefferson, Benjamin Franklin, George Washington, and other colonial representatives of the Continental Congress combined the energies of the thirteen colonies. The colonists fought for and earned independence from England after an eight-year struggle.

The growth of America after the American Revolution included the development of new states and new territories, along with westward movement during the years 1790 to 1830.

LITERATURE

1620 William Bradford begins to write *The History of Plymouth Plantation*

1650 Anne Dudley Bradstreet's poems, including "To My Dear and Loving Husband," are published

1732 Benjamin Franklin prints *Poor Richard's Almanac*, published annually until 1757

1620   1640   1660   1680   1700   1720   1740

HISTORY

1630 Puritans settle Massachusetts Bay Colony

1620 Pilgrims land at Plymouth, Massachusetts

British ships such as these brought soldiers to and from the colonies during the Revolutionary War.

Improvements in industry—mostly mills and factories—meant more jobs. Better transportation developed with the steamboat and the steam locomotive.

There were four literary styles in this time period. These include native literature, colonial literature, revolutionary literature, and early national literature.

The native literature in this unit includes American Indian poems and myths, originally passed down orally and later written down. The myth is titled "The Origin of Plumage." The colonial literature includes William Bradford's *The History of Plymouth Plantation*, which records the emotions of Pilgrims landing on a new shore in a new land. Anne Dudley Bradstreet's "To My Dear and Loving Husband" reflects the feelings of a Puritan woman for her husband. The selection from Ben Franklin's *Poor Richard's Almanac* is a group of clever sayings about life.

Revolutionary literature in this unit is represented by Thomas Paine's *The American Crisis, Number 1*. His writing brought Americans together in their struggle against the British. The early national period is reflected in this unit with Washington Irving's "Wouter Van Twiller," a story about a man who, in spite of his popularity, is not what he seems. There are two works in this unit by another early national writer, Edgar Allan Poe. These include the moving love poem "Annabel Lee" and the horrifying tale "The Black Cat." Irving's and Poe's writing marked the beginning of a truly American form of writing.

LITERATURE

1776 Thomas Paine writes *The American Crisis, Number 1*

1819 Washington Irving publishes his first stories

1843 Edgar Allan Poe's "The Black Cat" is first published

1849 Edgar Allan Poe's "Annabel Lee" is first published

1740   1760   1780   1800   1820   1840   1860

1754 French and Indian War begins

1775 Battles at Lexington and Concord begin the Revolutionary War

1776 America declares its independence from England

1783 Treaty of Paris ends the Revolutionary War

1800 U.S. census shows 5,308,483 people live in the United States

1812 United States declares war on England

1803 Louisiana Purchase doubles area of the United States

HISTORY

Forging America's Literary Tradition Unit 1   **11**

The History of Plymouth Plantation
William Bradford

William Bradford
1590–1657

Literary Terms

diary a daily record of personal events, thoughts, or feelings

nonfiction writing that explains or describes real events and is not meant to entertain

About the Author

William Bradford was born in England in 1590 the son of a farmer. As a young boy, Bradford joined a church that separated from the Church of England. The members of Bradford's church were not treated well by those of other religions, and eventually moved to Holland.

Although Bradford had no formal schooling, he was well educated. The church members were university trained. Bradford learned languages, literature, and the Bible.

The church members, later called Pilgrims, decided to go to America to set up a new religious colony. Bradford joined them. They traveled on the ship the *Mayflower* and landed at Plymouth, Massachusetts, in December of 1620. After the landing on Plymouth, John Carver was elected governor of the colony. After Carver died, Bradford was chosen governor. He led the colony for many years. Bradford's **diary** is one of the few remaining accounts of what happened on the Pilgrims' voyage and on their settlement in America. A diary is a daily record of personal events, thoughts, or feelings. It is **nonfiction**. Nonfiction is writing that explains or describes real events and is not meant to entertain.

About the Selection

The *History of Plymouth Plantation* is a diary written by William Bradford beginning in 1620. Bradford explains the feelings of the early settlers, the Pilgrims, as they land in America for the first time. This selection tells of the landing at Cape Cod, Massachusetts, after the sickness and hardship of a long sea trip.

This map shows the route the Pilgrims took to America. The Pilgrims left Plymouth, England, in September of 1620. They landed in Plymouth, Massachusetts, in December of 1620.

from The History of Plymouth Plantation

Of Their Safe Arrival at Cape Cod

Being thus arrived in a good harbor and brought safe to land, they fell upon their knees and blessed the God of heaven who had brought them over the vast and furious ocean, and delivered them from all perils and **miseries** thereof, again to set their feet on the firm and stable earth, their proper element. And no marvel if they were thus joyful, seeing wise Seneca was so affected with sailing a few miles on the coast of his own Italy, as he **affirmed**, that he had rather remain twenty years on his way by land than pass by sea to any place in a short time, so **tedious** and dreadful was the same unto him.

But here I cannot but stay and make a pause, and stand half amazed at this poor people's present condition; and so I think will the reader, too, when he well considers the same. Being thus past the vast ocean, and a sea of troubles before in their preparation (as may be remembered by that which went

How is William Bradford's diary like or unlike diaries you have written or read?

Seneca refers to Lucius Annaeus Seneca, who was a Roman statesman who lived about 4 B.C. to A.D. 65.

affirm to state positively

miseries things that cause one to suffer

tedious tiresome; boring

Scripture is a book or passage from the Bible. An *Apostle* is a biblical reference to a person sent out to preach the teachings of Jesus.

before), they had now no friends to welcome them nor inns to entertain or refresh their weatherbeaten bodies; no houses or much less towns to repair to, to seek for **succor**. It is recorded in Scripture as a mercy to the Apostle and his shipwrecked company, that the **barbarians** showed them no small kindness in refreshing them, but these savage barbarians, when they met with them (as after will appear) were readier to fill their sides full of arrows than otherwise. And for the season it was winter, and they that know the winters of that country know them to be sharp and violent, and subject to cruel and fierce storms, dangerous to travel to known places, much more to search an unknown coast. Besides, what could they see but a hideous and **desolate** wilderness, full of wild beasts and wild men—and what **multitudes** there might be of them they knew not. Neither could they, as it were, go up to the top of Pisgah to view from this wilderness a more goodly country to feed their hopes; for which way soever they turned their eyes (saved upward to the heavens) they could have little **solace** or content in respect of any outward objects. For summer being done, all things stand upon them with a weatherbeaten face, and the whole country, full of woods and thickets, represented a wild and savage hue. If they looked behind them, there was the mighty ocean which they had passed and was now as a main bar and gulf to separate them from all the civil parts of the world. . . .

The word *Pisgah* is the name of a mountain in Jordan from which Moses saw the Promised Land.

What could now **sustain** them but the Spirit of God and His grace? May not and ought not the children of these fathers rightly say "Our fathers were Englishmen which came over this great ocean, and were ready to perish in this wilderness; but they cried unto the Lord, and He heard their voice and looked on their **adversity**. Let them therefore praise the Lord, because He is good: and His mercies endure forever."

adversity a state of misfortune	**desolate** lacking inhabitants	**solace** relief; comfort
		succor to aid or help
barbarian one who is not thought to be civilized; Bradford was referring to American Indians here	**multitude** a great number	**sustain** to give support or relief

Directions Write the answers to these questions using complete sentences.

Comprehension: Identifying Facts

1. What did the people do when they reached land?

2. Which season of the year did the settlers face when they first arrived?

3. What separated the settlers from the "civil parts of the world"?

Comprehension: Understanding Main Ideas

4. What is the mood of Bradford's writing?

5. What things did the settlers fear in the new land?

6. How does the last paragraph seem more positive than others?

Understanding Literature: Diary

The History of Plymouth Plantation is a chronicle, or diary. This type of writing means that the story is a true account of the events told in the order in which they happened. A diary is usually a personal account; however, sometimes a diary is written for others to read. In this case, Bradford's diary is one of the very few records we have of life in 1620–1621 at Plymouth Plantation.

7. Does Bradford's diary give you a good idea about life at Plymouth? Why or why not?

8. In what ways does this diary seem like it was meant to be read by others?

Critical Thinking

9. What part of this story did you like best? Why?

10. Do you think you would have liked to be a Pilgrim? Why or why not?

Writing on Your Own Use your imagination to write a diary entry as if you are a colonist seeing America in the 1600s for the first time. Use what you have learned about a diary and about America in the 1600s to do one of the following: describe what you see, explain your fears, or tell what you have done recently.

To My Dear and Loving Husband
Anne Dudley Bradstreet

Anne Dudley
Bradstreet
1612–1672

Literary Terms

couplet a rhyming pair

end rhyme a feature of a poem in which the last words of two lines rhyme with one another

image a word that appeals to our senses

metaphor a figure of speech that makes a comparison

About the Author

Born in Northampton, England, to a wealthy family, Anne Dudley was hardly prepared for her future life in rugged Massachusetts. She married a well-educated man, Simon Bradstreet. At the age of eighteen, she sailed with him to the Massachusetts Bay Colony in America. The harsh land certainly was not suited for her, but she and her husband settled into this different life. Her husband became the governor of the Massachusetts Bay Colony. Together they had eight children.

Unlike most Puritan women, Bradstreet was quite well educated. She used writing as both an escape from her harsh surroundings and as a creative outlet. A collection of her poems, called *The Tenth Muse Lately Sprung up in America,* was published in London in 1650. She became well known for her poetry and for her account of early colonial life in America.

About the Selection

"To My Dear and Loving Husband" is thought to be one of Bradstreet's best poems. It is thought to be a sincere reflection of the love between her and her husband, Simon Bradstreet. The emotions she expresses in the poem show how close she was to her husband and her family.

This poem makes use of **metaphors**, **images**, and **end rhymes**. A metaphor is a figure of speech that makes a comparison. An image is a word that appeals to our senses. An end rhyme occurs when the last words of two lines rhyme with one another. Each rhyming pair is called a **couplet**.

To My Dear and Loving Husband

If ever two were one, then surely we.

If ever man were loved by wife, then thee;

If ever wife was happy in a man,

4 Compare with me, ye women, if you can.

I prize thy love more than whole mines of gold

Or all the riches that the East doth hold.

My love is such that rivers cannot **quench**,

8 Nor ought but love from thee give **recompense**.

Thy love is such I can no way repay,

The heavens reward thee **manifold**, I pray.

Then while we live in love, let's so **persevere**

12 That when we live no more, we may live ever.

Notice the end rhymes in every two lines of this poem. The rhyming pairs, such as *we* and *thee*, are a couplet.

Simon Bradstreet
1603–1697

---

manifold many times; a great deal

persevere to continue in the face of difficulties

quench to cause to lose heat or warmth; to relieve or satisfy with liquid

recompense a reward or compensation; an equivalent or return for something done

To My Dear and Loving Husband
Anne Dudley Bradstreet

Directions Write the answers to these questions using complete sentences.

Comprehension: Identifying Facts

1. Which lines prove that the poet is happy in her marriage?

2. Which lines prove that the poet knows that her husband loves her as well?

3. How does the poet compare herself to other women?

Comprehension: Understanding Main Ideas

4. In what ways does the poet make this poem interesting?

5. How is the writing in this poem different from writing today?

6. What does the last line of the poem mean?

Understanding Literature: End Rhyme, Couplet, Image, and Metaphor

This poem contains end rhymes, which means that the last words in each pair of lines rhymes. Each rhyming pair is called a couplet. In this poem, *we* and *thee* rhyme in lines 1 and 2; *man* and *can* rhyme in lines 3 and 4. In the final two lines, the word *persevere* should be pronounced to rhyme with *ever*. The poem also includes images and metaphors. Images are word pictures that appeal to our senses, such as the words in line 7 "that rivers cannot quench." A metaphor is a figure of speech that makes a comparison. For example, in line 5, the poet compares her love to mines of gold.

7. What is a couplet?

8. What is a metaphor?

Critical Thinking

9. Do you think that someone could write a poem expressing these same emotions today? Explain your answer.

10. How do you think Simon Bradstreet felt when he received such a poem from his wife?

Writing on Your Own Write a poem about a person. In your poem, use end rhymes, at least one image, and one metaphor. Use "To My Dear and Loving Husband" as a guide.

Poor Richard's Almanac
Benjamin Franklin

Benjamin Franklin
1706–1790

Literary Terms

almanac a calendar and date book

aphorism a wise and clever saying

About the Author

Benjamin Franklin was perhaps one of the most interesting men in American history. He was born in Boston, Massachusetts, in 1706. As the fifteenth child in the family, he could not expect to be well educated, but young Franklin taught himself reading, science, and mathematics. He worked as a printer in Philadelphia. In 1729 he began producing *The Pennsylvania Gazette*. Soon after, in hopes of making more money, he began to produce an **almanac**, which was the calendar and date book of the day. Because of the popularity of its clever sayings, *Poor Richard's Almanac* became profitable.

Franklin is also known as a scientist and a statesman. Many people remember him as the man who discovered the electrical nature of lightning. As a statesman, Franklin did much to ensure the success of the American Revolution. His fame extended well beyond Philadelphia to all of the United States and to Europe, especially France and England.

About the Selection

The colonial family almost always had an almanac. For a printer, the almanac was very profitable because it appeared yearly. Franklin decided to print an almanac in 1732 to save his new printing business. He published his almanac under the pen name of Richard Saunders. Called *Poor Richard's Almanac*, it was extremely successful because of the many useful and clever "Sayings of Poor Richard."

Franklin published this almanac for twenty-six years. Americans who could barely read enjoyed the wise and clever sayings, called **aphorisms**, of Poor Richard. Reading these aphorisms today makes it clear that much of the wisdom of the eighteenth century is also the wisdom of the present.

Poor Richard's Almanac

Poor Richard, 1733.

AN

Almanack

For the Year of Chrift

1 7 3 3,

Being the Firft after LEAP YEAR:

And makes fince the Creation	Years
By the Account of the Eaftern *Greeks*	7241
By the Latih Church, when ☉ ent. ♈	6932
By the Con.putation of *W.W*.	5742
By the *Roman* Chronology	5682
By the *Jewifh* Rabbies	5494

Wherein is contained

The Lunations, Eclipfes, Judgment of the Weather, Spring Tides, Planets Motions & mutual Afpects, Sun and Moon's Rifing and Setting, Length of Days, Time of High Water, Fairs, Courts, and obfervable Days.
Fitted to the Latitude of Forty Degrees, and a Meridian of Five Hours Weft from *London*, but may without fenfible Error, ferve all the adjacent Places, even from *Newfoundland* to *South-Carolina*.

By *RICHARD SAUNDERS*, Philom.

PHILADELPHIA:
Printed and fold by *B. FRANKLIN*, at the New Printing-Office near the Market.

The title page above is from the first edition of *Poor Richard's Almanac.*

Which of Poor Richard's sayings are familiar to you?

From the Sayings of Poor Richard

1 One today is worth two tomorrows.

2 He that is of the opinion that money will do everything may well be suspected of doing everything for money.

3 A truly great man will neither trample on a worm nor sneak to an emperor.

4 If you would know the value of money, go and try to borrow some; he that goes a-borrowing goes a-sorrowing.

5 The eye of a master will do more work than both his hands.

6 'Tis hard for an empty bag to stand upright.

7 If a man could have half his wishes, he would double his troubles.

8 If a man empties his purse into his head, no man can take it away from him. An **investment** in knowledge always pays the best interest.

9 People who are wrapped up in themselves make small packages.

investment money spent in a way that earns more money; doing something in order to receive something in return

Benjamin Franklin (center) used a printing press like the one shown here to print *Poor Richard's Almanac.*

10 Fools make feasts, and wise men eat them.

11 He that lives on hope will die fasting.

12 Glass, china, and reputation are easily cracked and never well mended.

13 Be slow in choosing a friend, slower in changing.

14 Love your neighbor; yet don't pull down your hedge.

15 They that won't be counseled can't be helped.

16 Three may keep a secret if two of them are dead.

17 Fish and visitors smell in three days.

18 The rotten apple spoils his companions.

19 Early to bed and early to rise makes a man healthy, wealthy, and wise.

20 An open foe may prove a curse; but a pretended friend is worse.

Do these sayings give good advice?

Poor Richard's Almanac
Benjamin Franklin

Directions Write the answers to these questions using complete sentences.

Comprehension: Identifying Facts

1. Which of Poor Richard's sayings prove that Franklin valued education?

2. Which saying suggests that a secret should not be told?

3. Which three sayings contain rhyming words?

Comprehension: Understanding Main Ideas

4. What does saying number 9 mean?

5. What does saying number 20 say about friendship?

6. From these sayings, explain what you can tell about Ben Franklin's personality.

Understanding Literature: Almanac and Aphorism

The "Sayings of Poor Richard" were designed to be brief fillers for the eighteenth-century date book, or almanac. Benjamin Franklin chose to write these sayings, also called aphorisms, as little pieces of advice for the somewhat uneducated reader of the day. Some of the sayings rhymed, but many did not. All of these sayings, however, teach a lesson about life.

7. What is the purpose of an aphorism?

8. What do aphorisms teach?

Critical Thinking

9. Which saying do you agree with most? Why?

10. Do you agree with saying number 13? Explain your answer.

Writing on Your Own Think of some lesson that you have learned in your life. Write an original one- or two-line aphorism that you believe would be useful to others. Use the same style Franklin used for his aphorisms.

The American Crisis, Number 1
Thomas Paine

Thomas Paine

1737–1809

Literary Term

pamphlet a short, unbound piece of writing with no cover or with a paper cover

About the Author

Thomas Paine, although an American, was actually born in England in 1737. He came to America at age thirty-seven after finding little success at a number of jobs in England. His wife had died also while he was still in England. Paine was ready for a new start in America.

He got his start in Philadelphia, where he became a successful journalist. There he wrote a **pamphlet** called *Common Sense*, which called for independence from Great Britain. A pamphlet is a short, unbound piece of writing with no cover or with a paper cover. *Common Sense* was a huge success—about a half a million copies were sold. When war broke out with Great Britain, Paine joined the Revolutionary Army where his writing once again captured the American spirit with *The American Crisis*.

Paine's popularity decreased after the war. He spent the final years of his life unhappy and poor. He died in New York in 1809.

About the Selection

The Revolutionary War was a long, difficult struggle. In 1776, the colonial army under George Washington retreated from the British. With winter setting in and the colonial army seemingly beaten, something was needed to raise the soldiers' spirits. It was about this time that Paine began writing *The American Crisis, Number 1*. This was the first of sixteen pamphlets. It was read to the colonial troops before they won the Battle of Trenton in December of 1776. Paine's writing had helped improve the soldiers' mood.

From The American Crisis, Number 1

General George Washington, the tall man with the green cloak, inspects his troops at Valley Forge.

What does Paine do in his writing to make his points clear?

These are the times that try men's souls. The summer soldier and the sunshine patriot will, in this crisis, shrink from the service of their country; but he that stands it now, deserves the love and thanks of man and woman. **Tyranny**, like hell, is not easily conquered; yet we have this consolation with us, that the harder the conflict, the more glorious the triumph. What we obtain too cheap, we **esteem** too lightly: it is dearness only that gives everything its value. Heaven knows how to put a proper price upon its goods; and it would be strange indeed if so **celestial** an article as freedom should not be highly rated. Britain, with an army to enforce her tyranny, has declared that she has a right (not only to tax) but "to bind us in all cases whatsoever," and if being bound in that manner is not slavery, then is there not such a thing as slavery upon earth. Even the expression is **impious**; for so unlimited a power can belong only to God. . . .

I have as little superstition in me as any man living, but my secret opinion has ever been, and still is, that God Almighty will

celestial supreme; heavenly

esteem to regard

impious lacking proper respect for God

tyranny unjust governmental control

not give up a people to military destruction, or leave them unsupportedly to perish, who have so earnestly and so repeatedly sought to avoid the calamities of war, by every decent method which wisdom could invent. Neither have I so much of the **infidel** in me, as to suppose that He has **relinquished** the government of the world, and given us up to the care of devils; and as I do not, I cannot see on what grounds the King of Britain can look up to heaven for help against us: a common murderer, a highwayman, or a house-breaker, has as good a **pretence** as he. . . .

I shall not now attempt to give all the particulars of our retreat to the Delaware; suffice it for the present to say, that both officers and men, though greatly harassed and fatigued, frequently without rest, covering, or provision, the **inevitable** consequences of a long retreat, bore it with a manly and **martial** spirit. All their wishes centered in one, which was that the country would turn out and help them to drive the enemy back. Voltaire has remarked that King William never appeared to full advantage but in difficulties and in action; the same remark may be made on General Washington, for the character fits him. There is a natural firmness in some minds which cannot be unlocked by trifles, but which, when unlocked, discovers a cabinet of **fortitude**; and I reckon it among those kind of public blessings, which we do not immediately see, that God hath blessed him with uninterrupted health, and given him a mind that can even flourish upon care. . . .

This is our situation, and who will may know it. By perseverance and fortitude we have the prospect of a glorious issue; by cowardice and submission, the sad choice of a variety of evils—a ravaged country—a depopulated city—habitations without safety, and slavery without hope—our homes turned into barracks . . . for Hessians, and a future race to provide for, whose fathers we shall doubt of. Look on this picture and weep over it! and if there yet remains one thoughtless wretch who believes it not, let him suffer it **unlamented**. . . .

In this paragraph, the author writes that he thinks God will be on the side of the colonies.

Voltaire refers to François-Marie Voltaire, a French writer who lived from 1694–1778.

Hessians were German soldiers who the British paid to fight the colonials in the Revolutionary War.

---

fortitude strength of mind

inevitable unable to be avoided

infidel one who has no religious beliefs

martial warlike; related to war or military life

pretence a feeling or an action that is not sincere

relinquish to give up

unlamented without grief, sorrow, or regret

Directions Write the answers to these questions using complete sentences.

Comprehension: Identifying Facts

1. Who does Thomas Paine say is the only one who has unlimited power?

2. Where did the American army retreat to?

3. What does Paine say will happen through "cowardice and submission"?

Comprehension: Understanding Main Ideas

4. What religious beliefs are revealed in this writing?

5. How does Paine view George Washington?

6. What is the mood of this writing?

Understanding Literature: Pamphlet

The American Crisis and *Common Sense* by Thomas Paine were both pamphlets. These were short, unbound writings that had no cover or had just a paper cover. The pamphlet was one of the first kinds of printed material to be used. Before Paine made the pamphlet popular in America, pamphlets had been used in Europe to spread religious or political ideas. Once newspapers, magazines, and books became more popular, people used these materials instead of pamphlets.

7. Why do you think pamphlets were popular?

8. Is there anything used today that is similar to a pamphlet? Explain.

Critical Thinking

9. Paine goes to great lengths to explain the importance of the American cause. Do you think he states his points effectively? Explain.

10. Do you think there is a message that still applies to Americans today in this writing? Explain.

Writing on Your Own Use the library or Internet to research a part of the American Revolution that interests you. Write a paragraph describing your topic. Include important dates, people, and events related to your topic.

Wouter Van Twiller

Washington Irving

Wasington Irving

1783–1859

Literary Terms

exaggeration stretching the truth to a great extent

satire a humorous form of writing that makes fun of some part of society

sketch a brief writing that often runs from subject to subject and is often humorous

About the Author

Born in 1783 in New York City, Washington Irving was named for George Washington. Irving was interested in reading and writing, but he quit school at the age of sixteen, as he was not a good student. He then traveled around New York, especially the area around the Hudson River. He liked visiting the Dutch farmers in the area and learning about their history. These experiences became a key part of his later writing.

When it became obvious that he would have to support himself, Irving began to write. He published some of his works under the pen name of Diedrich Knickerbocker. His most famous works are "The Legend of Sleepy Hollow" and "Rip Van Winkle."

Irving traveled around Europe for many years. He died a famous and wealthy writer in 1859. Irving was a well-liked and pleasant man with an excellent sense of humor. These qualities are reflected in his writing.

About the Selection

"Wouter Van Twiller" is commonly known as a **sketch**, one of Irving's best writing forms. A sketch is a brief writing that often runs from subject to subject and is often humorous. This kind of writing is also called **satire**. Satire is frequently used to make fun of some part of society, such as politicians. The author's sense of humor and his attempt to poke fun at certain types of people make reading this story interesting and enjoyable. In "Wouter Van Twiller," Irving uses **exaggeration**, which is stretching the truth to a great extent. Exaggeration about the main character in this story, a common form of satire, suggests that the author had a low regard for political figures.

Wouter Van Twiller

What kind of man is Wouter Van Twiller?

A *burgomaster* is a town leader, such as a mayor. *Magistracy*, or a magistrate, is a judge.

Here the author points out that many people who are not smart are thought by others to be smart. He gives the example of an owl, a stupid bird, but thought by many to be a symbol of intelligence. How does this relate to Wouter Van Twiller?

The **renowned** Wouter (or Walter) Van Twiller was descended from a long line of Dutch burgomasters, who had successively dozed away their lives, and grown fat upon the bench of magistracy in Rotterdam; and who had **comported** themselves with such singular wisdom and **propriety**, that they were never either heard or talked of—which, next to being universally applauded, should be the object of ambition of all magistrates and rulers. There are two opposite ways by which some men make a figure in the world: one, by talking faster than they think, and the other, by holding their tongues and not thinking at all. By the first, many a **smatterer** acquires the reputation of a man of quick parts; by the other, many a **dunderpate**, like the owl, the stupidest of birds, comes to be considered the very type of wisdom. This, by the way, is a casual remark, which I would not, for the universe, have it thought I apply to Governor Van Twiller. It is true he was a man shut up within himself, like an oyster, and rarely spoke, except in monosyllables; but then it was allowed he seldom said a foolish thing. So **invincible** was his gravity that he was never known to laugh or even to smile through the whole course of a long and prosperous life. Nay, if a joke were uttered in his presence, that set lightminded hearers in a roar, it was observed to throw him into a state of perplexity. Sometimes he would **deign** to inquire into the matter, and

comport to behave; to act according to what is expected

deign to do something in a snobbish way

dunderpate a stupid person; a dunce

invincible unable to be defeated

propriety following socially acceptable rules of acting and speaking

renowned famous

smatterer one who speaks about something but has a limited understanding of the topic

when, after much explanation, the joke was made as plain as a pikestaff, he would continue to smoke his pipe in silence, and at length, knocking out the ashes, would exclaim, "Well! I see nothing in all that to laugh about."

With all his reflective habits, he never made up his mind on a subject. His **adherents** accounted for this by the astonishing **magnitude** of his ideas. He conceived every subject on so grand a scale that he had not room in his head to turn it over and examine both sides of it. Certain it is, that, if any matter were **propounded** to him on which ordinary mortals would rashly determine at first glance, he would put on a vague, mysterious look, shake his **capacious** head, smoke some time in profound silence, and at length observe that "he had his doubts about the matter"; which gained him the reputation of a man slow of belief and not easily imposed upon. What is more, it gained him a lasting name; for to this habit of the mind has been **attributed** his **surname** of Twiller; which is said to be a corruption of the original Twijfler, or, in plain English, *Doubter*.

The person of this illustrious old gentleman was formed and proportioned, as though it had been moulded by the hands of some cunning Dutch statuary, as a model of majesty and lordly **grandeur**. He was exactly five feet six inches in height, and six feet five inches in circumference. His head was a perfect sphere, and of such stupendous dimensions, that Dame

A *pikestaff* is a spiked staff used for support when walking on slippery ground.

A *statuary* is a person who makes statues.

This paragraph is an example of exaggeration. The author describes Wouter Van Twiller as a large, short man with a big head.

adherent one who follows or supports something	**capacious** containing or able to contain a great deal	**magnitude** great size
		propound to offer
attribute to connect	**grandeur** the quality or state of being grand or magnificent	**surname** a family name or nickname

Nature, with all her sex's **ingenuity**, would have been puzzled to construct a neck capable of supporting it: wherefore she wisely declined the attempt, and settled it firmly on the top of his backbone, just between the shoulders. His body was oblong and particularly capacious at bottom; which was wisely ordered by Providence, seeing that he was a man of **sedentary** habits, and very averse to the idle labor of walking. His legs were short, but sturdy in proportion to the weight they had to sustain; so that when erect he had not a little the appearance of a beer barrel on skids. His face, that **infallible** index of the mind, presented a vast expanse, unfurrowed by any of those lines and angles which disfigure the human **countenance** with what is termed expression. Two small gray eyes twinkled feebly in the midst, like two stars of lesser magnitude in a hazy **firmament,** and his full-fed cheeks, which seemed to have taken toll of everything that went into his mouth, were curiously **mottled** and streaked with dusky red, like a spitzenberg apple.

His habits were as regular as his person. He daily took his four stated meals, appropriating exactly an hour to each; he smoked and doubted eight

countenance facial expression	**ingenuity** the ability to invent or to be clever
firmament sky; heavens	**mottled** full of spots or blotches
infallible unable to make errors	**sedentary** doing much sitting or not moving

hours, and he slept the remaining twelve of the four-and-twenty. Such was the renowned Wouter Van Twiller—a true philosopher, for his mind was either elevated above, or **tranquilly** settled below, the cares and perplexities of this world. He had lived in it for years, without feeling the least curiosity to know whether the sun revolved round it, or it round the sun; and he had watched, for at least half a century, the smoke curling from his pipe to the ceiling, without once troubling his head with any of those numerous theories by which a philosopher would have perplexed his brain, in accounting for its rising above the surrounding atmosphere.

In his council he presided with great state and solemnity. He sat in a huge chair of solid oak, **hewn** in the celebrated forest of the Hague, fabricated by an experienced timmerman of Amsterdam, and curiously carved about the arms and feet, into exact imitations of gigantic eagle's claws. Instead of a scepter, he swayed a long Turkish pipe, wrought with jasmine and amber, which had been presented to a stadtholder of Holland at the conclusion of a treaty with one of the **petty** Barbary powers. In this stately chair would he sit, and this magnificent pipe would he smoke, shaking his right knee with a constant motion, and fixing his eye for hours together upon a little print of Amsterdam, which hung in a black frame against the opposite wall of the council-chamber. Nay, it has even been said, that when any **deliberation** of extraordinary length and intricacy was on the carpet, the renowned Wouter would shut his eyes for full two hours at a time, that he might not be disturbed by external objects; and at such times the internal commotion of his mind was **evinced** by certain regular **guttural** sounds, which his admirers declared were merely the noise of conflict, made by his **contending** doubts and opinions.

A *timmerman* is a carpenter. A *scepter* is a staff or baton. A *stadtholder* is a Provincial governor.

contending struggling or contesting	**evince** to reveal	**petty** small or minor
deliberation a discussion for or against a certain idea	**guttural** coming from the throat	**tranquilly** calmly
	hewn cut	

Wouter Van Twiller
Washington Irving

Directions Write the answers to these questions using complete sentences.

Comprehension: Identifying Facts

1. What political position did Wouter Van Twiller hold?

2. From where did he descend?

3. What are two ways in which the author says men can "make a figure in the world"?

4. What is the English translation of the name "Wouter Van Twiller"?

5. How tall and how wide was Wouter?

6. How did Wouter spend the twenty-four hours in the day?

7. Where did Wouter like to sit?

8. For how long would Wouter shut his eyes during long deliberations?

9. Describe Wouter's chair.

10. What did Wouter like to hold in his hand?

Comprehension: Understanding Main Ideas

11. What things make Wouter a humorous character that could not possibly be real? Identify three examples of exaggeration.

12. What is Washington Irving's opinion of politicians?

13. Find a part in the story that suggests that Wouter was probably not too smart.

14. The final lines of this story tell that Wouter closed his eyes and made "guttural sounds" for two hours. His admirers believed that he was deep in thought. What are the guttural sounds?

15. What is Washington Irving suggesting about people?

16. What purpose is there in writing like this?

17. Why did people seem to like Wouter?

18. Are there people like Wouter in the world today? Explain.

19. What are some things that Irving makes fun of in this story?

20. What bad habits does Irving mention in this story?

Understanding Literature: Satire and Exaggeration

Washington Irving was a master of satire. This technique uses wit and humor to make fun of a subject. Satire is often used to make fun of some part of society, such as politicians. Exaggeration, or stretching the truth to make something appear more extreme than it is, is often a part of satire. Satire is not usually intended to harm, however. It is intended to express an opinion or to prove something to the reader. In "Wouter Van Twiller," the intention was to prove that people are not always what they seem, and that sometimes the people who are honored do not necessarily deserve the honor.

21. Do you think the story is a mean or bitter one? Defend your answer.

22. What are some examples of exaggeration that Irving uses to create humor?

23. How did Wouter react to jokes? What does this say about his character?

24. How did Wouter make decisions? Find the line in the second paragraph that shows that Wouter could or could not make decisions. What is satirized in this paragraph?

25. What purpose does satire serve?

Critical Thinking

26. Do you think that it is possible to have an overly high opinion of someone? Explain your answer.

27. Why do you think Irving chose to write this sketch? Explain.

28. Did you find this story humorous? Why or why not?

29. What do you think this sketch says about Washington Irving as a person?

30. Is a person like Wouter dangerous? Why or why not?

Writing on Your Own Write a humorous paragraph about an imaginary person or thing using exaggeration. To describe this person or thing, use comparisons and language that tell the reader that the person could not possibly be real. Read your paragraph to a partner.

American Indian Poetry
Anonymous

About the Authors

Before European colonists arrived in America, American Indians lived there. Each group had its own way of life. The Chippewa, also called the Ojibwa, lived near the Great Lakes. Wild rice, an important food, thrived in the shallow lakes and streams of the area. For control of the rice lands, the Ojibwa drove other groups onto the plains. The Omaha lived in what is now Nebraska. The Sioux moved from place to place. They followed buffalo on horseback across the large western plains. The buffalo provided meat for food, hides for tepee covers and clothing, bones and sinew for tools and weapons, and horns for ladles and powderhorns. The way of life of these skilled hunters has become part of the symbols and legends of the American West.

Literary Term

mood the feeling that writing creates

About the Selections

Some traditional culture has been passed on in the form of poetry. Many of the American Indian poems that we can read today were originally chants, songs, or speeches. These poems give us a view of an earlier time. They discuss life and death. They present a picture of a world in which people lived closely with nature. The Omaha selection comes from a speech delivered in 1813. In that year Big Elk, an Omaha, spoke at the funeral of Black Buffalo, a leader of the Teton Sioux.

Each of these poems suggests a **mood**. Mood is the feeling that writing creates, such as sadness, peacefulness, or fear. Look for the mood as you read these poems.

A Lone Wolf I am . . .
I roam in many places . . .
I am weary.

— *Sioux*

Death will come.
And always comes out of season.
It is the command of the Great Spirit.
All nations and people must obey.

— Big Elk, *Omaha*

Toward calm and shady places
I am walking on the earth.

— *Chippewa*

American Indian Poetry
Anonymous

Directions Write the answers to these questions using complete sentences.

Comprehension: Identifying Facts

1. According to Big Elk, what is the command that all people must obey?

2. Why is the Sioux poet weary?

3. Where is the Chippewa poet walking?

Comprehension: Understanding Main Ideas

4. Why do you think Big Elk says that death will come "out of season"?

5. How is the Sioux poet similar to a wolf?

6. How are these poems made more effective by the short sentence patterns?

Understanding Literature: Mood

Each of the poems by American Indians is brief, but each one suggests an emotion, or mood. The mood makes the reader feel what the poet is feeling. A strong sense of mood can make the poem effective even though it is short and simple.

7. Do you think that the mood of these poems is happy? Explain your answer.

8. How does the mood of each poem make you feel?

Critical Thinking

9. Do you think Big Elk's view of death is similar to the way we view death today? Why or why not?

10. Which poem do you like best? Why?

Writing on Your Own Choose one of the American Indian poems and write it down on a sheet of paper. Write three additional lines keeping the same mood of the poem, but telling more about the subject.

The Origin of Plumage

Anonymous

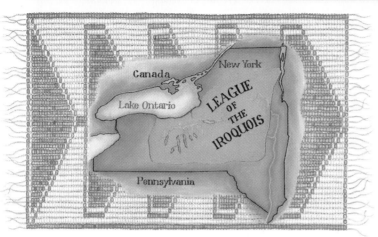

Literary Term

myth a story that explains how some things in the natural world came to be

About the Authors

The Iroquois lived in the eastern woodland area of the United States. In about 1400, one leader dreamed of a large tree that grew from the roots of the united Five Nations. As a result of this dream, five groups—the Cayuga, Oneida, Onondaga, Mohawk, and Seneca—joined together as one group. In about 1722, the Tuscarora joined the group, which became known as the League of the Iroquois, or the Six Nations. The Iroquois soon controlled the area from the Saint Lawrence River in Canada to what is now Tennessee and from Maine on the Atlantic Ocean to Michigan. They also controlled much fur trade and boat travel on the Great Lakes.

After maintaining power for two hundred years, the League was divided by the question of whether the Iroquois should side with the British or the Americans during the American Revolution. Many Iroquois chose to join the British. Some historians believe that the American government may have been patterned after the League of the Iroquois.

About the Selection

A **myth** is a story that explains how some things in the natural world came to be. "The Origin of Plumage" is an Iroquois myth about how birds got their feathers. This version is a retelling of the myth recorded by Erminnie A. Smith in *Myths of the Iroquois*.

The Origin of Plumage

What is the message in this myth? What can be learned from the story?

Plumage is another name for feathers. A *turkey buzzard* is a large bird, also called a turkey vulture, with black feathers, a bare red head, and a six-foot wingspan.

In the beginning, the birds, having been created without feathers, remained hidden. They were ashamed of their appearance. One day they assembled in a great meeting. They asked their gods to give them some kind of covering. They were told that these coverings were all ready but that they were a long distance away. The birds must send for them.

Accordingly, another meeting was held to encourage some bird to go in search of the plumage. However, each bird had some excuse for not going. At last, a turkey buzzard volunteered to go and to bring back the feathers. It was a long journey, but the bird was directed on his way by the gods.

Finally, the turkey buzzard found the coverings. He selfishly took the most beautiful one for himself. However, he found out that he could not fly in this covering. He continued to try on all of the feathered uniforms until he selected his present suit. This covering, although the least beautiful of all, allowed him to glide gracefully through the air. The good turkey buzzard returned and brought with him all of the feathery garments. Each bird chose his present colored suit.

Directions Write the answers to these questions using complete sentences.

Comprehension: Identifying Facts

1. Who told the birds that there were feathers made for them?

2. Which bird volunteered to go after these feathers?

3. What kind of covering did the turkey buzzard finally choose?

Comprehension: Understanding Main Ideas

4. What references to a belief in a higher power can be found in this myth?

5. What does this story have to say about American Indian beliefs?

6. What lesson is meant to be learned by this story?

Understanding Literature: Myth

As you have already learned, "The Origin of Plumage" is a myth. This kind of writing is a story that explains how some things in the natural world came to be.

7. What makes "The Origin of Plumage" a myth?

8. Do you like it better written down, or would you rather have heard the story told orally? Why or why not?

Critical Thinking

9. Why do you think that many birds made excuses when asked to go get the feathers?

10. What do you think could be another title for this tale? Why?

Writing on Your Own Research the turkey buzzard (also called turkey vulture) at the library. Write a paragraph in your own words describing what this bird looks like, where it can be found, how large it is, what it eats, and any other information you find useful.

The Black Cat
Edgar Allan Poe

Edgar Allan Poe
1809–1849

Literary Terms

fiction writing that is imaginitive and designed to entertain

first-person point of view written as if someone is telling the story

narrator one who tells a story

About the Author

Edgar Allan Poe was born in 1809 in Boston, Massachusetts. His father left the family, and his mother died when Poe was two years old. His foster father, John Allan, was a wealthy tobacco farmer from Virginia. However, Poe and Allan did not get along.

Poe attended college at the University of Virginia and at West Point, the nation's military college. He did not finish at either school. He eventually went to live with his aunt and her daughter (Poe's cousin), Virginia Clemm. In 1835, he married Virginia secretly when she was just thirteen years old.

Poe and his wife lived in poverty. He became an editor and a successful literary critic, but made very little money at it. Eventually some of his poems and short stories were published. By 1845, Poe had become fairly famous as a writer. Even so, he was never wealthy. When Virginia died in 1847, Poe fell apart mentally. His health also declined, and he drank heavily. He died in 1849.

Poe's works reflect imagination and horror. His stories often deal with strange plots and unexpected endings. His characters are often deeply disturbed. Some of Poe's best-known stories include "The Fall of the House of Usher," "The Tell-Tale Heart," and "The Pit and the Pendulum."

About the Selection

"The Black Cat" is typical of Poe's tales of horror and terror. It is **fiction**, which is writing that is imaginitive and designed to entertain. It is told in the **first-person point of view**. This means that it is written as if someone—in this case, the **narrator**—is telling the story. A narrator is one who tells a story. The feelings in this story are guilt and madness, both common to Poe's writings.

The Black Cat

For the most wild, yet most homely narrative which I am about to pen, I neither expect nor **solicit** belief. Mad indeed would I be to expect it, in a case where my very senses reject their own evidence. Yet, mad am I not—and very surely do I not dream. But tomorrow I die, and today I would unburden my soul. My immediate purpose is to place before the world plainly, **succinctly**, and without comment, a series of mere household events. In their consequences these events have terrified—have tortured—have destroyed me. Yet I will not attempt to **expound** them. To me they have presented little but horror; to many they will seem less terrible than baroques. Hereafter, perhaps, some intellect may be found which will reduce my **phantasm** to the commonplace—some intellect more calm, more logical, and far less excitable than my own, which will perceive in the circumstances I detail with awe, nothing more than an ordinary succession of very natural causes and effects.

From my infancy I was noted for the **docility** and humanity of my disposition. My tenderness of heart was even so conspicuous as to make me the jest of my companions. I was especially fond of animals, and was indulged by my parents with a great variety of pets. With these I spent most of my time, and never was so happy as when feeding and caressing them. This peculiarity of character grew with my growth, and, in my manhood, I derived from it one of my principal sources of pleasure. To those who have cherished an affection for a faithful and **sagacious** dog, I need hardly be at

> The narrator in this story tells the reader over and over again that he is not crazy. What do you think?

> A *baroque* is a form of literature common in the seventeenth century. It was elaborate and expressed an interest in the strange and unusual.

---

docility the quality of being easy to control; tameness

expound to explain

phantasm a spirit or ghost

sagacious wise; keen

solicit to approach with a request; to ask for

succinctly without wasting words

the trouble of explaining the nature or the intensity of the gratification thus derivable. There is something in the unselfish and self-sacrificing love of a brute, which goes directly to the heart of him who has had frequent occasion to test the paltry friendship and **gossamer fidelity** of mere *man*.

I married early, and was happy to find in my wife a disposition not **uncongenial** with my own. Observing my **partiality** for domestic pets, she lost no opportunity of **procuring** those of the most agreeable kind. We had birds, goldfish, a fine dog, rabbits, a small monkey, and *a cat*.

This latter was a remarkably large and beautiful animal, entirely black, and sagacious to an astonishing degree. In speaking of his intelligence, my wife, who at heart was not a little **tinctured** with superstition, made frequent **allusion** to the ancient popular notion, which regarded all black cats as witches in disguise. Not that she was ever *serious* upon this point—and I mention the matter at all for no better reason than that it happens, just now, to be remembered.

Pluto—this was the cat's name—was my favorite pet and playmate. I alone

allusion hints or hinting

fidelity loyalty or devotion

gossamer light or unimportant

partiality fondness

procure to obtain

tinctured having a quality of

uncongenial unsuited; unagreeable in nature, taste, or outlook

fed him, and he attended me wherever I went about the house. It was even with difficulty that I could prevent him from following me through the streets.

Our friendship lasted in this manner for several years, during which my general **temperament** and character—through the **instrumentality** of the Fiend **Intemperance**—had (I blush to confess it) experienced a radical alteration for the worse. I grew, day by day, more moody, more irritable, more regardless of the feelings of others. I suffered myself to use intemperate language to my wife. At length, I even offered her personal violence. My pets, of course, were made to feel the change in my disposition. I not only neglected, but ill-used them. For Pluto, however, I still retained sufficient regard to restrain me from maltreating him, as I made no **scruple** of maltreating the rabbits, the monkey, or even the dog, when by accident, or through affection, they came in my way. But my disease grew upon me—for what disease is like alcohol!—and at length even Pluto, who was now becoming old and consequently somewhat peevish—even Pluto began to experience the effects of my ill temper.

One night, returning home much intoxicated, from one of my haunts about town, I fancied that the cat avoided my presence. I seized him; when, in his fright at my violence, he inflicted a slight wound upon my hand with his teeth. The fury of a demon instantly possessed me. I knew myself no longer. My original soul seemed at once to take its flight from my body; and a more than fiendish **malevolence**, gin-nurtured, thrilled every fiber of my frame. I took from my waistcoat pocket a penknife, opened it, grasped the poor beast by the throat, and deliberately cut one of its eyes from the socket! I blush, I burn, I shudder while I pen the damnable **atrocity**.

The narrator explains here how his drinking has made him mistreat his pets.

atrocity a horrifying event

instrumentality the use of something

intemperance regular drinking of large amounts of alcohol

malevolence the state of being cruel or evil

scruple a hesitation to do something because it is wrong

temperament attitude; personality

When reason returned with the morning—when I had slept off the fumes of the night's **debauch**—I experienced a sentiment half of horror, half of remorse, for the crime of which I had been guilty; but it was at best a feeble and **equivocal** feeling, and the soul remained untouched. I again plunged into excess, and soon drowned in wine all memory of the deed.

In the meantime the cat slowly recovered. The socket of the lost eye presented, it is true, a frightful appearance, but he no longer appeared to suffer any pain. He went about the house as usual but, as might be expected, fled in extreme terror at my approach. I had so much of my old heart left as to be at first grieved by this evident dislike on the part of a creature which had once so loved me. But this feeling soon gave place to irritation. And then came, as if to my final and **irrevocable** overthrow, the spirit of Perverseness. Of this spirit philosophy takes no account. Yet I am not more sure that my soul lives than I am that perverseness is one of the primitive impulses of the human heart, one of the **indivisible** primary faculties, or sentiments, which give direction to the character of man. Who has not, a hundred times, found himself committing a vile or a silly action for no other reason than because he knows he should *not?* Have we not a perpetual **inclination**, in the teeth of our best judgment, to violate that which is *law*, merely because we understand it to be such? This spirit of Perverseness, I say, came to my final overthrow. It was this **unfathomable** longing of the soul to *vex itself*—to offer violence to its own nature—to do wrong for the wrong's sake—only that urged me to continue and finally to **consummate** the injury I had inflicted upon the unoffending brute. One morning, in cool blood, I slipped a noose about its

The word *perverseness* means turning away from what is right or good.

Here the narrator kills the cat by hanging it. Why do you think he does this?

consummate to complete

debauch an act that goes against morals, such as heavy drinking

equivocal uncertain

inclination a natural way of tending to do something

indivisible unable to be separated

irrevocable unable to be taken back

unfathomable not capable of being understood

neck and hung it to the limb of a tree; hung it with the tears streaming from my eyes and with the bitterest remorse at my heart; hung it *because* I knew that it had loved me and *because* I felt it had given me no reason of offense; hung it *because* I knew that in so doing I was committing a sin, a deadly sin that would so **jeopardize** my **immortal** soul as to place it—if such a thing were possible—even beyond the reach of the infinite mercy of the Most Merciful and Terrible God.

On the night of the day on which this cruel deed was done, I was aroused from sleep by the cry of fire. The curtains of my bed were in flames. The whole house was blazing. It was with great difficulty that my wife, a servant, and myself made our escape from the **conflagration**. The destruction was complete. My entire worldly wealth was swallowed up, and I resigned myself thenceforward to despair.

I am above the weakness of seeking to establish a sequence of cause and effect, between the disaster and the atrocity. But I am detailing a chain of facts—and wish not to leave even a possible link imperfect. On the day succeeding the fire, I visited the ruins. The walls, with one exception, had fallen in. This exception was found in a compartment wall, not very thick,

conflagration a large fire

immortal unable to be killed

jeopardize to expose to danger or risk

Here the narrator visits his home after it had burned. On a plaster wall he sees a mysterious image of a cat with a rope around its neck. How do you think this image got there?

which stood about the middle of the house, and against which had rested the head of my bed. The plastering had here, in great measure, resisted the action of the fire—a fact which I **attributed** to its having been recently spread. About this wall a dense crowd was collected, and many persons seemed to be examining a particular portion of it with very minute and eager attention. The words "strange!" "singular!" and other similar expressions excited my curiosity. I approached and saw as if graven in *bas-relief* upon the white surface, the figure of a gigantic *cat*. The impression was given with an accuracy truly marvelous. There was a rope about the animal's neck.

When I first beheld this **apparition**—for I could scarcely regard it as less—my wonder and my terror were extreme. But at length reflection came to my aid. The cat, I remembered, had been hung in a garden adjacent to the house. Upon the alarm of the fire, this garden had been immediately filled by the crowd—by some one of whom the animal must have been cut from the tree and thrown, through an open window, into my chamber. This had probably been done with the view of arousing me from sleep. The falling of other walls had compressed the victim of my cruelty into the substance of the freshly spread plaster; the lime of which, with the flames and the *ammonia* from the carcass, had then accomplished the **portraiture** as I saw it.

Although I thus readily accounted to my reason, if not altogether to my conscience, for the startling fact just detailed, it did not the less fail to make a deep impression upon my fancy. For months I could not rid myself of the phantasm of the cat; and, during this period, there came back into my spirit a half-sentiment that seemed, but was not, remorse. I went so far as to regret the loss of the animal, and to look about me, among the vile haunts which I now **habitually** frequented, for another pet of the same species, and of somewhat similar appearance, with which to supply its place.

What does this paragraph tell you about the narrator as a person?

---

apparition a ghost

attribute to explain by indicating a cause

habitually done out of habit

portraiture a drawing

One night as I sat, half **stupefied**, in a den of more than **infamy**, my attention was suddenly drawn to some black object, **reposing** upon the head of one of the immense hogsheads of gin, or of rum, which **constituted** the chief furniture of the apartment. I had been looking steadily at the top of this hogshead for some minutes, and what now caused me surprise was the fact that I had not sooner perceived the object thereupon. I approached it, and touched it with my hand. It was a black cat—a very large one—fully as large as Pluto, and closely resembling him in every respect but one. Pluto had not a white hair upon any portion of his body; but this cat had a large, although indefinite splotch of white, covering nearly the whole region of the breast.

Upon my touching him, he immediately arose, purred loudly, rubbed against my hand, and appeared delighted with my notice. This, then, was the very creature of which I was in search. I at once offered to purchase it of the landlord; but this person made no claim to it—knew nothing of it—had never seen it before.

I continued my caresses, and, when I prepared to go home, the animal evinced a disposition to accompany me. I permitted it to do so; occasionally stooping and patting it as I proceeded. When it reached the house it domesticated itself at once and became immediately a great favorite with my wife.

For my own part, I soon found a dislike to it arising within me. This was just the reverse of what I had anticipated; but—I know not how or why it was—its evident fondness for myself rather disgusted and annoyed. By slow degrees these feelings of disgust and annoyance rose into the bitterness of hatred. I avoided the creature; a certain sense of shame, and the remembrance of my former deed of cruelty, preventing me from physically abusing it. I did not, for some weeks, strike, or otherwise violently ill use it; but gradually—very gradually—I came to look upon it with unutterable **loathing**,

A *hogshead* is a large cask or barrel.

constitute to make up or form	shocking event	**reposing** resting
infamy evil reputation brought on by a	**loathing** extreme disgust	**stupefied** groggy; amazed

and to flee silently from its **odious** presence as from the breath of **pestilence**.

What added, no doubt, to my hatred of the beast, was the discovery, on the morning after I brought it home that, like Pluto, it also had been deprived of one of its eyes. This circumstance, however, only **endeared** it to my wife, who, as I have already said, possessed, in a high degree, that humanity of feeling which had once been my distinguishing trait, and the source of many of my simplest and purest pleasures.

With my **aversion** to this cat, however, its partiality for myself seemed to increase. It followed my footsteps with a **pertinacity** which it would be difficult to make the reader comprehend. Whenever I sat, it would crouch beneath my chair or spring upon my knees, covering me with its loathsome caresses. If I arose to walk it would get between my feet and thus nearly throw me down, or, fastening its long and sharp claws in my dress, clamber, in this manner, to my breast. At such times, although I longed to destroy it with a blow, I was yet withheld from so doing, partly by a memory of my former crime, but chiefly—let me confess it at once—by absolute *dread* of the beast.

This dread was not exactly a dread of physical evil—and yet I should be at a loss how otherwise to define it. I am almost ashamed to own—yes, even in this felon's cell, I am almost ashamed to own—that the terror and horror with which the animal inspired me, had been heightened by one of the merest **chimeras** it would be possible to conceive. My wife had called my attention, more than once, to the character of the mark of white hair, of which I have spoken, and which constituted the sole visible difference between the strange beast and the one I had destroyed. The reader will remember that this mark, although large, had been originally very indefinite; but by slow

The author is adding to the mystery of this story. The new cat is very much like Pluto, which the narrator had killed. What do you think will happen next?

aversion dislike	**endear** to cause to be loved	**pertinacity** stubbornness
chimera something made up by the mind; a dream	**odious** deserving hatred	**pestilence** disease; something that is destructive

degrees—degrees nearly **imperceptible**, and which for a long time my reason struggled to reject as fanciful—it had at length assumed a rigorous distinctness of outline. It was now the representation of an object that I shudder to name—and for this, above all, I loathed, and dreaded, and would have rid myself of the monster *had I dared*—it was now, I say, the image of a hideous—of a ghastly thing—of the Gallows!—oh, mournful and terrible engine of horror and of crime—of agony and of death!

A *gallows* is a structure, made of two upright posts and a crosspiece, from which criminals are hanged.

And now was I indeed wretched beyond the wretchedness of mere humanity. And a *brute beast*, whose fellow I had **contemptuously** destroyed—*a brute beast* to work out for me—for me a man fashioned in the imagine of the High God—so much of **insufferable** woe! Alas! neither by day nor by night knew I the blessing of rest any more! During the former the creature left me no moment alone; and, in the latter, I started hourly from dreams of unutterable fear to find the hot breath of *the thing* upon my face, and its vast weight, an incarnate nightmare that I had no power to shake off—**incumbent** eternally upon my *heart!*

Beneath the pressure of torments such as these, the feeble remnant of the good within me **succumbed**. Evil thoughts became my sole **intimates**—the darkest and most evil of thoughts. The moodiness of my usual temper increased to hatred of all things and of all mankind; while, from the sudden, frequent, and ungovernable outbursts of a fury to which I now blindly abandoned myself, my uncomplaining wife, alas! was the most usual and the most patient of sufferers.

One day she accompanied me upon some household errand, into the cellar of the old building which our poverty compelled us to inhabit. The cat followed me down the steep stairs, and, nearly throwing me headlong, **exasperated** me to

contemptuously in an uncaring or hateful manner	**imperceptible** unable to be sensed or imagined	**intimate** a person's very close friend
exasperate to excite into anger	**incumbent** resting on	**succumb** to yield to superior strength, force, or desire
	insufferable difficult to bear	

Forging America's Literary Tradition Unit 1 **49**

madness. Uplifting an axe, and forgetting, in my wrath, the childish dread which had hitherto stayed my hand, I aimed a blow at the animal which, of course, would have proved instantly fatal had it descended as I wished. But this blow was arrested by the hand of my wife. Goaded, by the interference, into a rage more than **demoniacal**, I withdrew my arm from her grasp and buried the axe in her brain. She fell dead upon the spot without a groan.

This hideous murder accomplished, I set myself forthwith, and with entire deliberation, to the task of concealing the body. I knew that I could not remove it from the house, either by day or by night, without the risk of being observed by the neighbors. Many projects entered my mind. At one period I thought of cutting the corpse into minute fragments and destroying them by fire. At another I resolved to dig a grave for it in the floor of the cellar. Again I deliberated about casting it in the well in the yard—about packing it in a box, as if merchandise, with the usual arrangements, and so getting a porter to take it from the house. Finally I hit upon what I considered a far better **expedient** than either of these. I determined to wall it up in the cellar—as the monks of the middle ages are recorded to have walled up their victims.

For a purpose such as this, the cellar was well adapted. Its walls were loosely constructed, and had lately been plastered throughout with a rough plaster, which the dampness of the atmosphere had prevented from hardening. Moreover, in one of the walls was a **projection**, caused by a false chimney or fireplace, that had been filled up, and made to resemble the rest of the cellar. I made no doubt that I could readily displace the bricks at this point, insert the corpse, and wall the whole up as before, so that no eye could detect anything suspicious.

And in this calculation I was not deceived. By means of a crowbar I easily dislodged the bricks, and, having carefully deposited the body against the inner wall, I propped it in that position, while, with little trouble, I relaid the whole structure

A *porter* is a person who is paid to carry heavy objects.

The narrator plans to wall up his murdered wife.

demoniacal possessed or influenced by a devil or an evil spirit

expedient a solution to a problem

projection a part that sticks out

as it originally stood. Having procured mortar, sand, and hair with every possible precaution, I prepared a plaster which could not be distinguished from the old, and with this I very carefully went over the new brickwork. When I had finished, I felt satisfied that all was right. The wall did not present the slightest appearance of having been disturbed. The rubbish on the floor was picked up with the minutest care. I looked around triumphantly and said to myself—"Here at least, then, my labor has not been in vain."

My next step was to look for the beast which had been the cause of so much wretchedness; for I had at length, firmly resolved to put it to death. Had I been able to meet with it, at the moment, there could have been no doubt of its fate; but it appeared that the crafty animal had been alarmed at the violence of my previous anger, and **forbore** to present itself in my present mood. It is impossible to describe, or to imagine, the deep, the **blissful** sense of relief which the absence of the **detested** creature occasioned in my **bosom**. It did not make its appearance during the night—and thus for one night at least, since its introduction into the house, I soundly and tranquilly slept; aye, *slept* even with the burden of murder upon my soul!

blissful happy	**detested** hated
bosom the human chest, often thought of as the seat of emotions	**forbore** avoided

The second and the third day passed, and still my tormentor came not. Once again I breathed as a free man. The monster, in terror, had fled the **premises** forever! I should behold it no more! My happiness was supreme! The guilt of my dark deed disturbed me but little. Some few **inquiries** had been made, but these had been readily answered. Even a search had been instituted—but of course nothing was to be discovered. I looked upon my future **felicity** as secured.

Upon the fourth day of the assassination, a party of the police came, very unexpectedly, into the house, and proceeded again to make rigorous investigation of the premises. Secure, however, in the **inscrutability** of my place of concealment, I felt no embarrassment whatever. The officers bade me accompany them in their search. They left no nook or corner unexplored. At length, for the third or fourth time, they descended into the cellar. I quivered not in a muscle. My heart beat calmly as that of one who slumbers in innocence. I walked the cellar from end to end. I folded my arms upon my bosom and roamed easily to and fro. The police were thoroughly satisfied and prepared to depart. The glee at my heart was too strong to be restrained. I burned to say if but one word, by way of triumph, and to render doubly sure their assurance of my guiltlessness.

"Gentlemen," I said at last, as the party ascended the steps. "I delight to have **allayed** your suspicions. I wish you all health, and a little more courtesy. By the by, gentlemen, this—this is a very well constructed house." (In the **rabid** desire to say something easily, I scarcely knew what I uttered at all.) "I may say an *excellently* well constructed house. These walls—are you going, gentlemen?—these walls are solidly put together;" and here, through the mere frenzy of **bravado**, I rapped heavily, with a cane which I held in my hand, upon

> The narrator acts very calm and confident in this paragraph, though the police are searching for his missing wife in his home. Why do you think he acts this way?

allay to calm or reduce	**inquiry** a question	**premises** a building or part of a building
bravado a show of bravery	**inscrutability** an inability to be easily found out or understood	**rabid** going to extreme lengths
felicity a state of happiness		

that very portion of the brickwork behind which stood the corpse of the wife of my bosom.

But may God shield and deliver me from the fangs of the **archfiend**! No sooner had the **reverberation** of my blows sunk into silence, than I was answered by a voice from within the tomb!—by a cry, at first muffled and broken, like the sobbing of a child, and then quickly swelling into one long, loud, and continuous scream, utterly **anomalous** and inhuman—a howl—a wailing shriek, half of horror and half of triumph, such as might have arisen only out of hell, **conjointly** from the throats of the damned in their agony and of the demons that **exult** in the **damnation**.

Of my own thoughts it is folly to speak. Swooning, I staggered to the opposite wall. For one instant the party upon the stairs remained motionless, through extremity of terror and of awe. In the next, a dozen stout arms were toiling at the wall. It fell bodily. The corpse, already greatly decayed and clotted with gore, stood erect before the eyes of the spectators. Upon its head, with red extended mouth and solitary eye of fire, sat the hideous beast whose craft had seduced me into murder, and whose informing voice had **consigned** me to the hangman. I had walled the monster up within the tomb!

The narrator explains here that he has accidently walled up the cat with his murdered wife. The reader is left to wonder what will happen to the narrator. What do you think will happen?

anomalous unusual

archfiend a chief demon or devil, especially Satan

conjointly combined

consign to give someone over to the control of another

damnation the act of being sent to hell

exult to be extremely joyful

reverberation an echo

Directions Write the answers to these questions using complete sentences.

Comprehension: Identifying Facts

1. What relationship did the narrator have with pets when he was a child?

2. What caused the narrator to become violent toward his wife and animals?

3. Who was Pluto? What two horrible things did the narrator do to him?

4. After the fire in the house, what was the clear image on the wall?

5. How was the second black cat different from the first?

6. What did the narrator do in a rage while on the cellar steps?

7. What caused the narrator's rage on the steps?

8. How did he hide the body of his wife?

9. What did the police discover in the basement?

10. What "monster" had the narrator walled up?

Comprehension: Understanding Main Ideas

11. Did the narrator love his wife?

12. How did the narrator react to the visit by the police? How can you explain his behavior?

13. Is the narrator mad? In what ways does he seem sane? In what ways does he seem insane?

14. Is the narrator ever sorry for his actions? Find sentences from the story that support your answer.

15. At what point in this story does the narrator get into trouble first?

16. When events or actions in a story go against what is thought to be normal or natural, it is called "supernatural." What parts of this story seemed supernatural?

17. At what point in this story do we realize the narrator is telling the story from a jail cell?

18. Why does the narrator say the things he says to the police as they are leaving the cellar?

19. Much of this story seems hard to believe, yet the author makes the reader feel that the action is real. How? Explain.

20. What will become of the narrator?

Understanding Literature: Grotesque and Arabesque

When he published his works in 1840, Edgar Allan Poe divided his works into two categories. He called his works *Tales of the Grotesque and Arabesque*. The word *grotesque* is usually thought of as dealing with the supernatural, such as ghosts and monsters. *Arabesque*, however, refers to the "terror of the soul." Usually, the mental and emotional state of the character is not normal. Grotesque is usually physical, while arabesque is usually about spiritual or mental agony. "The Black Cat" was not published until 1843, so Poe did not identify it in either category.

21. What does grotesque mean?

22. What does arabesque mean?

23. How do grotesque and arabesque differ?

24. Which type of story do you think "The Black Cat" is? Why?

25. Could "The Black Cat" be both grotesque and arabesque? Explain.

Critical Thinking

26. Is "The Black Cat" a good title for this tale? Why or why not? What might be another good title for this story?

27. What kind of woman do you think the narrator's wife was? Explain your answer.

28. Do you think it was the cat who made the narrator do the things he did, or something else? Explain.

29. Did this story have a satisfying ending? Why or why not?

30. Did you like this story? Why or why not?

Writing on Your Own Choose *grotesque* or *arabesque* as a starting point for a story. Write a paragraph describing a story you would like to write, explaining how it fits into one of the two story types. Then write the story. It does not need to be long, but it should tell about a main character and something that happens to this character.

Annabel Lee
Edgar Allan Poe

Edgar Allan Poe
1809–1849

Literary Terms

end rhyme a feature of a poem in which the last words of two lines rhyme with one another

mood the feeling that writing creates

refrain repetition of words or phrases to create mood or emphasis

rhythm a regular pattern of stressed and unstressed syllables

About the Author

As you have already learned, Edgar Allan Poe married his young cousin, Virginia Clemm. The two lived in poverty, and Virginia died in 1847 after a five-year illness. Although his life contained much sorrow and disappointment, Poe continued to edit and to write. However, two years after his wife's death, Poe was found near death in Baltimore, Maryland. He died in a hospital four days later.

Out of the sorrow of Poe's life came success with his writing. As one of America's most gifted poets, short story writers, and literary critics, Poe has had a lasting influence on modern writers. Today, some of his best-known poems include "Ulalume," "Lenore," "The Raven," and "Annabel Lee."

About the Selection

Edgar Allan Poe was not only a highly unusual teller of tales but also a remarkable poet. His works are known for their **end rhymes, mood,** and **rhythm.** An end rhyme occurs when the last words of two lines rhyme. Mood is the feeling writing creates. Rhythm is a regular pattern of stressed and unstressed syllables. His poems are also sad and emotional. They often discuss death. Poe's favorite topic in poetry was to describe the death of a beautiful woman. Some poems also describe a lasting loyalty to a perfect woman. The narrators in these poems speak of grief over the loss of an ideal love.

This selection, "Annabel Lee," is typical of Poe's theme that only love can save one from despair. This work was Poe's last poem and was written shortly before his death. It was inspired by Poe's love for his wife, Virginia Clemm, who died of tuberculosis in 1847. You will notice that this poem repeats some words or phrases. This is called a **refrain**. Refrains are used to create mood or to emphasize words.

Grand Manan Sunset, **Alfred Thompson Bricher**

Annabel Lee

It was many and many a year ago,
    In a kingdom by the sea
That a maiden there lived whom you may know.
4   By the name of Annabel Lee;
And this maiden she lived with no other thought
    Than to love and be loved by me.

I was a child and *she* was a child,
8   In this kingdom by the sea;
But we loved with a love that was more than love—
    I and my Annabel Lee—
With a love that the wingéd seraphs of heaven
12   **Coveted** her and me.

How did Annabel Lee die in this poem? Who was blamed for her death?

A *seraph* is an angel.

covet to wish for heavily

And this was the reason that, long ago,
    In this kingdom by the sea,
A wind blew out of a cloud, chilling
16   My beautiful Annabel Lee;
So that her highborn kinsmen came
    And bore her away from me,
To shut her up in a sepulchre

20   In this kingdom by the sea.

The angels, not half so happy in heaven,
    Went envying her and me—
Yes!—that was the reason (as all men know,
24   In this kingdom by the sea)
That the wind came out of the cloud by night,
    Chilling and killing my Annabel Lee.

But our love it was stronger by far than the love
28   Of those who were older than we—
    Of many far wiser than we—
And neither the angels in heaven above,
    Nor the demons down under the sea,
32 Can ever **dissever** my soul from the soul
    Of the beautiful Annabel Lee.

For the moon never beams, without bringing me dreams
    Of the beautiful Annabel Lee;
36 And the stars never rise, but I feel the bright eyes
    Of the beautiful Annabel Lee.
And so, all the night tide, I lie down by the side
Of my darling—my darling—my life and my bride,
40   In her sepulchre there by the sea—
    In her tomb by the sounding sea.

dissever to separate

Directions Write the answers to these questions using complete sentences.

Comprehension: Identifying Facts

1. Which lines show the love between the poet and Annabel Lee?

2. What words refer to death in this poem?

3. How did Annabel Lee die?

Comprehension: Understanding Main Ideas

4. How does the poem illustrate the concept of eternal love?

5. What is meant by the "kingdom by the sea"?

6. What is meant by the lines, "But our love it was stronger by far than the love/Of those who were older than we—/Of many far wiser than we—"?

Understanding Literature: Mood and Refrain

In poetry, the plot is not as important as the mood. The attempt is made to make the reader feel emotion. Repetition of certain words or phrases is one way of creating a mood. Such repetition of lines is called a refrain.

7. What are some examples of words, phrases, or lines that appear more than once in the poem "Annabel Lee"?

8. How does this device help to create a mood?

Critical Thinking

9. What is the mood of the poem? Explain your answer.

10. What part of the poem indicates that the poet is still grieving for his lost love? Do you think that this is healthy grieving or not? Explain your answer.

Writing on Your Own Write a poem using at least six lines. Use at least one refrain—repetition of a word or phrase—to create a mood in your poem.

Metaphor

A metaphor is a figure of speech that makes a comparison. A metaphor does not use the words *like* or *as*. The comparisons are made between two things that are alike only in some small way. For example:

> They were **drowning** in **money.**
>
> **She** is a **breath of fresh air.**

These examples compare having money to drowning and a woman to fresh air. Notice metaphors state the comparison rather than use *like* or *as*.

Metaphors are useful in writing because they provide images and make comparisons for the reader. Metaphors challenge the reader to picture the image or make the comparison the author is trying to give. Metaphors also make writing more interesting.

In the next column are some metaphors Edgar Allan Poe used in "The Black Cat."

> But I am detailing a **chain of facts**— and wish not to leave even a possible link imperfect.
>
> During the former the **creature** left me no moment alone; and, in the latter, I started hourly from dreams of unutterable fear to find the hot breath of *the thing* upon my face, and its vast weight, an **incarnate nightmare** that I had no power to shake off— incumbent eternally upon my *heart*!

The first sentence compares facts to a chain. The second sentence compares the cat to a living nightmare.

Review

1. What is a metaphor?

2. Do metaphors use *like* or *as*?

3. Do you think Poe's metaphors make the writing more interesting? Why or why not?

4. How do metaphors improve writing?

5. Why do you think authors use metaphors?

Writing on Your Own Write three metaphors of your own describing a person, place, or thing. Do not use *like* or *as*.

UNIT 1 SUMMARY

Unit 1 covers 1620 to 1849. The development of new colonies, the struggle between Europeans and American Indians, and the American Revolution took place during this time.

Four styles of literature—native, colonial, revolutionary, and early national—represent early America. Native literature in this unit includes American Indian poems and a myth that had been passed down orally. Colonial literature in this unit includes the works of William Bradford, Anne Dudley Bradstreet, and Benjamin Franklin. These writings copied European styles. The revolutionary literature in this unit is by Thomas Paine, a writer during the American Revolution. Early national literature came about in the 1800s. Two professional writers, Washington Irving and Edgar Allan Poe, were part of this movement. They studied the inner workings of people and society. Early national literature began to replace letters, essays, and speeches that were popular in the past.

Selections

■ *The History of Plymouth Plantation* by William Bradford is a diary describing the Pilgrims' first landing in America.

■ "To My Dear and Loving Husband" by Anne Dudley Bradstreet is a love poem from a wife to her husband.

■ The selection from *Poor Richard's Almanac* by Benjamin Franklin is a list of aphorisms, or clever sayings.

■ *The American Crisis, Number 1* by Thomas Paine is a pamphlet that expresses the desire for freedom and urges Americans to continue their struggle against England.

■ "Wouter Van Twiller" by Washington Irving is a sketch that uses satire and exaggeration to poke fun at a man's undeserved fame.

■ Three American Indian poems by the Omaha, Sioux, and Chippewa express American Indian attitudes toward death and love for the land.

■ "The Origin of Plumage" is an Iroquois myth, or story that explains how something in the natural world came to be. This myth explains how all birds got their feathers.

■ "The Black Cat" by Edgar Allan Poe is a horror short story about one man's madness and his cat.

■ "Annabel Lee" by Edgar Allan Poe is a poem about the grief caused by the death of a lover.

UNIT 1 REVIEW

Directions Write the answers to these questions using complete sentences.

Comprehension: Identifying Facts

1. Why did the Puritans and Pilgrims leave England?

2. What was established in the South?

3. Who were three political leaders of the 1700s?

4. Which two authors in this unit represent the time after the American Revolution?

5. Who were the very first people to live in America?

Comprehension: Understanding Main Ideas

6. What similarities and differences can you see in the works of Washington Irving and Edgar Allan Poe? How did each writer's background affect his works?

7. Describe the similarities and differences found in the poetry of Anne Dudley Bradstreet and Edgar Allan Poe.

8. How does Benjamin Franklin's writing differ from William Bradford's? Are their writings similar in any way? Explain your answer.

9. In what ways are the American Indian poems in this unit similar to and different from the other poetry in this unit?

10. What are three common themes of the selections in this unit?

Understanding Literature: Fiction and Nonfiction

Most early American literature is nonfiction and based on writing styles used in Europe. Nonfiction describes actual people and real events. Toward the middle of the nineteenth century, fiction was introduced. Fiction describes imaginary characters and made-up events. An American style of writing also developed.

11. Identify each selection in Unit 1 by genre (poem, short story, essay, etc.). If the work is not a poem, tell whether the selection is fiction or nonfiction.

12. Choose two works from Unit 1. How are these two works different? Compare these two selections for language, style, content, and characters.

13. Write the name of the selection from Unit 1 that surprised you the most. Explain the reasons for your choice.

14. Which selection from this unit describes life in America best? Why?

15. Is it important for a nation to have its own style of writing? Explain.

Critical Thinking

16. Anne Dudley Bradstreet is the only woman represented in this unit. Do you think she would be admired today? Explain your answer.

17. Do you like the early American literature from this unit? Why or why not?

18. Explain what you think is most important about early American literature.

19. Which author from this unit did you like best? Why?

20. Which poem from this unit did you like best? Why?

Speak and Listen

Think how society has changed since the 1800s. What are some ways in which modern life is different from the life of a young person who lived 150 to 200 years ago? What is the one thing that you would miss most if you were to go back in time to the 1800s? For your class, prepare a brief speech that answers these questions. Think about what you will say. Make a few notes to help you remember what to say. Practice by giving your speech to a partner. Listen to your partner's speech and give each other suggestions. Then you are ready to give your speech to the class.

Beyond Words

Review the selections included in Unit 1. Think about how you might illustrate one poem or story. Draw a picture or poster that illustrates some selection in this unit.

Writing on Your Own Write an essay describing your favorite selection from Unit 1. Explain why you liked the selection, how it made you feel, and what you learned by reading it. Include an introductory sentence, a body, and a conclusion.

Test-Taking Tip

Avoid waiting until the night before a test to study. Plan your time so that you can get a good night's sleep the night before a test.

"If I read a book and it makes my whole body so cold no fire can ever warm me, I know that is poetry. If I feel physically as if the top of my head were taken off, I know that is poetry. These are the only ways I know it. Is there any other way?"

—Emily Dickinson

"There are two classes of poets—the poets by education and practice, these we respect; and poets by nature, these we love."

—Ralph Waldo Emerson, *Parnassus*, 1874

UNIT 2 *The Inspiration of New England: 1837–1860*

Much of the best early American literature came from the northeastern part of the United States called New England. Several excellent writers lived in this area, particularly in Massachusetts. These writers not only contributed to the wealth of American writing, but also offered many exciting new ideas to the American people.

In this unit, you will learn about the New England authors and their writing.

This time in American literary history is sometimes called the Golden Age of New England. Beginning in the 1830s, the sense of greatness in the United States was growing. Transportation was developing by the building of roads, canals, steamboats, and railroads. People and goods could expand to the West and South. The age of industry gave work to the common person: the builder, the laborer, the farmer. The belief in the basic goodness of people was growing.

The individual became very important. In this land of the free, great writers like Ralph Waldo Emerson and Henry David Thoreau were turning people on to the ideas of individual freedom. Industry was growing. Much opportunity for all men and women existed. However, some harsh realities existed at this time, too. Industrial growth in the North meant poor working conditions.

Industry was ugly; towns were dirty and crowded. Even children were forced to work hard, long hours.

Slavery in the South also became more and more difficult to accept. How could slavery fit in with the statements in the Declaration of Independence? If "all men were created equal," then how could slavery exist? Slowly, more and more great thinkers in this country were drawn to the antislavery cause.

New England was the center for culture in the early 1800s. This area was rich with colleges and artistic expression. The excitement of learning, the sense of hopefulness, the spirit of individual freedom, and strong morals were all a part of romanticism. The writers in Unit 2 were all part of the romantic movement. Some qualities represented by romantics include deeply personal thoughts and emotions, an interest in nature, and an interest in the unusual

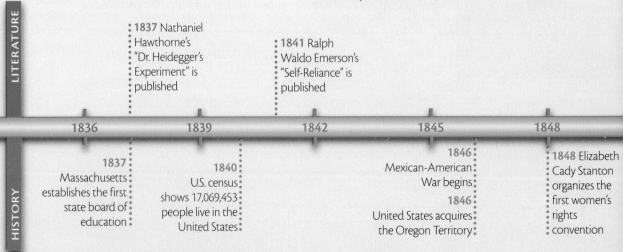

LITERATURE

1837 Nathaniel Hawthorne's "Dr. Heidegger's Experiment" is published

1841 Ralph Waldo Emerson's "Self-Reliance" is published

1836　1839　1842　1845　1848

HISTORY

1837 Massachusetts establishes the first state board of education

1840 U.S. census shows 17,069,453 people live in the United States

1846 Mexican-American War begins

1846 United States acquires the Oregon Territory

1848 Elizabeth Cady Stanton organizes the first women's rights convention and the original. New Englanders were also influenced by transcendentalism. This belief said that the spiritual world had greater value than the material world and that the individual was of great importance.

Some writers of this time, such as Emerson and Thoreau, thought that people were basically good. Emerson's "Self-Reliance" celebrates being true to oneself. Thoreau's *Walden* stresses the simple life and an appreciation for nature.

Other writers, such as Nathaniel Hawthorne and Herman Melville, felt that there was a kind of evil in people. Hawthorne's "Dr. Heidegger's Experiment" shows how people might behave if they had a second chance at youth. Melville's "The Fiddler" discusses the nature of happiness and success, while his poem "Shiloh" describes the scene of a just-completed

New England includes the states of Maine, New Hampshire, Vermont, Massachusetts, Rhode Island, and Connecticut.

battle. Finally, Emily Dickinson's poems represent the expression of innermost thoughts and feelings. Her poems are brief but meaningful looks at death, separation, and life after death. New England was the setting for all of these artists. Many of them were neighbors. New England became a special literary center during this important period.

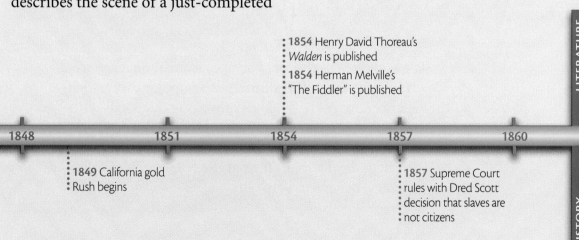

LITERATURE

1854 Henry David Thoreau's *Walden* is published

1854 Herman Melville's "The Fiddler" is published

1848   1851   1854   1857   1860

1849 California gold Rush begins

1857 Supreme Court rules with Dred Scott decision that slaves are not citizens

HISTORY

Self-Reliance
Ralph Waldo Emerson

Ralph Waldo
Emerson

1803–1882

Literary Terms

essay a kind of writing that deals with one main subject and states facts and opinions to support the author's beliefs

excerpt a short passage from a longer piece of writing

About the Author

Ralph Waldo Emerson was born in Boston, Massachusetts, in 1803. His father died when Emerson was eight years old. The family was then quite poor. The eight children were raised in a strict, sheltered home in Concord, Massachusetts. The family struggled, but four sons, including Emerson, were able to go to college at Harvard. He graduated in 1821 and became a minister. He was later named pastor of a Boston church. He married, but his wife died just over a year after the wedding. An independent thinker, Emerson felt uncomfortable with his role as a church leader. He left the ministry in 1832.

Emerson then traveled to Europe where he met many famous writers. They encouraged him to try writing. He discovered that he was not only a talented writer, but also a gifted speaker. He developed a belief that stressed the importance of an independent spirit. He encouraged people to feel a sense of worth and to think for themselves.

Emerson believed in the basic goodness of people. His writing is often thought to be among the greatest in American literature. When his health began to fail, Emerson returned to Concord. He died in 1882.

About the Selection

These **excerpts**, or short passages from a longer piece of writing, are taken from Emerson's popular **essay**, "Self-Reliance." An essay is a kind of writing that deals with one main subject. In an essay, the author usually tries to state several facts and opinions in support of a certain belief. As the title suggests, the main idea of "Self-Reliance" is to know, trust, and believe in yourself.

Self-Reliance

1. I read the other day some verses written by an **eminent** painter which were original and not **conventional**. Always the soul hears an **admonition** in such lines, let the subject be what it may. The sentiment they instill is of more value than any thought they may contain. To believe your own thought, to believe that what is true for you in your private heart is true for all men—that is genius. . . .

What is Emerson's main idea in this essay?

2. There is a time in every man's education when he arrives at the conviction that envy is ignorance; that imitation is suicide; that he must take himself for better, for worse, as his portion; that though the wide universe is full of good, no kernel of **nourishing** corn can come to him but through his toil **bestowed** on that plot of ground which is given to him to till. The power which resides in him is new in nature, and none but he knows what that is which he can do, nor does he know until he has tried. Not for nothing one face, one character, one fact, makes much impression on him, and another none. . . .

Here the author is stating his belief that people should do what they do best and not copy others.

3. Trust thyself: every heart vibrates to that iron string. Accept the place the divine **providence** has found for you; the society of your **contemporaries**, the connection of events. Great men have always done so . . .

---

admonition a gentle warning

bestow to give as a gift

contemporaries people of the same or nearly the same age

conventional ordinary; commonplace

eminent famous

nourishing providing energy from food

providence help from God

Here the author refers to several important people in history who were often misunderstood. *Pythagoras* was a Greek philosopher and mathematician (about 580–500 B.C.); *Socrates* was a Greek philosopher (about 470–399 B.C.); *Martin Luther* was a German Reformation leader (1483–1546); *Nicolaus Copernicus* was a Polish astronomer (1473–1543); *Galileo Galilei* was an Italian astronomer and physicist (1564–1642); and *Sir Isaac Newton* was an English mathematician and physicist (1642–1727).

Do you think it is important to be yourself? Why?

14. A foolish consistency is the **hobgoblin** of little minds, adored by little statesmen and philosophers and divines. With consistency a great soul has simply nothing to do. He may as well concern himself with his shadow on the wall. . . . Speak what you think today in words as hard as cannon balls, and tomorrow speak what tomorrow thinks in hard words again, though it **contradict** everything you said today. Ah, then, exclaim the aged ladies, you shall be sure to be misunderstood. Misunderstood! It is a right fool's word. Is it so bad then to be misunderstood? Pythagoras was misunderstood, and Socrates, and Jesus, and Luther, and Copernicus, and Galileo, and Newton, and every pure and wise spirit that ever took flesh. To be great is to be misunderstood.

43. Insist on yourself; never imitate. Your own gifts you can present every moment with the **cumulative** force of a whole life's **cultivation**; but of the adopted talent of another, you have only an **extemporaneous** half possession. . . .

50. A political victory, a rise of rents, the recovery of your sick, or the return of your absent friend, or some other favorable event raises your spirits, and you think good days are preparing for you. Do not believe it. . . . Nothing can bring you peace but yourself. Nothing can bring you peace but the triumph of principles.

---

contradict to go against

cultivation growth

cumulative combined

extemporaneous done on the spur of the moment

hobgoblin an imaginary fear; something that causes fear

Self-Reliance
Ralph Waldo Emerson

Directions Write the answers to these questions using complete sentences.

Comprehension: Identifying Facts

1. How does Emerson define genius? (paragraph 1)

2. What does Emerson say ignorance is? (paragraph 2)

3. Does the author believe that it is a bad thing to be misunderstood? (paragraph 14)

Comprehension: Understanding Main Ideas

4. Explain the title of this essay. What does self-reliance mean?

5. What does this essay reveal about Emerson?

6. What does the final line of the essay mean? ("Nothing can bring you peace but the triumph of principles.")

Understanding Literature: Essay

You have probably written or read an essay before. An essay is any piece of writing that states an opinion or belief about a given topic. Emerson's full essay was much longer than what you have just read—it was fifty paragraphs. This longer, more in-depth type of essay is called a formal essay. However, not all essays are that long and formal. Informal or personal essays are much shorter and treat the subject more lightly.

7. How is this essay different from other kinds of writing you have read in this book so far?

8. What is Emerson's main point in "Self-Reliance"?

Critical Thinking

9. Do you think that the message in this essay might especially benefit any particular age group? Explain your answer.

10. Identify two ways in which you could show how you are different from others.

Writing on Your Own Think of an idea for an informal essay. The topic does not need to be extremely important, as long as it is something you have a strong belief about. Write a paragraph describing your topic. At least one of the sentences should express your opinion about the topic.

Walden
Henry David Thoreau

Henry David
Thoreau
1817–1862

Literary Term

simile a comparison that uses the words *like* or *as*

About the Author

Henry David Thoreau lived almost his entire life in various small towns of Massachusetts, especially Concord. He was one of four children in a fairly poor family. He attended Harvard College and graduated in 1837. Then he became a school teacher. He did not enjoy teaching, so he decided to write. He was influenced by another New Englander, Ralph Waldo Emerson. Thoreau decided to practice Emerson's teachings and to live close to nature.

Thoreau moved to a small cabin in the woods on Walden Pond, about a mile from Concord. Here he kept only the things he needed and lived simply. For two years he observed nature, lived alone, and thought about the universe. The essays he wrote about these two years were put together in a book called *Walden*. The collection was published in 1854, one of only two books published during Thoreau's own lifetime. His entire collection of works, twenty volumes, was not published until 1906.

Although Thoreau had several loves, he never married and he never traveled far from Concord. He died of tuberculosis at age 44.

About the Selection

Walden is a book about Thoreau's two years of life alone in the woods. His writing shows that observing nature, avoiding society, and living simply can indeed be delightful. *Walden* is thought to be his best work. The following is a selection taken from "Where I Lived and What I Lived For," a chapter from *Walden*.

This selection includes **similes**. A simile is a comparison that uses the words *like* or *as*. For example: "He was as cold as ice."

Walden

FROM Where I Lived and What I Lived For

The present was my next experiment of this kind, which I purpose to describe more at length; for convenience, putting the experience of two years into one. As I have said, I do not propose to write an ode to **dejection** but to brag as lustily as chanticleer in the morning, standing on his roost, if only to wake my neighbors up.

When first I took up my **abode** in the woods, that is, began to spend my nights as well as days there, which, by accident, was on Independence Day, or the Fourth of July, 1845, my house was not finished for winter, but was merely a defense against the rain, without plastering or chimney, the walls being of rough, weather-stained boards, with wide **chinks**, which made it cool at night. The upright white hewn studs and freshly planed door and window casings gave it a clean and airy look, especially in the morning, when its timbers were **saturated** with dew, so that I fancied that by noon some sweet gum would **exude** from them. To my imagination it retained throughout the day more or less of this **auroral** character, reminding me of a certain house on a mountain which I had visited a year before. This was an airy and unplastered cabin, fit to

What were Thoreau's home and surrounding areas like at Walden?

A *chanticleer* is a rooster.

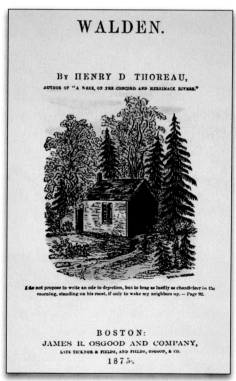

WALDEN.

BY HENRY D THOREAU,

AUTHOR OF "A WEEK ON THE CONCORD AND MERRIMACK RIVERS."

I do not propose to write an ode to dejection, but to brag as lustily as chanticleer in the morning, standing on his roost, if only to wake my neighbors up. — Page 92.

BOSTON:
JAMES R. OSGOOD AND COMPANY,
LATE TICKNOR & FIELDS, AND FIELDS, OSGOOD, & CO.
1875.

The cover above from the 1875 edition of *Walden* shows what Thoreau's small cabin looked like.

abode a home

auroral referring to arches of light that appear in the upper atmosphere of a planet's polar regions

chink a small opening between the logs of a cabin

dejection sadness

exude to ooze out

saturated filled completely with something

entertain a traveling god, and where a goddess might trail her garments. The winds which passed over my dwelling were such as sweep over the ridges of mountains, bearing the broken strains, or celestial parts only, of **terrestrial** music. The morning wind forever blows, the poem of creation is uninterrupted; but few are the ears that hear it. Olympus is but the outside of the earth everywhere.

The only house I had been the owner of before, if I except a boat, was a tent, which I used occasionally when making **excursions** in the summer, and this is still rolled up in my garret; but the boat, after passing from hand to hand, has gone down the stream of time. With this more **substantial** shelter about me, I had made some progress toward settling in the world. This frame, so slightly clad, was a sort of crystallization around me, and reacted on the builder. It was suggestive somewhat as a picture in outlines. I did not need to go outdoors to take the air, for the atmosphere within had lost none of its freshness. It was not so much within doors as behind a door where I sat, even in the rainiest weather. The Harivansa says, "An abode without birds is like a meat without seasoning." Such was not my abode, for I found myself suddenly neighbor to the birds; not by having imprisoned one, but having caged myself near them. I was not only nearer to some of those which commonly frequent the garden and the orchard, but to those wilder and more thrilling songsters of the forest which never, or rarely, **serenade** a villager—the wood thrush, the veery, the scarlet tanager, the field sparrow, the whippoorwill, and many others.

I was seated by the shore of a small pond, about a mile and a half south of the village of Concord and somewhat higher than it, in the midst of an extensive wood between that town and Lincoln, and about two miles south of that our only field known to fame, Concord Battle Ground; but I was so

excursion a short trip	**substantial** firmly constructed; large
serenade to sing or play music, often outdoors at night to court a loved one	**terrestrial** of or relating to the earth

low in the woods that the opposite shore, half a mile off, like the rest, covered with wood, was my most distant horizon. For the first week, whenever I looked out on the pond it impressed me like a **tarn** high up on the side of a mountain, its bottom far above the surface of other lakes, and, as the sun arose, I saw it throwing off its nightly clothing of mist, and here and there, by degrees, its soft ripples or its smooth reflecting surface was revealed, while the mists, like ghosts, were **stealthily** withdrawing in every direction into the woods, as at the breaking up of some **nocturnal conventicle**. The very dew seemed to hang upon the trees later into the day than usual, as on the sides of mountains.

This small lake was of most value as a neighbor in the intervals of a gentle rainstorm in August, when, both air and

Walden Pond still exists today. This 1908 photograph above shows the view of Walden Pond from Thoreau's cabin.

conventicle a meeting; a secret meeting	**stealthily** slowly and secretly	**tarn** a small, steep-banked mountain lake or pool
nocturnal of, relating to, or occurring in the night		

water being perfectly still, but the sky overcast, midafternoon had all the serenity of evening, and the wood thrush sang around, and was heard from shore to shore. A lake like this is never smoother than at such a time; and the clear portion of the air above it being shallow and darkened by clouds, the water, full of light and reflections, becomes a lower heaven itself so much the more important. From a hilltop nearby, where the wood had been recently cut off, there was a pleasing vista southward across the pond, through a wide indentation in the hills which form the shore there, where their opposite sides sloping toward each other suggested a stream flowing out in that direction through a wooded valley, but stream there was none. That way I looked between and over the near green hills to some distant and higher ones in the horizon, **tinged** with blue. Indeed, by standing on tiptoe I could catch a glimpse of some of the peaks of the still bluer and more distant mountain ranges in the northwest, those true-blue coins from heaven's own mint, and also of some portion of the village. But in other directions, even from this point, I could not see over or beyond the woods which surrounded me. It is well to have some water in your neighborhood, to give **buoyancy** to and float the earth. One value even of the smallest well is that when you look into it you see that earth is not continent but **insular**. This is as important as that it keeps butter cool. When I looked across the pond from this peak toward the Sudbury meadows, which in time of flood I distinguished elevated perhaps by a **mirage** in their seething valley, like a coin in a basin, all the earth beyond the pond appeared like a thin crust **insulated** and floated even by this small sheet of **intervening** water, and I was reminded that this on which I dwelt was but *dry land.* . . .

The author uses a simile in this sentence. "Like a coin in a basin" is a simile that describes the way the flooded meadows look.

buoyancy a tendency to float in liquid

insular of, relating to, or being an island

insulated kept from transferring heat

intervening occurring between two things

mirage the appearance of water that is not really there, caused by the bending or reflection of rays of light

tinged having a slight amount or shading of color

Walden
Henry David Thoreau

Directions Write the answers to these questions using complete sentences.

Comprehension: Identifying Facts

1. How long did Thoreau live in the woods?

2. On what date did the author move into his cabin in the woods?

3. Copy the sentence that proves that this cabin was the author's first house.

4. Who were his "neighbors"?

5. How wide was the pond he overlooked?

6. What was the view toward the northwest?

7. How far away did he live from the Concord Battle Ground?

8. What kinds of birds were around his cabin?

9. What could Thoreau see from a nearby hilltop?

10. At what time of year did rainstorms occur?

Comprehension: Understanding Main Ideas

11. Describe the cabin that became Thoreau's home.

12. Did Thoreau feel "caged," or like he was in a prison? Why or why not?

13. What things was Thoreau able to enjoy that people in a town or village didn't have?

14. To what does Thoreau compare the pond in the fourth paragraph?

15. Why did Thoreau like the pond?

16. Does it seem like Thoreau enjoyed where he lived? Why or why not?

17. How does Thoreau describe the mountains in the distance?

18. What was the weather often like where he lived?

19. Did Thoreau seem to lead a comfortable life at Walden Pond? Explain.

20. What does this writing seem to say about nature?

Review Continued on Next Page

Understanding Literature: Simile

As you have learned, one way to make writing more interesting is by using certain figures of speech. Such techniques are especially useful in descriptive writing because they can suggest new meanings for words. One common figure of speech is simile. A simile is a comparison that uses the words *like* or *as*.

21. What is a simile and why is it used?

22. Find three similes in *Walden*. Write them on your own paper.

23. Identify each comparison by underlining the appropriate words.

24. Do these similes make the sentences more interesting? Why or why not?

25. Choose one of the sentences that uses a simile. Rewrite the sentence using a simile of your own.

Critical Thinking

26. Would you like to live alone in such a place as Walden Pond? Explain both the good and the bad sides of this experiment of living close to nature.

27. Why do you think Thoreau wanted to live where he lived? Explain.

28. Do you think it would be possible for someone to live today as Thoreau did? Why or why not?

29. How does this writing make you feel about Thoreau as a person? Explain.

30. Is Thoreau's view of nature similar to your own? Why or why not?

Writing on Your Own Thoreau described Walden Pond in great detail. Choose a place that you enjoy and describe it as Thoreau described Walden. Write a paragraph describing a specific part you like best about the place.

Dr. Heidegger's Experiment
Nathaniel Hawthorne

Nathaniel
Hawthorne
1804–1864

Literary Terms

fable a story with a message or moral

mood the feeling that writing creates

moral a message in a story

About the Author

Nathaniel Hawthorne was born in Salem, Massachusetts, on July 4, 1804. Salem had been a town of witch hunts in the 1690s, and Hawthorne's past relatives had taken part in these trials. Hawthorne was troubled by his family's background, and he became very interested in the history of the New England area.

Hawthorne's father was a sea captain who died when Hawthorne was four. The family lived an unhappy life. Hawthorne graduated from college in 1825 and later turned to writing as a career. He spent ten years learning to be a writer. He married in 1842 and settled in Concord, where he and his wife raised four children.

Hawthorne's first collection of stories was called *Twice Told Tales*, published in 1837. "Dr. Heidegger's Experiment" is taken from this collection. However, his later novels, such as *The House of Seven Gables* and *The Scarlet Letter*, made him famous. He became known as a writer of good and evil. Hawthorne's themes include sin and "the truth of the human heart."

About the Selection

"Dr. Heidegger's Experiment" is a story of four elderly people who are the subjects of a strange experiment. The story is an example of the magical world of romantic literature. It gives the reader much to think about concerning human nature.

Like many of Hawthorne's stories, "Dr. Heidegger's Experiment" teaches a lesson. Such a lesson in literature is sometimes taught in a certain style called a **fable**. This story is a fable because there is a message, or **moral**. Sometimes the moral of a story is stated directly, but often the reader must arrive at the moral. Notice also how this story creates a **mood** of mystery. Mood is the feeling that writing creates.

Dr. Heidegger's Experiment

Hawthorne makes a moral statement in this story. What is it? Is it a good statement?

That very singular man, old Dr. Heidegger, once invited four **venerable** friends to meet him in his study. There were three whitebearded gentlemen, Mr. Medbourne, Colonel Killigrew, and Mr. Gascoigne, and a withered gentlewoman, whose name was the Widow Wycherly. They were all melancholy old creatures, who had been unfortunate in life, and whose greatest misfortune it was that they were not long ago in their graves. Mr. Medbourne, in the vigor of his age, had been a prosperous merchant, but had lost his all by a frantic speculation, and was now little better than a **mendicant**. Colonel Killigrew had wasted his best years, and his health and substance, in the pursuit of sinful pleasures, which had given birth to a brood of pains, such as the gout and **divers** other torments of soul and body. Mr. Gascoigne was a ruined politician, a man of evil fame, or at least had been so, till time had buried him from the knowledge of the present generation, and made him **obscure** instead of **infamous**. As for the Widow Wycherly, tradition tells us that she was a great beauty in her day; but, for a long while past, she had lived in deep **seclusion**, on account of certain scandalous stories, which had prejudiced the **gentry** of the town against her. It is a circumstance worth mentioning, that each of these three old gentlemen, Mr. Medbourne, Colonel Killigrew, and Mr. Gascoigne, were early lovers of the Widow

Gout is a disease marked by pain and swelling in the joints.

divers various

gentry members of the ruling or upper class

infamous having a reputation of the worst kind

mendicant a beggar

obscure relatively unknown

seclusion the act of being alone or away from others

venerable old and respected

Wycherly, and had once been on the point of cutting each other's throats for her sake. And, before proceeding further, I will merely hint, that Dr. Heidegger and all his four guests were sometimes thought to be a little beside themselves; as is not unfrequently the case with old people, when worried either by present troubles or woeful recollections.

"My dear old friends," said Dr. Heidegger, motioning them to be seated, "I am desirous of your assistance in one of those little experiments with which I amuse myself here in my study."

If all stories were true, Dr. Heidegger's study must have been a very curious place. It was a dim, old-fashioned chamber, **festooned** with cobwebs and besprinkled with antique dust. Around the walls stood several oaken bookcases, the lower shelves of which were filled with rows of gigantic folios and black-letter quartos, and the upper with little parchment-covered duodecimos. Over the central bookcase was a bronze bust of Hippocrates, with which, according to some authorities, Dr. Heidegger was accustomed to hold consultations, in all difficult cases of his practice.

Folios, quartos, and *duodecimos* are different sizes of books. *Hippocrates* was a Greek physician and the father of medicine (about 460–377 B.C.).

festooned decorated

In the obscurest corner of the room stood a tall and narrow oaken closet, with its door ajar, within which doubtfully appeared a skeleton. Between two of the bookcases hung a looking glass, presenting its high and dusty plate within a **tarnished gilt** frame. Among many wonderful stories related of this mirror, it was fabled that the spirits of all the doctor's deceased patients dwelt within its verge, and would stare him in the face whenever he looked **thitherward**. The opposite side of the chamber was ornamented with the full-length portrait of a young lady, arrayed in the faded magnificence of silk, satin, and brocade, and with a **visage** as faded as her dress. Above half a century ago, Dr. Heidegger had been on the point of marriage with this young lady; but, being affected with some slight disorder, she had swallowed one of her lover's prescriptions, and died on the bridal evening. The greatest curiosity of the study remains to be mentioned; it was a ponderous folio volume, bound in black leather, with massive silver clasps. There were no letters on the back, and nobody could tell the title of the book. But it was well known to be a book of magic; and once, when a chambermaid had lifted it, merely to brush away the dust, the skeleton had rattled in its closet, the picture of the young lady had stepped one foot upon the floor, and several ghastly faces had peeped forth from the mirror; while the **brazen** head of Hippocrates frowned, and said, "Forbear!"

Such was Dr. Heidegger's study. On the summer afternoon of our tale, a small round table, as black as **ebony**, stood in the center of the room, sustaining a cut-glass vase, of beautiful form and elaborate workmanship. The sunshine came through the window, between the heavy festoons of two faded damask curtains, and fell directly across this vase; so that a mild splendor was reflected from it on the ashen

The words *ponderous folio volume* describe a heavy book of great size.

What is the mood of the study? How does this add to the mysterious feeling of this story?

brazen made of brass	**gilt** gold, or looking like gold	**thitherward** toward that place
ebony a kind of hard, dark wood	**tarnished** dulled or destroyed in luster by air, dust, or dirt	**visage** face; appearance

visages of the five old people who sat around. Four champagne glasses were also on the table.

"My dear old friends," repeated Dr. Heidegger, "may I reckon on your aid in performing an exceedingly curious experiment?"

Now Dr. Heidegger was a very strange old gentleman, whose **eccentricity** had become the **nucleus** for a thousand fantastic stories. Some of these fables, to my shame be it spoken, might possibly be traced back to mine own **veracious** self; and if any passages of the present tale should startle the reader's faith, I must be content to bear the **stigma** of a fictionmonger.

A *fictionmonger* is a liar or a teller of tall tales.

When the doctor's four guests heard him talk of this proposed experiment, they anticipated nothing more wonderful than the murder of a mouse in an air-pump, or the examination of a cobweb by the microscope, or some similar nonsense, with which he was constantly in the habit of pestering his intimates. But without waiting for a reply, Dr. Heidegger hobbled across the chamber, and returned with the same ponderous folio, bound in black leather, which common report affirmed to be a book of magic. Undoing the silver clasps, he opened the volume, and took from among its black-letter pages a rose, or what was once a rose, though now the green leaves and crimson petals had assumed one brownish hue, and the ancient flower seemed ready to crumble to dust in the doctor's hands.

"This rose," said Dr. Heidegger, with a sigh, "this same withered and crumbling flower, blossomed five-and-fifty years ago. It was given me by Sylvia Ward, whose portrait hangs yonder; and I meant to wear it in my bosom at our wedding. Five-and-fifty years it has been treasured between the leaves of this old volume. Now, would you **deem** it possible that this rose of half a century could ever bloom again?"

deem to think or judge; to consider	**nucleus** a central point, group, or mass	**veracious** truthful; honest
eccentricity an odd or abnormal behavior	**stigma** a mark of shame	

What does this tell you about the Widow Wycherly as a person?

"Nonsense!" said the Widow Wycherly, with a peevish toss of her head. "You might as well ask whether an old woman's wrinkled face could ever bloom again."

"See!" answered Dr. Heidegger.

He uncovered the vase, and threw the faded rose into the water which it contained. At first, it lay lightly on the surface of the fluid, appearing to **imbibe** none of its moisture. Soon, however, a singular change began to be visible. The crushed and dried petals stirred, and assumed a deepening tinge of crimson, as if the flower were reviving from a death-like slumber; the slender stalk and twigs of **foliage** became green; and there was the rose of half a century, looking as fresh as when Sylvia Ward had first given it to her lover. It was scarcely full blown; for some of its delicate red leaves curled modestly around its moist bosom, within which two or three dewdrops were sparkling.

"That is certainly a very pretty **deception**," said the doctor's friends; carelessly, however, for they had witnessed greater miracles at a **conjurer's** show; "pray how was it effected?"

conjurer a magician

deception a trick

foliage leaves, flowers, and branches

imbibe to take in; to drink

"Did you never hear of the 'Fountain of Youth,'" asked Dr. Heidegger, "which Ponce de Leon, the Spanish adventurer, went in search of, two or three centuries ago?"

"But did Ponce de Leon ever find it?" said the Widow Wycherly.

"No," answered Dr. Heidegger, "for he never sought it in the right place. The famous Fountain of Youth, if I am rightly informed, is situated in the southern part of the Floridian peninsula, not far from Lake Macaco. Its source is overshadowed by several gigantic magnolias, which, though numberless centuries old, have been kept as fresh as violets, by the **virtues** of this wonderful water. An acquaintance of mine, knowing my curiosity in such matters, has sent me what you see in the vase."

"Ahem!" said Colonel Killigrew, who believed not a word of the doctor's story; "and what may be the effect of this fluid on the human frame?"

"You shall judge for yourself, my dear Colonel," replied Dr. Heidegger; "and all of you, my respected friends, are welcome to so much of this admirable fluid as may restore to you the bloom of youth. For my own part, having had much trouble in growing old, I am in no hurry to grow young again. With your permission, therefore, I will merely watch the progress of the experiment."

While he spoke, Dr. Heidegger had been filling the four champagne glasses with the water of the Fountain of Youth. It was apparently **impregnated** with an **effervescent** gas, for little bubbles were continually ascending from the depths of the glasses, and bursting in silvery spray at the surface. As the liquor **diffused** a pleasant perfume, the old people doubted not that it possessed **cordial** and comfortable properties; and, though utter **sceptics** as to its **rejuvenescent** power, they were inclined to swallow it at once. But Dr. Heidegger besought them to stay a moment.

Juan Ponce de Leon explored Florida in 1513. He was looking for gold and some say the Fountain of Youth. Water from this fountain, some believed, turned people young again.

---

cordial tending to revive or cheer

diffuse to scatter or spread freely

effervescent bubbling

impregnated filled with

rejuvenescent causing a return of youthfulness

sceptic one who doubts

virtue a good quality or trait

Dr. Heidegger is trying to make his friends think about what they have learned in life before they begin the experiment. He wants them to have rules to guide them when they become young again.

"Before you drink, my respectable old friends," said he, "it would be well that, with the experience of a lifetime to direct you, you should draw up a few general rules for your guidance, in passing a second time through the perils of youth. Think what a sin and shame it would be, if, with your peculiar advantages, you should not become patterns of virtue and wisdom to all the young people of the age."

The doctor's four venerable friends made him no answer, except by a feeble and **tremulous** laugh; so very ridiculous was the idea, that, knowing how closely **repentance** treads behind the steps of error, they should ever go astray again.

"Drink, then," said the doctor, bowing. "I rejoice that I have so well selected the subjects of my experiment."

Here the author is referring to *palsy,* a medical condition marked by uncontrollable shaking. Palsied hands are hands that shake.

With palsied hands, they raised the glasses to their lips. The liquor, if it really possessed such virtues as Dr. Heidegger **imputed** to it, could not have bestowed on four human beings who needed it more woefully. They looked as if they had never known what youth or pleasure was, but had been the offspring of Nature's **dotage**, and always the gray, **decrepit**, sapless, miserable creatures who now sat stooping round the doctor's table, without life enough in their souls or bodies to be animated even by the prospect of growing young again. They drank off the water, and replaced their glasses on the table.

Assuredly there was an almost immediate improvement in the aspect of the party, not unlike what might have been produced by a glass of generous wine, together with a sudden glow of cheerful sunshine, brightening over all their visages at once. There was a healthful **suffusion** on their cheeks, instead of the ashen hue that had made them look so corpse-like. They gazed at one another, and fancied that some magic power had really begun to smooth away the deep and sad **inscriptions** which Father Time had been so long engraving

decrepit old	**impute** to claim as a cause	**repentance** the act of turning away from sin or feeling regret
dotage a state of mental decay or decrease in alertness	**inscription** something written or engraved	**suffusion** a blush
		tremulous nervous

on their brows. The Widow Wycherly adjusted her cap, for she felt almost like a woman again.

"Give us more of this wondrous water!" cried they, eagerly. "We are younger,—but we are still too old! Quick,—give us more!"

"Patience, patience!" quoth Dr. Heidegger, who sat watching the experiment, with philosophic coolness. "You have been a long time growing old. Surely, you might be content to grow young in half an hour! But the water is at your service."

Again he filled their glasses with the liquor of youth, enough of which still remained in the vase to turn half the old people in the city to the age of their own grandchildren. While the bubbles were yet sparkling on the brim, the doctor's four guests snatched their glasses from the table, and swallowed the contents at a single gulp. Was it **delusion**? Even while the **draught** was passing down their throats, it seemed to have wrought a change on their whole systems. Their eyes grew clear and bright; a dark shade deepened among their silvery locks; they sat around the table, three gentlemen of middle age, and a woman, hardly beyond her **buxom** prime.

"My dear widow, you are charming!" cried Colonel Killigrew, whose eyes had been fixed upon her face, while the shadows of age were flitting from it like darkness from the crimson daybreak.

The fair widow knew, of old, that Colonel Killigrew's compliments were not always measured by sober truth; so she started up and ran to the mirror, still dreading that the ugly visage of an old woman would meet her gaze. Meanwhile, the three gentlemen behaved in such a manner, as proved that the water of the Fountain of Youth possessed some intoxicating qualities; unless, indeed, their **exhilaration** of spirits were merely a lightsome dizziness, caused by the sudden removal of the weight of years. Mr. Gascoigne's mind seemed to run on political topics, but whether relating to the past, present,

buxom healthily plump	**delusion** a false belief about the self, others, or objects	**draught** a drink
		exhilaration the feeling of being excited

or future, could not easily be determined, since the same ideas and phrases have been in **vogue** these fifty years. Now he rattled forth full-throated sentences about patriotism, national glory, and the people's right; now he muttered some perilous stuff or other, in a sly and doubtful whisper, so cautiously that even his own conscience could scarcely catch the secret; and now, again, he spoke in measured accents, and a deeply **deferential** tone, as if a royal ear were listening to his well-turned periods. Colonel Killigrew all this time had been trolling forth a jolly bottle-song, and ringing his glass in symphony with the chorus, while his eyes wandered toward the buxom figure of the Widow Wycherly. On the other side of the table, Mr. Medbourne was involved in a calculation of dollars and cents, with which was strangely **intermingled** a project for supplying the East Indies with ice, by harnessing a team of whales to the polar icebergs.

After drinking the water, the four become young again. What else has changed about these people?

As for the Widow Wycherly, she stood before the mirror **curtsying** and **simpering** to her own image, and greeting it as the friend whom she loved better than all the world beside. She thrust her face close to the glass, to see whether some long-remembered wrinkle or crow's foot had indeed vanished. She examined whether the snow had so entirely melted from her hair, that the venerable cap could be safely thrown aside. At last, turning briskly away, she came with a sort of dancing step to the table.

"My dear old doctor," cried she, "pray favor me with another glass!"

"Certainly, my dear madam, certainly!" replied the **complaisant** doctor; "see! I have already filled the glasses."

There, in fact, stood the four glasses, brimful of this wonderful water, the delicate spray of which, as it effervesced from the surface, resembled the tremulous glitter of diamonds. It was now so nearly sunset, that the chamber had

complaisant willing to please	**curtsy** to show respect by a slight lowering of the body with bended knees	**intermingled** mixed in
		simper to smile in a silly manner
	deferential respectful	**vogue** popularity

grown duskier than ever; but a mild and moonlike splendor gleamed from within the vase, and rested alike on the four guests, and on the doctor's venerable figure. He sat in a highbacked, elaborately carved oaken armchair, with a gray dignity of aspect that might have well befitted that very Father Time, whose power had never been disputed, save by this fortunate company. Even while **quaffing** the third draught of the Fountain of Youth, they were almost awed by the expression of his mysterious visage.

But, the next moment, the exhilarating gush of young life shot through their veins. They were now in the happy prime of youth. Age, with its miserable train of cares, and sorrows, and diseases, was remembered only as the trouble of a dream, from which they had joyously awoke. The fresh gloss of the soul, so early lost, and without which the world's successive scenes had been but a gallery of faded pictures, again threw its enchantment over all their prospects. They felt like new-created beings, in a new-created universe.

"We are young! We are young!" they cried exultingly.

Youth, like the **extremity** of age, had **effaced** the strongly marked characteristics of middle life, and mutually **assimilated** them all. They were a group of merry youngsters, almost maddened with the **exuberant** frolicsomeness of their years. The most singular effect of their gayety was an impulse to mock the **infirmity** and decrepitude of which they had so lately been the victims. They laughed loudly at their old-fashioned attire, the wide-skirted coats and flapped waistcoats of the young men, and the ancient cap and gown of the blooming girl. One limped across the floor, like a gouty grandfather; one set a pair of spectacles astride of his nose, and pretended to pore over the black-letter pages of the book of magic; a third seated himself in an armchair, and strove to imitate the venerable dignity of Dr. Heidegger. Then all shouted **mirthfully**, and leaped about the room. The Widow

> Does Dr. Heidegger seem like a good man? What do you think?

assimilate to make similar	**extremity** intense degree	**infirmity** being feeble or frail; old
efface to erase, wipe away, or rub out	**exuberant** joyously unrestrained	**mirthfully** gladly
		quaff to drink deeply

Wycherly—if so fresh a damsel could be called a widow—tripped up to the doctor's chair, with a mischievous merriment in her rosy face.

"Doctor, you dear old soul," cried she, "get up and dance with me!" And then the four young people laughed louder than ever, to think what a queer figure the poor old doctor would cut.

"Pray excuse me," answered the doctor, quietly. "I am old and rheumatic, and my dancing days were over long ago. But either of these gay young gentlemen will be glad of so pretty a partner."

"Dance with me, Clara!" cried Colonel Killigrew.

"No, no, I will be her partner!" shouted Mr. Gascoigne.

"She promised me her hand, fifty years ago!" exclaimed Mr. Medbourne.

They all gathered round her. One caught both her hands in his **passionate** grasp,—another threw his arm about her waist,—the third buried his hand among the glossy curls that clustered beneath the widow's cap. Blushing, panting, struggling, **chiding**, laughing, her warm breath fanning each of their faces by turns, she strove to **disengage** herself, yet still remained in their triple **embrace**. Never was there a livelier picture of youthful rivalship, with **bewitching** beauty for the prize. Yet, by a strange deception, owing to the duskiness of the chamber, and the antique dresses which they still wore, the tall mirror is said to have reflected the figures of the three old, gray, withered grandsires, ridiculously contending for the skinny ugliness of a shriveled grandam.

But they were young: their burning passions proved them so. Inflamed to madness by the **coquetry** of the girl-widow, who neither granted nor quite withheld her favors, the three rivals began to interchange threatening glances. Still keeping hold of the fair prize, they grappled fiercely at one another's throats. As they struggled to and fro, the table was over-

The word *rheumatic* refers to rheumatism, or having inflamed muscles or joints.

The mirror mysteriously shows that the four elderly people are in fact still old. What do you think is happening here?

bewitching attractive in a mysterious way	coquetry flirting	embrace a hug
chiding scolding	disengage to break loose	passionate with intense feeling

turned, and the vase dashed in a thousand fragments. The precious Water of Youth flowed in a bright stream across the floor, moistening the wings of a butterfly, which, grown old in the decline of summer, had alighted there to die. The insect fluttered lightly through the chamber, and settled on the snowy head of Dr. Heidegger.

"Come, come, gentlemen!—come, Madam Wycherly," exclaimed the doctor, "I really must protest this riot."

This paragraph explains that the struggling causes the vase of liquid to fall and break. A dead butterfly magically comes back to life when the spilled liquid touches it.

They stood still and shivered; for it seemed as if gray Time were calling them back from their sunny youth, far down into the chill and darksome vale of years. They looked at old Dr. Heidegger, who sat in his carved armchair, holding the rose of half a century, which he had rescued from among the fragments of the shattered vase. At the motion of his hand, the four rioters resumed their seats; the more readily, because their violent exertions had wearied them, youthful though they were.

"My poor Sylvia's rose!" ejaculated Dr. Heidegger, holding it in the light of the sunset clouds; "it appears to be fading again."

And so it was. Even while the party were looking at it, the flower continued to shrivel up, till it became as dry and fragile as when the doctor had first thrown it into the vase. He shook off the few drops of moisture which clung to its petals.

"I love it as well thus, as in its dewy freshness," observed he, pressing the withered rose to his withered lips. While he spoke, the butterfly fluttered down from the doctor's snowy head, and fell upon the floor.

His guests shivered again. A strange chillness, whether of the body or spirit they could not tell, was creeping gradually over them all. They gazed at one another, and fancied that each fleeting moment snatched away a charm, and left a deepening furrow where none had been before. Was it an illusion? Had the changes of a lifetime been crowded into so brief a space, and were they now four aged people, sitting with their old friend, Dr. Heidegger?

"Are we grown old again, so soon?" cried they, **dolefully**.

In truth, they had. The Water of Youth possessed merely a virtue more **transient** than that of wine. The **delirium** which it created had effervesced away. Yes! they were old again. With a shuddering impulse, that showed her a woman still, the widow clasped her skinny hands before her face, and wished that the coffin lid were over it, since it could be no longer beautiful.

delirium wild excitement	**dolefully** sadly	**transient** passing very quickly

"Yes, friends, ye are old again," said Dr. Heidegger; "and lo! the Water of Youth is **lavished** on the ground. Well, I **bemoan** it not; for if the fountain gushed at my very doorstep, I would not stoop to bathe my lips in it; no, though its delirium were for years instead of moments. Such is the lesson ye have taught me!"

But the doctor's four friends had taught no such lesson to themselves. They resolved forthwith to make a **pilgrimage** to Florida, and quaff at morning, noon, and night from the Fountain of Youth.

> This paragraph explains the moral of this story. What do you think the moral is? Does this change what you thought of Dr. Heidegger as a person?

NOTE—In an English Review, not long since, I have been accused of **plagiarizing** the idea of this story from a chapter in one of the novels of Alexander Dumas. There has undoubtedly been a plagiarism on one side or the other, but as my story was written a good deal more than twenty years ago, and as the novel is of considerably more recent date, I take pleasure in thinking that M. Dumas has done me the honor to appropriate one of the fanciful conceptions of my earlier days. He is heartily welcome to it; nor is it the only instance, by many, in which the great French romancer has exercised the privilege of commanding genius by **confiscating** the intellectual property of less famous people to his own use and behoof.

Nathaniel Hawthorne
September, 1860

> Hawthorne added this paragraph to respond to someone who accused him of stealing this story, or *plagiarizing*. He explains here that he did not steal the story.

---

bemoan to express deep grief

confiscate to take

lavished wasted

pilgrimage a journey to a sacred place

plagiarize to copy someone else's writing

Dr. Heidegger's Experiment
Nathaniel Hawthorne

Directions Write the answers to these questions using complete sentences.

Comprehension: Identifying Facts

1. Name Dr. Heidegger's four guests. Tell how each had spent his or her youth.

2. In which room do the guests gather?

3. What happens to the flower when Dr. Heidegger drops it into the vase?

4. Where had the mysterious fluid come from?

5. What happens as the group of guests drink the fluid?

6. What is Dr. Heidegger doing while the others drink?

7. How does the vase break?

8. Is Dr. Heidegger upset over what happens to the liquid?

9. How does Widow Wycherly react to becoming old again?

10. What do the elderly people decide to do at the end of the experiment?

Comprehension: Understanding Main Ideas

11. What supernatural events are in this story?

12. Describe the room in which the experiment took place. Identify the items that made the experiment seem strange or even scary.

13. What is the reason for including a narrator in the story?

14. What do you know about Dr. Heidegger's one love?

15. Why does Dr. Heidegger not want to drink the liquid himself?

16. Describe how the liquid changes each person.

17. Do the characters experience good changes or bad changes after drinking the liquid? Explain.

18. What does Dr. Heidegger prove with his experiment?

19. What does this story say about growing old?

20. What does this story say about behaviors?

Understanding Literature: Fable and Moral

This story is told in the style of a fable. It has a message, or moral. Sometimes a moral is actually stated in a story. Other times, the reader must try to find the moral by thinking about what was just read. Writers use morals to make a statement about society, often about a particular behavior or belief. Morals allow readers to think more deeply about the topic. However, not all stories have morals, or at least such a strong moral message as "Dr. Heidegger's Experiment" contains.

21. At the very end of the story, Dr. Heidegger states that his friends have taught him a lesson. Write down the line that shows that the doctor has learned a lesson. Read the line and explain what it means. The final paragraph of the story again mentions this lesson. Was this lesson also taught to the four friends?

22. What is the moral of this story? Do you agree with this moral?

23. Should elderly people "become patterns of virtue and wisdom to all the young people of the age"? Why or why not?

24. Were Dr. Heidegger's guests good examples of this pattern of virtue and wisdom? Why or why not?

25. Can you think of any examples of elderly people in public life who have or have not been examples of virtue and wisdom? Explain your answer.

Critical Thinking

26. Why do you think Dr. Heidegger selected these particular friends for this experiment?

27. If you could magically be younger or older than you are now, would you do it? Why or why not?

28. What do you think about the Fountain of Youth?

29. In your opinion, does our society respect the elderly as much as it should? Explain.

30. Did you like this story? Why or why not?

> **Writing on Your Own**
>
> Think about the moral of "Dr. Heidegger's Experiment." Write a paragraph about your opinion of this moral. Do you agree or disagree with the moral? Why? Be sure to give reasons to support your opinion.

The Fiddler
Herman Melville

Herman Melville

1819–1891

Literary Terms

first-person point of view written as if someone is telling the story

point of view the position from which the author or storyteller chooses to tell the story

About the Author

Herman Melville was born in New York City in 1819. He was one of eight children in a rather wealthy family. However, his father had business failings when Melville was twelve years old. Suddenly, the family was poor, and then Melville's father died. Melville left school to help support his family. He worked as a bank clerk, teacher, and later as a sailor where he traveled to many interesting places. He eventually married in 1847.

Melville wrote many novels and stories, but most works were not successful during his life and his writing did not bring him much money. Not until after his death in 1891 did people begin to think of his works as great literature. Some of his best known stories include *Moby Dick, Typee*, and *Billy Budd*.

Melville's works look at life, human experiences, and social problems. His characters seek answers to the meaning of life. Melville was able to show people's efforts to be free in an evil world.

About the Selection

"The Fiddler" tells a story of three men who meet for a few hours. In the short time covered in the story, one man has a great impact on another. The story examines happiness and success.

The **point of view** in any story is the position from which the author or storyteller chooses to tell the story. This story is told in the **first-person point of view,** or as if someone is telling the story. In this story, the "I" or "me" refers to the character of Helmstone.

From The Fiddler

So my poem is damned, and immortal fame is not for me! I am nobody forever and ever. Intolerable fate!

Snatching my hat, I dashed down the criticism, and rushed out into Broadway, where enthusiastic **throngs** were crowding to a circus in a side street nearby, very recently started, and famous for a capital clown.

Presently my old friend Standard rather **boisterously accosted** me.

"Well met, Helmstone, my boy! Ah! what's the matter? Haven't been committing murder? Ain't flying justice? You look wild!"

"You have seen it, then?" said I, of course referring to the criticism.

"Oh yes; I was there at the morning performance. Great clown, I assure you. But here comes Hautboy. Hautboy—Helmstone."

Without having time or inclination to resent so **mortifying** a mistake, I was instantly soothed as I gazed on the face of the new acquaintance so **unceremoniously** introduced. His person was short and full, with a juvenile, animated cast to it. His complexion rurally **ruddy**; his eye sincere, cheery, and gray. His hair alone betrayed that he was not an overgrown boy. From his hair I set him down as forty or more.

"Come, Standard," he gleefully cried to my friend, "are you not going to the circus? The clown is **inimitable**, they say.

What does the narrator of this story learn from his two friends?

What does Helmstone think of Hautboy?

accost to speak to in an intense, harsh way	**inimitable** unable to be copied	**throng** crowd of people
boisterously noisily; loudly	**mortifying** shameful	**unceremoniously** not formally
	ruddy reddish in color	

Equestrian Circus Ring,
Gifford Beal

Come; Mr. Helmstone, too—come both; and circus over, we'll take a nice stew and punch at Taylor's. . . ."

During the circus performance I kept my eye more on Hautboy than on the celebrated clown. Hautboy was the sight for me. Such genuine enjoyment as his struck me to the soul with a sense of the reality of the thing called happiness. . . . In a man of forty I saw a boy of twelve; and this too without the slightest abatement of my respect. . . .

But much as I gazed upon Hautboy, and much as I admired his air, yet that desperate mood in which I had first rushed from the house had not so entirely departed as not to molest me with **momentary** returns. But from these **relapses** I would rouse myself, and swiftly glance round the broad amphitheatre of eagerly interested and all-applauding human faces. Hark! claps, thumps, deafening huzzas; the vast assembly seemed frantic with **acclamation**; and what, **mused** I, has caused all this? Why, the clown only comically grinned with one of his extra grins. . . .

An *amphitheatre* is a theater or an auditorium where something is performed.

acclamation applause; a loud, eager expression of approval

momentary from time to time

muse to become absorbed in thought

relapse a slip or fall to a previous worse state

Again my eye swept the circus, and fell on the ruddy **radiance** of the countenance of Hautboy. But its clear honest cheeriness disdained my disdain. My intolerant pride was **rebuked**. . . .

Circus over, we went to Taylor's. Among crowds of others, we sat down to our stews and punches at one of the small marble tables. Hautboy sat opposite to me. Though greatly subdued from its former hilarity, his face still shone with gladness. But added to this was a quality not so prominent before: a certain serene expression of leisurely, deep good sense. Good sense and good humor in him joined hands. As the conversation proceeded between the brisk Standard and him—for I said little or nothing—I was more and more struck with the excellent judgment he evinced. In most of his remarks upon a variety of topics Hautboy seemed **intuitively** to hit the exact line between enthusiasm and **apathy**. It was plain that while Hautboy saw the world pretty much as it was, yet he did not theoretically **espouse** its bright side nor its dark side. . . . It was plain, then—so it seemed at that moment, at least—that his extraordinary cheerfulness did not arise either from **deficiency** of feeling or thought.

Suddenly remembering an engagement, he took up his hat, bowed pleasantly, and left us.

"Well, Helmstone," said Standard, **inaudibly** drumming on the slab, "what do you think of your new acquaintance?"

The two last words tingled with a peculiar and novel significance.

"New acquaintance indeed," echoed I. "Standard, I owe you a thousand thanks for introducing me to one of the most singular men I have ever seen. It needed the optical sight of such a man to believe in the possibility of his existence."

"You rather like him, then," said Standard, with ironical dryness.

Here Hautboy remembers that he has to be somewhere else, and so leaves Helmstone and Standard.

apathy a lack of feeling or emotion	**inaudibly** not able to be heard	**radiance** brightness; a glow
deficiency lack	**intuitively** naturally	**rebuke** to turn back or keep down
espouse to take up and support as a cause		

"I hugely love and admire him, Standard. I wish I were Hautboy."

"Ah? That's a pity, now. There's only one Hautboy in the world."

This last remark set me to pondering again, and somehow it revived my dark mood.

"His wonderful cheerfulness, I suppose," said I, sneering with spleen, "originates not less in a **felicitous** fortune than in a felicitous temper. . . . Much more, cheerfulness. Unpossessed of genius, Hautboy is eternally blessed."

"Ah? You would not think him an extraordinary genius, then?"

"Genius? What! such a short, fat fellow a genius! Genius, like Cassius, is lank."

Cassius Longinus was a Roman general who helped plan the killing of Julius Caesar.

"Ah? But could you not fancy that Hautboy might formerly have had genius, but luckily getting rid of it, at last fatted up?"

"For a genius to get rid of his genius is as impossible as for a man in the galloping **consumption** to get rid of that."

"Ah? You speak very decidedly."

"Yes, Standard," cried I, increasing in spleen, "your cheery Hautboy, after all, is no pattern, no lesson for you and me. With average abilities; opinions clear, because **circumscribed**; passions docile, because they are feeble; a temper hilarious, because he was born to it—how can your Hautboy be made a reasonable example to a heady fellow like you, or an **ambitious** dreamer like me? . . .

"Ah?"

How has Helmstone's opinion of Hautboy changed?

"Why do you *Ah* to me so strangely whenever I speak?"

"Did you ever hear of Master Betty?"

"The great English **prodigy**, who long ago ousted the Siddons and the Kembles from Drury Lane, and made the whole town run mad with acclamation?"

---

ambitious having desire to achieve a goal

circumscribe to define clearly

consumption the wasting away of the body caused by tuberculosis

felicitous very well suited; pleasant or delightful

prodigy a highly talented child

"The same," said Standard, once more inaudibly drumming on the slab.

I looked at him perplexed. He seemed to be holding the master key of our theme in mysterious reserve; seemed to be throwing out his Master Betty, too, to puzzle me only the more.

"What under heaven can Master Betty, the great genius and prodigy, an English boy twelve years old, have to do with the poor commonplace plodder, Hautboy, an American of forty?"

"Oh, nothing in the least. I don't imagine that they ever saw each other. Besides, Master Betty must be dead and buried long ere this. . . .

"Proceed with your observations on Hautboy. You think he never had genius, quite too contented, and happy and fat for that—ah? You think him no pattern for men in general? affording no lesson of value to neglected merit, genius ignored, or **impotent presumption** rebuked?—all of which three amount to much the same thing. You admire his cheerfulness, while scorning his commonplace soul. Poor Hautboy, how sad that your very cheerfulness should, by a by-blow, bring you despite!"

What is the disagreement between Standard and Helmstone?

"I don't say I scorn him; you are unjust. I simply declare that his is no pattern for me."

A sudden noise at my side attracted my ear. Turning, I saw Hautboy again, who very **blithely** reseated himself on the chair he had left.

"I was behind time with my engagement," said Hautboy, "so thought I would run back and rejoin you. But come, you have sat long enough here. Let us go to my rooms. It is only a five minutes' walk."

"If you will promise to fiddle for us, we will," said Standard.

Fiddle! thought I—he's a jiggumbob *fiddler*, then? No wonder genius declines to measure its pace to a fiddler's bow. My spleen was very strong on me now.

---

blithely happily and with little thought

impotent helpless; incapable of restraining oneself

presumption an attitude or belief based on a rude sense of self importance

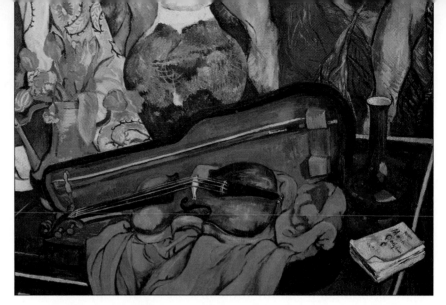

The Violin Box,
Suzanne Valadon

"I will gladly fiddle you your fill," replied Hautboy to Standard. "Come on."

In a few minutes we found ourselves in the fifth story of a sort of storehouse, in a lateral street to Broadway. It was curiously furnished with all sorts of odd furniture which seemed to have been obtained, piece by piece, at auctions of old-fashioned household stuff. But all was charmingly clean and cozy.

Pressed by Standard, Hautboy forthwith got out his dented old fiddle and, sitting down on a tall rickety stool, played away right merrily at "Yankee Doodle" and other offhanded, dashing, and **disdainfully** carefree airs. But common as were the tunes, I was **transfixed** by something miraculously superior in the style. Sitting there on the old stool, his rusty hat sideways cocked on this head, one foot dangling adrift, he plied the bow of an enchanter. All my moody discontent, every **vestige** of peevishness, fled. My whole **splenetic** soul **capitulated** to the magical fiddle. . . .

When, leaving him, Standard and I were in the street once more, I earnestly conjured him to tell me who, in sober truth, this marvelous Hautboy was.

Helmstone likes Hautboy's violin playing. What effect does it have on Helmstone?

capitulate to surrender; to yield	**splenetic** full of feelings of anger or ill will	**transfix** to be held motionless
disdainfully proudly		**vestige** a trace; a tiny bit

"Why, haven't you seen him? And didn't you yourself lay his whole **anatomy** open on the marble slab at Taylor's? What more can you possibly learn? Doubtless, your own masterly insight has already put you in possession of all."

"You mock me, Standard. There is some mystery here. Tell me, I **entreat** you, who is Hautboy?"

"An extraordinary genius, Helmstone," said Standard, with sudden **ardor**, "who in boyhood drained the whole **flagon** of glory; whose going from city to city was a going from triumph to triumph. One who has been an object of wonder to the wisest, been caressed by the loveliest, received the open **homage** of thousands and thousands of the **rabble**. But today he walks Broadway and no man knows him. With you and me, the elbow of the hurrying clerk, and the pole of the remorseless omnibus, shove him. He who has a hundred times been crowned with laurels, now wears, as you see, a bunged beaver. Once fortune poured showers of gold into his lap, as showers of laurel leaves upon his brow. Today, from house to house he hies, teaching fiddling for a living. Crammed once with fame, he is now hilarious without it. *With* genius and *without* fame, he is happier than a king. More a prodigy now than ever."

"His true name?"

"Let me whisper it in your ear."

"What! Oh, Standard, myself, as a child, have shouted myself hoarse applauding that very name in the theatre."

"I have heard your poem was not very handsomely received," said Standard, now suddenly shifting the subject.

"Not a word of that, for Heaven's sake!" cried I. . . .

Next day I tore all my manuscripts, bought me a fiddle, and went to take regular lessons of Hautboy.

An *omnibus* is a vehicle designed to carry large numbers of passengers. *Laurels* is a crown used to honor someone. It is made out of a kind of evergreen called laurel.

Standard is referring to Helmstone's poem that was criticized, which was revealed at the beginning of the story.

anatomy the physical makeup of a living thing	**entreat** to plead	**homage** respect
ardor intensity	**flagon** a bottle or flask, often used for wine	**rabble** the lowest class of people; a mob

The Fiddler
Herman Melville

Directions Write the answers to these questions using complete sentences.

Comprehension: Identifying Facts

1. Why is a crowd on the street on this particular morning?

2. What old friend "boisterously accosts" Helmstone, the narrator?

3. What is the name of the man who is introduced to Helmstone?

4. Describe this new acquaintance.

5. What is the main attraction at the circus?

6. Where do the three men go after the circus performance?

7. Who is the subject of discussion after the new acquaintance leaves Taylor's?

8. What does Hautboy do for a living?

9. What secret does Standard keep from Helmstone until almost the end of the story?

10. What does Helmstone do at the very end of the story?

Comprehension: Understanding Main Ideas

11. Why is Helmstone in such a "spleendish," or nasty mood on this day?

12. Hautboy leaves the story at one point and then returns. What is the reason for this brief absence?

13. How does Hautboy's violin playing affect Helmstone?

14. What is the mystery of Hautboy's past?

15. Why does Standard at first not want to tell Helmstone the truth about Hautboy?

16. How does Helmstone's impression of Hautboy change throughout the story?

17. Why is Hautboy happier now than when he was younger?

18. What is the lesson about success, genius, and fame that Hautboy teaches?

19. Does Helmstone learn this lesson?

20. Does it seem as if Standard has also learned this lesson? Explain.

Understanding Literature: First-Person Point of View

You have learned how the point of view in a story is the position from which the author or storyteller chooses to tell the story. One point of view is the first person. This point of view uses pronouns such as "I" or "me" to relate events. First-person point of view is one of several points of view writers use to tell a story.

21. From whose point of view is this story told?

22. How does the use of the first person make this story effective?

23. Which character in the story do you most identify with? Was your answer affected by use of the first person? Explain.

24. Helmstone switches his opinions about people and things in the course of this story. Does the first-person point of view make the change of opinion natural? Explain.

25. How do you think this story would have been different if it were told from Hautboy's or Standard's point of view?

Critical Thinking

26. Helmstone is upset because someone did not like his poem. Why do you think being passed over or not liked can be so difficult for some people?

27. Why do you think Melville used the circus and the clowns as part of this story?

28. Why do you think Helmstone tears up his manuscripts at the end of the story? Do you think this was wise? Explain.

29. This story focuses on recognizing and acting on what is really important in life. When have you changed your way of thinking or acting because of something you experienced in life? Was the change for the better? Explain.

30. Does this story have a good moral? Why or why not?

Writing on Your Own Choose a sentence from "The Fiddler" that shows the use of the first person. Write a paragraph explaining why this sentence is an example of the first person and how the sentence expresses the narrator's point of view.

Shiloh
Herman Melville

Herman Melville
1819–1891

Literary Terms

requiem a prayer for the dead; a work that has been written in honor of the dead

subtitle a second, less important title under the first that gives more information about the writing

About the Author

Herman Melville used his many unusual experiences as a sailor and traveler for his stories. However, Melville was also a very talented poet. He did not begin to write poetry until age forty. He wrote poems for his own enjoyment and often published them using his own money.

Just as with his books and stories, Melville's poems examine life and death, human experiences, and social problems. His works seek answers to the meaning and struggles of life. His collection of poems called *Battle-Pieces and Aspects of the War*, published in 1866, contains poems such as "Shiloh" that deal with the Civil War. You will learn more about this war in Unit 3.

About the Selection

The Civil War was a difficult time for America. Many soldiers from both Union and Confederate armies were injured or died fighting in this war. One particularly bloody battle took place on April 6 and 7, 1862, near Pittsburgh Landing, Tennessee. Both the Union and Confederate armies lost 25 percent of their men. This battle, called the Battle of Shiloh, was named after a church that stood on the battlefield.

Melville describes war in very real terms. "Shiloh" describes the scene of a battle after it has ended. The silence of the battlefield Melville describes is far different from the patriotic scenes some people picture with war.

Sometimes poems or stories have a second, less important title under the first that gives more information about the writing. This is a **subtitle**. The subtitle of this poem is called "A **Requiem**," which is a prayer for the dead or a work that has been written in honor of the dead.

SHILOH

A REQUIEM —
(April, 1862)

Skimming lightly, wheeling still,
  The swallows fly low
Over the field in clouded days,
4   The forest-field of Shiloh—
Over the field where April rain
Solaced the **parched** ones stretched in pain
Through the pause of night
8   That followed the Sunday fight
  Around the church of Shiloh—
The church so lone, the log-built one,
That echoed to many a parting groan
12   And natural prayer
  Of dying **foemen mingled** there—
Foemen at morn, but friends at eve—
  Fame or country least their care:
16   (What like a bullet can undeceive!)
  But now they lie low,
While over them the swallows skim,
  And all is hushed at Shiloh.

Union forces at the
Battle of Shiloh.

How is war portrayed
in this poem?

foemen enemies
mingle to mix together

parched very dry; very
thirsty

Directions Write the answers to these questions using complete sentences.

Comprehension: Identifying Facts

1. In what month, year, and days did the Battle of Shiloh take place?

2. What lone building is at the scene of this battle?

3. What birds are flying over the battlefield?

Comprehension: Understanding Main Ideas

4. Why are the soldiers "foemen at morn, but friends at eve"?

5. In line 15, why do the soldiers no longer care about fame or country?

6. Reread the ending to this poem. Why is all hushed at Shiloh?

Understanding Literature: Subtitle

A subtitle is a separate, less important title to a work. Subtitles are often an important clue to the subject matter or the theme of a poem. Notice the subtitle that is used with this particular poem: "A Requiem—(April, 1862)."

7. A requiem is a mass or prayer for the dead. In what ways is this poem a tribute to the dead?

8. Which lines do you think are especially suggestive of death or dying?

Critical Thinking

9. What do you think would be the "natural prayer of dying foemen"?

10. How does this poem make you feel about war? Explain.

Writing on Your Own Research the Battle of Shiloh using the library or the Internet. Find information about the battle that was not included in "About the Selection." Write a few paragraphs describing in your own words what happened, who the leaders in the battle were, and why the battle was important.

Poems
by Emily Dickinson

Emily Dickinson
1830–1886

Literary Terms

stanza a group of lines within a poem that forms a unit and often has the same rhythm and rhyme pattern

symbol a person, place, or thing that represents an idea or thought

About the Author

Born in 1830 in Amherst, Massachusetts, Emily Dickinson was the shy daughter of a well-known lawyer. She was well educated and had a happy early family life. It is thought that Dickinson fell in love with a married preacher and that the disappointment of that failed love caused her to live away from others. By the age of thirty, she rarely left her father's house.

Dickinson spent much of her time writing poetry. However, only seven poems were published during her lifetime, and all without her name on them. When Dickinson died in 1886, she left behind over 1,700 poems. Not until years after her death were all of her poems published or popular. Now Dickinson is widely known as a special talent.

About the Selections

Much of Dickinson's poetry deals with death and life after death. She often observed simple things and wrote about them in very moving ways. Her poetry suggests a knowledge of grief and death. One of her skills was in making an idea that is hard to understand, like death, seem real.

Dickinson's poems are written in **stanzas**. A stanza is a group of lines within a poem that forms a unit and often has the same rhythm and rhyme pattern. Her poetry also uses **symbols**. A symbol is a person, place, or thing that represents an idea or a thought. "Because I could not stop for Death" is filled with symbols. For example, "Death" and "He" are symbols of God.

"I never saw a moor" shows the poet's certainty of a better afterlife. "My life closed twice before its close" examines death and the sadness of parting.

Notice that each set of four lines in the poem below forms a stanza. What attitude does the poet have toward death in this poem?

Reflection of the Sun in the Sea, **Nicolas Tarkhoff**

Because I could not stop for Death

Because I could not stop for Death—
He kindly stopped for me—
The Carriage held but just Ourselves—
4 And Immortality.

We slowly drove—He knew no **haste**
And I had put away
My labor and my leisure too,
8 For His **Civility**—

We passed the School, where Children strove
At Recess—in the Ring—
We passed the Fields of Gazing Grain—
12 We passed the Setting Sun—

Or rather—He passed Us—
The Dews drew quivering and chill—
For only Gossamer, my Gown—
16 My **Tippet** only **Tulle**—

We paused before a House that seemed
A Swelling of the Ground—
The Roof was scarcely visible—
20 The **Cornice**—in the Ground—

Since then—'tis Centuries—and yet
Feels shorter than the Day
I first **surmised** the Horses' Heads
24 Were toward **Eternity**—

civility courtesy; politeness	**eternity** endless life; the everlasting	**surmise** to guess or imagine	**tulle** a sheer net used for veils
cornice the very top piece of a building, often overhanging	**haste** swiftness	**tippet** a shoulder cape, often with hanging ends	

I never saw a moor

I never saw a **moor**,
I never saw the sea;
Yet know I how the **heather** looks,
4 And what a wave must be.

I never spoke with God,
Nor visited in heaven;
Yet certain am I of the spot
8 As if the chart were given.

What does this poem
say about a belief in a
higher power?

My life closed twice before its close

My life closed twice before its close—
It yet remains to see
If **Immortality** unveil
4 A third event to me

So huge, so hopeless to conceive
As these that twice befell.
Parting is all we know of heaven,
8 And all we need of hell.

What is the poet's
feeling toward parting?

heather a flowering plant that grows on a moor	**immortality** the quality or state of living forever	**moor** a wide area of open land, often high but poorly drained

Poems
by Emily Dickinson

Directions Write the answers to these questions using complete sentences.

Comprehension: Identifying Facts

"Because I could not stop for Death"

1. Name the things that the poet and the driver of the carriage pass on their ride.

2. Where are the poet and the driver going?

3. How is the poet dressed?

"I never saw a moor"

4. What has the poet not seen in this poem?

5. This poem moves from the concrete to the abstract. Concrete places are physical ones that a person can see or touch. Abstract places cannot be seen or touched. Which places does the poet mention that are concrete? Which places are abstract?

6. What is the poet certain of in this poem?

"My life closed twice before its close"

7. What does the poet claim has happened during her life?

8. What does the poem say about parting?

Comprehension: Understanding Main Ideas

"Because I could not stop for Death"

9. What do the carriage and the driver represent?

10. Stanza five describes a "Swelling in the Ground," a reference to a grave. Does the poet seem afraid of it? Explain your answer.

"I never saw a moor"

11. What things is Dickinson comparing in this poem?

12. What does this poem say about faith in a higher power?

13. How is heaven like a moor?

"My life closed twice before its close"

14. Explain the first line in this poem.

15. The poet refers to some "huge" and "hopeless" events that must have occurred. What do you think these events could have been?

16. Explain the last two lines of this poem.

Understanding Literature: Stanza and Symbol

You have learned about two common parts of poetry: stanzas and symbols. A stanza is a group of lines within a poem that forms a unit. The poems you have just read each have four-line stanzas. The number of lines in a stanza can range from two to eight. A symbol is a person, place, or thing that represents an idea or thought. Poets like to use symbols to make comparisons or to help the reader create images. Symbols can be very simple and obvious, but sometimes they can be difficult to notice and understand in writing.

17. How many stanzas does each Dickinson poem have?

18. What do you notice about the rhyming within these stanzas?

19. Do you think stanzas make poems easier to read? Why or why not?

20. Find a symbol in one of the poems. What is being symbolized?

21. How can symbols make writing more effective?

Critical Thinking

22. Does the poet suggest a fear of death? Explain your answer.

23. In "My life closed twice before its close," Dickinson says that parting is both heaven and hell. Explain what she might have meant by this. Do you agree?

24. Do you think that the poet has a relationship with God? Explain your answer.

25. Which poem did you like best? Why?

Writing on Your Own Choose the Emily Dickinson poem you liked best. Write a paragraph describing what you think the poet is trying to say in the poem. (Remember, there is no incorrect meaning for a poem.)

A simile is a figure of speech. It compares two different things using the words *like* or *as*. Similes very often describe a living thing or an action. You have probably used similes in everyday speech. Here are some examples.

Her **hands** were as cold as **icicles**.

The **man** was like a **giant**.

In these examples, hands are compared to icicles and a man is compared to a giant.

Many authors use similes. Similes help make sentences interesting. They create images in the reader's mind that are entertaining and descriptive. Similes can help describe something that is hard for the reader to understand by comparing it to something more simple. Without similes and other figures of speech, writing might not be as interesting or easy to understand.

Following are some similes from "Dr. Heidegger's Experiment" by Nathaniel Hawthorne.

On the summer afternoon of our tale, a small round table, **as black as ebony**, stood in the center of the room, sustaining a cut-glass vase, of beautiful form and elaborate workmanship.

"My dear widow, you are charming!" cried Colonel Killigrew, whose eyes had been fixed upon her face, while the shadows of age were flitting from it **like darkness from the crimson daybreak**.

In the first sentence, the blackness of the table is compared to ebony. In the second sentence, age is compared to the darkness of the crimson daybreak.

Review

1. What two words do similes use?

2. What is a simile? Write two examples of your own.

3. Why are similes useful in writing?

4. How did Hawthorne's similes improve his writing?

5. Do you think similes improve writing? Why or why not?

Writing on Your Own Write a paragraph describing a person. Use at least three similes. At least one simile should use *like* and at least one should use *as*.

UNIT 2 SUMMARY

In Unit 2, you have read and discussed the works of Ralph Waldo Emerson, Henry David Thoreau, Nathaniel Hawthorne, Herman Melville, and Emily Dickinson. They all were New Englanders. The 1830s to the 1860s was a time of great growth in American literature. New England was an area rich with the growth of ideas and literature.

The literature of this time is called romanticism. The writing was mostly positive. Romantic writing had a strong sense of the individual and an interest in nature. Writings were known for deep feelings, original thoughts, and mystery.

New England writers also were affected by transcendentalism. This belief said that the spiritual world had a greater value than the material world and that the individual was very important.

Selections

■ "Self-Reliance" by Ralph Waldo Emerson is an essay about knowing, trusting, and believing in yourself.

■ *Walden* by Henry David Thoreau is a journal about Thoreau's two years of living alone at Walden Pond. The journal expresses an appreciation for nature and describes Thoreau's cabin and surroundings.

■ "Dr. Heidegger's Experiment" by Nathaniel Hawthorne is a story about three elderly people who become young again for a short time after drinking Dr. Heidegger's magic liquid. However, Dr. Heidegger realizes that even with a chance to start over and become young again, people will not necessarily learn from their mistakes.

■ "The Fiddler" by Herman Melville is a story about a struggling poet who realizes that his idea of fame and genius is not what it should be.

■ "Shiloh" by Herman Melville is one of many poems describing the horrors of the American Civil War. This poem tells about the battlefield after the Battle of Shiloh.

■ Three poems by Emily Dickinson reveal Dickinson's varying beliefs about life and death. "Because I could not stop for Death" is about death and immortality; "I never saw a moor" discusses faith and a belief in the afterlife; and "My life closed twice before its close" reflects the poet's view on death and parting.

UNIT 2 REVIEW

Directions Write the answers to these questions using complete sentences.

Comprehension: Identifying Facts

1. What period of time is covered in this unit?

2. Which region of the United States is studied?

3. What opportunities existed for people during this time?

4. Why are the writers in this unit called romantics?

5. What social problems were there during this time period?

Comprehension: Understanding Main Ideas

6. How did each author's background contribute to his or her style of writing?

7. Which two authors believed in the individual and in the basic goodness of people? How did these authors explain this message?

8. What was Emily Dickinson's view of death?

9. Compare "Dr. Heidegger's Experiment" and "The Fiddler." How were these two stories alike and different?

10. What are the main themes of the literature in this unit?

Understanding Literature: Transcendentalism, Romanticism, Prose, and Poetry

The New England writers in this unit were influenced by transcendentalism. This said that the spiritual world was more important than the material world. Transcendentalism also expressed the value of the individual and the importance of self-reliance. Freedom and strong morals were main ideas behind another movement in this period called romanticism.

The works in this unit represent two forms of writing: prose and poetry. Prose is written in sentences and paragraphs. It can appear in essays, journals, speeches, letters, myths, short stories, and novels. Poetry is written in lines and stanzas. A stanza is a group of lines in a poem.

11. List the names of the selections included in Unit 2.

12. Identify each selection in Unit 2 as either prose or poetry.

13. Identify the genre of each prose selection.

14. How do prose and poetry differ?

15. Do you prefer to read prose or poetry? Why?

Critical Thinking

16. Do you think that Emily Dickinson and Herman Melville might have enjoyed knowing each other? Explain.

17. Which selection from this unit did you like best? Why?

18. Do you agree with Emerson's ideas about self-reliance? Why or why not?

19. How is the romantic literature in this unit different from colonial literature in the first unit?

20. The romantics had an appreciation for nature. Is nature still an important subject today? Explain.

Speak and Listen

Go to your school or public library. Find another selection by a writer in Unit 2, or locate another author from this time period, such as Oliver Wendell Holmes, Henry Wadsworth Longfellow, James Russell Lowell, or John Greenleaf Whittier. Prepare to read the selection to the class. When you are confident that you can read the selection well, read it to the class. Identify the selection, author, and the date the work was written.

Beyond Words

Draw a map of the New England states. Use reference books or an atlas to locate a map. Identify the large cities and state capitals. Try to locate the towns that were mentioned in connection with the authors and selections in this unit.

Writing on Your Own

Choose your favorite author from Unit 2. Find out more information about this author using the library, the Internet, and the information already given in this unit. Write a 500-word report about this author explaining his or her life, the major works this author has written, and why this author is well known today.

Test-Taking Tip

Before you begin a test, look it over quickly. Try to set aside enough time to complete each section.

"The songs of the slave represent the sorrows of his heart; and he is relieved by them, only as an aching heart is relieved by its tears."

—Frederick Douglass, *Narrative of the Life of Frederick Douglass*, 1845

"I hear America singing, the varied carols I hear."

—Walt Whitman, "I Hear America Singing," 1860

UNIT 3 *Local Color in America: 1849–1889*

There was a time in American literature when people began to value local places and local voices. This was called local color. War, rebuilding, and growth were all a part of this difficult time. In this unit, you will learn about local color and this time in American history.

This period in American history was very difficult. A main event was the Civil War. This was perhaps the greatest struggle in the nation's history. As you learned in the last unit, slavery had been dividing the nation. As the United States approached the middle of the 1800s, it became clear that the problem would not be solved peacefully. By the time Abraham Lincoln became President in 1861, most southern states had left the Union. They wanted to become independent from the United States. On April 12, 1861, a battle broke out at Fort Sumter in South Carolina. The Civil War had begun. Many battles unlike America had ever seen before were fought. The war took thousands of lives and destroyed millions of dollars worth of property. The war ended in 1865, leaving the nation to grieve, heal, and become one again. By the time the war ended, all of the enslaved Africans had become free.

The problems did not end there. President Lincoln was shot and killed five days after the end of the Civil War. Surviving the war and the loss of its President forced America to come of age. However, the country was no longer as enthusiastic as it had been in the romantic period before the war. The government started a rebuilding plan called Reconstruction. Eventually, people rebuilt.

This period also saw the end of the American Indian way of life. With the Civil War over, Americans moved westward and continued to drive American Indians from their land. As more states were added to the Union, American Indians were forced to live on reservations.

Despite the many problems during this time, literature continued. A kind of writing called local color became important. Local color was written by the common person for the common person. It reflected the way people spoke and dressed, the way people behaved, and the customs in certain places.

LITERATURE

1849 "Thirty-Five" by Sarah Josepha Hale appears in *Godey's Lady's Book*

1850 James W. C. Pennington's *The Fugitive Blacksmith* is published

1854 Chief Seattle presents "This Sacred Soil" speech after giving up land to settlers

1864 President Abraham Lincoln writes "A Letter to Mrs. Bixby"

| 1840 | 1845 | 1850 | 1855 | 1860 | 1865 |

HISTORY

1861 Civil War begins with a battle at Fort Sumter

1863 President Lincoln issues the Emancipation Proclamation, freeing slaves in the South

Westward the Course of Empire Takes Its Way, 1868

Walt Whitman's two poems in this unit, "Beat! Beat! Drums!" and "Come Up from the Fields Father," record the awful realities of the Civil War. Abraham Lincoln's "A Letter to Mrs. Bixby" shows how the war affected everyone, not just soldiers.

At first, local color took the form of writings about and for women. In this unit, Sarah Josepha Hale's poem "Thirty-Five" is an example of this kind of writing.

Literature about slavery was also a part of local color. Spirituals in this unit express the feelings and dreams of a better life for an enslaved people. Also in this unit, James W. C. Pennington tells of his life as an enslaved man who flees to freedom in *The Fugitive Blacksmith*. In addition, Frederick Douglass's speech "What the Black Man Wants" expresses the hopes and desires for the future of African Americans.

Toward the later years of the local color period, Mark Twain became very popular. This unit features part of the story of his own life called *Life on the Mississippi*.

Another source of local color was the American West. Songs such as "The Old Chisholm Trail" in this unit give a glimpse of life on the frontier. In contrast, Chief Seattle's speech "This Sacred Soil" expresses the sadness American Indians felt at the loss of their land. American Indian lullabies in this unit capture the beauty and simplicity of American Indian life.

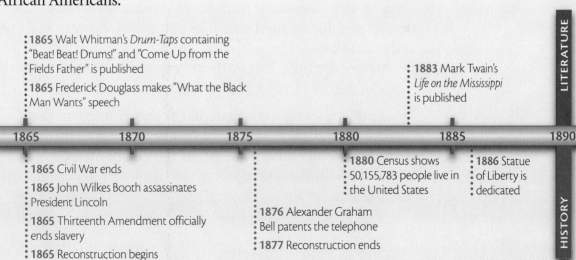

LITERATURE

1865 Walt Whitman's *Drum-Taps* containing "Beat! Beat! Drums!" and "Come Up from the Fields Father" is published

1865 Frederick Douglass makes "What the Black Man Wants" speech

1883 Mark Twain's *Life on the Mississippi* is published

| 1865 | 1870 | 1875 | 1880 | 1885 | 1890 |

HISTORY

1865 Civil War ends

1865 John Wilkes Booth assassinates President Lincoln

1865 Thirteenth Amendment officially ends slavery

1865 Reconstruction begins

1876 Alexander Graham Bell patents the telephone

1877 Reconstruction ends

1880 Census shows 50,155,783 people live in the United States

1886 Statue of Liberty is dedicated

Thirty-Five
Sarah Josepha Hale

Sarah Josepha Hale

1788–1879

Literary Term

figurative language
language that makes a
comparison and is not
meant to be taken
literally

About the Author

Sarah Josepha Hale was born in Newport, New Hampshire, in 1788. After becoming a widow in 1822, she began to write for a living. Her belief in good literature helped to shape the thoughts of many women writers and readers during the 1800s.

The first women's magazine in the United States, *Godey's Lady's Book*, appeared in 1830 in Philadelphia. This magazine hired many women artists and writers. Hale became an editor and writer for this magazine in 1841.

Hale's own works include several women's poems and an early history of famous women. She also wrote the nursery rhyme "Mary Had a Little Lamb." Hale is also known for helping convince President Abraham Lincoln to make Thanksgiving a national holiday in 1863. She died in Philadelphia in 1879.

About the Selection

Writings about and for women became popular in eastern cities from 1850 to 1900. Women's magazines contained poems, short stories, essays, and sewing projects. "Thirty-Five" is a good example of the poetry found in women's magazines during the 1800s. The language is flowery and the ideas are simple. The celebration of the poem appealed to women of the time. It is interesting to note that this poem appeared in 1849 when Hale was sixty-one, not thirty-five.

This poem uses **figurative language**. This is language that makes a comparison and is not meant to be taken literally. For example, stanza one mentions the link of Memory's chain. The author is comparing the memories in her mind to the links in a chain.

Thirty-Five

How does the author describe life at thirty-five? Notice the use of figurative language in the second stanza. How does the poet compare the moon to memories?

I'm thirty-five—I'm thirty-five!
    Nor would I make it less,
For not a year has passed away
4   Unmarked by happiness.
I would not drop a single link
    Of Memory's golden chain,
Since distance brightens all the joy
8   And softens all the pain.
Why should I grieve that youth is gone?
    Its better hopes survive;
I know the **gilding** from the gold,
12   Now I am thirty-five.

I see the old moon softly rest
    Within the new moon's rays,
And cradled thus within my heart
16   I hold my early days;
And every gentle, generous thought
    Is living in my mind,—
The planets in their onward course
20   Ne'er leave their light behind:
And sorrows, like the dews of night
    That keep the flowers alive,
Ah! I can value these aright,
24   Now I am thirty-five.

I know the young have hopes more bright,
    Nor would I shadow these—
A **wildering** charm is in the light
28   Which **fervent Fancy** sees.
The rose is lovely in the bud,
    And lovelier when 'tis blown,
Yet never till its bloom is passed
32   Is half its sweetness known.
And in the garden of my soul,
    While Faith's white flowers revive,
The holier charm of youth is mine,
36   Though I am thirty-five.

I'm thirty-five—I'm thirty-five!
    I would not make it less,
For not a year has passed away
40   Unmarked by happiness.
And who would drop affection's link
    From Memory's golden chain?
Or lose a sorrow, losing too
44   The love that soothed the pain!
And oh! may Heaven within my soul
    Keep truth and love alive,
Then angel graces will be mine,
48   Though over thirty-five.

fancy imagination; a liking formed by chance rather than reason

fervent marked by intense feeling

gilding a thin coating of gold; something that gives an attractive but often false appearance

wildering wandering; moving with no set path

Directions Write the answers to these questions using complete sentences.

Comprehension: Identifying Facts

1. What has marked each year of the author's life?

2. What does the author cradle within her heart?

3. Which phrase is repeated in this poem? How many times?

Comprehension: Understanding Main Ideas

4. What is the mood of this poem?

5. In what ways does the author make thirty-five seem old?

6. What advantages to growing older does the author mention?

Understanding Literature: Figurative Language

Figurative language is an expression of comparison. Usually, the comparison is between two seemingly unlike things. "Thirty-Five" contains many examples of figurative language. For example, stanza two tells of early days "cradled thus within my heart." The author compares holding her fond memories of her early days to a woman holding a baby.

7. Read the poem again. Identify two examples of figurative language in "Thirty-Five" that have not already been pointed out to you. Write down these examples.

8. What seemingly unlike things is the author comparing in each case? Discuss the meaning of each example of figurative language.

Critical Thinking

9. Do you think this poem would be popular if it appeared in a modern women's magazine? Why or why not?

10. Do you agree that older people should not be sorry that youth is gone? Explain.

Writing on Your Own Write a poem of at least two stanzas using your own age as the title. The poem should reflect what your age means to you and why this age is important.

This nineteenth century engraving shows cotton picking in Alabama.

Literary Terms

dialect a regional variety of language

refrain the repetition of words or phrases to create mood or emphasis

spiritual a religious and emotional song developed among enslaved Africans in the South during the middle of the 1800s

About the Authors

"Swing Low, Sweet Chariot" and "Deep River" are two examples of **spirituals**. A spiritual is a religious and often deeply emotional song. These songs were first sung by enslaved Africans during the 1800s. Spirituals have been passed down from generation to generation, and the words may have changed somewhat over the years. No one person is credited with making up these songs.

About the Selections

Spirituals helped to develop a feeling of faith for enslaved Africans. Spirituals also offered hope for a better life. A spiritual was sung in a steady pattern or rhythm. It was sometimes used to send a message about an escape route for enslaved Africans. Often the language had double meanings. This way, enslaved Africans could move from plantation to plantation while they sang or chanted a message in code. It is clear from the spirituals on the following two pages that the deep religious faith and the hope for a better life had a big impact on enslaved Africans.

Today, many spirituals are still sung in churches. Often, a person with a strong voice sings lines while the rest of the group responds with the **refrain**. A refrain is the repeating of words or phrases for mood or emphasis. The combination of a single voice and the refrain makes a unique song.

These spirituals use **dialect**—a regional variety of language. In written dialect, words are often spelled exactly as they are pronounced.

Local Color in America Unit 3   **125**

Spirituals and music were important for religion and ceremonies of enslaved Africans.

Swing Low, Sweet Chariot

Swing low, sweet chariot,
Comin' for to carry me home.

Jordan is a river in Palestine. This is a reference to heaven, or the Promised Land.

I looked over Jordan and what did I see,
Comin' for to carry me home?
A band of angels comin' aftah me,
Comin' for to carry me home.

Notice the dialect in this spiritual. Words like "comin'" and "git" are written exactly as they are pronounced.

If you git there before I do,
Comin' for to carry me home,
Tell all my frien's I'm a-comin', too,
Comin' for to carry me home.

The brightes' day that ever I saw,
Comin' for to carry me home,
When Jesus washed my sins away,
Comin' for to carry me home.

I'm sometimes up an' sometimes down,
Comin' for to carry me home,
But still my soul feel heavenly-boun',
Comin' for to carry me home.

Deep River

Deep river, my home is over Jordan.
Deep river, Lord, I want to cross over into Campground.
Oh, chillun, oh, don't you want to go
To that gospel feast, that promised land,
That land where all is peace?
Walk into heaven and take my seat
And cast my crown at Jesus' feet. Lord,
Deep river, my home is over Jordan.
Deep river, Lord, I want to cross over into Campground.

What emotions does
this spiritual contain?

Gospel means the
message of God.

Picking Cotton, **William Aiken Walker**

Spirituals
Anonymous

Directions Write the answers to these questions using complete sentences.

Comprehension: Identifying Facts

1. In "Swing Low, Sweet Chariot," what line is repeated over and over? How many times does this line appear?

2. How many stanzas are there in "Swing Low, Sweet Chariot"?

3. What words are repeated in "Deep River"?

Comprehension: Understanding Main Ideas

4. In "Swing Low, Sweet Chariot," what lines contain words or phrases that show the hope of enslaved Africans?

5. Explain how spirituals might have been useful to enslaved Africans as they worked on the plantations.

6. Explain the meaning of line three in "Deep River."

Understanding Literature: Spiritual and Refrain

Spirituals are important because they are one of the voices of enslaved Africans. We can learn how enslaved Africans must have felt by reading spirituals. As you have already learned, some poetry repeats phrases or lines—this is a refrain. Spirituals also use refrains. These provide emphasis to certain lines or phrases.

7. How do you think a spiritual is similar to and different from a poem? Explain.

8. Identify the refrain in each of the two spirituals. Explain how these spirituals can be better remembered because of the repeated words.

Critical Thinking

9. Why do you think these songs have remained popular for over one hundred years?

10. Do you think these spirituals have the same impact being read rather than sung?

Writing on Your Own Choose the spiritual you liked best. Write a paragraph explaining why you liked the spiritual and how the spiritual made you feel.

The Fugitive Blacksmith
James W. C. Pennington

James W. C.
Pennington
1809–1870

Literary Terms

autobiography a story about a person's life written by that person

setting the place and time in a story

About the Author

James W. C. Pennington was an enslaved African in Maryland who became a blacksmith. At about twenty-one years of age, he left his large family to escape to the North where he could be free. After a long, difficult escape, he eventually arrived in Pennsylvania. There he was taken in by a Quaker man named William Wright, who was against slavery. Pennington stayed with the Wright family for six months. There he learned to read and write and was introduced to Christianity.

Pennington later became a teacher, an antislavery supporter, and a pastor. He spent years trying to convince the nation to stop slavery and was a leader in this movement. In 1850, Pennington went to Europe to escape capture from his former master. He returned to America only when his freedom was guaranteed. His **autobiography**, *The Fugitive Blacksmith*, was published in 1850 in England. An autobiography is a story about a person's life written by that person. Pennington's was one of many horrifying tales formerly enslaved Africans wrote about their experiences.

About the Selection

"Escape: A Slave Narrative" is a chapter from *The Fugitive Blacksmith*. The excerpts that you will read describe the six long days that Pennington spent in search of freedom.

The **setting**, or the place and time in a story, adds to the detail of this story. The setting changes throughout. Most of the settings are outside on roads as Pennington makes his way to the North. The time period for the story is the early to the middle 1800s, when slavery existed in America.

From The Fugitive Blacksmith

Escape: A Slave Narrative

Why does James Pennington decide to escape? What dangers does he face on his way to Pennsylvania?

It was now two o'clock. I stepped into the quarter; there was a strange and **melancholy** silence **mingled** with the **destitution** that was apparent in every part of the house. The only **morsel** I could see in the shape of food, was a piece of Indian-flour bread, it might be half-a-pound in weight. This I placed in my pocket, and giving a last look at the aspect of the house, and at a few small children who were playing at the door, I sallied forth thoughtfully and melancholy, and after crossing the barnyard, a few moments' walk brought me to a small cave, near the mouth of which lay a pile of stones, and into which I had deposited my clothes. From this, my course lay through thick and heavy woods and back lands to town, where my brother lived. This town was six miles distance. It was now near three o'clock, but my object was neither to be seen on the road, or to approach the town by daylight, as I was well known there, and as any intelligence of my having been seen there would at once put the pursuers on my track. The first six miles of my flight, I not only traveled very slowly, therefore, so as to avoid carrying any daylight to this town; but during this walk another very **perplexing** question was **agitating** my mind. Shall I call on my brother as I pass through, and shew him what I am about! My brother was

agitate to bother	**mingle** to mix together	**perplexing** complicated; very puzzling or confusing
destitution extreme poverty	**morsel** a small piece of food	
melancholy very sad		

older than I, we were much attached; I had been in the habit of looking to him for counsel.

I entered the town about dark, resolved, all things in view, *not* to shew myself to my brother. Having passed through the town without being recognized, I now found myself under cover of night, a **solitary** wanderer from home and friends; my only guide was the North Star, by this I knew my general course northward, but at what point I should strike Pennsylvania, or when and where I should find a friend I knew not. . . .

The night was fine for the season, and passed on with little interruption for want of strength, until, about three o'clock in the morning, I began to feel the chilling effects of the dew.

At this moment, gloom and melancholy again spread through my whole soul. The prospect of utter destitution which threatened me was more than I could bear, and my heart began to melt. What substance is there in a piece of dry Indian-bread? What **nourishment** is there in it to warm the nerves of one already chilled to the heart? Will this afford a sufficient **sustenance** after the toil of the night? But while these thoughts were agitating my mind, the day dawned upon me, in the midst of an open extent of country, where the only shelter I could find,

nourishment energy from food

solitary single

sustenance enough food or drink to keep the body strong

A *corn shock* is a pile of corn stalks placed end down in a field.

A *turnpike* is a road used by paying a toll. A *tollgate* is the point where a person must pay a fee to use a road.

The *Mason and Dixon's line* is the boundary line between Pennsylvania and Maryland that once divided free states and slave states and later became the dividing line of the North and South. Most people today call it the Mason-Dixon line.

without risking my travel by daylight, was a corn shock, but a few hundred yards from the road, and here I must pass my first day out. The day was an unhappy one; my hiding place was extremely **precarious**. I had to sit in a squatting position the whole day, without the least chance to rest. But, besides this, my scanty **pittance** did not afford me that nourishment which my hard night's travel needed. Night came again to my relief, and I sallied forth to pursue my journey. By this time, not a crumb of my crust remained, and I was hungry and began to feel the desperation of distress. . . .

At the dawn of the third day I continued my travel. As I had found my way to a public turnpike road during the night, I came very early in the morning to a tollgate where the only person I saw, was a lad about twelve years of age. I inquired of him where the road led to. He informed me it led to Baltimore. I asked him the distance, he said it was eighteen miles.

This intelligence was perfectly astounding to me. My master lived eighty miles from Baltimore. I was now sixty-two miles from home. That distance in the right direction, would have placed me several miles across Mason and Dixon's line, but I was evidently yet in the state of Maryland. . . .

When I had walked a mile on this road, and when it had now gotten to be about nine o'clock, I met a young man with a load of hay. He drew up his horses, and addressed me in a very kind tone, when the following **dialogue** took place between us.

"Are you traveling any distance, my friend?"

"I am on my way to Philadelphia."

"Are you free?"

"Yes, sir."

"I suppose, then, you are provided with free papers?"

"No, sir. I have no papers."

"Well, my friend, you should not travel on this road: you will be taken up before you have gone three miles. There are

| **dialogue** a discussion | **pittance** a small amount | **precarious** dangerous; depending on chance events |

men living on this road who are constantly on the lookout for your people; and it is seldom that one escapes them who attempts to pass by day."

He then very kindly gave me advice where to turn off the road at a certain point, and how to find my way to a certain house, where I would meet with an old gentleman who would further advise me whether I had better remain till night, or go on. . . .

I went about a mile, making in all two miles from the spot where I met my young friend, and about five miles from the tollgate to which I have referred, and I found myself at the twenty-four miles' stone from Baltimore. It was now about ten o'clock in the **forenoon**; my strength was greatly exhausted by reason of the want of suitable food; but the excitement that was then going on in my mind, left me little time to think of my *need* of food. Under ordinary

Here the author refers to a stone. These were posts that were once used to mark distances along roads.

forenoon late morning

circumstances as a traveler, I should have been glad to see the "Tavern," which was near the mile-stone; but as the case stood with me, I deemed it a dangerous place to pass, much less to stop at. I was therefore passing it as quietly and as rapidly as possible, when from the lot just opposite the house, or sign-post, I heard a coarse stern voice cry, "Halloo!"

I turned my face to the left, the direction from which the voice came, and observed that it proceeded from a man who was digging potatoes. I answered him politely; when the following occurred:—

"Who do *you* belong to?"

"I am free, sir."

"Have you got papers?"

"No, sir."

"Well, you must stop here."

By this time he had got astride the fence, making his way into the road. I said,

"My business is onward, sir, and I do not wish to stop."

"I will see then if you don't stop, you black rascal."

He was now in the middle of the road, making after me in a brisk walk.

I saw that a crisis was at hand; I had no weapons of any kind, not even a pocketknife; but I asked myself, shall I surrender without a struggle? The instinctive answer was, "No." What will you do? continue to walk; if he runs after you, run; get him as far from the house as you can, then turn suddenly and **smite** him on the knee with a stone; that will render him, at least, unable to pursue you.

This was a desperate scheme, but I could think of no other, and my habits as a blacksmith had given my eye and hand such mechanical skill, that I felt quite sure that if I could only get a stone in my hand, and have time to wield it, I should not miss his knee-pan.

He began to breathe short. He was evidently **vexed** because I did not halt, and I felt more and more **provoked** at

circumstance condition	**provoked** excited into anger	**smite** to strike sharply
		vexed irritated; annoyed

the idea of being thus pursued by a man to whom I had not done the least injury. I had just began to glance my eye about for a stone to grasp, when he made a tiger-like leap at me. This of course brought us to running. At this moment he yelled out "Jake Shouster!" and at the next moment the door of a small house standing to the left was opened, and out jumped a shoemaker **girded** up in this leather apron, with his knife in hand. He sprang forward and seized me by the collar, while the other seized my arms behind. I was now in the grasp of two men, either of whom were larger bodied than myself, and one of whom was armed with a dangerous weapon.

Why do you think these men want to capture Pennington?

Standing in the door of the shoemaker's shop, was a third man; and in the potato lot I had passed, was still a fourth man. Thus surrounded by superior physical force, the fortune of the day it seemed to me was gone.

My heart melted away, I sunk resistlessly into the hands of my captors, who dragged me immediately into the tavern which was near. I ask my reader to go in with me, and see how the case goes. . . .

"Come now, this matter may easily be settled without you going to jail; who do you belong to, and where did you come from?". . .

I resolved, therefore, to insist that I was free. This not being **satisfactory** without other evidence, they tied my hands and set out, and went to a magistrate who lived about half a mile distant. It so happened, that when we arrived at his house he was not at home. This was to them a disappointment, but to me it was a relief; but I soon learned by their conversation, that there was still another magistrate in the neighborhood, and that they would go to him. In about twenty minutes, and after climbing fences and jumping ditches, we, captors and captive, stood before his door, but it was the same manner as before—he was not at home. By this time the day had worn away to one or two o'clock, and my captors evidently began to

A *magistrate* is a local official with limited powers over criminal cases.

---

girded bound up

satisfactory good enough

feel somewhat impatient of the loss of time. We were about a mile and a quarter from the tavern. As we set out on our return they began to **parley**. Finding it was difficult for me to get over fences with my hands tied, they untied me, and said, "Now John," that being the name they had given me, "if you have run away from any one it would be much better for you to tell us!" but I continued to **affirm** that I was free. I knew, however, that my situation was very critical, owing to the shortness of the distance I must be from home: my advertisement might overtake me at any moment. . . .

We got to the tavern at three o'clock. Here they again cooled down, and made an appeal to me to make a **disclosure**. I saw that my attempt to escape strengthened their belief that I was a **fugitive**. I said to them, "If you will not put me in jail, I will now tell you where I am from." They promised. "Well," said I, "a few weeks ago, I was sold from the eastern shore to a slave trader, who had a large gang, and set out for Georgia, but when he got to a town in Virginia, he was taken sick, and died with the smallpox. Several of his gang also died with it, so that the people in the town became alarmed, and did not wish the gang to remain among them. No one claimed us, or wished to have anything to do with us; I left the rest, and thought I would go somewhere and get work."

When I said this, it was evidently believed by those who were present, and notwithstanding the unkind feeling that had existed, there was a murmur of **approbation**. At the same time I perceived that a panic began to seize some, at the idea that I was one of a smallpox gang. Several who had clustered near me, moved off to a respectful distance. . . .

I was now left alone with the man who first called to me in the morning. In a sober manner, he made this proposal to me: "John, I have a brother living in Risterstown, four miles off, who keeps a tavern; I think you had better go and live

Pennington lies to the men by saying he was exposed to smallpox, a disease that spreads to others and at the time was deadly. The lie works, as the men move away from Pennington after hearing his story. What does this part of the story reveal about Pennington?

affirm to state positively	**disclosure** the act of making something known	**fugitive** a person who is fleeing or trying to escape
approbation approval; praise		**parley** to speak to one another

with him, till we see what will turn up. He wants an ostler. I at once **assented** to this. "Well," said he, "take something to eat, and I will go with you."

Although I had so completely frustrated their designs for the moment, I knew that it would by no means answer for me to go into that town, where there were prisons, handbills, newspapers, and travelers. My intention was, to start with him, but not to enter town alive. . . .

[The narrator of the tale escapes from his captor while being taken to Risterstown. He again attempts to make his way to freedom.]

It was Thursday morning; the clouds that had veiled the sky during the latter part of the previous day and the previous night were gone. It was not until about an hour after the sun rose that I heard any outdoor movements about the house. As soon as I heard those movements, I was satisfied there was but one man about the house, and that he was preparing to go some distance to work for the day. . . .

I cannot now, with pen or tongue, give a correct idea of the feeling of wretchedness I experienced, every nerve in my system quivered, so that not a particle of my flesh was at rest. In this way I passed the day. . . .

After several hours I found my way back to the road, but the hope of making any thing like clever speed was out of the question. All I could do was to keep my legs in motion, and this I continued to do with the utmost difficulty. The latter part of the night I suffered extremely from cold. There came a heavy frost; I expected at every moment to fall on the road and perish. I came to a cornfield covered with heavy shocks of Indian corn that had been cut; I went into this and got an ear, and then crept into one of the shocks; ate as much of it as I could, and thought I would rest a little and start again, but weary nature could not sustain the operation of grinding hard corn for its own nourishment, and I sunk to sleep.

When I awoke, the sun was shining around; I started with alarm, but it was too late to think of seeking any other shelter;

An *ostler* is a person who takes care of horses.

Handbills were small printed sheets passed out by hand. They were often used to advertise something.

What problems does Pennington have at this point in the story?

assent to agree

I therefore nestled myself down, and concealed myself as best I could from the light of day. After recovering a little from my fright, I commenced again eating my whole corn. Grain by grain I worked away at it; when jaws grew tired, as they often did, I would rest, and then begin afresh. Thus, although I began an early breakfast, I was nearly the whole of the forenoon before I had done. . . .

My strength was considerably renewed; though I was far from being nourished, I felt that my life was at least safe from death by hunger. Thus encouraged, I set out with better speed than I had made since Sunday and Monday night. I had a **presentiment**, too, that I must be near free soil. I had not yet the least idea where I should find a home or friend, still my spirits were so highly **elated**, that I took the whole of the road to myself; I ran, hopped, skipped, jumped, clapped my hands, and talked to myself. . . .

After an hour or two of such freaks of joy, a gloom would come over me in connection with these questions, "But where are you going? What are you going to do? What will you do with freedom without father, mother, sisters, and brothers? What will you say when you are asked where you were born? You know nothing of the world; how will you explain the fact of your ignorance?"

These questions made me feel deeply the **magnitude** of the difficulties yet before me.

Saturday morning dawned upon me; and although my strength seemed yet considerably fresh, I began to feel a hunger somewhat more destructive and pinching, if possible, than I had before. I resolved, at all risk, to continue my travel by daylight, and to ask information of the first person I met. . . .

The resolution of which I informed the reader at the close of the last chapter, being put into practice, I continued my flight on the public road; and a little after the sun rose, I came in sight of a tollgate again. For a moment all the events which followed my passing a tollgate on Wednesday morning, came

Here Pennington asks himself some very serious questions. How do you think he will solve these problems?

---

elated marked by high spirits

magnitude great size

presentiment a feeling that something is about to happen

fresh to my **recollection,** and produced some hesitation; but at all events, said I, I will try again.

On arriving at the gate, I found it attended by an elderly woman, whom I afterwards learned was a widow, and an excellent Christian woman. I asked her if I was in Pennsylvania. On being informed that I was, I asked her if she knew where I could get employ? She said she did not; but advised me to go to W. W., a Quaker, who lived about three miles from her, whom I would find to take an interest in me. She gave me directions which way to take; I thanked her, and bade her good morning, and was very careful to follow her directions.

In about half an hour I stood trembling at the door of W. W. After knocking, the door opened upon a comfortably spread table; the sight of which seemed at once to increase my hunger sevenfold. Not daring to enter, I said I had been sent to him in search of employ. "Well," said he, "Come in and take thy breakfast, and get warm, and we will talk about it; thee

Quakers were members of a religious group who believed in nonviolence. They often helped enslaved Africans to freedom.

As you learned in "About the Author," W. W. stands for William Wright, the Quaker man who takes in Pennington.

recollection memory

must be cold without any coat." *"Come in and take thy breakfast, and get warm!"* These words spoken by a stranger, but with such an air of simple sincerity and fatherly kindness, made an overwhelming impression upon my mind. They made me feel, spite of all my fear and **timidity**, that I had, in the **providence** of God, found a friend and a home. . . .

From that day to this, whenever I discover the least disposition in my heart to **disregard** the wretched condition of any poor or distressed persons with whom I meet, I call to mind these words—*"Come in and take thy breakfast, and get warm."* They **invariably** remind me of what I was at that time; my condition was as wretched as that of any human being can possibly be, with the exception of the loss of health or reason. I had but four pieces of clothing about my person, having left all the rest in the hands of my captors. I was a starving fugitive, without home or friends—a reward offered for my person in the public papers—pursued by cruel man-hunters, and no claim upon him to whose door I went. Had he turned me away, I must have perished. Nay, he took me in, and gave me of his food, and shared with me his own garments. Such treatment I had never before received at the hands of any white man.

disregard to pay no attention to

invariably constantly

providence help from God

timidity a lack of courage or self-confidence

Directions Write the answers to these questions using complete sentences.

Comprehension: Identifying Facts

1. What food is Pennington able to take with him?

2. What is Pennington's guide on his way to Pennsylvania?

3. Toward what city is the author heading?

4. When Pennington reaches the turnpike on the third day, how many miles is he from his home?

5. Some men capture Pennington. Why are they alarmed by his story?

6. Who finally invites the author into his home?

7. Why is Pennington grateful to this man?

8. What does Pennington say would have happened to him if he had not been taken in?

9. What things does the man share with Pennington?

10. Had any other white man treated Pennington so well?

Comprehension: Understanding Main Ideas

11. Explain the emotional state of the author as he decides to leave his family and try to escape to the North.

12. What fears does Pennington have to face during his trip?

13. How is the North Star important in this story?

14. Describe the physical problems that the author has during the six-day trip.

15. In what way is this selection told in a conversational tone?

16. Pennington meets several people during his trip. Each person treats him in a different way. What does this say about people's attitudes toward slavery at the time?

17. Pennington tells a lie to the men about being exposed to smallpox. Why?

18. How does Pennington manage to get enough to eat throughout his trip?

Review Continued on Next Page

19. What does Pennington learn in this story?

20. What is this story's message about slavery?

Understanding Literature: Setting

The place and time, or setting, in a story can be extremely important. Place tells the "where" of a story. Time tells the "when" of the story. In *The Fugitive Blacksmith*, the place and time add to the detail of the events.

21. What is the state in which Pennington was a slave?

22. What is the state to which he is heading for freedom?

23. What is the kind of place in which most of the action takes place?

24. What is the day of the week Pennington escapes and the day of the week he reaches safety in Pennsylvania?

25. During what time period does this story take place?

Critical Thinking

26. Pennington had a large family. How do you think he felt about leaving his relatives behind as he tried to escape?

27. What emotions do you think the author felt during his escape?

28. What would be your biggest fear if you had to make an escape such as Pennington did? Why?

29. How do you feel about slavery after reading this story? Explain.

30. Was this an effective antislavery story? Why or why not?

Writing on Your Own Choose a paragraph from this story that describes a setting. Write your own paragraph telling what you think the setting looks like based on the information the author provides. Fill in your own details about the setting. Describe what the author did not tell about.

Poems
by Walt Whitman

Walt Whitman

1819–1892

Literary Term

free verse poetry that does not have a strict rhyming pattern or regular line length, and uses actual speech patterns for the rhythms of sound

About the Author

Walt Whitman was born in New York in 1819 to a poor family. At ten he worked in a newspaper and printing shop. Later he wrote, printed, edited, and even delivered newspapers. He was also a teacher for a short time.

When he was thirty-five, Whitman's first book of poetry, *Leaves of Grass*, was published. His poems celebrated the United States. They were original, bold, and positive. However, *Leaves of Grass* sold poorly. Whitman had to return to newspaper work to support himself.

Whitman's experiences as a nurse in the Civil War led to war poems that were added to *Leaves of Grass* in later editions. After the war, Whitman held several government jobs until he had a stroke in 1873. He continued to live in New York until his death in 1892. Whitman later became known as the national poet of America. His poems express America's values, its working class, and its democracy.

About the Selections

Whitman wrote several poems about the horrors of the Civil War based on his experiences as a nurse. He once wrote: "The real war will never get in the books." "Beat! Beat! Drums!" describes the stir before the fighting. "Come Up from the Fields Father" describes the tragedy for those at home.

Whitman created a form of poetry that he believed told his ideas better than the strict rhyming patterns of most poetry. His new form, called **free verse**, used actual speech patterns for the rhythms of sound. It did not have a strict rhyming pattern or regular line length. Free verse was not accepted at first. However, by the end of Whitman's life, other writers began using this new form.

Beat! Beat! Drums!

The photo above shows a Civil War marching band.

Beat! beat! drums!—blow! bugles! blow!
Through the windows—through doors—burst like a ruthless force,
3 Into the solemn church, and scatter the **congregation**,
Into the school where the scholar is studying;
Leave not the bridegroom quiet—no happiness must he have now with his bride,
6 Nor the peaceful farmer any peace, plowing his field or gathering his grain.
So fierce you whir and pound you drums—so shrill you bugles blow.

Beat! beat! drums!—blow! bugles! blow!
9 Over the traffic of cities—over the rumble of wheels in the streets;
Are beds prepared for sleepers at night in the houses? no sleepers must sleep in those beds,
No bargainers' bargains by day—no **brokers** or **speculators**—would they continue?
12 Would the talkers be talking? would the singer attempt to sing?
Would the lawyer rise in the court to state his case before the judge?
Then rattle quicker, heavier drums—you bugles wilder blow.

15 Beat! beat! drums!—blow! bugles! blow!
Make no parley—stop for no **expostulation**,
Mind not the timid—mind not the weeper or prayer,
18 Mind not the old man **beseeching** the young man,
Let not the child's voice be heard, nor the mother's **entreaties**,
Make even the trestles to shake the dead where they lie awaiting the hearses,
21 So strong you thump O terrible drums—so loud you bugles blow.

---

beseech to beg

broker an agent who handles sales and purchases for other people

congregation a group of people gathered for worship

entreaty a plea

expostulation discussion

speculator a person who assumes business risks in hopes of gain; one who buys or sells in the hopes of profiting from market changes

In both poems, notice that the line lengths differ and that there is no rhyming pattern. They are written in free verse. What do these poems say about war?

How does each family member react to the news in the letter in "Come Up from the Fields Father"?

Come Up from the Fields Father

Come up from the fields Father, here's a letter from our Pete,
And come to the front door, Mother, here's a letter from thy dear son.

3 Lo, 'tis autumn,
Lo, where the trees, deeper green, yellower and redder,
Cool and sweeten Ohio's villages with leaves fluttering in the **moderate** wind,
6 Where apples ripe in the orchards hang and grapes on the **trellised** vines,
(Smell you the smell of grapes on the vines?
Smell you the buckwheat where the bees were lately buzzing?)
9 Above all, lo, the sky so calm, so transparent after the rain, and with
        wondrous clouds,
Below too, all calm, all **vital** and beautiful, and the farm prospers well.

Down in the fields all prospers well,
12 But now from the fields come Father, come at the daughter's call,
And come to the entry, Mother, to the front door come right away.
Fast as she can she hurries, something **ominous**, her steps trembling,
15 She does not **tarry** to smooth her hair nor adjust her cap.

Open the envelope quickly,
O this is not our son's writing, yet his name is signed,
18 O a strange hand writes for our dear son, O stricken mother's soul!
All swims before her eyes, flashes with black, she catches the main words only,
Sentences broken, *gunshot wound in the breast, cavalry skirmish, taken to hospital,*
21 *At present low, but will soon be better.*

moderate calm	**tarry** to delay	**trellised** supported on a frame of latticework	**vital** full of life
ominous forbidding or alarming			

Field hospitals such as this were set up to care for wounded soldiers after battles.

Ah, now the single figure to me,
Amid all **teeming** and wealthy Ohio with all its cities and farms,
24 Sickly white in the face and dull in the head, very faint,
By the **jamb** of a door leans.
Grieve not so, dear Mother (the just-grown daughter speaks through her sobs,
27 The little sisters huddle around speechless and dismayed).
See, dearest Mother, the letter says Pete will soon be better.

Alas, poor boy, he will never be better (nor maybe needs to be better, that brave
and simple soul),
30 While they stand at home at the door he is dead already,
The only son is dead.

But the mother needs to be better,
33 She with thin form presently dressed in black,
By day her meals untouched, then at night fitfully sleeping, often waking,
In the midnight waking, weeping, longing with one deep longing,
36 O that she might withdraw unnoticed, silent from life escape and withdraw,
To follow, to seek, to be with her dear dead son.

---

jamb the upright pieces
forming the sides of the
opening for a door

teeming filled to
overflowing

Poems
by Walt Whitman

Directions Write the answers to these questions using complete sentences.

Comprehension: Identifying Facts

"Beat! Beat! Drums!"

1. Which places and buildings are invaded by the war effort?

2. In which stanza are the sounds of the bugles and drums loudest?

3. In stanza two, what question is asked about the talkers and the singers?

4. How many lines are there in this poem? How many stanzas?

"Come Up from the Fields Father"

5. Which season of the year is mentioned?

6. Who sends a letter home?

7. What are the words that describe the condition of the son?

8. How do the daughters react to the news? How does the mother react to the news?

9. What might be another descriptive title for this poem?

10. Does this poem contain any rhymes?

Comprehension: Understanding Main Ideas

"Beat! Beat! Drums!"

11. The drums and bugles represent the calling of young men to war. Why does the poet tell of so many different kinds of men?

12. The sound of the drums differs in each stanza. How do the drums change? Why?

13. Which lines make the war seem more personal?

14. Which line indicates that death will be certain for some men?

15. What would you say is the mood of this poem?

"Come Up from the Fields Father"

16. Certain phrases describe the farm in detail. What are some of these descriptive phrases?

17. Why does the mother hurry to open the letter? How does she feel as she reads?

18. Who wrote the letter?

19. Which stanza shows that the poet knows something that the family does not know?

20. What happens to the son?

Review Continued on Next Page

Understanding Literature: Free Verse

Walt Whitman used free verse for these two poems. Free verse is poetry that does not have a strict rhyming pattern or regular line length and use actual speech patterns for rhythm of sound. The result is a poem that sounds more like normal speech than a rhyming poem. Free verse allows the poet more freedom to write because there are no limits caused by a rhyme pattern or a certain line length.

21. Even though "Beat! Beat! Drums!" is written in free verse, did you still detect a certain rhythm? Explain.

22. Without rhyming and regular line lengths, how is free verse still poetry?

23. Which poem do you think is more effective than the other as a free verse poem? Why?

24. Why do you think people did not like free verse at first?

25. Do you think free verse is more or less effective than more traditional poetry? Why or why not?

Critical Thinking

26. Do these poems show the positive side or negative side of war? Explain.

27. What images did you picture when you read "Beat! Beat! Drums!"

28. What images did you picture when you read "Come Up from the Fields Father"?

29. How do these poems make you feel about war? Explain.

30. Which poem is a more effective Civil War poem? Explain.

Writing on Your Own Write a paragraph comparing "Beat! Beat! Drums!" and "Come Up from the Fields Father." Explain how the poems are alike and how they are different. Think about the writing style, content, and emotions present in these poems when comparing the two.

A Letter to Mrs. Bixby
Abraham Lincoln

Abraham Lincoln
1809–1865

Literary Term

sequence the order of events in a literary work

About the Author

Abraham Lincoln was born in Kentucky in 1809. When he was nine, his mother died; his father soon remarried. Lincoln had less than one year of education, but he borrowed books and worked to learn all that he could on his own. He soon discovered his talent as a speaker. He told stories in the country store and drew audiences for his funny tales.

Lincoln's political career began with a position with the Illinois local government. Later he became a successful lawyer in Springfield, Illinois. There he was married to Mary Todd.

Lincoln became the sixteenth President of the United States in 1861. The Civil War began just after he took office. He wanted to save the nation. However, this happened only after the Union won the long, bloody Civil War in 1865. It was during the war that Lincoln gave one of this best-known speeches, the "Gettysburg Address."

Shortly after the war ended, Lincoln was shot and killed while attending a play at Ford's Theater in Washington, D.C. The nation mourned the loss. He has become known as one of America's greatest Presidents.

About the Selection

Lincoln's writings and speeches reached the hearts of many people. He wrote "A Letter to Mrs. Bixby" to a woman whose sons had died in the Civil War. It is a sample of the kindness Lincoln showed to others.

The order of events in a story is called **sequence**. "A Letter to Mrs. Bixby" contains an organization of thoughts similar to sequencing. Lincoln suggests five thoughts to Mrs. Bixby: praying for her, expressing sorrow, thanking her, offering comfort, and stating that he feels weak in his ability to comfort her.

President Lincoln is the tall man wearing the top hat in the photo above. The photo shows him meeting with his officers after the Battle of Antietam.

A Letter to Mrs. Bixby

Executive Mansion
Washington, November 21, 1864

Mrs. Bixby, Boston, Massachusetts

Dear Madam:

I have been shown in the files of the War Department a statement of the Adjutant-General of Massachusetts that you are the mother of five sons who have died gloriously on the field of battle. I feel how weak and fruitless must be any words of mine which should attempt to **beguile** you from the grief of a loss so overwhelming. But I cannot **refrain** from **tendering** to you the **consolation** that may be found in the thanks of the Republic they died to save. I pray that our heavenly Father may **assuage** the **anguish** of your **bereavement**, and leave you only the cherished memory of the loved and lost, and the solemn pride that must be yours to have laid so costly a sacrifice upon the altar of freedom.

Yours very sincerely and respectfully,

Abraham Lincoln

What does this letter reveal about the suffering a war causes?

anguish extreme pain or distress

assuage to lessen

beguile to deceive or trick

bereavement the feeling of loss, especially in the death of a loved one

consolation comfort

refrain to keep oneself from doing

tender to offer

A Letter to Mrs. Bixby
Abraham Lincoln

Directions Write the answers to these questions using complete sentences.

Comprehension: Identifying Facts

1. How many of Mrs. Bixby's sons died in battle?

2. What prayer does Lincoln offer to Mrs. Bixby?

3. On what altar did Lincoln say that Mrs. Bixby laid her sacrifice?

Comprehension: Understanding Main Ideas

4. Often the President gives someone on his staff the task of writing letters. Do you think Lincoln did that in this case? Explain your answer.

5. After reading the kind of personal letter that President Lincoln wrote to a woman who had lost her sons in battle, what personality traits would you use to describe Abraham Lincoln?

6. Lincoln knew that his letter would not stop the grief that Mrs. Bixby feels. In what ways might his letter still have been a comfort to her?

Understanding Literature: Sequence

The way writing is organized is important. The order of events in a piece of writing is called sequence. Often a sequence in a story represents events in the order in which they occur. This was the case with "A Letter to Mrs. Bixby."

7. Reread Lincoln's letter. Place these five thoughts in the correct sequence in which they appear in the letter: expressing sorrow, praying for her, thanking her, offering comfort in memories, and stating that he feels unable to comfort her.

8. Do you think that the organization of this letter could be rearranged in some better way? Explain your answer.

Critical Thinking

9. Do you think Mrs. Bixby might have been helped by this letter? Explain.

10. Do you like Lincoln's writing style? Why or why not?

> **Writing on Your Own** Research more about Abraham Lincoln's presidency using the library or the Internet. Write two or three paragraphs explaining his accomplishments as President. Include important dates and other details about his presidency.

What the Black Man Wants
Frederick Douglass

Frederick Douglass

1817–1895

About the Author

Born in Maryland in 1817, Frederick Douglass was an enslaved African. Because he worked for a Baltimore family as a house servant, he was able to learn reading and writing. The idea of escape was never far from his mind. This desire added to his early efforts to learn.

Eventually, Douglass was successful in his escape. He moved to New York, where he married in 1838. He then became active in the antislavery movement. He is also known for starting an independent black newspaper, the *North Star*. Douglass met Abraham Lincoln several times to discuss the problems of slavery. During the Civil War, Douglass also organized African American soldiers. When the war was over, he worked for the civil rights of formerly enslaved Africans.

As a speaker and writer, Douglass was active in the struggle of African Americans for independence. His autobiography *Narrative of the Life of Frederick Douglass*, published in 1845, is his most well-known writing.

About the Selection

The selection that follows is an excerpt from a speech Frederick Douglass gave in 1865 at the yearly meeting of the Massachusetts Anti-Slavery Society in Boston. This speech deals with the question of the right of African Americans to vote. (It was not until the Fifteenth Amendment was passed in 1870 that African Americans were given this right.) Douglass had just been asked the question "Why does the Negro want to be able to vote?" His answer explains not only why African Americans should vote but how they should be given justice in America.

Douglass uses **symbols** in this speech. A symbol is a person, place, or thing that represents an idea or a thought.

FROM

What the Black Man Wants

I will tell you why we want it. We want it because it is our right, first of all. No class of men can, without insulting their own nature, be content with any **deprivations** of their rights. We want it, again, as a means for educating our race. Men are so **constituted** that they derive their **conviction** of their own possibilities largely from the estimate formed of them by others. If nothing is expected of a people, that people will find it difficult to **contradict** that **expectation**. By depriving us of suffrage, you affirm our incapacity to form an intelligent judgment respecting public men and public measures; you declare before the world that we are unfit to exercise the elective **franchise**, and by this means lead us to undervalue ourselves, to put a low estimate upon ourselves, and to feel that we have no possibilities like other men.

Again, I want the elective franchise, for one, as a colored man, because ours is a peculiar government, based upon a peculiar idea, and that idea is universal suffrage. If I were in a monarchical government, or an autocratic or aristocratic government, where the few bore rule and the many were subject, there would be no special **stigma** resting upon me, because I did not exercise the elective franchise. It would do me no great violence. Mingling with the mass, I should partake of the strength of the mass; . . . and I should have the

In 1865 many people were seeking to extend the right to vote to women and to African Americans. Why does Douglass say that African Americans want the right to vote?

Suffrage is the right to vote. Douglass explains his opinion here that not having the right to vote makes people have less respect for themselves. Do you agree with this idea?

Douglass refers to three kinds of government here. *Monarchical* refers to a society ruled by a king. *Autocratic* refers to a society ruled by a person with unlimited power. An *aristocratic* society is ruled by a noble and an upper class.

constituted made up; set up

contradict to go against

conviction a strong belief; an opinion

deprivation loss or removal

expectation something that is expected

franchise a right given to people, especially the right to vote

stigma a mark of shame

The First Vote, 1867

same **incentives** to **endeavor** with the mass of my fellow men; it would be no particular burden, no particular deprivation; but here, where universal suffrage is the rule, where that is the **fundamental** idea of the government, to rule us out is to

| **endeavor** to strive to reach or achieve something | **fundamental** main or basic | **incentive** something that excites someone into action |

make us an exception, to brand us with the stigma of **inferiority**, and to invite to our heads the missiles of those about us; therefore, I want the franchise for the black man. . . .

I ask my friends who are apologizing for not insisting upon this right, where can the black man look, in this country, for the **assertion** of his right, if he may not look to the Massachusetts Anti-Slavery Society? Where under the whole heavens can he look for sympathy in asserting this right, if he may not look to this platform? Have you lifted us up to a certain height to see that we are men, and then are any disposed to leave us there, without seeing that we are put in possession of all our rights? We look naturally to this platform for the assertion of all our rights, and for this one especially.

I understand the antislavery societies of this country to be based on two principles—first, the freedom of the blacks in this country; and, second, the elevation of them. Let me not be misunderstood here. I am not asking for sympathy at the hands of abolitionists, sympathy at the hands of any. I think the American people are disposed often to be generous rather than just. I look over this country at the present time, and I see educational societies, **sanitary** commissions, freedmen's associations and the like,—all very good: but in regard to the colored people there is always more that is **benevolent**, I perceive, than just, **manifested** towards us. What I ask for the Negro is not benevolence, not pity, not sympathy, but simple justice. The American people have always been anxious to know what they shall do with us. . . .

Everybody has asked the question, and they learned to ask it early of abolitionists, "What shall we do with the Negro?" I have had but one answer from the beginning. Do nothing with us! Your doing with us has already played the mischief

This paragraph expresses Douglass's feeling that the Massachusetts Anti-Slavery Society should help African Americans gain the right to vote.

An *abolitionist* was one who wanted to end slavery and free the slaves. Groups such as the Massachusetts Anti-Slavery Society were abolitionist groups.

Here Douglass explains that it is justice that he wants for his people. What kind of justice does Douglass want?

assertion the act of stating positively or standing up for	**inferiority** being of lower status or of less importance	**sanitary** relating to health
benevolent marked by goodwill; marked by doing good	**manifest** to display or make obvious	

This paragraph has many symbols. The main symbol mentions apples on an apple tree. The apples are symbols for Douglass's people and the apple tree is a symbol for America.

with us. Do nothing with us! If the apples will not remain on the tree of their own strength, if they are worm-eaten at the core, if they are early ripe and disposed to fall, let them fall! I am not for tying or fastening them on the tree in any way, except by nature's plan, and if they will not stay there, let them fall. And if the Negro cannot stand on his own legs, let him fall also. All I ask is, give him a chance to stand on his own legs! Let him alone! If you see him on his way to school, let him alone, don't disturb him. If you see him going to the dinner table at a hotel, let him go! If you see him going to the ballot-box, let him alone, don't disturb him! If you see him going into a workshop, just let him alone,—your interference is doing him a positive injury. . . . Let him fall if he cannot stand alone! If the Negro cannot live by the line of **eternal** justice, . . . the fault will not be yours, it will be his who made the Negro, and established that line for his government. Let him live or die by that. If you will only untie his hands, and give him a chance, I think he will live. . . .

PROSPECTUS
FOR AN ANTI-SLAVERY PAPER, TO BE ENTITLED
NORTH STAR.

FREDERICK DOUGLASS

Proposes to publish, in ROCHESTER, N. Y., a **WEEKLY ANTI-SLAVERY PAPER**, with the above title.

The object of the NORTH STAR will be to attack SLAVERY in all its forms and aspects; advocate UNIVERSAL EMANCIPATION; exalt the standard of PUBLIC MORALITY; promote the Moral and Intellectual Improvement of the COLORED PEOPLE; and hasten the day of FREEDOM to the Three Millions of our ENSLAVED FELLOW COUNTRYMEN.

The Paper will be printed upon a double medium sheet, at $2,00 per annum, if paid in advance, or $2,50, if payment be delayed over six months.

The names of Subscribers may be sent to the following named persons, and should be forwarded, as far as practicable, by the first of November, proximo.

FREDERICK DOUGLASS, Lynn, Mass.
SAMUEL BROOKE, Salem, Ohio.
M. R. DELANY, Pittsburgh, Pa.
VALENTINE NICHOLSON, Harveysburgh, Warren Co. O.
Mr. WALCOTT, 21 Cornhill, Boston.

JOEL P. DAVIS, Economy, Wayne County, Ind.
CHRISTIAN DONALDSON, Cincinnati, Ohio.
J. M. M'KIM, Philadelphia, Pa.
AMARANCY PAINE, Providence, R. I.
Mr. GAY, 142 Nassau Street, New York.

SUBSCRIBERS' NAMES.	RESIDENCE.	NO. OF COPIES.

Frederick Douglass published an African American newspaper called the *North Star*. The statements to the left describe its purpose.

eternal lasting forever

What the Black Man Wants
Frederick Douglass

Directions Write the answers to these questions using complete sentences.

Comprehension: Identifying Facts

1. What is the first reason Frederick Douglass gives for wanting African Americans to have the right to vote?

2. What kind of government does Douglass believe especially demands the right to vote for all?

3. To what organization does Douglass look for asserting this right?

4. What does Douglass ask of society when African Americans go to the ballot box?

5. What does Douglass feel is doing "positive injury" to African Americans?

6. What forms of government are mentioned in this speech?

7. What does Douglass want instead of pity and sympathy?

8. What is an abolitionist?

9. What is Douglass's answer to the question of what should be done with African Americans?

10. What does Douglass believe will happen if African Americans are given a chance?

Comprehension: Understanding Main Ideas

11. Explain why Douglass believed that being deprived of the right to vote would make his people have low self-esteem.

12. Describe how another form of government might not make the author believe that African Americans should vote.

13. Explain the meaning of these words: ". . . but here, where universal suffrage is the rule, where that is the fundamental idea of the government, to rule us out is to make us an exception. . . ."

14. What is the author's general opinion of the American people?

15. What does Douglass think about the "benevolence" toward African Americans shown by the American people?

16. What is the main message of this speech?

17. What is the mood of this speech?

18. How does Douglass compare African Americans to an apple tree?

Review Continued on Next Page

19. Why does Douglass want nothing done with African Americans?

20. Douglass explains that if the black man "falls," so be it. Does Douglass believe that African Americans will fall? Explain your answer.

Understanding Literature: Symbol

Some sentences mean exactly what they say. For example: "The lion is a large cat with a tawny body and a tufted tail." Other sentences have a symbolic meaning. They stand for or suggest something else. For example: "The general was a lion during battle." This sentence uses the lion as a symbol for courage.

Frederick Douglass uses symbolic phrases in his speech. He says, "If you only untie his hands, and give him a chance, I think he will live. . . ." This quotation from the end of the selection contains a phrase of symbolic meaning.

21. Does anyone actually have his hands tied?

22. Why does Douglass use this expression? To what is he referring, if not actually "hands tied"?

23. What other phrase would mean almost the same thing?

24. How does the meaning of the "hands tied" phrase make it especially effective? Explain your answer.

25. Find another symbol in this speech and write it down. Then explain what it means.

Critical Thinking

26. Why do you think that most African Americans of the time might have wanted the right to vote?

27. Do you think this speech is effective? Explain your answer.

28. How does this speech explain why voting is important to everyone?

29. Douglass was a former slave. How do you think this made him a good spokesperson for the rights of African Americans?

30. Do you think Douglass is like any African American leaders today? Explain.

Writing on Your Own Write a sentence or paragraph using a symbolic phrase. Then write a sentence explaining what is being symbolized in your sentence or paragraph.

Life on the Mississippi
Mark Twain

Mark Twain
1835–1910

Literary Terms

autobiography a story about a person's life written by that person

dialect a regional variety of language

About the Author

Mark Twain was born Samuel Langhorne Clemens in 1835. "Mark Twain" was a term of measurement steamboat pilots used to describe about twelve feet of water. Mark Twain became the name Clemens used as an author.

Twain was born in Missouri and grew up near the Mississippi River. Later he worked as a printer and newspaperman in eastern cities. He returned to the South to try to be a steamboat pilot. The Civil War, however, interrupted his career. In 1861 Twain traveled west. His humorous newspaper writings made him famous. He also became a popular speaker. He later moved back east and married, settling down first in New York and later in Connecticut. Eventually, Twain gave up newspaper writing to write books. He is best known for his stories *Tom Sawyer* and *The Adventures of Huckleberry Finn*.

When Twain's wife and two daughters died, his works changed to a heavy, violent mood. Unsuccessful business deals left him in debt at age sixty, but he earned money speaking and paid his debts. He died in Connecticut in 1910.

About the Selection

Much of Twain's **autobiography**, a story about a person's life published by that person, recalls the happiest days of his childhood. This selection, the fourth chapter of his autobiography, is a good example of his humorous writing style. It also shows how important the river steamer was in a small American town in the 1800s.

Twain uses **dialect**, or a regional variety of language, in this and other stories. Certain words express the flavor of the times. They are spelled the way they are pronounced.

Life on the Mississippi

The Boys' Ambition

What does this story tell you about life during this time period?

When I was a boy, there was but one permanent ambition among my comrades in our village on the west bank of the Mississippi River. That was, to be a steamboatman. We had **transient** ambitions of other sorts, but they were only transient. When a circus came and went, it left us all burning to become clowns; the first Negro **minstrel** show that ever came to our section left us all suffering to try that kind of life; now and then we had a hope that if we lived and were good, God would permit us to be pirates. These ambitions faded out, each in its turn; but the ambition to be a steamboatman always remained.

Once a day a cheap, **gaudy** packet arrived upward from St. Louis, and another downward from Keokuk. Before these events, the day was glorious with expectancy; after them, the day was a dead and empty thing. Not only the boys, but the whole village, felt this. After all these years I can picture that old time to myself now, just as it was then: the white town **drowsing** in the sunshine of a summer's morning; the streets empty, or pretty nearly so; one or two clerks sitting in front of the Water Street stores, with their splint-bottomed chairs tilted back against the walls, chins on breasts, hats slouched

What descriptions does the author give of the town?

drowse to be drowsy or tired

gaudy flashy; showy; having tasteless design

minstrel one of a group of performers giving a program of melodies, jokes, and skits

transient passing very quickly

Mississippi in Time of Peace

over their faces, asleep—with shingle-shavings enough around to show what broke them down; a sow and a litter of pigs loafing along the sidewalk, doing a good business in watermelon rinds and seeds; two or three lonely little freight piles scattered about the levee; a pile of skids on the slope of the stone-paved wharf, and the fragrant town **drunkard** asleep in the shadow of them; two or three wood flats at the head of the wharf, but nobody to listen to the peaceful lapping of the wavelets against them; the great Mississippi, the majestic, the magnificent Mississippi, rolling its mile-wide tide along, shining in the sun; the dense forest away on the other side; the point above the town, and the point below, bounding the river-glimpse and turning it into a sort of sea, and withal a very still and brilliant and lonely one.

Presently a film of dark smoke appears above one of those remote points: instantly a Negro drayman, famous for his quick eye and **prodigious** voice, lifts up the cry, "S-t-e-a-m-

A *levee* is a landing place for boats on a river. A *flat* is a small, flat-bottomed boat.

A *drayman* is a person who hauls goods using a cart or wagon called a dray.

drunkard one who is continuously drunk

prodigious unusual; causing amazement or wonder

boat a-comin'!" and the scene changes! The town drunkard stirs, the clerks wake up, a furious clatter of drays follows, every house and store pours out a human contribution, and all in a twinkling the dead town is alive and moving. Drays, carts, men, boys, all go hurrying from many quarters to a common center, the wharf.

Assembled there, the people fasten their eyes upon the coming boat as upon a wonder they are seeing for the first time. And the boat is rather a handsome sight, too. She is long and sharp and trim and pretty; she has two tall, fancy-topped chimneys, with a **gilded** device of some kind swung between them; a fanciful pilot house, all glass and gingerbread, perched on top of the texas deck behind them; the paddle boxes are gorgeous with a picture or with gilded rays above the boat's name; the boiler deck, the hurricane deck, and the texas deck are fenced and ornamented with clean white railings; there is a flag gallantly flying from the jack staff; the furnace doors are open and the fires glaring bravely; the upper decks are black with passengers; the captain stands by the big bell, calm, imposing, the envy of all; great volumes of the blackest smoke are rolling and tumbling out of the chimneys—a husbanded **grandeur** created with a bit of pitch pine just before arriving at a town; the crew are grouped on the forecastle; the broad stage is run far out over the port bow, and a deck hand stands picturesquely on the end of it with a coil of rope in his hand; the pent steam is screaming through the gauge cocks, the captain lifts his hand, a bell rings, the wheels stop; then they turn back, churning the water to foam, and the steamer is at rest. Then such a scramble as there is to get aboard and to get ashore, and to take in freight and to **discharge** freight, all at one and the same time; and such a yelling and a cursing as the mates **facilitate** it all with! Ten minutes later the steamer is under way again, with no flag on the jack staff and no black smoke issuing from the chimneys. After ten more minutes the

Often times when people refer to a boat, the boat is called "she," as the author does here.

The author uses several terms in this paragraph to describe the steamboat. *Gingerbread* refers to the fancy ornamental shapes on the boat. The *texas deck* was a place on a steamboat containing officers' quarters and the pilot house. The *paddle box* was a wooden covering built over the upper part of the paddle wheels of the steamboat. A *boiler deck* was the deck containing the steam engine that propelled the steamboat. The *hurricane deck* was a light deck extending over the main deck. The *jack staff* was a stick on the front of a ship used to hold the ship's flag. The *forecastle* was the forward part of a boat where the crew was housed.

discharge to take off; to remove or let go

facilitate to help bring about; to make easier

gilded giving the false appearance of gold

grandeur the quality or state of being grand or magnificent

town is dead again, and the town drunkard asleep by the skids once more.

My father was a justice of the peace, and I supposed he possessed the power of life and death over all men, and could hang anybody that offended him. This was **distinction** enough for me as a general thing; but the desire to be a steamboatman kept **intruding**, nevertheless.

I first wanted to be a cabin boy, so that I could come out with a white apron on and shake a tablecloth over the side, where all my old comrades could see me; later I thought I would rather be the deck hand who stood on the end of the stage-plank with the coil of rope in his hand, because he was particularly **conspicuous**. But these were only daydreams— they were too heavenly to be **contemplated** as real possibilities.

By and by one of our boys went away. He was not heard of for a long time. At last he turned up as **apprentice** engineer or "striker" on a steamboat. This thing shook the bottom out of all my Sunday-school teachings. That boy had been **notoriously** worldly, and I just the reverse; yet he was **exalted** to this eminence, and I left in obscurity and misery. There was nothing generous about this fellow or his greatness. He would always manage to have a rusty bolt to scrub while his boat tarried at our town, and he would sit on the inside guard and scrub it, where we all could see him and envy him and loathe him. And whenever his boat was laid up he would come home and swell around the town in his blackest and greasiest clothes, so that nobody could help remembering that he was a steamboatman; and he used all sorts of steamboat technicalities in his talk, as if he were so used to them that he forgot common people could not understand them. He

This is an example of Twain's humorous writing style. Does Twain really mean that his father could hang anyone who upset him?

apprentice one who works for a professional for a certain period of time to learn the professional's art or trade

conspicuous obvious; noticeable

contemplate to think about

distinction worthiness; a special honor

exalt to raise in rank, power, or character

intrude to force in or upon without permission

notoriously generally known and talked of

Labboard is the same as "larboard," or the left side of a ship when looking forward from the back of the ship. Notice "St. Looy" in the next sentence. This is an example dialect. *St. Looy* means the city of St. Louis, Missouri.

would speak of the labboard side of a horse in an easy, natural way that would make one wish he was dead. And he was always talking about "St. Looy" like an old citizen; he would refer casually to occasions when he was "coming down Fourth Street," or when he was "passing by the Planter's House," or when there was a fire and he took a turn on the brakes of "the old Big Missouri"; and then he would go on and on about how many towns the size of ours were burned down there that day.

Two or three boys had long been persons of consideration among us because they had been to St. Louis once and had a vague general knowledge of its wonders, but the day of their glory was over now. They **lapsed** into a humble silence, and learned to disappear when the ruthless cub engineer approached. This fellow had money, too, and hair oil. Also an ignorant silver watch and a showy brass watch chain. He wore a leather belt and used no suspenders. If ever a youth was cordially admired and hated by his comrades, this one was. No girl could withstand his charms. He "cut out" every boy in the village.

Here the author explains that the boat the boy worked on exploded for some reason. However, living through the explosion makes the boy a hero.

When his boat blew up at last, it diffused a **tranquil** contentment among us such as we had not known for months. But when he came home the next week, alive, **renowned**, and appeared in church all battered up and bandaged, a shining hero, stared at and wondered over by everybody, it seemed to us that the **partiality** of **Providence** for an undeserving reptile had reached a point where it was open to **criticism**.

This creature's career could produce but one result, and it speedily followed. Boy after boy managed to get on the river. The minister's son became an engineer. The doctor's and the postmaster's sons became mud clerks; the wholesale liquor dealer's son became a barkeeper on a boat; four sons of the chief merchant, and two sons of the county judge, became

A *mud clerk* was a second clerk on a river steamer. The name came from the duty to go ashore at unimportant stops, often mud banks, to handle freight.

criticism judgment by others	**partiality** fondness	**renowned** famous
lapse to slip away gradually	**providence** help from God	**tranquil** calm

pilots. Pilot was the grandest position of all. The pilot, even in those days of **trivial** wages, had a princely salary—from a hundred and fifty to two hundred and fifty dollars a month, and no board to pay. Two months of his wages would pay a preacher's salary for a year. Now some of us were left **disconsolate**. We could not get on the river—at least our parents would not let us.

So, by and by, I ran away. I said I would never come home again till I was a pilot and could come in glory. But somehow I could not manage it. I went meekly aboard a few of the boats that lay packed together like sardines at the long St. Louis wharf, and humbly inquired for the pilots, but got only a cold shoulder and short words from mates and clerks. I had to make the best of this sort of treatment for the time being, but I had comforting daydreams of a future when I should be a great and honored pilot, with plenty of money, and could kill some of these mates and clerks and pay for them.

The author explains in the final paragraph that he never was able to fulfill his dream of becoming a pilot. What does he do to make himself feel better for this failure?

disconsolate dejected; downcast; cheerless

trivial of little worth

Directions Write the answers to these questions using complete sentences.

Comprehension: Identifying Facts

1. What are three "transient ambitions" mentioned in the first paragraph?

2. In his description of the town, Twain tells what is happening in the street before the steamboat arrives. What citizens are mentioned in paragraph two?

3. How long does the steamboat stay in town?

4. Which jobs on a steamboat does the author wish to have eventually?

5. The story focuses on one "creature" who does manage to get a job on a steamboat. What job does he get? What eventually happens to his boat?

6. What seems to the author to be the grandest job of all?

7. How much salary did a pilot get?

8. Why does Twain run away from home?

9. What comfort does Twain mention in the final paragraph?

10. Does Twain fulfill his dreams to work on a steamboat?

Comprehension: Understanding Main Ideas

11. How old do you think the author was at the time of the events in this selection? Explain your answer.

12. Describe the differences of the town before the arrival of the steamboat, during its short stay, and after it leaves.

13. How does the author describe the ways in which the steamboat is a "handsome sight"? What words does he use?

14. How does the success of one local boy bother the other boys? What humor does the author introduce at this point in the story?

15. How does the explosion help the one local boy become even more admired?

16. There are several characters in this story. Describe each one.

17. What sense of place does Twain portray in this story?

18. What reasons keep Twain from reaching his goal of working on a steamboat?

19. Does it seem like Twain is being serious when he says he wants to kill some of his mates and clerks?

20. An autobiography is a story that a person writes about his or her own life. How can you tell that this story is autobiographical?

Understanding Literature: Dialect

One part of local color is the use of ordinary language common to a certain place. This is called dialect. Because cities, towns, and states were separated by distance, people spoke differently. For example, someone in the South used different words or expressions than those in the North, East, or West. Dialect is one way to give a local feeling to writing. Twain was very well known for adding dialect to his writing to capture a local feeling.

21. Find some examples of dialect in this story. Write three examples.

22. Write what you think each example of dialect means. (Note: Some of these words may have been defined for you in the story already.)

23. How does this language add to the mood and image of the story?

24. Do you think dialect is still important in writing today? Explain.

25. What are some examples of dialect used in the area where you live?

Critical Thinking

26. Does this story glamorize the life of a steamboat worker? Explain.

27. Would you have liked to work on a steamboat? Why or why not?

28. You have learned that local color reflects the way people speak and dress, the way people behave, and the customs popular in certain locations. How is this story an example of local color?

29. What message do you think this story contains that people can still use today?

30. Do you think people envy other people as the boys all envy this one local boy? Give an example from your own experience.

Writing on Your Own Twain describes in this chapter of *Life on the Mississippi* something that he wanted to do but never did: work on a steamboat. Write a paragraph describing something in life that you have always wanted to do but have not done. Explain why you want to do this thing and whether you think you will do it at some point.

The Old Chisholm Trail
Anonymous

About the Author

During the late nineteenth century, the Great Plains of North America became home to millions of steers. Steers are in the same family as bulls and cows that the Spanish brought to America hundreds of years ago. These animals ran wild in southeastern Texas. When cattle worth four dollars a head in Texas eventually brought forty dollars in Missouri, cowhands and cattle drives provided a way for ranchers to make money.

Cowhands often sang simple tunes to pass the time and to calm cattle during long drives from ranches to cities. Like spirituals, these cowhand songs have become part of this country's rich and varied history.

Literary Terms

ballad a simple song that often uses a refrain and sometimes uses rhyme and is passed from person to person

dialect a regional variety of language

end rhyme a feature of a poem or song in which the last words of two lines rhyme with one another

refrain the repetition of words or phrases to create mood or emphasis

About the Selection

Those who traveled to the West in the 1800s and later settled it were brave men and women who faced many hardships. They described their way of life in songs called **ballads.** These ballads often had a **refrain** and **end rhymes.** A refrain is the repetition of words or phrases to create mood or emphasis. End rhymes occur when the last words of two lines rhyme with one another.

Cowhand songs were passed from person to person. Those who sang these songs often made minor changes. The following selection is one version of a song about the work of the cowhand. It describes a cattle drive over the Chisholm Trail, which ran from ranches in Texas to railroads in Kansas. Notice the use of **dialect** in this song. Dialect is a regional variety of language. In written dialect, words are spelled as they are pronounced.

The Old Chisholm Trail

Come along, boys, and listen to my tale,
I'll tell you of my troubles on the old Chisholm trail.

Chorus
Come ti yi youpy, youpy yea, youpy yea,
Coma ti yi youpy, youpy yea.

I started up the trail October twenty-third,
I started up the trail with the 2-U herd.

Oh, a ten-dollar hoss and a forty-dollar saddle,
And I'm goin' to punchin' Texas cattle.

I woke up one morning on the old Chisholm trail,
Rope in my hand and a cow by the tail.

I'm up in the mornin' afore daylight
And afore I sleep the moon shines bright.

My hoss throwed me off at the creek called Mud,
My hoss throwed me off round the 2-U herd.

Last time I saw him he was goin' cross the level
A-kicking up his heels and a-running like the devil.

Last night I was on guard and the leader broke the
ranks, I hit my horse down the shoulders and I spurred
him in the flanks.

The wind commenced to blow, and the rain began to fall,
It looked, by grab, like we was goin' to lose 'em all.

My slicker's in the wagon and I'm gittin' mighty cold,
And these longhorn sons-o'-guns are gittin' hard to hold.

Saddle up, boys, and saddle up strong
For I think these cattle have scattered along.

What are the "troubles on the old Chisholm Trail"?

Notice the use of dialect in this line. "Hoss" is referring to a horse. "Goin'" and "punchin'" are also examples of dialect.

A *slicker* is a raincoat. A *longhorn* is any type of long-horned cattle formerly common in the southwestern United States.

This 1871 engraving shows cattle being loaded into a Kansas-Pacific Railway car.

With my blanket and my gun and my rawhide rope,
I'm a-slidin' down the trail in a long, keen **lope**.

Don't give a hoot if they never do stop;
I ride as long as an eight-day clock.

We rounded 'em up and put 'em on the cars,
And that was the last of the old Two Bars.

Well, it's bacon and beans most every day—
I'd as soon be a-eatin' prairie hay.

I went to the boss to draw my roll,
He had it figgered out I was nine dollars in the hole.

I'll sell my outfit just as soon as I can,
I won't punch cattle for no other man.

With my knees in the saddle and my seat in the sky,
I'll quit punching cows in the sweet by-and-by.

Fare you well, old trail-boss, I don't wish you any harm,
I'm a-quittin' this business to go on the farm.

lope the way in which a horse moves forward

The Old Chisholm Trail
Anonymous

Directions Write the answers to these questions using complete sentences.

Comprehension: Identifying Facts

1. During what time of year does this cowhand face his troubles on the cattle drive?

2. What does the cowhand eat almost every day?

3. What job does the cowhand say that he wishes to have?

Comprehension: Understanding Main Ideas

4. What does this song suggest about the life of a cowhand?

5. What is the basic story of this song? Write down events in your own words.

6. Explain the ways in which this song is like a poem.

Understanding Literature: Dialect

Several words used in "The Old Chisholm Trail" show that this tune is a regional song. The use of dialect makes the song sound as if it were sung by a cowhand. This is another example of how dialect is an important part of local color literature.

7. Identify five words that are written as dialect—just as if a person in the old West were saying or singing them. List these words on your paper. How do they contribute to your impression of the West?

8. This song is not grammatically correct. Do you think the song should be grammatically correct? Explain your answer.

Critical Thinking

9. Do you think being a cowhand sounds like fun or like hard work? Explain your answer.

10. Do you think that the cowhand who sings will actually quit working with cattle to go work on a farm? Give reasons to support your answer.

Writing on Your Own Write a paragraph describing whether you think songs should be considered literature. List examples of recent songs and use "The Old Chisholm Trail" to support your opinion. Clearly state your opinion at the beginning of the paragraph, and then add at least three statements to support your opinion.

This Sacred Soil
Chief Seattle

Chief Seattle
1786–1866

Literary Term

setting the time and place in a story

About the Author

Chief Seattle was a leader of the Duwamish and had close ties with the Suquamish nations in the coastal areas of the Pacific Northwest. He was friendly toward the first white settlers in this area. Later he became a Roman Catholic and made some Catholic ways part of American Indian life.

Chief Seattle's people were experts at fishing and earned their living from the sea. The land was also very important to them. However, Seattle, Washington, was developed in the area of Seattle's birth. He did not want the city to be named after him. He believed that after his death his spirit would be troubled every time his name was spoken. According to tradition, Chief Seattle was offered gifts to pay for the trouble that might be caused by the naming of the city after him.

About the Selection

In 1855 Chief Seattle signed a treaty that gave his people's land to the white settlers. The Governor of Washington, Isaac Stevens, received the territory for the settlers. The following selection is an excerpt from the speech Seattle made in 1854. The selection shows how Seattle's people strongly believed that this land would always belong to their people. His simple **setting** descriptions allow the reader to picture his people's land very clearly. Setting is the time and place in a story. The speech is short, yet very memorable.

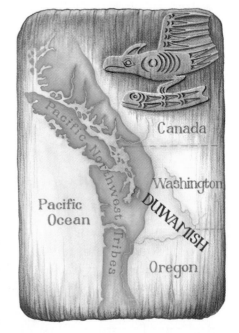

From This Sacred Soil

Every part of this soil is sacred in the estimation of my people. Every hillside, every valley, every plain and grove, has been **hallowed** by some sad or happy event in days long vanished. The very dust upon which you now stand responds more lovingly to their footsteps than to yours, because it is rich with the blood of our ancestors and our bare feet are conscious of the sympathetic touch. Even the little children who lived here and rejoiced here for a brief season will love these **somber solitudes** and at **eventide** they greet shadowy returning spirits. And when the last Red Man shall have perished, and the memory of my tribe shall have become a myth among the White Men, these shores will swarm with the invisible dead of my tribe, and when your children's children think themselves alone in the field, the store, the shop, upon the highway, or in the silence of the pathless woods, they will not be alone. At night when the streets of your cities and villages are silent and you think them deserted, they will throng with the returning hosts that once filled and still love this beautiful land. The White Man will never be alone.

Let him be just and deal kindly with my people, for the dead are not powerless. Dead, did I say? There is no death, only a change of worlds.

> Why do American Indians think of their land as sacred?

> Why will the "White Man" never be alone?

eventide evening

hallow to be made sacred or holy

solitude the state of being alone or isolated

somber dark colored

173

Directions Write the answers to these questions using complete sentences.

Comprehension: Identifying Facts

1. What word is used to describe the soil?

2. Why does the land respond more lovingly to the footsteps of the American Indians?

3. What does Seattle say will eventually happen to his people?

Comprehension: Understanding Main Ideas

4. Which sentences include phrases or words that show how much the Duwamish and Suquamish loved their land?

5. What does Seattle predict for the area?

6. How does Seattle indicate that he believes in an afterlife?

Understanding Literature: Setting

Regional literature gives the reader a sense of place, or setting. The reader can picture what the place looks like and what kinds of things happen in this place. Chief Seattle's speech gives the reader a sense of the land in the Pacific Northwest. His speech also presents how his people view the land. His view of the land is much different than the sense of place in "The Old Chisholm Trail."

7. Explain how Seattle creates a sense of place in his speech.

8. How is Seattle's sense of place different from the sense of place created in "The Old Chisholm Trail."

Critical Thinking

9. Do you believe that an injustice took place in 1855? Explain your answer.

10. Do you sense the sadness in this speech? Explain your answer.

Writing on Your Own All American Indians lost their land to the United States. Chief Seattle's speech makes it clear how valuable this land was to his people. Write a paragraph explaining how this speech made you feel about what happened to the American Indians and to their land.

Lullabies
Zuni and Makah

About the Authors

The Zuni are American Indians who live in the Southwest. Many Zuni are farmers and herders today. They belong to the Pueblo group. Hundreds of years ago, the Zuni lived in the desert and mesa areas of the American Southwest. In what is now New Mexico, the Zuni built large houses, often many stories tall, of adobe and rocks. The Zuni raised crops and sheep. They created a highly developed civilization in a harsh land. Today, much ancient Zuni culture still exists. Ceremony is an important part of close-knit Pueblo life.

The Makah were American Indians from the Northwest Pacific Coast. They settled in what is now Washington and were part of the Nootka people. Trees provided wood for their homes and their canoes. Rivers and the ocean provided food. The Nootka were great whalers. Hunting whales was dangerous work that involved the skills of many men. A successful hunt provided food and whale oil for the entire village. Today, many American Indians living along the Northwest Pacific Coast still earn their living from the sea, but now use modern equipment.

Literary Term

lullaby a soothing song or poem sung to a baby

About the Selections

American Indian songs are usually based on the experiences of the people of a certain area. Such songs were passed on for generations. The language has changed as the songs have been handed down. The following selections are **lullabies**. A lullaby is a soothing song or poem sung to a baby. These two lullabies show different ways of life in different locations. Yet both songs are full of love, hope, and comfort.

Mother and Child, Sandra Bierman

What similarities and differences do you see in these two lullabies?

My Son

My little son,
You will put a whale harpoon and a sealing spear into your canoe,
Not knowing what use you will make of them.

—*A Makah Lullaby from Washington*

Lullaby

Go to sleep, my little baby,
I will work.
Father will bring the sheep home soon.
Go to sleep, my little beetle.
Go to sleep, my little one,
My little jackrabbit.

—*A Zuni Lullaby from New Mexico*

Directions Write the answers to these questions using complete sentences.

Comprehension: Identifying Facts

1. In "Lullaby," what does the mother want the baby to do?

2. Where is the father?

3. In "My Son," what things will the child put in his canoe?

Comprehension: Understanding Main Ideas

4. In "Lullaby," how old do you think the child is? Explain your answer.

5. In "My Son," explain where this mother and son live.

6. What kind of life does this mother see for her son?

Understanding Literature: Lullaby

A lullaby is a soothing song or poem sung to a baby. The name comes from the root word "lull," meaning to make quiet or to give a brief time of quiet. Both of these lullabies, Zuni and Makah, are sung by a mother to her child.

7. Read these two lullabies again. What are the comforting words that the mother uses in each song?

8. What are other words that a parent might use in singing and rocking a baby to sleep?

Critical Thinking

9. How are these lullabies similar to or different from lullabies you have heard before?

10. What do you think these lullabies reveal about the Zuni and the Makah? Explain.

Writing on Your Own Choose the lullaby you liked best. Think of a sentence you could add to the lullaby. Copy down the lullaby on your own paper. Add your sentence, being careful to follow the same writing style and mood.

Dialect

Dialect is the way of speaking or writing common to a certain place. Writers use dialect to show the reader how people actually talk. You may have seen words like those listed below. These are all examples of dialect.

goin'	dunno	ain't	git
agin	'em	runnin'	doin'

Dialect is often used when a character in a story is speaking. Words are misspelled on purpose so that the reader reads the words as they would actually sound. Writers use dialect to make writing more realistic. The reader can get an idea about what a place in a story is like by hearing how someone in that place speaks.

Some authors in this unit used dialect. Here are some examples.

"S-t-e-a-m-boat a-comin'!"

I was therefore passing it as quietly and as rapidly as possible, when from the lot just opposite the house, or sign-post, I heard a coarse stern voice cry, "Halloo!"

My hoss throwed me off at the creek called Mud, . . .

The first sentence is from Mark Twain's *Life on the Mississippi*. In this sentence, the reader can imagine how the drayman sounded as he let everyone know of the steamboat's arrival. The second sentence is from James W. C. Pennington's *The Fugitive Blacksmith*. "Halloo" means "hello." The final sentence is from "The Old Chisholm Trail." "Hoss" means "horse." "Throwed" is not correct; it should be "threw," but dialect makes the sentence sound as if it were spoken by a cowhand.

Review

1. What is dialect?

2. What does dialect add to writing?

3. Do you think the use of dialect improves writing? Why or why not?

4. What dialect have you noticed when listening to others speak?

5. How does dialect give the reader a sense of place?

Writing on Your Own Write three sentences of your own using dialect. Underline words in your sentences that are clearly examples of dialect.

UNIT 3 SUMMARY

Unit 3 covers 1849 to 1889, an important time in American history. Slavery, the Civil War, the death of President Abraham Lincoln, and the removal of American Indians from their land made this a difficult time.

Slavery and the Civil War especially divided the country. However, the Civil War ended slavery. Americans began to look west for growth. The nation began to grow and come together again. Literature continued to grow, too. A new kind of writing called local color became important. Local color focused on the way people spoke and dressed, the way people behaved, and the customs popular in certain areas. Sarah Josepha Hale, James W. C. Pennington, Walt Whitman, Abraham Lincoln, Frederick Douglass, Mark Twain, Chief Seattle, and several anonymous writers all added to this local color movement.

Selections

■ "Thirty-Five" is a poem by Sarah Josepha Hale about the enjoyment of life at middle age.

■ "Swing Low, Sweet Chariot" and "Deep River" are spirituals that express the sorrow of slavery and the hope for a better life.

■ *The Fugitive Blacksmith* by James W. C. Pennington is an autobiography of Pennington's escape from slavery.

■ "Beat! Beat! Drums!" and "Come Up from the Fields Father" by Walt Whitman are Civil War poems that tell of the loss and grief the war caused.

■ "A Letter to Mrs. Bixby" by former President Abraham Lincoln shows Lincoln's compassion for a woman who lost five sons in the Civil War.

■ "What the Black Man Wants" is a speech by Frederick Douglass expressing the need to grant African Americans the right to vote.

■ *Life on the Mississippi* is Mark Twain's autobiography. The selection from it in this unit is about Twain's childhood dream to work on a riverboat.

■ "The Old Chisholm Trail" is a song about cowhands and the old West.

■ "This Sacred Soil" is a speech by Chief Seattle expressing the importance of his people's land.

■ "Lullaby" and "My Son" are two lullabies of the Zuni and the Makah, both American Indian tribes.

Directions Write the answers to these questions using complete sentences.

Comprehension: Identifying Facts

1. What war was fought during this time period?

2. During which years was this war fought?

3. What event happened after the war?

4. What happened to American Indians during this time?

5. What happened to African Americans during this time?

Comprehension: Understanding Main Ideas

6. Explain the struggles represented by the speeches of Frederick Douglass and Chief Seattle. Why are their stories an important part of American literature?

7. Describe the differences in writing style between Mark Twain and Abraham Lincoln.

8. The African American spirituals, "The Old Chisholm Trail," and the Zuni and Makah lullabies were all songs. How are all of these songs alike and different?

9. Why is James W. C. Pennington's *The Fugitive Blacksmith* an important story about slavery?

10. What does Walt Whitman's poetry communicate about the Civil War?

Understanding Literature: First-Person and Third-Person Point of View

Two main points of view are the first person and the third person. The first person uses the author/character as the narrator, or speaker, in the story. Writers use the pronouns *I*, *me*, and *my* in stories written in the first person. First person can make the reader feel closer to the narrator. The third person does not have a narrator who uses the pronouns *I*, *me*, and *my*. Sometimes there is a narrator who knows all that happens in the story, plus the thoughts and feelings of all of the characters. The narrator may also tell the story from the limited point of view of certain characters. Pronouns used in the third person include *he*, *she*, *his*, *her*, and *they*.

11. Which authors in this unit use the first-person point of view?

12. Did the first-person point of view make you feel closer to the narrators in these stories? Why or why not?

13. Which authors in this unit use the third-person point of view?

14. How does the use of third person make these stories different from those told in the first person?

15. Do you prefer to read stories written in the first person or in the third person? Explain.

Critical Thinking

16. Notice how each style of writing in this unit differs. Which writing style do you think would be the most difficult to match? Why?

17. There are many issues presented by writings in this unit. Which piece of literature do you think does the best job communicating about an issue? Why?

18. This unit presents local color literature. Which selection do you think is the best example of local color? Why?

19. Which selection in this unit do you like best? Why?

20. Do you think reading the literature in this unit helps you as a person today? Why or why not?

Speak and Listen

Several selections in this unit are meant to be read aloud or sung. These selections include speeches, lullabies, and spirituals. Choose one of these works. Prepare to read it to the class as intended by the author. If you choose a long speech, present only one or two paragraphs. Practice reading your selection aloud. Present the selection to the class.

Beyond Words

Choose a character from a selection in Unit 3. Think about how this character might look. Draw a picture of the character doing something from the selection. If possible, research details such as historically correct clothing or objects for the background of your picture.

Writing on Your Own
Unit 3 features local color literature. Write an essay explaining what local color literature is. Include a statement of purpose for your essay. Include at least three examples of local color literature using quotes from the selections in Unit 3. Then write a conclusion.

Test-Taking Tip
Always read directions more than once. Underline words that tell how many examples or items you must provide.

"As the boat bounced from the top of each wave, the wind tore through the hair of the hatless men, and as the craft plopped her stern down again the spray splashed them. . . . It was probably glorious, this play of the free sea, wild with emerald and white and amber."

—Stephen Crane, "The Open Boat," 1897

"There was no mistake about it, it *was* cold. He strode up and down, stamping his feet and threshing his arms, until reassured by the returning warmth. Then he got out matches and proceeded to make a fire."

—Jack London, "To Build a Fire," 1908

UNIT 4 *The Harvest of Realism and Naturalism: 1890–1908*

Toward the end of the nineteenth century, a new kind of literature became important. For the first time, writers began writing about very real events. Unlike the romantic writers of the past, writers now chose to write in very believable styles. The mood of this literature was often grim. These writings often focused on survival. It was a new style for a very new century.

In this unit, you will learn about two new literary movements and read two selections from these movements.

Toward the end of the 1800s, industry grew in the United States. The Civil War and Reconstruction were over. The North and South had to learn to be one nation again. The country was about to become one of the most powerful nations in the world.

By the 1890s, movement west continued. Farming and industry were important. Industry was changing the lives of many Americans. Inventions such as the telephone, the electric light, and many new machines made the United States the land of opportunity. The middle class became interested in reading. Book and newspaper publishing became successful. People came to America from other countries by the thousands to be a part of American growth and success.

Along with opportunities, however, came problems. Factory jobs were difficult, and pay was low. The success of farming was uncertain. Many people in cities were poor. People who came to America from other countries met up with hard labor and long hours in industry. Many politicians were dishonest and did things to harm the American people. Men and women faced the reality that life was a struggle.

Much of the literature of the time reflected unhappy events in life. New short stories, novels, and poetry were much different from writings of the earlier, romantic period. This new movement in literature was called realism. Writers now wrote about life as it was, not as they wished it to be. Life was looked at as never before—honestly and in great detail. Common events and personal experiences became the subjects of the realists. How people lived, how they reacted to events in life, and how they fit into the universe were all common ideas in realist literature.

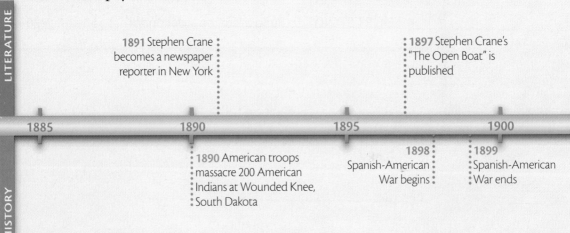

LITERATURE

1891 Stephen Crane becomes a newspaper reporter in New York

1897 Stephen Crane's "The Open Boat" is published

1885   1890   1895   1900

1890 American troops massacre 200 American Indians at Wounded Knee, South Dakota

1898 Spanish-American War begins

1899 Spanish-American War ends

HISTORY

Similar to realism was a literary movement called naturalism. Its message can be described as survival of the fittest against nature: the stronger survive, while the weaker do not. This kind of writing included characters who were helpless to understand nature and to defend themselves against it.

The two authors in this unit fit into the realist and naturalist movements. Stephen Crane's writing shows a very realistic and naturalistic point of view. He accurately tells about events in life. He examines the inner nature of humans as well. His characters are victims of cold and grim fate. Many of his characters are never named and therefore represent all people. No writer more accurately reflects the realistic movement than does Crane. His selection "The Open Boat" is perhaps one of the best short stories ever written.

Jack London also wrote with a realist and naturalist point of view. His story

In 1890, American soldiers massacred 200 American Indians at Wounded Knee, South Dakota. The memorial above marks where the massacre occurred.

"To Build a Fire" in this unit is an example of a character struggling to survive. This is a common theme in London's writings. His stories give readers an exciting, yet tragic, view of characters facing some force beyond their control and understanding—usually nature.

1900 Jack London's first novel is published

1908 Jack London's "To Build a Fire" is published

LITERATURE

1900   1905   1910   1915

1900
U.S. census shows 75,994,575 people live in the United States

1900
Hawaiian Islands are made an American territory

1903
Orville and Wilbur Wright fly the first powered, controlled, heavier-than-air airplane at Kitty Hawk, North Carolina

1908
Henry Ford introduces the Model T, the first mass-produced automobile

HISTORY

The Open Boat
Stephen Crane

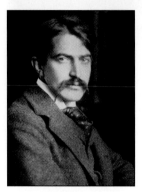

Stephen Crane
1871–1900

Literary Terms

personification a figure of speech that gives human qualities to something that is not human, such as a place or an object

plot the series of events in a story

refrain the repetition of words or phrases to create mood or emphasis

rising action a technique authors use to build tension and suspense

About the Author

Born in Newark, New Jersey, in 1871, Stephen Crane was the son of a Methodist minister. After attending college for two years, Crane went to New York in 1891 to become a newspaper reporter. He eventually wrote books. In 1895, he published a novel about the Civil War called *The Red Badge of Courage*. This story made him very famous and wealthy.

During the next five years, Crane continued working as a reporter. He wrote about the Greco-Turkish War in 1897 and the Spanish-American War in 1898. These assignments had many hardships. However, the experiences allowed him to write several great stories and poems in his short life.

Crane's busy life may have led to his early death. He died in Germany of tuberculosis at twenty-eight.

About the Selection

"The Open Boat" is a short story based on one of Crane's real-life events. In 1897, Crane traveled to Cuba to write about a revolt there. His ship, the *Commodore*, sank off the coast of Florida in January of 1897. His adventure is detailed in "The Open Boat." Because of its length, "The Open Boat" is divided into seven sections or chapters. These chapters are numbered throughout the story.

Crane uses **rising action** in this story. Authors use rising action to build suspense. Rising action makes the reader continue to read to see how the **plot** will develop. Plot is the series of events in a story. Crane also uses **personification** and **refrain** in this story. Personification is a figure of speech that gives human qualities to something that is not human, such as a place or an object. Refrain is the repetition of words or phrases to create mood or emphasis.

The pen Boat

A tale intended to be after the fact, being the experience of four men from the sunk steamer *Commodore*.

– I –

None of them knew the color of the sky. Their eyes glanced level, and were fastened upon the waves that swept toward them. These waves were of the hue of slate, save for the tops, which were of foaming white, and all of the men knew the colors of the sea. The horizon narrowed and widened, and dipped and rose, and at all times its edge was jagged with waves that seemed thrust up in points like rocks.

What struggles do the four men face?

Many a man ought to have a bathtub larger than the boat which here rode upon the sea. These waves were most wrongfully and **barbarously abrupt** and tall, and each froth-top was a problem in small-boat navigation.

The cook squatted in the bottom and looked with both eyes at the six inches of gunwale which separated him from the ocean. His sleeves were rolled over his fat forearms, and the two flaps of his unbuttoned vest dangled as he bent to bail out the boat. Often he said: "Gawd! That was a narrow clip." As he remarked it he **invariably** gazed eastward over the broken sea.

The gunwale *is the upper edge of a boat's side.*

The oiler, steering with one of the two oars in the boat, sometimes raised himself suddenly to keep clear of water that swirled in over the stern. It was a thin little oar and it seemed often ready to snap.

The stern *is the rear of a boat.*

---

abrupt characterized by changing without warning

barbarously harshly or cruelly

invariably constantly

A *correspondent* is a newspaper reporter. A correspondent often writes articles from a distant place. The author of this story, Stephen Crane, was a correspondent.

The *bow* is the front part of a boat.

The correspondent, pulling at the other oar, watched the waves and wondered why he was there.

The injured captain, lying in the bow, was at this time buried in that **profound dejection** and **indifference** which comes, temporarily at least, to even the bravest and most enduring when, willy nilly, the firm fails, the army loses, the ship goes down. The mind of the master of a vessel is rooted deep in the timbers of her, though he commands for a day or a decade; and this captain had on him the stern impression of a scene in the grays of dawn of seven turned faces, and later a stump of a topmast with a white ball on it that slashed to and fro at the waves, went low and lower, and down. Thereafter there was something strange in his voice. Although steady, it was deep with mourning, and of a quality beyond **oration** or tears.

"Keep 'er a little more south, Billie," said he.

"A little more south, sir," said the oiler in the stern.

A seat in this boat was not unlike a seat upon a bucking bronco, and by the same token, a bronco is not much smaller. The craft pranced and reared and plunged like an animal. As each wave came, and she rose for it, she seemed like a horse making at a fence outrageously high. The manner of her scramble over these walls of water is a **mystic** thing, and, moreover, at the top of them were ordinarily these problems in white water, the foam racing down from the summit of each wave, requiring a new leap, and a leap from the air. Then, after scornfully bumping a crest, she would slide, and race, and splash down a long incline, and arrive bobbing and nodding in front of the next menace.

A **singular** disadvantage of the sea lies in the fact that after successfully **surmounting** one wave you discover that there is another behind it just as important and just as nervously anxious to do something effective in the way of swamping boats. In a ten-foot dinghy one can get an idea of the

A *dinghy* is a small boat or lifeboat with oars or sails.

dejection sadness	**mystic** mysterious	**singular** unique
indifference the state of feeling no concern or interest about anything	**oration** formal speech	**surmount** to get to the top of
	profound complete	

resources of the sea in the line of waves that is not **probable** to the average experience, which is never at sea in a dinghy. As each slatey wall of water approached, it shut all else from the view of the men in the boat, and it was not difficult to imagine that this particular wave was the final outburst of the ocean, the last effort of the grim water. There was a terrible grace in the move of the waves, and they came in silence, save for the snarling of the crests.

In the **wan** light the faces of the men must have been gray. Their eyes must have glinted in strange ways as they gazed steadily astern. Viewed from a balcony, the whole thing would doubtless have been weirdly **picturesque**. But the men in the boat had no time to see it, and if they had had leisure, there were other things to occupy their minds. The sun swung steadily up the sky, and they knew it was broad day because the color of the sea changed from slate to emerald green, streaked with amber lights, and the foam was like tumbling snow. The process of the breaking day was unknown to them. They were aware only of this effect upon the color of the waves that rolled toward them.

In **disjointed** sentences the cook and the correspondent argued as to the difference between a lifesaving station

disjointed lacking order; hard to understand

picturesque charming or quaint in appearance

probable very likely

wan dim

and a house of refuge. The cook had said: "There's a house of refuge just north of the Mosquito Inlet Light, and as soon as they see us, they'll come off in their boat and pick us up."

"As soon as who see us?" said the correspondent.

"The crew," said the cook.

"Houses of refuge don't have crews," said the correspondent. "As I understand them, they are only places where clothes and grub are stored for the benefit of shipwrecked people. They don't carry crews."

"Oh, yes, they do," said the cook.

"No, they don't," said the correspondent.

"Well, we're not there yet, anyhow," said the oiler, in the stern.

"Well," said the cook, "perhaps it's not a house of refuge that I'm thinking of as being near Mosquito Inlet Light. Perhaps it's a lifesaving station."

"We're not there yet," said the oiler, in the stern.

– II –

What gives the men hope in this chapter?

As the boat bounced from the top of each wave, the wind tore through the hair of the hatless men, and as the craft plopped her stern down again the spray splashed past them. The crest of each of these waves was a hill, from the top of which the men surveyed, for a moment, a broad **tumultuous expanse**, shining and wind-riven. It was probably splendid, it was probably glorious, this play of the free sea, wild with lights of emerald and white and amber.

"Bully good thing it's an onshore wind," said the cook. "If not, where would we be? Wouldn't have a show."

"That's right," said the correspondent.

The busy oiler nodded his **assent**.

Then the captain, in the bow, chuckled in a way that expressed humor, **contempt, tragedy**, all in one. "Do you think we've got much of a show now, boys?" said he.

assent agreement	**expanse** a great extent of something spread out	**tumultuous** violent; marked by noisy movement
contempt deep dislike or scorn	**tragedy** a terrible event	

Whereupon the three were silent, save for a trifle of hemming and hawing. To express any particular **optimism** at this time they felt to be childish and stupid, but they all doubtless possessed this sense of the situation in their minds. A young man thinks **doggedly** at such times. On the other hand, the **ethics** of their condition was decidedly against any open suggestion of hopelessness. So they were silent.

"Oh, well," said the captain, soothing his children, "we'll get ashore all right."

But there was that in his tone which made them think; so the oiler quoth, "Yes! If this wind holds!"

The cook was bailing: "Yes! If we don't catch hell in the surf."

Canton flannel gulls flew near and far. Sometimes they sat down on the sea, near patches of brown seaweed that rolled on the waves with a movement like carpets on a line in a gale. The birds sat comfortably in groups, and they were envied by some in the dinghy, for the wrath of the sea was no more to them than it was to a covey of prairie chickens a thousand miles inland. Often they came very close and stared at the men with black bead-like eyes. At these times they were **uncanny** and **sinister** in their unblinking **scrutiny**, and the men hooted angrily at them, telling them to be gone. One came, and evidently decided to alight on the top of the captain's head. The bird flew parallel to the boat and did not circle, but made short sidelong jumps in the air in chicken fashion. His black eyes were **wistfully** fixed upon the captain's head. "Ugly brute," said the oiler to the bird. "You look as if you were made with a jackknife." The cook and the correspondent swore darkly at the creature. The captain naturally wished to knock it away with the end of the heavy painter; but he did not dare do it, because anything

> A *covey* is a small flock.

doggedly stubbornly	**optimism** the state of believing in the best possible outcome	**sinister** suggesting a feeling of fear; evil
ethics principles guiding a person or group; the study of good and bad	**scrutiny** a searching look or close watch	**uncanny** peculiar; unnatural
		wistfully longingly

Why do you think the
men do not like the
birds?

resembling an **emphatic** gesture would have capsized this freighted boat; and so, with his open hand, the captain gently and carefully waved the gull away. After it had been discouraged from the pursuit the captain breathed easier on account of his hair, and others breathed easier because the bird struck their minds at this time as being somehow gruesome and **ominous**.

In the meantime the oiler and the correspondent rowed. And also they rowed. They sat together in the same seat, and each rowed an oar. Then the oiler took both oars; then the correspondent took both oars; then the oiler; then the correspondent. They rowed and they rowed. The very ticklish part of the business was when the time came for the reclining one in the stern to take his turn at the oars. By the very last star of truth, it is easier to steal eggs from under a hen than it was to change seats in the dinghy. First the man in the stern slid his hand along the thwart and moved with care, as if he were of Sèvres. Then the man in the rowing seat slid his hand along the other thwart. It was all done with the most extraordinary care. As the two sidled past each other, the whole party kept watchful eyes on the coming wave, and the captain cried: "Look out now! Steady there!"

A *thwart* is a rower's
seat extending across a
boat. *Sèvres* is a French
city known for its
decorated porcelain,
called Sèvres porcelain.

The brown mats of seaweed that appeared from time to time were like islands, bits of earth. They were traveling, apparently, neither one way nor the other. They were, to all intents, stationary. They informed the men in the boat that it was making progress slowly toward the land.

The captain, rearing cautiously in the bow, after the dinghy soared on a great swell, said that he had seen the lighthouse at Mosquito Inlet. Presently the cook remarked that he had seen it. The correspondent was at the oars then, and for some reason he too wished to look at the lighthouse, but his back was toward the far shore, and the waves were important, and for some time he could not seize an opportunity to turn his head. But at last there came a wave

emphatic forceful; attracting special attention	**ominous** having a forbidding or alarming character

more gentle than the others, and when at the crest of it he swiftly scoured the western horizon.

"See it?" said the captain.

"No," said the correspondent slowly, "I didn't see anything."

"Look again," said the captain. He pointed. "It's exactly in that direction."

At the top of another wave, the correspondent did as he was bid, and this time his eyes chanced on a small, still thing on the edge of the swaying horizon. It was precisely like the point of a pin. It took an anxious eye to find a lighthouse so tiny.

"Think we'll make it, captain?"

"If this wind holds and the boat don't swamp, we can't do much else," said the captain.

The little boat, lifted by each towering sea, and splashed viciously by the crests, made progress that in the absence of seaweed was not apparent to those in her. She seemed just a wee thing wallowing, miraculously top up, at the mercy of five oceans. Occasionally a great spread of water, like white flames, swarmed into her.

"Bail her, cook," said the captain **serenely**.

"All right, captain," said the cheerful cook.

– III –

It would be difficult to describe the **subtle** brotherhood of men that was here established on the seas. No one said that it was so. No one mentioned it. But it dwelt in the boat, and each man felt it warm him. They were a captain, an oiler, a cook, and a correspondent, and they were friends—friends in a more curiously ironbound degree than may be common. The hurt captain, lying against the water jar in the bow, spoke always in a low voice and calmly, but he could never command a more ready and swiftly obedient crew than the **motley** three of the dinghy. It was more than a mere

What pleasant surprise occurs at the end of this chapter?

motley made up of a varied mixture	**serenely** calmly	**subtle** difficult to understand or detect

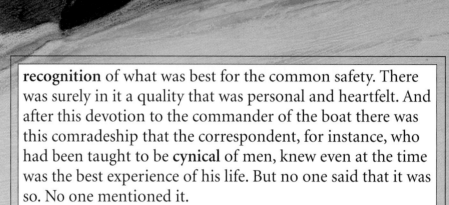

recognition of what was best for the common safety. There was surely in it a quality that was personal and heartfelt. And after this devotion to the commander of the boat there was this comradeship that the correspondent, for instance, who had been taught to be **cynical** of men, knew even at the time was the best experience of his life. But no one said that it was so. No one mentioned it.

"I wish we had a sail," remarked the captain. "We might try my overcoat on the end of an oar and give you two boys a chance to rest." So the cook and the correspondent held the mast and spread wide the overcoat. The oiler steered, and the little boat made good way with her new rig. Sometimes the oiler had to scull sharply to keep a sea from breaking into the boat, but otherwise sailing was a success.

Meanwhile the lighthouse had been growing slowly larger. It had now almost assumed color, and appeared like a little gray shadow on the sky. The man at the oars could not be prevented from turning his head rather often to try for a glimpse of this little gray shadow.

At last, from the top of each wave the men in the tossing boat could see land. Even as the lighthouse was an upright shadow on the sky, this land seemed but a long black shadow on the sea. It certainly was thinner than paper. "We must be about opposite New Smyrna," said the cook, who had coasted this shore often in schooners. "Captain, by the way, I

cynical deeply distrustful

recognition the act of understanding or realizing something

believe they abandoned that lifesaving station there about a year ago."

"Did they?" said the captain.

The wind slowly died away. The cook and the correspondent were not now obliged to slave in order to hold high the oar. But the waves continued their old **impetuous** swooping at the dinghy, and the little craft, no longer under way, struggled woundily over them. The oiler or the correspondent took the oars again.

Shipwrecks are **apropos** of nothing. If men could only train for them and have them occur when the men had reached pink condition, there would be less drowning at sea. Of the four in the dinghy none had slept any time worth mentioning for two days and two nights previous to embarking in the dinghy, and in the excitement of clambering about the deck of a foundering ship they had also forgotten to eat heartily.

For these reasons, and for others, neither the oiler nor the correspondent was fond of rowing at this time. The correspondent wondered **ingenuously** how in the name of all that was sane could there be people who thought it amusing to row a boat. It was not an amusement; it was a **diabolical** punishment, and even a genius of mental

apropos to the purpose; at the right time

diabolical devilish; relating to the devil

impetuous marked by force of movement or action

ingenuously innocently; with childlike simplicity

aberrations could never conclude that it was anything but a horror to the muscles and a crime against the back. He mentioned to the boat in general how the amusement of rowing struck him, and the weary-faced oiler smiled in full sympathy. Previously to the foundering, by the way, the oiler had worked double watch in the engine room of the ship.

"Take her easy, now, boys," said the captain. "Don't spend yourselves. If we have to run a surf you'll need all your strength, because we'll sure have to swim for it. Take your time."

Slowly the land arose from the sea. From a black line it became a line of black and a line of white—trees and sand. Finally, the captain said that he could make out a house on the shore. "That's the house of refuge, sure," said the cook. "They'll see us before long, and come out after us."

The distant lighthouse reared high. "The keeper ought to be able to make us out now, if he's looking through a glass," said the captain. "He'll notify the lifesaving people."

"None of those other boats could have got ashore to give word of the wreck," said the oiler, in a low voice. "Else the lifeboat would be out hunting us."

Slowly and beautifully the land loomed out of the sea. The wind came again. It had **veered** from the northeast to the southeast. Finally, a new sound struck the ears of the men in the boat. It was the low thunder of the surf on the shore. "We'll never be able to make the lighthouse now," said the captain. "Swing her head a little more north, Billie," said he.

"A little more north, sir," said the oiler.

Whereupon the little boat turned her nose once more down the wind, and all but the oarsman watched the shore grow. Under the influence of this expansion doubt and **direful apprehension** were leaving the minds of the men. The management of the boat was still most absorbing, but it could not prevent a quiet cheerfulness. In an hour, perhaps, they would be ashore.

The men in the boat are unable to make it to shore because there are waves crashing on shore.

aberration a belief that goes against what is common or normal	**apprehension** understanding **direful** dreadful	**veer** to change direction or course

Their backbones had become thoroughly used to balancing in the boat, and they now rode this wild colt of a dinghy like circus men. The correspondent thought that he had been drenched to the skin, but happening to feel in the top pocket of his coat, he found therein eight cigars. Four of them were soaked with seawater; four were perfectly **scatheless**. After a search, somebody produced three dry matches, and thereupon the four **waifs** rode **impudently** in their little boat, and, with an assurance of an **impending** rescue shining in their eyes, puffed at the big cigars and judged well and ill of all men. Everybody took a drink of water.

– IV –

"Cook," remarked the captain, "there don't seem to be any signs of life about your house of refuge."

"No," replied the cook. "Funny they don't see us!"

A broad stretch of lowly coast lay before the eyes of the men. It was of dunes topped with dark vegetation. The roar of the surf was plain, and sometimes they could see the white lip of a wave as it spun up the beach. A tiny house was blocked out black upon the sky. Southward, the slim lighthouse lifted its little gray length.

Tide, wind, and waves were swinging the dinghy northward. "Funny they don't see us," said the men.

The surf's roar was here dulled, but its tone was nevertheless thunderous and mighty. As the boat swam over the great rollers, the men sat listening to this roar. "We'll swamp sure," said everybody.

It is fair to say here that there was not a lifesaving station within twenty miles in either direction, but the men did not know this fact, and in **consequence** they made dark and **opprobrious** remarks concerning the eyesight of the nation's

What thoughts do the men have in this chapter?

consequence result	**impudently** in a manner marked by boldness or cockiness	**scatheless** unharmed; uninjured
impending about to occur		**waif** a stray person
	opprobrious disrespectful	

An *epithet* is an abusive word or phrase.

lifesavers. Four scowling men sat in the dinghy and **surpassed** records in the invention of epithets.

"Funny they don't see us."

The lightheartedness of a former time had completely faded. To their sharpened minds it was easy to conjure pictures of all kinds of **incompetency** and blindness and, indeed, cowardice. There was the shore of the populous land, and it was bitter and bitter to them that from it came no sign.

"Well," said the captain, ultimately, "I suppose we'll have to make a try for ourselves. If we stay out here too long, we'll none of us have strength left to swim after the boat swamps."

And so the oiler, who was at the oars, turned the boat straight for the shore. There was a sudden tightening of muscle. There was some thinking.

"If we don't all get ashore," said the captain. "If we don't all get ashore, I suppose you fellows know where to send news of my finish?"

They then briefly exchanged some addresses and **admonitions**. As for the reflections of the men, there was a great deal of rage in them. Perchance they might be **formulated** thus: "If I am going to be drowned—if I am going to be drowned—if I am going to be drowned, why in the name of the seven mad gods who rule the sea, was I allowed to come thus far and **contemplate** sand and trees? Was I brought here merely to have my nose dragged away as I was about to nibble the sacred cheese of life? It is **preposterous**. If this old ninny woman, Fate, cannot do better than this, she should be **deprived** of the management of men's fortunes. She is an old hen who knows not her intention. If she has decided to drown me, why did she not do it in the beginning and save me all this trouble? The whole affair is absurd. . . .

The woman in this paragraph is not really a woman. The author is using personification to give life to nature or "fate" by referring to it as a woman.

admonition a gentle warning	**formulate** to organize into a statement	**preposterous** against nature, reason, or common sense
contemplate to think about	**incompetency** the inability to act due to a lack of needed skills or qualities	**surpass** to become better, greater, or stronger than
deprive to take something away		

But no, she cannot mean to drown me. She dare not drown me. She cannot drown me. Not after all this work." Afterward the man might have had an impulse to shake his fist at the clouds: "Just you drown me, now, and then hear what I call you!"

The billows that came at this time were more **formidable**. They seemed always just about to break and roll over the little boat in a **turmoil** of foam. There was a preparatory and long growl in the speech of them. No mind unused to the sea would have concluded that the dinghy could ascend these sheer heights in time. The shore was still afar. The oiler was a wily surfman. "Boys," he said swiftly, "she won't live three minutes more, and we're too far out to swim. Shall I take her to sea again, captain?"

"Yes! Go ahead!" said the captain.

This oiler, by a series of quick miracles and fast and steady oarsmanship, turned the boat in the middle of the surf and took her safely to sea again.

There was a considerable silence as the boat bumped over the furrowed sea to deeper water. Then somebody in gloom spoke: "Well, anyhow, they must have seen us from the shore by now."

The gulls went in slanting flight up the wind toward the gray **desolate** east. A squall, marked by dingy clouds, and clouds brick red, like smoke from a burning building, appeared from the southeast.

"What do you think of those lifesaving people? Ain't they peaches?"

"Funny they haven't seen us."

"Maybe they think we're out here for sport! Maybe they think we're fishin'. Maybe they think we're damned fools."

It was a long afternoon. A changed tide tried to force them southward, but wind and wave said northward. Far ahead, where coastline, sea, and sky formed their mighty angle, there were little dots which seemed to indicate a city on the shore.

How do the men feel at this point in the story?

desolate lacking inhabitants	**formidable** causing fear or dread	**turmoil** extreme confusion or rapid movement

"St. Augustine?"

The captain shook his head. "Too near Mosquito Inlet."

And the oiler rowed, and then the correspondent rowed. Then the oiler rowed. It was a weary business. The human back can become the seat of more aches and pains than are registered in books for the **composite anatomy** of a regiment. It is a limited area, but it can become a theater of **innumerable** muscular conflicts, tangles, wrenches, knots, and other comforts.

"Did you ever like to row, Billie?" asked the correspondent.

"No," said the oiler. "Hang it!"

When one exchanged the rowing seat for a place in the bottom of the boat, he suffered a bodily **depression** that caused him to be careless of everything save an **obligation** to wiggle one finger. There was cold seawater swashing to and fro in the boat, and he lay in it. His head, pillowed on a thwart, was within an inch of the swirl of a wave crest, and sometimes a particularly **obstreperous** sea came inboard and drenched him once more. But these matters did not annoy him. It is almost certain that if the boat had capsized he would have tumbled comfortably out upon the ocean as if he felt sure that it was a great soft mattress.

"Look! There's a man on the shore!"

"Where?"

"There! See 'im? See 'im?"

"Yes, sure! He's walking along."

"Now he's stopped. Look! He's facing us!"

"He's waving at us!"

"So he is! By thunder!"

"Ah, now we're all right! Now we're all right! There'll be a boat out here for us in half an hour."

"He's going on. He's running. He's going up to that house there."

Notice how the author does not tell the reader who is speaking here. The reader must imagine which person is speaking.

anatomy the physical makeup of a living thing	**depression** the lowering of activity	**obligation** a duty or responsibility
composite made up of several parts	**innumerable** too many to be numbered	**obstreperous** marked by loud noise

The remote beach seemed lower than the sea, and it required a searching glance to **discern** the little black figure. The captain saw a floating stick and they rowed to it. A bath towel was by some weird chance in the boat, and, tying this on the stick, the captain waved it. The oarsman did not dare turn his head, so he was obliged to ask questions.

"What's he doing now?"

"He's standing still again. He's looking, I think. . . . There he goes again. Toward the house. . . . Now he's stopped again."

"Is he waving at us?"

"No, not now! He was, though."

"Look! There comes another man!"

"He's running."

"Look at him go, would you!"

"Why, he's on a bicycle. Now he's met the other man. They're both waving at us. Look!"

"There comes something up the beach."

"What the devil is that thing?"

"Why, it looks like a boat."

"Why, certainly, it's a boat."

"No, it's on wheels."

"Yes, so it is. Well, that must be the lifeboat. They drag them along shore on a wagon."

"That's the lifeboat, sure."

"No, by God, it's—it's an omnibus."

"I tell you it's a lifeboat."

discern to detect with the eyes

An *omnibus* is a kind a vehicle that is used to carry a large number of passengers.

"It is not! It's an omnibus. I can see it plain. See? One of those big hotel omnibuses."

"By thunder, you're right. It's an omnibus, sure as fate. What do you suppose they are doing with an omnibus? Maybe they are going around collecting the life crew, hey?"

"That's it, likely. Look! There's a fellow waving a little black flag. He's standing on the steps of the omnibus. There come those other two fellows. Now they're all talking together. Look at the fellow with the flag. Maybe he ain't waving it."

"That ain't a flag, is it? That's his coat. Why, certainly, that's his coat."

"So it is. It's his coat. He's taken it off and is waving it around his head. But would you look at him swing it!"

"Oh, say, there isn't any lifesaving station there. That's just a winter resort hotel omnibus that has brought over some of the boarders to see us drown."

"What's that idiot with the coat mean? What's he signaling, anyhow?"

"It looks as if he were trying to tell us to go north. There must be a lifesaving station up there."

"No! He thinks we're fishing. Just giving us a merry hand. See? Ah, there, Willie!"

"Well, I wish I could make something out of those signals. What do you suppose he means?"

"He don't mean anything. He's just playing."

"Well, if he'd just signal us to try the surf again, or to go to sea and wait, or go north, or go south, or go to hell, there would be some reason in it. But look at him! He just stands there and keeps his coat revolving like a wheel. The ass!"

"There come more people."

"Now there's quite a mob. Look! Isn't that a boat?"

"Where? Oh, I see where you mean. No, that's no boat."

"That fellow is still waving his coat."

"He must think we like to see him do that. Why don't he quit it? It don't mean anything."

"I don't know. I think he is trying to make us go north. It must be that there's a lifesaving station there somewhere."

"Say, he ain't tired yet. Look at 'im wave."

"Wonder how long he can keep that up. He's been revolving his coat ever since he caught sight of us. He's an idiot. Why aren't they getting men to bring a boat out? A fishing boat—one of those big yawls—could come out here all right. Why don't he do something?"

A *yawl* is a small boat.

"Oh, it's all right now."

"They'll have a boat out here for us in less than no time, now that they've seen us."

A faint yellow tone came into the sky over the low land. The shadows on the sea slowly deepened. The wind bore coldness with it, and the men began to shiver.

"Holy smoke!" said one, allowing his voice to express his **impious** mood, "if we keep on monkeying out here! If we've got to flounder out here all night!"

"Oh, we'll never have to stay here all night! Don't you worry. They've seen us now, and it won't be long before they'll come chasing out after us."

The shore grew dusky. The man waving a coat blended gradually into this gloom, and it swallowed in the same manner the omnibus and the group of people. The spray, when it dashed uproariously over side, made the voyagers shrink and swear like men who were being branded.

"I'd like to catch the chump who waved the coat. I feel like socking him one, just for luck."

"Why? What did he do?"

"Oh, nothing, but then he seemed so damned cheerful."

In the meantime the oiler rowed, and then the correspondent rowed, and then the oiler rowed. Gray faced and bowed forward, they mechanically, turn by turn, plied the leaden oars. The form of the lighthouse had vanished from the southern horizon, but finally a pale star appeared, just lifting from the sea. The streaked saffron in the west passed before the all-merging darkness, and the sea to the east was black. The land had vanished, and was expressed only by the low and drear thunder of the surf.

Saffron is a slight orange or orange-yellow color.

impious lacking proper respect

"If I am going to be drowned—if I am going to be drowned—if I am going to be drowned, why, in the name of the seven mad gods who rule the sea, was I allowed to come thus far and contemplate sand and trees? Was I brought here merely to have my nose dragged away as I was about to nibble the sacred cheese of life?"

The patient captain, drooped over the water jar, was sometimes obliged to speak to the oarsman.

"Keep her head up! Keep her head up!"

"Keep her head up, sir." The voices were weary and low.

This was surely a quiet evening. All save the oarsman lay heavily and **listlessly** in the boat's bottom. As for him, his eyes were just capable of noting the tall black waves that swept forward in a most sinister silence, save for an occasional subdued growl of a crest.

The cook's head was on a thwart, and he looked without interest at the water under his nose. He was deep in other scenes. Finally he spoke. "Billie," he murmured, dreamfully, "what kind of pie do you like best?"

– V –

"Pie," said the oiler and the correspondent, **agitatedly**. "Don't talk about those things, blast you!"

"Well," said the cook, "I was just thinking about ham sandwiches and—"

A night on the sea in an open boat is a long night. As darkness settled finally, the shine of the light, lifting from the sea in the south, changed to full gold. On the northern horizon a new light appeared, a small bluish gleam on the edge of the waters. These two lights were the furniture of the world. Otherwise there was nothing but waves.

Two men huddled in the stern, and distances were so magnificent in the dinghy that the rower was enabled to keep his feet partly warmed by thrusting them under his

These lines were used earlier in this story. They are repeated here for effect. This is an example of a refrain. Who do you think is thinking these thoughts?

In this chapter, why does the correspondent want to wake the others?

agitatedly being upset	**listlessly** without interest, energy, or spirit

companions. Their legs indeed extended far under the rowing seat until they touched the feet of the captain forward.

Sometimes, despite the efforts of the tired oarsman, a wave came piling into the boat, an icy wave of the night, and the chilling water soaked them anew. They would twist their bodies for a moment and groan, and sleep the dead sleep once more, while the water in the boat gurgled about them as the craft rocked.

The plan of the oiler and the correspondent was for one to row until he lost the ability, and then arouse the other from his seawater couch in the bottom of the boat.

The oiler plied the oars until his head drooped forward and the overpowering sleep blinded him. And he rowed yet afterward. Then he touched a man in the bottom of the boat, and called his name. "Will you spell me for a little while?" he said meekly.

"Sure, Billie," said the correspondent, awakening and dragging himself to a sitting position. They exchanged places carefully, and the oiler, cuddling down in the seawater at the cook's side, seemed to go to sleep instantly.

The particular violence of the sea had ceased. The waves came without snarling. The obligation of the man at the oars was to keep the boat headed so that the tilt of the rollers would not capsize her, and to preserve her from filling when the crests rushed past. The black waves were silent and hard to be seen in the darkness. Often one was almost upon the boat before the oarsman was aware.

In a low voice the correspondent addressed the captain. He was not sure that the captain was awake, although this iron man seemed to be always awake. "Captain, shall I keep her making for that light north, sir?"

The same steady voice answered him. "Yes. Keep it about two points off the port bow."

The cook had tied a life belt around himself in order to get even the warmth which this clumsy cork **contrivance** could donate, and he seemed almost stove-like when a rower,

contrivance an artificial arrangement

Port is the left side of a boat looking forward. Since the bow is the front of a boat, the port bow is forward and to the left of the boat.

whose teeth invariably chattered wildly as soon as he ceased his labor, dropped down to sleep.

The correspondent, as he rowed, looked down at the two men sleeping underfoot. The cook's arm was around the oiler's shoulders, and, with their **fragmentary** clothing and **haggard** faces, they were the babes of the sea—a **grotesque** rendering of the old babes in the wood.

Later he must have grown stupid at his work, for suddenly there was growling of water, and a crest came with a roar and a swash into the boat, and it was a wonder that it did not set the cook afloat in his life belt. The cook continued to sleep, but the oiler sat up, blinking his eyes and shaking with the new cold.

"Oh, I'm awful sorry, Billie," said the correspondent **contritely**.

"That's all right, old boy," said the oiler, and lay down again and was asleep.

Presently it seemed that even the captain dozed, and the correspondent thought that he was the one man afloat on all the oceans. The wind had a voice as it came over the waves, and it was sadder than the end.

There was a long, loud swishing astern of the boat, and a gleaming trail of **phosphorescence**, like blue flame, was furrowed on the black waters. It might have been made by a monstrous knife.

Then there came a stillness, while the correspondent breathed with the open mouth and looked at the sea.

Suddenly there was another swish and another long flash of bluish light, and this time it was alongside the boat, and might almost have been reached with an oar. The correspondent saw an enormous fin speed like a shadow through the water, hurling the **crystalline** spray and leaving the long glowing trail.

> Here the correspondent sees a shark.

contritely regretfully	**fragmentary** incomplete	**haggard** having a worn-out appearance
crystalline clear or sparkling	**grotesque** horrible; not natural; strange	**phosphorescence** a lasting light without heat

The correspondent looked over his shoulder at the captain. His face was hidden, and he seemed to be asleep. He looked at the babes of the sea. They certainly were asleep. So, being bereft of sympathy, he leaned a little way to one side and swore softly into the sea.

But the thing did not then leave the vicinity of the boat. Ahead or astern, on one side or the other, at intervals long or short, fled the long sparkling streak, and there was to be heard the *whirroo* of the dark fin. The speed and power of the thing was greatly to be admired. It cut the water like a gigantic and keen **projectile**.

The presence of this biding thing did not affect the man with the same horror that it would if he had been a picnicker. He simply looked at the sea dully and swore in an undertone.

How does the correspondent react to seeing the shark?

Nevertheless, it is true that he did not wish to be alone with the thing. He wished one of his companions to awaken by chance and keep him company with it. But the captain hung motionless over the water jar, and the oiler and the cook in the bottom of the boat were plunged in slumber.

projectile a self-propelling weapon; a missile

– VI –

In this chapter, how is the correspondent like the soldier in Algiers?

"If I am going to be drowned—if I am going to be drowned—if I am going to be drowned, why, in the name of the seven mad gods who rule the sea, was I allowed to come thus far and contemplate sand and trees?"

During this dismal night, it may be remarked that a man would conclude that it was really the intention of the seven mad gods to drown him, despite the **abominable** injustice of it. For it was certainly an abominable injustice to drown a man who had worked so hard, so hard. The man felt it would be a crime most unnatural. Other people had drowned at sea since galleys swarmed with painted sails, but still—

When it occurs to a man that nature does not regard him as important, and that she feels she would not **maim** the universe by disposing of him, he at first wishes to throw bricks at the temple, and he hates deeply the fact that there are no bricks and no temples. Any visible expression of nature would surely be pelleted with his jeers.

Then, if there be no **tangible** thing to hoot he feels, perhaps, the desire to confront a **personification** and **indulge** in pleas, bowed to one knee, and with hands **supplicant**, saying: "Yes, but I love myself."

A high cold star on a winter's night is the word he feels that she says to him. Thereafter he knows the **pathos** of his situation.

The men in the dinghy had not discussed these matters, but each had, no doubt, reflected upon them in silence and according to his mind. There was seldom any expression upon their faces save the general one of complete weariness. Speech was devoted to the business of the boat.

abominable quite disagreeable or unpleasant	**maim** to batter, mangle, or harm seriously	**personification** something meant to represent a person or a human form
indulge to take pleasure in or yield to the desire of	**pathos** something in an experience that brings on a feeling of pity	**supplicant** begging
		tangible able to be sensed, especially by touch

To chime the notes of his emotion, a verse mysteriously entered the correspondent's head. He had even forgotten that he had forgotten this verse, but it suddenly was in his mind.

> A soldier of the Legion lay dying in Algiers;
> There was a lack of woman's nursing, there was
>   dearth of woman's tears;
> But a comrade stood beside him, and he took
>   that comrade's hand;
> And he said: "I never more shall see my own,
>   my native land."

Here the correspondent remembers a poem. Why is this poem significant?

In his childhood, the correspondent had been made acquainted with the fact that a soldier of the Legion lay dying in Algiers, but he had never regarded the fact as important. **Myriads** of his schoolfellows had informed him of the soldier's **plight**, but the dinning had naturally ended by making him perfectly indifferent. He had never considered it his affair that a soldier of the Legion lay dying in Algiers, nor had it appeared to him as a matter of sorrow. It was less to him than the breaking of a pencil's point.

Now, however, it quaintly came to him as a human, living thing. It was no longer merely a picture of a few throes in the breast of a poet, meanwhile drinking tea and warming his feet at the grate; it was an actuality—stern, mournful, and fine.

The correspondent plainly saw the soldier. He lay on the sand with his feet out straight and still. While his pale left hand was upon his chest in an attempt to thwart the going of his life, the blood came between his fingers. In the far Algerian distance, a city of low square forms was set against a sky that was faint with the last sunset hues. The correspondent, plying the oars and dreaming of the slow and slower movements of the lips of the soldier, was moved by a profound and perfectly **impersonal** comprehension. He was sorry for the soldier of the Legion who lay dying in Algiers.

The thing which had followed the boat and waited had evidently grown bored at the delay. There was no longer to be heard the slash of the cut-water, and there was no longer the

The correspondent feels sorry for the dying soldier in the poem. Struggling for his own life, the correspondent can feel what it is like to be near death.

impersonal not personal	**myriad** a great number	**plight** a difficult situation

flame of the long trail. The light in the north still glimmered, but it was apparently no nearer to the boat. Sometimes the boom of the surf rang in the correspondent's ears, and he turned the craft seaward then and rowed harder. Southward, someone had evidently built a watch fire on the beach. It was too low and too far to be seen, but it made a shimmering, **roseate** reflection upon the bluff back of it, and thus could be discerned from the boat. The wind came stronger, and sometimes a wave suddenly raged out like a mountain cat, and there was to be seen the sheen and sparkle of a broken crest.

The captain, in the bow, moved on his water jar and sat erect. "Pretty long night," he observed to the correspondent. He looked at the shore. "Those lifesaving people take their time."

"Did you see that shark playing around?"

"Yes, I saw him. He was a big fellow, all right."

"Wish I had known you were awake."

Later the correspondent spoke into the bottom of the boat. "Billie!" There was a slow and gradual **disentanglement**. "Billie, will you spell me?"

"Sure," said the oiler.

As soon as the correspondent touched the cold, comfortable seawater in the bottom of the boat, and had huddled close to the cook's lifebelt he was deep in sleep, despite the fact that his teeth played all the popular airs. This sleep was so good to him that it was but a moment before he heard a voice call his name in a tone that demonstrated the last stages of exhaustion. "Will you spell me?"

"Sure, Billie."

The light in the north had mysteriously vanished, but the correspondent took his course from the wide-awake captain.

Later in the night they took the boat farther out to sea, and the captain directed the cook to take one oar at the stern and keep the boat facing the seas. He was to call out if he should hear the thunder of the surf. This plan enabled the oiler and the correspondent to get **respite** together. "We'll give

disentanglement the act of freeing something from being tangled	**respite** rest	**roseate** rose colored

those boys a chance to get into shape again," said the captain. They curled down and, after a few **preliminary** chatterings and trembles, slept once more the dead sleep. Neither knew they had **bequeathed** to the cook the company of another shark, or perhaps the same shark.

As the boat caroused on the waves, spray occasionally bumped over the side and gave them a fresh soaking, but this had not power to break their **repose**. The ominous slash of the wind and the water affected them as it would have affected mummies.

"Boys," said the cook, with the notes of every **reluctance** in his voice, "she's drifted in pretty close. I guess one of you had better take her to sea again." The correspondent, aroused, heard the crash of the toppled crests.

> How has the rising action in this story been built up since the beginning?

As he was rowing, the captain gave him some whiskey-and-water, and this steadied the chills out of him. "If I ever get ashore and anybody shows me even a photograph of an oar—"

At last there was a short conversation.

"Billie . . . Billie, will you spell me?"

"Sure," said the oiler.

– VII –

When the correspondent again opened his eyes, the sea and the sky were each of the gray hue of the dawning. Later, carmine and gold was painted upon the waters. The morning appeared finally, in its splendor, with a sky of pure blue, and the sunlight flamed on the tips of the waves.

> What happens to the four men at the end of this story?

On the distant dunes were set many little black cottages, and a tall white windmill reared above them. No man, nor dog, nor bicycle appeared on the beach. The cottages might have formed a deserted village.

The voyagers scanned the shore. A conference was held in the boat. "Well," said the captain, "if no help is coming, we

bequeath to give or leave by will	**preliminary** coming before something else	**reluctance** unwillingness
		repose rest

might better try a run through the surf right away. If we stay out here much longer we will be too weak to do anything for ourselves at all." The others silently **acquiesced** in this reasoning. The boat was headed for the beach. The correspondent wondered if none ever ascended the tall wind tower, and if then they never looked seaward. This tower was a giant, standing with its back to the plight of the ants. It represented in a degree, to the correspondent, the serenity of nature amid the struggles of the individual—nature in the wind, and nature in the vision of men. She did not seem cruel to him then, nor **beneficent**, nor treacherous, nor wise. But she was indifferent, flatly indifferent. It is, perhaps, **plausible** that a man in this situation, impressed with the unconcern of the universe, should see the innumerable flaws of his life, and have them taste wickedly in his mind, and wish for another chance. A distinction between right and wrong seems absurdly clear to him, then, in this new ignorance of the grave edge, and he understands that if he were given another opportunity he would mend his conduct and his words, and be better and brighter during an introduction or at a tea.

"Now, boys," said the captain, "she is going to swamp sure. All we can do is to work her in as far as possible, and then when she swamps, pile out and scramble for the beach. Keep cool now, and don't jump until she swamps sure."

> The men decide here that their only chance to survive is to risk passing through the surf to shore. What do you think will happen?

The oiler took the oars. Over his shoulders he scanned the surf. "Captain," he said, "I think I'd better bring her about, and keep her head-on to the seas and back her in."

"All right, Billie," said the captain. "Back her in." The oiler swung the boat then and, seated in the stern, the cook and the correspondent were obliged to look over their shoulders to contemplate the lonely and indifferent shore.

The monstrous inshore rollers heaved the boat high until the men were again enabled to see the white sheets of water scudding up the slanted beach. "We won't get in very close," said the captain. Each time a man could wrest his attention from the rollers, he turned his glance toward the shore, and in

---

acquiesce to accept   **beneficent** kind; charitable   **plausible** reasonable

the expression of the eyes during this contemplation there was a singular quality. The correspondent, observing the others, knew that they were not afraid, but the full meaning of their glances was shrouded.

As for himself, he was too tired to grapple fundamentally with the fact. He tried to **coerce** his mind into thinking of it, but the mind was dominated at this time by the muscles, and the muscles said they did not care. It merely occurred to him that if he should drown it would be a shame.

There were no hurried words, no **pallor**, no plain agitation. The men simply looked at the shore. "Now, remember to get well clear of the boat when you jump," said the captain.

Seaward the crest of a roller suddenly fell with a thunderous crash, and the long white **comber** came roaring down upon the boat.

"Steady now," said the captain. The men were silent. They turned their eyes from the shore to the comber and waited. The boat slid up the incline, leaped at the furious top, bounced over it, and swung down the long back of the wave. Some water had been shipped and the cook bailed it out.

But the next crest crashed also. The tumbling, boiling flood of white water caught the boat and whirled it almost **perpendicular**. Water swarmed in from all sides. The correspondent had his hands on the gunwale at this time, and when the water entered at the place he swiftly withdrew his fingers, as if he objected to wetting them.

The little boat, drunken with this weight of water, reeled and snuggled deeper into the sea.

"Bail her out, cook! Bail her out!" said the captain.

"All right, captain," said the cook.

"Now, boys, the next one will do for us sure," said the oiler. "Mind to jump clear of the boat."

coerce to force	**pallor** paleness; lack of color, especially in the face	**perpendicular** being at a right angle to a given line or plane
comber a long, curling wave of the sea		

The third wave moved forward, huge, furious, **implacable**. It fairly swallowed the dinghy, and almost **simultaneously** the men tumbled into the sea. A piece of life belt had lain in the bottom of the boat, and as the correspondent went overboard he held this to his chest with his left hand.

The January water was icy, and he reflected immediately that it was colder than he had expected to find it on the coast of Florida. This appeared to his dazed mind as a fact important enough to be noted at the time. The coldness of the water was sad; it was tragic. This fact was somehow so mixed and confused with his opinion of his own situation, so that it seemed almost a proper reason for tears. The water was cold.

When he came to the surface he was conscious of little but the noisy water. Afterward he saw his companions in the sea.

Here a wave overturns the boat. The men fall into the water. Was this what you thought would happen?

implacable unable to be changed or resisted	**simultaneously** at the same time

The oiler was ahead in the race. He was swimming strongly and rapidly. Off to the correspondent's left, the cook's great white and corked back bulged out of the water, and in the rear the captain was hanging with his one good hand to the keel of the overturned dinghy.

There is a certain immovable quality to a shore, and the correspondent wondered at it amid the confusion of the sea.

It seemed also very attractive, but the correspondent knew that it was a long journey, and he paddled leisurely. The piece of life preserver lay under him, and sometimes he whirled down the incline of a wave as if he were on a hand sled.

But finally he arrived at a place in the sea where travel was beset with difficulty. He did not pause swimming to inquire what manner of current had caught him, but there his progress ceased. The shore was set before him like a bit of scenery on a stage, and he looked at it and understood with his eyes each detail of it.

As the cook passed, much farther to the left, the captain was calling to him, "Turn over on your back, cook! Turn over on your back and use the oar."

"All right, sir." The cook turned on his back, and, paddling with an oar, went ahead as if he were a canoe.

Presently the boat also passed to the left of the correspondent with the captain clinging with one hand to the keel. He would have appeared like a man raising himself to look over a board fence, if it were not for the extraordinary gymnastics of the boat. The correspondent marveled that the captain could still hold to it.

The captain is hanging onto the keel, the bottom part of the overturned boat.

They passed on, nearer to shore—the oiler, the cook, the captain—and following them went the water jar, bouncing gaily over the seas.

The correspondent remained in the grip of this strange new enemy—a current. The shore, with its white slope of sand and its green bluff, topped with little silent cottages, was spread like a picture before him. It was very near to him then, but he was impressed as one who, in a gallery, looks at a scene from Brittany or Algiers.

He thought: "I am going to drown? Can it be possible? Can it be possible? Can it be possible?" Perhaps an individual must consider his own death to be the final **phenomenon** of nature.

But later a wave perhaps whirled him out of this small, deadly current, for he found suddenly that he could again make progress toward the shore. Later still, he was aware that the captain, clinging with one hand to the keel of the dinghy, had his face turned away from the shore and toward him, and was calling his name. "Come to the boat! Come to the boat!"

In his struggle to reach the captain and the boat, he reflected that when one gets properly wearied, drowning must really be a comfortable arrangement—a **cessation** of **hostilities** accompanied by a large degree of relief; and he was glad of it, for the main thing in his mind for some months had been horror of the temporary **agony**. He did not wish to be hurt.

The man on shore is undressing because he intends to enter the water to save the men.

Presently he saw a man running along the shore. He was undressing with most remarkable speed. Coat, trousers, shirt, everything flew magically off him.

"Come to the boat!" called the captain.

"All right, captain." As the correspondent paddled, he saw the captain let himself down to the bottom and leave the boat. Then the correspondent performed his one little marvel of the voyage. A large wave caught him and flung him with ease and supreme speed completely over the boat and far beyond it. It struck him even then as an event in gymnastics, and a true miracle of the sea. An overturned boat in the surf is not a plaything to a swimming man.

The correspondent arrived in water that reached only to his waist, but his condition did not enable him to stand for more than a moment. Each wave knocked him into a heap, and the undertow pulled at him.

---

agony extreme pain of mind or body

cessation stopping

hostilities violent acts

phenomenon a rare or unusual event

Then he saw the man who had been running and undressing, and undressing and running, come bounding into the water. He dragged ashore the cook, and then waded toward the captain; but the captain waved him away, and sent him to the correspondent. He was naked—naked as a tree in winter; but a halo was about his head, and he shone like a saint. He gave a strong pull, and a long drag, and a bully heave at the correspondent's hand. The correspondent, schooled in the minor **formulae**, said: "Thanks, old man." But suddenly the man cried: "What's that?" He pointed a swift finger. The correspondent said: "Go."

In the shallows, face downward, lay the oiler. His forehead touched sand that was **periodically**, between each wave, clear of the sea.

Here the author reveals that the oiler has drowned.

The correspondent did not know all that **transpired** afterward. When he achieved safe ground he fell, striking the sand with each particular part of his body. It was as if he had dropped from a roof, but the thud was grateful to him.

It seems that instantly the beach was populated with men with blankets, clothes, and flasks, and women with coffeepots and all the remedies sacred to their minds. The welcome of the land to the men from the sea was warm and generous, but a still and dripping shape was carried slowly up the beach, and the land's welcome for it could only be the different and sinister hospitality of the grave.

When it came night, the white waves paced to and fro in the moonlight, and the wind brought the sound of the great sea's voice to the men on shore, and they felt that they could then be interpreters.

---

formulae a set form of words for use in a ceremony

periodically from time to time

transpire to take place

The Open Boat
Stephen Crane

Directions Write the answers to these questions using complete sentences.

Comprehension: Identifying Facts

1. Who are the four men in the dinghy?

2. Who in the group is injured?

3. What company do the men have in Chapter 2? What is their attitude toward this company?

4. Which person in the group seems to be the leader?

5. What do the men see on land in Chapter 4?

6. What fearful thing does the correspondent see during his turn at the oars?

7. What poem does the correspondent think about during his turn at the oars?

8. Why do the men fear staying out too long?

9. When the men head toward the shore in Chapter 7, what does the captain tell the others?

10. Which of the men does not survive the swim to the shore?

Comprehension: Understanding Main Ideas

11. Explain the meaning of the first sentence in this story: "None of them knew the color of the sky."

12. Describe the size and condition of the dinghy.

13. How does the author indicate the passage of time?

14. List some events that lead the men to believe that they will be saved.

15. What refrain, or statement that appears over and over, is used in this story? Explain what this statement means.

16. This story describes the conflict and struggle of people against nature. Explain this conflict and give at least two examples of struggle in the story.

17. This story is told from the point of view of one character. Which one?

18. What is the author's view of nature as described in this story?

19. Why can each man feel like an "interpreter" of the sea's voice at the end of the story?

20. In what ways does this story seem realistic?

Understanding Literature: Rising Action

Stephen Crane's use of rising action builds tension and suspense in this story. This technique is often used in mystery stories. In these stories, the question of who commits the crime is revealed in the last chapter or paragraph. This style can also be used effectively in adventure stories. Crane sets the scene, establishes the contrast between nature and the men in the boat, and constantly raises the reader's hopes that the men will be saved. Something happens in every section that explains either a new hope or a new fear. These hopes and fears are the steps of the rising action.

21. List what happens to build the suspense in each of the seven chapters.

22. At what point is the suspense at its highest?

23. At what point is the suspense over?

24. How did you feel when the suspense was over?

25. Did rising action make the story more effective for you? Why or why not?

Critical Thinking

26. How do you think you would have felt if you were lost at sea?

27. Why doesn't Stephen Crane tell us more about the personal lives of each of the men? Do you think he should have? Explain your answer.

28. Were you fearful that the men would not make it during the story? Did the story hold your interest? Explain your answers.

29. How do you feel about the final scene? How did the ending of the story affect you emotionally?

30. Did you like this story? Why or why not?

Writing on Your Own Using what you know about realism, write a paragraph explaining why this story is an example of realism. What events, writing style, and subject matter make the story realistic?

To Build a Fire
Jack London

Jack London
1876–1916

About the Author

Jack London was born in San Francisco, California. He was raised in Oakland, California. He quit school at fourteen to live a life of adventure. He explored San Francisco Bay by boat, then went to Japan as a sailor. At nineteen, he attended high school, then attended the University of California at Berkeley. He quit college to search for gold in Alaska, but was not successful. He then decided to try to earn a living as a writer.

London wrote fifty books in just seventeen years. He soon became the highest-paid writer in the United States. However, he spent freely and was forced to keep writing to pay off his debts. Toward the end of his life, money problems and heavy drinking had taken their toll. He killed himself at age forty.

London's works remain popular throughout the world for their adventure. Many of his stories focus on the struggle of people against nature. His best-known works are *The Call of the Wild*, *White Fang*, and *The Sea Wolf*.

About the Selection

"To Build a Fire" is one of many stories that London wrote using his experiences during the Klondike Gold Rush of 1897–1898 in Canada and Alaska. This story is about survival in a very cold and dangerous place. Like many of London's stories, "To Build a Fire" is a grim tale about one man against nature.

This story has a **protagonist** and an **antagonist**. A protagonist is the main character in a story. Most of the action centers around this main character. An antagonist is a person or thing in the story struggling against the protagonist. In this story, the man is the protagonist and nature is the antagonist.

To Build a Fire

Day had broken cold and gray, exceedingly cold and gray, when the man turned aside from the main Yukon trail and climbed the high earth-bank, where a dim and little-traveled trail led eastward through the fat spruce timberland. It was a steep bank, and he paused for breath at the top, excusing the act to himself by looking at his watch. It was nine o'clock. There was no sun nor hint of sun, though there was not a cloud in the sky. It was a clear day, and yet there seemed an **intangible** pall over the face of things, a **subtle** gloom that made the day dark, and that was due to the absence of sun. This fact did not worry the man. He was used to the lack of sun. It had been days since he had seen the sun, and he knew that a few more days must pass before that cheerful orb, due south, would just peep above the skyline and dip immediately from view.

The man flung a look back along the way he had come. The Yukon lay a mile wide and hidden under three feet of ice. On top of this ice were as many feet of snow. It was all pure white, rolling in gentle **undulations** where the ice jams of the freeze-up had formed. North and south, as far as his eye could see, it was unbroken white, save for a dark hairline that curved and twisted from around the spruce-covered island to the south, and that curved and twisted away into the north, where it disappeared behind another spruce-covered island. This dark hairline was the trail—the main trail—that led south five hundred miles to the Chilcoot Pass, Dyea, and salt water; and that led north seventy miles to Dawson, and still on to the north a thousand miles to Nulato, and finally to St. Michael, on Bering Sea, a thousand miles and half a thousand more.

This story is about a struggle between a man and nature. As you read, look for ways the author makes this struggle clear in the story.

Yukon refers to the Yukon Territory in northwestern Canada that is east of Alaska. The Yukon is known for its very cold winters. The Yukon trail extends through Alaska, the Yukon Territory, and to the Bering Sea.

intangible not able to be perceived; not real   **subtle** difficult to understand or detect   **undulation** a wave-like appearance

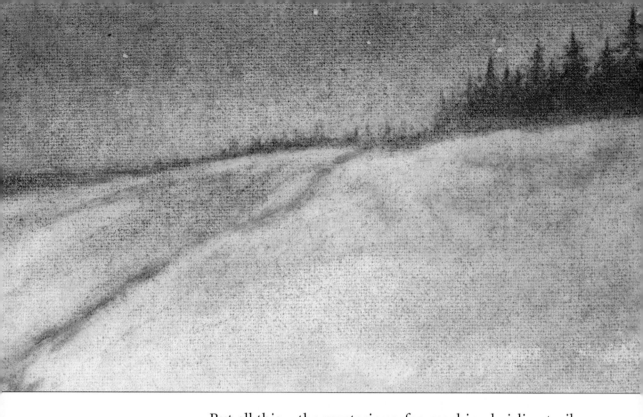

Chechaquo means "newcomer."

But all this—the mysterious, far-reaching hairline trail, the absence of sun from the sky, the tremendous cold, and the strangeness and weirdness of it all—made no impression on the man. It was not because he was long used to it. He was a newcomer in the land, a *chechaquo*, and this was his first winter. The trouble with him was that he was without imagination. He was quick and alert in the things of life, but only in the things, and not in the significances. Fifty degrees below zero meant eighty-odd degrees of frost. Such fact impressed him as being cold and uncomfortable, and that was all. It did not lead him to **meditate** upon his frailty as a creature of temperature, and upon man's frailty in general, able only to live within certain narrow limits of heat and cold; and from there on it did not lead him to the **conjectural** field of **immortality** and man's place in the universe. Fifty degrees below zero stood for a bite of frost that hurt and that must be guarded against by the use of mittens, ear flaps, warm

| **conjectural** guessed at or unproven | **immortality** the quality or state of living forever | **meditate** to think deeply |

moccasins, and thick socks. Fifty degrees below zero was to him just precisely fifty degrees below zero. That there should be anything more to it than that was a thought that never entered his head.

As he turned to go on, he spat **speculatively**. There was a sharp, explosive crackle that startled him. He spat again. And again, in the air, before it could fall to the snow, the spittle crackled. He knew that at fifty below spittle crackled on the snow, but this spittle had crackled in the air. Undoubtedly it was colder than fifty below—how much colder he did not know. But the temperature did not matter. He was bound for the old claim on the left fork of Henderson Creek, where the boys were already. They had come over across the divide from the Indian Creek country, while he had come the roundabout way to take a look at the possibilities of getting out logs in the spring from the islands in the Yukon. He would be in to camp by six o'clock; a bit after dark, it was true, but the boys would be there, a fire would be going, and a hot supper would be ready. As for lunch, he pressed his hand against the **protruding** bundle under his jacket. It was also under his shirt, wrapped up in a handkerchief and lying against the naked skin. It was the only way to keep the biscuits from freezing. He smiled agreeably to himself as he thought of those biscuits, each cut open and sopped in bacon grease, and each enclosing a generous slice of fried bacon.

He plunged in among the big spruce trees. The trail was faint. A foot of snow had fallen since the last sled had passed over, and he was glad he was without a sled, traveling light. In fact, he carried nothing but the lunch wrapped in the handkerchief. He was surprised, however, at the cold. It certainly was cold, he concluded, as he rubbed his numb nose and cheekbones with his mittened hand. He was a warm-whiskered man, but the hair on his face did not protect the high cheekbones and the eager nose that thrust itself **aggressively** into the frosty air.

Fifty below means fifty degrees below zero on a Fahrenheit thermometer. Water freezes at thirty-two degrees above zero Fahrenheit. This paragraph explains that it is so cold that the man's spit freezes.

aggressively forcefully	**protruding** sticking out	**speculatively** in a manner marked by curiosity

At the man's heels trotted a dog, a big native husky, the proper wolf dog, gray-coated and without any visible or **temperamental** difference from its brother, the wild wolf. The animal was **depressed** by the tremendous cold. It knew that it was no time for traveling. Its instinct told it a truer tale than was told to the man by the man's judgment. In reality, it was not merely colder than fifty below zero; it was colder than sixty below, than seventy below. It was seventy-five below zero. Since the freezing point is thirty-two above zero, it meant that one hundred and seven degrees of frost obtained. The dog did not know anything about thermometers. Possibly in its brain there was no sharp consciousness of a condition very cold such as was in the man's brain. But the brute had its instinct. It experienced a vague but menacing **apprehension** that **subdued** it and made it slink along at the man's heels, and that made it question eagerly every **unwonted** movement of the man as if expecting him to go into camp or to seek shelter somewhere and build a fire. The dog had learned fire, and it wanted fire, or else to burrow under the snow and cuddle its warmth away from the air.

The frozen moisture of its breathing had settled on its fur in a fine powder of frost, and especially were its jowls, muzzle, and eyelashes whitened by its crystalled breath. The man's red beard and mustache were likewise frosted, but more solidly, the deposit taking the form of ice and increasing with every warm, moist breath he exhaled. Also, the man was chewing tobacco, and the muzzle of ice held his lips so rigidly that he was unable to clear his chin when he **expelled** the juice. The result was that a crystal beard of the color and solidity of amber was increasing its length on his chin. If he fell down it would shatter itself, like glass, into brittle fragments. But he did not mind the **appendage**. It was the penalty all tobacco chewers paid in that country, and he had been out before in

Notice how the author is writing about what the dog is thinking. How does this help you relate to the dog as a character?

---

appendage a smaller part that sticks out from something larger

apprehension fear

depressed saddened

expel to force out

subdue to conquer; to bring under control

temperamental of or relating to how one thinks or behaves

unwonted unusual

two cold snaps. They had not been so cold as this, he knew, but by the spirit thermometer at Sixty Mile he knew they had been registered at fifty below and at fifty-five.

He held on through the level stretch of woods for several miles, crossed a wide flat, and dropped down a bank to the frozen bed of a small stream. This was Henderson Creek, and he knew he was ten miles from the forks. He looked at his watch. It was ten o'clock. He was making four miles an hour, and he **calculated** that he would arrive at the forks at half-past twelve. He decided to celebrate that event by eating his lunch there.

The dog dropped in again at his heels, with a tail drooping discouragement, as the man swung along the creek bed. The furrow of the old sled trail was plainly visible, but a dozen inches of snow covered the marks of the last runners. In a month no man had come up or down that silent creek. The man held steadily on. He was not much given to thinking, and just then particularly he had nothing to think about save that he would eat lunch at the forks and that at six o'clock he would be in camp with the boys. There was nobody to talk to; and, had there been, speech would have been impossible because of the ice muzzle on his mouth. So he continued **monotonously** to chew tobacco and to increase the length of his amber beard.

Once in a while the thought **reiterated** itself that it was very cold and that he had never experienced such cold. As he walked along he rubbed his cheekbones and nose with the back of his mittened hand. He did this automatically now and again changing hands. But rub as he would, the instant he stopped his cheekbones went numb, and the following instant the end of his nose went numb. He was sure to frost his cheeks; he knew that, and experienced a pang of regret that he had not **devised** a nose strap of the sort Bud wore in cold snaps. Such a strap passed across the cheeks, as well, and saved them. But it didn't matter much, after all. What were frosted cheeks? A bit painful, that was all; they were never serious.

The man is rubbing his face here so his cheeks will not freeze. He is afraid of getting frostbite, which happens when skin is exposed to extreme cold.

calculate to figure out, often by use of mathematics

devise to invent

monotonously varying very little

reiterate to state or do over again

Empty as the man's mind was of thoughts, he was keenly observant, and he noticed the changes in the creek, the curves and bends and timber jams, and always he sharply noted where he placed his feet. Once, coming around a bend, he shied **abruptly**, like a startled horse, curved away from the place where he had been walking, and retreated several paces back along the trail. The creek he knew was frozen clear to the bottom—no creek could contain water in that arctic winter—but he knew also that there were springs that bubbled out from the hillsides and ran along under the snow and on top the ice of the creek. He knew that the coldest snaps never froze these springs, and he knew likewise their danger. They were traps. They hid pools of water under the snow that might be three inches deep, or three feet. Sometimes a skin of ice half an inch thick covered them, and in turn was covered by the snow. Sometimes there were alternate layers of water and ice skin, so that when one broke through he kept on breaking through for a while, sometimes wetting himself to the waist.

That was why he had shied in such panic. He had felt the give under his feet and heard the crackle of a snow-hidden ice skin. And to get his feet wet in such a temperature meant trouble and danger. At the very least it meant delay, for he would be forced to stop and build a fire, and under its protection to bare his feet while he dried his socks and moccasins. He stood and studied the creek bed and its banks, and decided that the flow of water came from the right. He reflected awhile, rubbing his nose and cheeks, then skirted to the left, stepping gingerly and testing the footing for each step. Once clear of the danger, he took a fresh chew of tobacco and swung along at his four-mile **gait**.

In the course of the next two hours he came upon several similar traps. Usually the snow above the hidden pools had a sunken, candied appearance that advertised the danger. Once again, however, he had a close call; and once, suspecting danger, he **compelled** the dog to go on in front. The dog did not want to go. It hung back until the man shoved it forward,

Here the man is afraid of falling through the ice covering the creek.

abruptly without warning	**compel** to drive or urge forcefully	**gait** a manner of walking

and then it went quickly across the white, unbroken surface. Suddenly it broke through, **floundered** to one side, and got away to firmer footing. It had wet its forefeet and legs, and almost immediately the water that clung to it turned to ice. It made quick efforts to lick the ice off its legs, then dropped in the snow and began to bite out the ice that had formed between the toes. This was matter of instinct. To permit the ice to remain would mean sore feet. It did not know this. It merely obeyed the mysterious prompting that arose from the deep crypts of its being. But the man knew, having achieved a judgment on the subject, and he removed the mitten from his right hand and helped tear out the ice **particles**. He did not expose his fingers more than a minute, and was astonished at the swift numbness that smote them. It certainly was cold. He pulled on the mitten hastily, and beat the hand savagely across his chest.

In this paragraph, the dog falls through the ice. What kind of relationship do the man and the dog have?

---

flounder to struggle to move or get proper footing

particle a very small piece

At twelve o'clock the day was at its brightest. Yet the sun was too far south on its winter journey to clear the horizon. The bulge of the earth **intervened** between it and Henderson Creek, where the man walked under a clear sky at noon and cast no shadow. At half-past twelve, to the minute, he arrived at the forks of the creek. He was pleased at the speed he had made. If he kept it up, he would certainly be with the boys by six. He unbuttoned his jacket and shirt and drew forth his lunch. The action **consumed** no more than a quarter of a minute, yet in that brief moment the numbness laid hold of the exposed fingers. He did not put the mitten on, but, instead, struck the fingers a dozen sharp smashes against his leg. Then he sat down on a snow-covered log to eat. The sting that followed upon the striking of his fingers against his leg ceased so quickly that he was startled. He had had no chance to take a bit of biscuit. He struck the fingers repeatedly and returned them to the mitten, baring the other hand for the purpose of eating. He tried to take a mouthful, but the ice muzzle prevented. He had forgotten to build a fire and thaw out. He chuckled at his foolishness, and as he chuckled he noted the numbness creeping into the exposed fingers. Also, he noted that the stinging which had first come to his toes when he sat down was already passing away. He moved them inside the moccasins and decided that they were numb.

Notice how the author is building the suspense in this story. What do you think will happen next?

He pulled the mitten on hurriedly and stood up. He was a bit frightened. He stamped up and down until the stinging returned into the feet. It certainly was cold, was his thought. That man from Sulphur Creek had spoken the truth when telling how cold it sometimes got in the country. And he had laughed at him at the time! That showed one must not be too sure of things. There was no mistake about it, it *was* cold. He strode up and down, stamping his feet and threshing his arms, until reassured by the returning warmth. Then he got out matches and proceeded to make a fire. From the undergrowth, where high water of the previous spring had lodged a supply of seasoned twigs, he got his firewood.

---

consume to use up   **intervene** to come between

Working carefully from a small beginning, he soon had a roaring fire, over which he thawed the ice from his face and in the protection of which he ate his biscuits. For the moment the cold of space was outwitted. The dog took satisfaction in the fire, stretching out close enough for warmth and far enough away to escape being **singed**.

When the man had finished, he filled his pipe and took his comfortable time over a smoke. Then he pulled on his mittens, settled the ear flaps of his cap firmly about his ears, and took the creek trail up the left fork. The dog was disappointed and **yearned** back toward the fire. This man did not know cold. Possibly all the generations of his ancestry had been ignorant of cold, of real cold, of cold one hundred and seven degrees below freezing point. But the dog knew; all its ancestry knew, and it had inherited the knowledge. And it knew that it was not good to walk abroad in such fearful cold. It was the time to lie snug in a hole in the snow and wait for a curtain of cloud to be drawn across the face of outer space when this cold came. On the other hand, there was no keen **intimacy** between the dog and the man. The one was the toil slave of the other, and the only **caresses** it had ever received were the caresses of the whiplash and of harsh and menacing throat sounds that threatened the whiplash. So the dog made no effort to communicate its apprehension to the man. It was not concerned in the welfare of the man; it was for its own sake that it yearned back toward the fire. But the man whistled, and spoke to it with the sound of whiplashes, and the dog swung in at the man's heels and followed after.

The man took a chew of tobacco and proceeded to start a new amber beard. Also, his moist breath quickly powdered with white his mustache, eyebrows, and lashes. There did not seem to be so many springs on the left fork of the Henderson, and for half an hour the man saw no signs of any. And then it happened. At a place where there were no signs, where the soft, unbroken snow seemed to advertise solidity beneath, the

What does this tell you about how the man treats his dog?

caress a light stroking, rubbing, or patting	**intimacy** very close friendship or contact	**singe** to burn slightly
		yearn to long for

Here the man falls through the ice. He is now in great danger because his legs are wet and it is very cold.

man broke through. It was not deep. He wet himself half way to the knees before he floundered out to the firm crust.

He was angry, and cursed his luck aloud. He had hoped to get into camp with the boys at six o'clock, and this would delay him an hour, for he would have to build a fire and dry out his footgear. This was **imperative** at that low temperature—he knew that much; and he turned aside to the bank, which he climbed. On top, tangled in the underbrush about the trunks of several small spruce trees, was a high-water deposit of dry firewood—sticks and twigs, principally, but also large portions of seasoned branches and fine dry, last year's grasses. He threw down several large pieces on top of the snow. This served for a foundation and prevented the young flame from drowning itself in the snow it otherwise would melt. The flame he got by touching a match to a small shred of birch bark that he took from his pocket. This burned even more readily than paper. Placing it on the foundation, he fed the young flame with wisps of dry grass and with the tiniest dry twigs.

He worked slowly and carefully, keenly aware of his danger. Gradually, as the flame grew stronger, he increased the size of the twigs with which he fed it. He squatted in the snow, pulling the twigs out from their **entanglement** in the brush and feeding directly to the flame. He knew there must be no failure. When it is seventy-five below zero, a man must not fail in his first attempt to build a fire—that is, if his feet are wet. If his feet are dry, and he fails, he can run along the trail for half a mile and restore his **circulation**. But the circulation of wet and freezing feet cannot be restored by running when it is seventy-five below. No matter how fast he runs, the wet feet will freeze the harder.

All this the man knew. The old-timer on Sulphur Creek had told him about it the previous fall, and now he was appreciating the advice. Already all sensation had gone out of his feet. To build the fire he had been forced to remove his

circulation the orderly movement of blood through the body	entanglement the state of being tangled	imperative extremely necessary

mittens, and the fingers had quickly gone numb. His pace of four miles an hour had kept his heart pumping blood to the surface of his body and to all the **extremities**. But the instant he stopped, the action of the pump eased down. The cold of space smote the unprotected tip of the planet, and he, being on that unprotected tip, received the full force of the blow. The blood of his body **recoiled** before it. The blood was alive, like the dog, and like the dog it wanted to hide away and cover itself up from the fearful cold. So long as he walked four miles an hour, he pumped that blood, willy-nilly, to the surface; but now it **ebbed** away and sank down into the recesses of his body. The extremities were the first to feel its absence. His wet feet froze the faster, and his exposed fingers numbed the faster, though they had not yet begun to freeze. Nose and cheeks were already freezing, while the skin of all his body chilled as it lost its blood.

Willy-nilly means without choice or in a way that is lacking order.

But he was safe. Toes and nose and cheeks would be only touched by the frost, for the fire was beginning to burn with strength. He was feeding it with twigs the size of his finger. In another minute he would be able to feed it with branches the size of his wrist, and then he could remove his wet footgear, and, while it dried, he could keep his naked feet warm by the fire, rubbing them at first, of course, with snow. The fire was a success. He was safe. He remembered the advice of the old-timer on Sulphur Creek, and smiled. The old-timer had been very serious in laying down the law that no man must travel alone in the Klondike after fifty below. Well, here he was; he had had the accident; he was alone; and he had saved himself. Those old-timers were rather womanish, some of them, he thought. All a man had to do was to keep his head, and he was all right. Any man who was a man could travel alone. But it was surprising, the rapidity with which his cheeks and nose were freezing. And he had not thought his fingers could go lifeless in so short a time. Lifeless they were, for he could scarcely make them move together to grip a twig, and they seemed remote from his body and from him. When he

The *Klondike* is an area in the Yukon Territory. From 1897–1898, the Klondike Gold Rush took place there.

ebb to fall from a higher to a lower level	**extremity** a limb of the body	**recoil** to fall back under pressure; to shrink

touched a twig, he had to look and see whether or not he had hold of it. The wires were pretty well down between him and his finger ends.

All of which counted for little. There was the fire, snapping and crackling and promising life with every dancing flame. He started to untie his moccasins. They were coated with ice; the thick German socks were like sheaths of iron halfway to the knees; and the moccasin strings were like rods of steel all twisted and knotted as by some **conflagration**. For a moment he tugged with his numb fingers, then, realizing the folly of it, he drew his sheath knife.

But before he could cut the strings, it happened. It was his own fault or, rather, his mistake. He should not have built the fire under the spruce tree. He should have built it in the open. But it had been easier to pull the twigs from the brush and drop them directly on the fire. Now the tree under which he had done this carried a weight of snow on its boughs. No wind had blown for weeks and each bough was fully freighted. Each time he had pulled a twig he had communicated a slight **agitation** to the tree—an **imperceptible** agitation, so far as he was concerned, but an agitation sufficient to bring about the disaster. High up in the tree one bough capsized its load of snow. This fell on the boughs beneath, capsizing them. This process continued, spreading out and involving the whole tree. It grew like an avalanche, and it descended without warning upon the man and the fire, and the fire was blotted out! Where it had burned was a mantle of fresh and disordered snow.

Here snow falls from a tree and puts out the man's fire.

The man was shocked. It was as though he had just heard his own sentence of death. For a moment he sat and stared at the spot where the fire had been. Then he grew very calm. Perhaps the old-timer on Sulphur Creek was right. If he had only had a trail mate he would have been in no danger now. The trail mate could have built the fire. Well, it was up to him to build the fire over again, and this second time there must be no failure. Even if he succeeded, he would most likely lose

agitation movement; the act of disturbing something

conflagration a conflict or war; a terrible fire

imperceptible not able to be sensed

some toes. His feet must be badly frozen by now, and there would be some time before the second fire was ready.

Such were his thoughts, but he did not sit and think them. He was busy all the time they were passing through his mind. He made a new foundation for a fire, this time in the open, where no **treacherous** tree could blot it out. Next he gathered dry grasses and tiny twigs from the high-water flotsam. He could not bring his fingers together to pull them out, but he was able to gather them by the handful. In this way he got many rotten twigs and bits of green moss that were undesirable, but it was the best he could do. He worked **methodically**, even collecting an armful of the larger branches to be used later when the fire gathered strength. And all the while the dog sat and watched him, a certain yearning **wistfulness** in its eyes, for it looked upon him as the fire provider, and the fire was slow in coming.

When all was ready, the man reached in his pocket for a second piece of birch bark. He knew the bark was there, and, though he could not feel it with his fingers, he could hear its crisp rustling as he fumbled for it. Try as he would, he could not clutch hold of it. And all the time, in his consciousness, was the knowledge that each instant his feet were freezing. This thought tended to put him in a panic, but he fought against it and kept calm. He pulled on his mittens with his teeth, and threshed his arms back and forth, beating his hands with all his might against his sides. He did this sitting down, and he stood up to do it; and all the while the dog sat in the snow, its wolf brush of a tail curled around warmly over its forefeet, its sharp wolf ears pricked forward intently as it watched the man. And the man, as he beat and threshed with his arms and hands, felt a great **surge** of envy as he regarded the creature that was warm and secure in its natural covering.

Flotsam is a group of objects that collect together on shore next to a body of water.

methodically performed with a certain method or order	surge a sudden rush	wistfulness the state of being full of longing
	treacherous dangerous	

After a time he was aware of the first faraway signals of sensation in his beaten fingers. The faint tingling grew stronger till it **evolved** into a stinging ache that was **excruciating**, but which the man hailed with satisfaction. He stripped the mitten from his right hand and fetched forth the birch bark. The exposed fingers were quickly going numb again. Next he brought out his bunch of sulphur matches. But the tremendous cold had already driven the life out of his fingers. In his effort to separate one match from the others, the whole bunch fell in the snow. He tried to pick it out of the snow, but failed. The dead fingers could neither touch nor clutch. He was very careful. He drove the thought of his freezing feet, and nose, and cheeks, out of his mind, devoting his whole soul to the matches. He watched, using the sense of vision in place of that of touch, and when he saw his fingers on each side of the bunch, he closed them—that is, he willed to close them, for the wires were down, and the fingers did not obey. He pulled the mitten on the right hand, and beat it fiercely against his knee. Then, with both mittened hands, he scooped the bunch of matches, along with much snow, into his lap. Yet he was no better off.

After some **manipulation** he managed to get the bunch between the heels of his mittened hands. In this fashion he carried it to his mouth. The ice crackled and snapped when by a violent effort he opened his mouth. He drew the lower jaw in, curled the upper lip out of the way, and scraped the bunch with his upper teeth in order to separate a match. He succeeded in getting one, which he dropped on his lap. He was no better off. He could not pick it up. Then he devised a way. He picked it up in his teeth and scratched it on his leg. Twenty times he scratched before he succeeded in lighting it. As it flamed he held it with his teeth to the birch bark. But the burning brimstone went up his nostrils and into his lungs,

Brimstone is another name for sulphur, which is used in matches.

evolve to develop; to become

excruciating causing great pain

manipulation the act of working with the hands to complete a task

causing him to cough **spasmodically**. The match fell into the snow and went out.

The old-timer on Sulphur Creek was right, he thought in the moment of controlled despair that **ensued**: after fifty below, a man should travel with a partner. He beat his hands, but failed in exciting any sensation. Suddenly he bared both hands, removing the mittens with his teeth. He caught the whole bunch between the heels of his hands. His arm muscles not being frozen enabled him to press the hand heels tightly against the matches. Then he scratched the bunch along his leg. It flared into flame, seventy sulphur matches at once! There was no wind to blow them out. He kept his head to one side to escape the strangling fumes, and held the blazing bunch to the birch bark. As he so held it, he became aware of sensation in his hand. His flesh was burning. He could smell it. Deep down below the surface he could feel it. The sensation developed into pain that grew **acute**. And still he endured it, holding the flame of matches clumsily to the bark that would not light readily because his own burning hands were in the way, absorbing most of the flame.

At last, when he could endure no more, he jerked his hands apart. The blazing matches fell sizzling into the snow, but the birch bark was alight. He began laying dry grasses and the tiniest twigs on the flame. He could not pick and choose, for he had to lift the fuel between the heels of his hands. Small pieces of rotten wood and green moss clung to the twigs, and he bit them off as well as he could with his teeth. He cherished the flame carefully and awkwardly. It meant life, and it must not perish. The withdrawal of blood from the surface of his body now made him begin to shiver, and he grew more awkward. A large piece of green moss fell squarely on the little fire. He tried to poke it out with his fingers, but his shivering frame made him poke too far, and he disrupted the **nucleus** of the little fire, the burning grasses and tiny twigs separating and

The man is so cold that he can't feel his hands. He can hardly even tell that his own hands are burning.

acute sharp and severe	**nucleus** the center; the core	**spasmodically** with muscles jerking violently and uncontrollably
ensue to follow		

scattering. He tried to poke them together again, but in spite of the tenseness of the effort, his shivering got away with him, and the twigs were hopelessly scattered. Each twig gushed a puff of smoke and went out. The fire provider had failed. As he looked **apathetically** about him, his eyes chanced on the dog, sitting across the ruins of the fire from him, in the snow, making restless, hunching movements, slightly lifting one forefoot and then the other, shifting its weight back and forth on them with wistful eagerness.

The sight of the dog put a wild idea into his head. He remembered the tale of the man, caught in a blizzard, who killed a steer and crawled inside the **carcass**, and so was saved. He would kill the dog and bury his hands in the warm body until the numbness went out of them. Then he could build another fire. He spoke to the dog, calling it to him; but in his voice was a strange note of fear that frightened the animal, who had never known the man to speak in such a way before. Something was the matter, and its suspicious nature sensed danger—it knew not what danger, but somewhere, somehow, in its brain arose an apprehension of the man. It flattened its ears down at the sound of the man's voice, and its restless, hunching movements and the liftings and shiftings of its forefeet became more pronounced; but it would not come to the man. He got on his hands and knees and crawled toward the dog. This unusual posture again excited suspicion, and the animal sidled **mincingly** away.

The man sat up in the snow for a moment and struggled for calmness. Then he pulled on his mittens, by means of his teeth, and got upon his feet. He glanced down at first in order to assure himself that he was really standing up, for the absence of sensation in his feet left him unrelated to the earth. His erect position in itself started to drive the webs of suspicion from the dog's mind; and when he spoke **peremptorily**, with the sound of whiplashes in his voice, the

---

apathetically with little or no emotion

carcass a dead body

mincingly in a delicate way

peremptorily sternly; with a sense of urgency or command

dog **rendered** its customary allegiance and came to him. As it came within reaching distance, the man lost his control. His arms flashed out to the dog, and he experienced genuine surprise when he discovered that his hands could not clutch, that there was neither bend nor feeling in the fingers. He had forgotten for the moment that they were frozen and that they were freezing more and more. All this happened quickly, and before the animal could get away, he encircled its body with his arms. He sat down in the snow, and in this fashion held the dog, while it snarled and whined and struggled.

But it was all he could do, hold its body encircled in his arms and sit there. He realized that he could not kill the dog. There was no way to do it. With his helpless hands he could neither draw nor hold his sheath knife nor throttle the animal. He released it, and it plunged wildly away, with tail between its legs, and still snarling. It halted forty feet away and surveyed him curiously, with ears sharply pricked forward.

The man looked down at his hands in order to locate them, and found them hanging on the ends of his arms. It struck him as curious that one should have to use his eyes in order to find out where his hands were. He began threshing his arms back and forth, beating the mittened hands against his sides. He did this for five minutes, violently, and his heart pumped enough blood up to the surface to put a stop to his shivering. But no sensation was aroused in the hands. He had an impression that they hung like weights on the ends of his arms, but when he tried to run the impression down, he could not find it.

A certain fear of death, dull and **oppressive**, came to him. This fear quickly became **poignant** as he realized that it was no longer a mere matter of freezing his fingers and toes, or of losing his hands and feet, but that it was a matter of life and death with the chances against him. This threw him into a panic, and he turned and ran up the creek bed along the old, dim trail. The dog joined in behind and kept up with him. He ran blindly, without intention, in fear such as he had never

This part of the story shows how desperate the man has become. He is willing to kill his dog and use the dog's warmth to survive.

The man chooses to run because he thinks it might make him warm again.

| oppressive overpowering | poignant emotionally moving, touching, or painful | render to give up |

known in his life. Slowly, as he plowed and floundered through the snow, he began to see things again—the banks of the creek, the old timber jams, the leafless aspens, and the sky. The running made him feel better. He did not shiver. Maybe, if he ran on, his feet would thaw out; and, anyway, if he ran far enough, he would reach camp and the boys. Without doubt he would lose some fingers and toes and some of his face; but the boys would take care of him, and save the rest of him when he got there. And at the same time there was another thought in his mind that said he would never get to the camp and the boys; that it was too many miles away, that the freezing had too great a start on him, and that he would soon be stiff and dead. This thought he kept in the background and refused to consider. Sometimes it pushed itself forward and demanded to be heard, but he thrust it back and strove to think of other things.

> The man believes that he will lose some toes, fingers, and part of his face because of frostbite.

It struck him as curious that he could run at all on feet so frozen that he could not feel them when they struck the earth and took the weight of his body. He seemed to himself to skim along above the surface, and to have no connection with the earth. Somewhere he had once seen a winged Mercury, and he wondered if Mercury felt as he felt when skimming over the earth.

> *Mercury* was a messenger of the gods who was thought to have wings on his feet, according to Roman myth.

His theory of running until he reached camp and the boys had one flaw in it: he lacked the endurance. Several times he stumbled, and finally he tottered, crumpled up, and fell. When he tried to rise, he failed. He must sit and rest, he decided, and next time he would merely walk and keep on going. As he sat and regained his breath, he noted that he was feeling quite warm and comfortable. He was not shivering, and it even seemed that a warm glow had come to his chest and trunk. And yet, when he touched his nose or cheeks, there was no sensation. Running would not thaw them out. Nor would it thaw out his hands and feet. Then the thought came to him that the frozen portions of his body must be extending. He tried to keep this thought down, to forget it, to think of something else; he was aware of the panicky feeling that it caused, and he was afraid of the panic. But the thought

asserted itself, and **persisted**, until it produced a vision of his body totally frozen. This was too much, and he made another wild run along the trail. Once he slowed down to a walk, but the thought of the freezing extending itself made him run again.

And all the time the dog ran with him, at his heels. When he fell down a second time, it curled its tail over its forefeet and sat in front of him, facing him, curiously eager and intent. The warmth and security of the animal angered him, and he cursed it till it flattened down its ears **appeasingly**. This time the shivering came more quickly upon the man. He was losing in his battle with the frost. It was creeping into his body from all sides. The thought of it drove him on, but he ran no more than a hundred feet, when he staggered and pitched headlong. It was his last panic. When he had recovered his breath and control, he sat up and entertained in his mind the **conception** of meeting death with dignity. However, the conception did not come to him in such terms. His idea of it was that he had been making a fool of himself, running around like a chicken with its head cut off—such was the simile that occurred to him. Well, he was bound to freeze anyway, and he might as well take it decently. With this new-found peace of mind came the first glimmerings of drowsiness. A good idea, he thought, to sleep off to death. It

An *anesthetic* is a drug that causes loss of feeling, often used for surgery.

was like taking an anesthetic. Freezing was not so bad as people thought. There were lots worse ways to die.

He pictured the boys finding his body next day. Suddenly he found himself with them, coming along the trail and looking for himself. And, still with them, he came around a turn in the trail and found himself lying in the snow. He did not belong with himself anymore, for even he was out of himself, standing with the boys looking at himself in the snow. It certainly was cold, was his thought. When he got back to the States he could tell the folks what real cold was.

appeasingly in a way that calms or gives in	**assert** to state positively	**persist** to go on in spite of opposition
	conception idea	

He drifted on from this to a vision of the old-timer on Sulphur Creek. He could see him quite clearly, warm and comfortable, and smoking a pipe.

"You were right, old hoss; you were right," the man mumbled to the old-timer of Sulphur Creek.

Then the man drowsed off into what seemed to him the most comfortable and satisfying sleep he had ever known. The dog sat facing him and waiting. The brief day drew to a close in a long, slow twilight. There were no signs of a fire to be made, and, besides, never in the dog's experience had it known a man to sit like that in the snow and make no fire. As the twilight drew on, its eager yearning for the fire mastered it, and with a great lifting and shifting of forefeet, it whined softly, then flattened its ears down in **anticipation** of being **chidden** by the man. But the man remained silent. Later, the dog whined loudly. And still later it crept close to the man and caught the scent of death. This made the animal bristle and back away. A little longer it delayed, howling under the stars that leaped and danced and shone brightly in the cold sky. Then it turned and trotted up the trail in the direction of the camp it knew, where were the other food providers and fire providers.

anticipation an expectation that something will happen

chide to scold

241

Directions Write the answers to these questions using complete sentences.

Comprehension: Identifying Facts

1. Where is the man going?

2. What kind of dog is traveling with the man?

3. What evidence is there that this is a very cold day?

4. How does the dog get wet?

5. Why does the man decide to light a fire at first?

6. What happens to the man that makes it necessary for him to build another fire?

7. What mistake does the man make in building his second fire? What happens as a result?

8. Why does the man have trouble lighting the matches?

9. Why does the man decide to run?

10. What does the dog do that tells the reader the man has died?

Comprehension: Understanding Main Ideas

11. The man often refers to the "old-timer at Sulphur Creek." Why is the old-timer important?

12. The dog and the man have an interesting relationship. How could this relationship be described?

13. What is the main struggle in this story?

14. What kind of man is the main character?

15. Why doesn't the dog like the man?

16. The man does a good job of remaining calm throughout most of the story. At what point does he begin to panic? Why?

17. Why does the man want to kill his dog? What does this show about the man's state of mind?

18. The man makes the mistake of building his fire under a tree. What other mistake does the man admit to making?

19. The man has visions of his own death before dying. What are those visions?

20. Who is the winner of this struggle? Why?

Understanding Literature: Protagonist and Antagonist

There are at least two kinds of characters in most stories: a protagonist and an antagonist. A protagonist is the main character in a story. You can usually identify the protagonist by looking for the character around whom the action centers. An antagonist is a person or thing in the story struggling against the protagonist. In this story, the man is the protagonist. The antagonist is not a person, but nature. More specifically, the antagonist is the cold weather.

21. Why is it important for a story to have an antagonist and a protagonist?

22. Do you think a story can have more than one antagonist or protagonist? How?

23. Would "To Build a Fire" be a very interesting story without a protagonist? Explain your answer.

24. Why is it usually necessary for a story to have a main character?

25. Do you think the dog in this story is a protagonist, an antagonist, or something else?

Critical Thinking

26. What do you think of the main character in this story?

27. Why do you think the author included the dog in this story?

28. What moral message do you think London was intending to communicate in this story?

29. Did the ending surprise you? Explain how you felt about the outcome.

30. How does this story make you feel about the power of nature?

Writing on Your Own Write two or three paragraphs about a time in your life when something in nature surprised you. How did you feel? Did the event change you in some way? Answer these questions in your paragraphs.

Skills Lesson: Personification

Have your ever read a poem or story in which something that is not human is described as if it were a person? This is called personification. It describes something that is not human, such as an idea, object, or animal, as if it were a person. Below are examples.

The **clouds danced** across the sky.

Her **feeling of terror strangled** her from within.

From beneath the dark water, the **fish smiled** up at the fisherman.

In these examples, clouds are dancing, terror is strangling a woman, and a fish is smiling. However, the reader needs to know that in personification, meanings are not always to be taken as written. We all know that clouds do not really dance. Terror does not have the ability to strangle. Fish cannot smile. Personification tries to tell about something in a new and interesting way, even though it stretches the truth. It is up to the reader to think about how a cloud might seem like it dances as it moves.

In the next column is an example of personification from Stephen Crane's "The Open Boat."

If this old ninny woman, Fate, cannot do better than this, she should be deprived of the management of men's fortunes. She is an old hen who knows not her intention. If she has decided to drown me, why did she not do it in the beginning and save me all this trouble?

The reader can really sense the anger the men felt at being lost at sea in these sentences. The author uses personification to describe fate, which is just an idea, not a person. Fate is a power that makes things happen a certain way. Here, fate is given the human character of an old woman.

Review

1. What is personification?

2. What kinds of things are described with personification?

3. Is personification meant to be taken as it is written? Explain.

4. What is being personified in the example from "The Open Boat"?

5. How does personification add to writing?

Writing on Your Own Use personification to describe an object, idea, and animal. Write one sentence for each category.

UNIT 4 SUMMARY

From 1890 to 1908, the United States became a very powerful nation. Industry and farming were very important parts of the American way of life. Inventions changed the way people lived. However, life at this time was not without problems. Working in factories was very difficult and pay was low. Political leaders were often dishonest and difficult to trust. Many people coming to America from other countries found that life in the United States was not all that easy.

The writing during this time can be placed into two groups: realism and naturalism. Realism looked at life the way it was, not as people wished it to be. Realism also looked at common events and how the common person fit into the universe. Naturalism, similar to realism, focused on the survival of the fittest against nature. In naturalism, characters are helpless to understand nature and to defend themselves against it. The writers in this unit, Stephen Crane and Jack London, were two among many writers in the realism and naturalism movements.

Selections

■ "The Open Boat" by Stephen Crane is based on a true story of four men lost at sea. The reader gets a realistic look at how these men feel when facing death and gains an understanding of the powers of the sea. The story also tells of the classic struggle between humans and nature.

■ "To Build a Fire" by Jack London is a story about a man and his dog who travel on a cold winter day in the Yukon Territory. The story quickly becomes a tale of survival against nature. The man and his dog realize that their one hope to survive is in the man's ability to build a fire.

Directions Write the answers to these questions using complete sentences.

Comprehension: Identifying Facts

1. What good things were happening in America from 1890 to 1908?

2. What problems were there at this time?

3. What inventions changed the American way of life?

4. What kind of literature became popular?

5. What class of people took an interest in reading?

Comprehension: Understanding Main Ideas

6. What is the plot of "The Open Boat"?

7. What is the plot of "To Build a Fire"?

8. How are "The Open Boat" and "To Build a Fire" similar?

9. Explain how Stephen Crane's and Jack London's writing styles are alike.

10. Explain how "To Build a Fire" is an example of naturalism.

Understanding Literature: Realism and Naturalism

Two kinds of writing began in the late 1800s that looked at life in a much more realistic way. These forms are realism and naturalism. Realism looked at common events and the common person. Realist writings were very true to life. Naturalism focused on the "survival of the fittest" against nature in which characters are helpless to understand nature and to defend themselves against it. Realism and naturalism are similar. They often discuss nature and events that are very real and natural.

11. What is the main idea of realism?

12. What is the main idea of naturalism?

13. How are realism and naturalism similar?

14. Which do you like better, realism or naturalism? Why?

15. Which do you think did a better job of using realism, "The Open Boat" or "To Build a Fire"? Why?

Critical Thinking

16. "The Open Boat" was written over a hundred years ago. Do you think people would still like this story today if it were published in a magazine or made into a movie? Explain.

17. How has reading "The Open Boat" and "To Build a Fire" helped you gain a better understanding of life?

18. Why do you think realism and naturalism became important at this time?

19. Crane and London seem to have a gloomy view of the world. Explain why you agree or disagree with this view.

20. What will you remember most about "To Build a Fire"? Why?

Speak and Listen

Pretend that either "The Open Boat" or "To Build a Fire" has been made into a movie. To advertise the movie, a preview will appear on television and in movie theaters. A script must be written for this preview. Choose one of the stories; then write the movie preview script. Think of actors who might play the characters, and add their names to your script. Include a brief description of the plot. When finished, practice reading the script as if you are the preview announcer. Then read the script to your class.

Beyond Words

You have learned about realism in literature. Did you know that there was also a kind of art called realism? It became popular in America in the late 1800s. Realist paintings often focused on nature or showed objects or people in realistic ways. One artist, Winslow Homer, was part of this movement. One of his paintings called *A Summer Squall* can be seen on pages 182–183 of this textbook. Use what you know about realism to make your own realist drawing. For example, the drawing could actually show an event in a very real way or it could show a scene from "The Open Boat" or "To Build a Fire."

Writing on Your Own The endings of both selections in Unit 4 are very important to the stories. Write an essay describing why the ending of a short story is often the most important part. Begin your essay with a general statement about the importance of endings in stories. Add statements to support your opinion. Refer to "The Open Boat" or "To Build a Fire" in your essay. End the essay with a conclusion.

Test-Taking Tip

Try to answer all questions as completely as possible. When asked to explain your answer, do so in complete sentences.

"Drum on your drums, batter on your banjos, sob on the long cool winding saxophones. Go to it, O jazzmen."

—Carl Sandburg, "Jazz Fantasia," 1920

"I, too, sing America.
I am the darker brother. . . .
I, too, am America."

—Langston Hughes, "I, Too," 1925

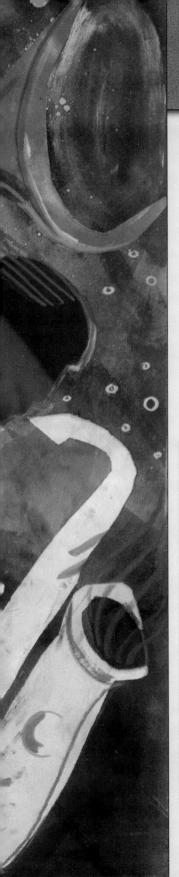

UNIT 5 | *American Literature Comes of Age: 1905–1940*

What do you think of when you hear the word *modern?* Do you think of cities and technology? New and exciting times? All of these and more describe the first part of the 1900s. With the good and bad times of the modern age came a new kind of literature called modernism.

In this unit, you will learn about the first half of the twentieth century in America and about the development of modernist literature.

The early twentieth century in America was a very busy and unusual time. There were many contrasts: wealth and poverty, war and peace, social well-being and social problems, city life and farm life, old ways and news ways of thinking.

The main event of this time was World War I. It was the most costly and bloodiest war the world had seen. It began in Europe in 1914. Later, the United States entered this war, which lasted until 1918. Working together to win this war helped to make firm partners of the United States and European nations. It also helped make the United States a world power.

After the war came the Roaring Twenties, the name used to describe the 1920s in America. It was a time of youthful energy. Developments in radio, magazines, newspapers, talking movies, and airplanes made these years exciting. The population became better educated. Many people moved to the city.

Change came for most Americans in 1929 with a huge stock market crash. It left many people poor or homeless. Throughout the 1930s, millions of Americans were forced to deal with the problems of society. This time came to be known as the Great Depression. People could not find work and did not have enough money for their basic needs. The American dream had ceased to be.

Through the good and bad times of the twentieth century, a new age of literature emerged. It was called modernism. It was much different from former writings. Modernist writers used very new ideas and styles to explain the many changes the modern world had caused. American writers

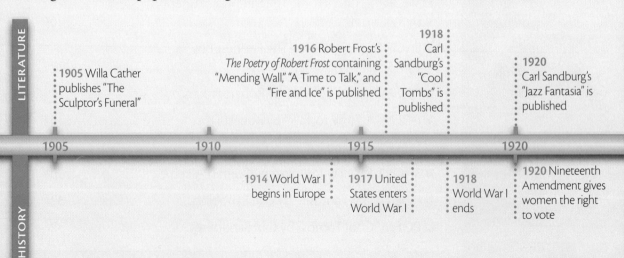

LITERATURE

1905 Willa Cather publishes "The Sculptor's Funeral"

1916 Robert Frost's *The Poetry of Robert Frost* containing "Mending Wall," "A Time to Talk," and "Fire and Ice" is published

1918 Carl Sandburg's "Cool Tombs" is published

1920 Carl Sandburg's "Jazz Fantasia" is published

1905   1910   1915   1920

1914 World War I begins in Europe

1917 United States enters World War I

1918 World War I ends

1920 Nineteenth Amendment gives women the right to vote

HISTORY

The automobile was mass-produced for the first time in the early 1900s.

were challenged by the 1930s and 1940s. New magazines, newspapers, and public readings kept literature alive. The literature of this time period looked at feelings of being alone and attempted to pull society together.

In this unit, you will study examples of struggle—of an engineer in Thomas Wolfe's "The Far and the Near," of a student in F. Scott Fitzgerald's "The Freshest Boy," and of a poor man in Conrad Aiken's "Impulse." You will examine some of the problems and joys of relationships as described in Robert Frost's "A Time to Talk" and "Mending Wall." Several works in this unit consider the effects of death: of one man in Willa Cather's "The Sculptor's Funeral," of historical figures in Carl Sandburg's "Cool Tombs," and of the world in Frost's "Fire and Ice." Sandburg's "Jazz Fantasia" celebrates the good times of the jazz age.

Another movement within modern literature was the Harlem Renaissance. Harlem is an area of New York City. The Harlem Renaissance focused on African American pride. Langston Hughes was just one of the creative voices and leaders in this movement. In this unit, his poem "Theme for English B" expresses much of the mood of the Harlem Renaissance.

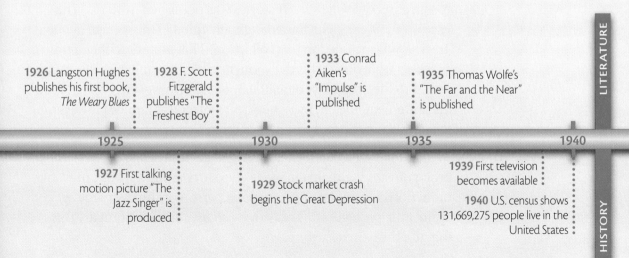

LITERATURE

1926 Langston Hughes publishes his first book, *The Weary Blues*

1928 F. Scott Fitzgerald publishes "The Freshest Boy"

1933 Conrad Aiken's "Impulse" is published

1935 Thomas Wolfe's "The Far and the Near" is published

1925　　　　1930　　　　1935　　　　1940

1927 First talking motion picture "The Jazz Singer" is produced

1929 Stock market crash begins the Great Depression

1939 First television becomes available

1940 U.S. census shows 131,669,275 people live in the United States

HISTORY

Thomas Wolfe

1900–1938

Literary Terms

antagonist a person or thing in the story struggling against the protagonist

protagonist the main character in a story around whom most of the action centers

simile a comparison that uses the words *like* or *as*

About the Author

Thomas Wolfe was born in Asheville, North Carolina, in 1900. His parents did not get along, and the family was divided. Wolfe lived with his mother and his brother in a boarding house. Wolfe spent much of his time reading. An excellent student, he entered college at fifteen. He was interested in theater and decided to be a playwright. He graduated and then attended Harvard to study drama.

Finding that writing plays was not where his talents lay, Wolfe began a novel. His works were often thought to be too wordy and long. Still, his first novel, *Look Homeward, Angel*, was a great success. It made him famous, but also made enemies of the people of his hometown. They were upset with the novel's negative view of Asheville and its people. Wolfe wrote several other successful novels, such as *You Can't Go Home Again* and *Of Time and the River*.

In 1938 Wolfe became ill with tuberculosis. He died at age thirty-eight.

About the Selection

A collection of Wolfe's short stories was published in 1935. "The Far and the Near," which was originally titled "The Cottage by the Tracks," was included in this collection. This story describes a train engineer who, during his daily journey, has blown his whistle and waved to the occupants of a little house for over twenty years. After his retirement, the engineer decides to meet this family. However, the family is not how he imagines them to be.

In this story, there is a **protagonist** and an **antagonist**. A protagonist is the main character in a story around whom most of the action centers. An antagonist is a person or thing struggling against the protagonist. This story also uses **similes**, comparisons that use the words *like* or *as*.

The Far and the Near

On the **outskirts** of a little town upon a rise of land that swept back from the railway there was a tidy little cottage of white boards, trimmed vividly with green blinds. To one side of the house there was a garden neatly patterned with plots of growing vegetables, and an arbor for the grapes that ripened late in August. Before the house there were three mighty oaks which sheltered it in their clean and **massive** shade in summer, and to the other side there was a border of gay flowers. The whole place had an air of tidiness, thrift, and modest comfort.

Every day, a few minutes after two o'clock in the afternoon, the limited express between two cities passed this spot. At that moment, the great train, having halted for a breathing space at the town near by, was beginning to lengthen evenly into its stroke, but it had not yet reached the full drive of its terrific speed. It swung into view **deliberately**, swept past with a powerful swaying motion of the engine, a low smooth rumble of its heavy cars upon pressed steel, and then it vanished in the cut. For a moment the progress of the engine could be marked by heavy bellowing puffs of smoke that burst at spaced intervals above the edges of the meadow grass, and finally nothing could be heard but the solid clacking **tempo** of the wheels **receding** into the drowsy stillness of the afternoon.

What does this story tell us about what we sometimes think about the world and what is reality?

An *arbor* is a structure of crossed strips of wood covered with vines or branches.

deliberately slowly; without hurrying

massive forming or consisting of a large mass

outskirts an area away from the center or near a border

recede to move back or away

tempo the rate or motion of an activity; pace

Every day for more than twenty years, as the train had approached this house, the engineer had blown on the whistle, and every day, as soon as she heard this signal, a woman had appeared on the back porch of the little house and waved to him. At first she had a small child clinging to her skirts, and now this child had grown to full womanhood, and every day she, too, came with her mother to the porch and waved.

The engineer had grown old and gray in the service. He had driven his great train, loaded with its weight of lives, across the land ten thousand times. His own children had grown up and married, and four times he had seen before him on the tracks the ghastly dot of **tragedy converging** like a cannon ball to its eclipse of horror at the boiler head—a light spring wagon filled with children, with its clustered row of small stunned faces; a cheap automobile stalled upon the tracks, set with the wooden figures of people **paralyzed** with fear; a battered hobo walking by the rail, too deaf and old to hear the whistle's warning; and a form flung past his window with a scream—all this the man had seen and known. He had known all the grief, the joy, the peril and the labor such a man could know; he had grown seamed and weathered in his loyal service, and now, schooled by the qualities of faith and courage and humbleness that attended his labor, he had grown old, and had the **grandeur** and the wisdom that these men have.

But no matter what peril or tragedy he had known, the vision of the little house and the women waving to him with a brave free motion of the arm had become fixed in the mind of the engineer as something beautiful and enduring, something beyond all change and ruin, and something that would always be the same, no matter what **mishap**, grief, or error might break the iron schedule of his days.

Notice the simile here. The author compares the train's movement toward tragedy to the swiftness of a cannon ball.

What does this paragraph tell you about the protagonist in this story—the engineer?

converge to come together	**mishap** bad luck or misfortune; an unfortunate accident	**paralyze** powerless; unable to move
grandeur grandness; greatness; magnificence		**tragedy** a terrible event

The sight of the little house and of these two women gave him the most **extraordinary** happiness he had ever known. He had seen them in a thousand lights, a hundred weathers. He had seen them through the harsh bare light of wintry gray across the brown and frosted stubble of the earth, and he had seen them again in the green **luring sorcery** of April.

He felt for them and for the little house in which they lived such tenderness as a man might feel for his own children, and at length the picture of their lives was carved so sharply in his heart that he felt that he knew their lives completely, to every hour and moment of the day, and he resolved that one day, when his years of service should be ended, he would go and find these people and speak at last with them whose lives had been so wrought into his own.

That day came. At last the engineer stepped from a train onto the station platform of the town where these two women lived. His years upon the rail had ended. He was a **pensioned**

extraordinary beyond what is usual	**luring** tempting; attracting with a hint of pleasure	**pensioned** paid a regular, fixed sum following retirement
		sorcery magic

servant of his company, with no more work to do. The engineer walked slowly through the station and out into the streets of the town. Everything was as strange to him as if he had never seen this town before. As he walked on, his sense of bewilderment and confusion grew. Could this be the town he had passed ten thousand times? Were these the same houses he had seen so often from the high windows of his cab? It was all as unfamiliar, as disquieting as a city in a dream, and the **perplexity** of his spirit increased as he went on.

Presently the houses thinned into the straggling outposts of the town, and the street faded into a country road—the one on which the women lived. And the man plodded on slowly in the heat and dust. At length he stood before the house he sought. He knew at once that he had found the proper place. He saw the lordly oaks before the house, the flower beds, the garden and the arbor, and farther off, the **glint** of rails.

Yes, this was the house he sought, the place he had passed so many times, the destination he had longed for with such happiness. But now that he had found it, now that he was here, why did his hand **falter** on the gate; why had the town, the road, the earth, the very entrance to this place he loved turned unfamiliar as the landscape of some ugly dream? Why did he now feel this sense of confusion, doubt, and hopelessness?

At length he entered by the gate, walked slowly up the path and in a moment more had mounted three short steps that led up to the porch, and was knocking at the door. Presently he heard steps in the hall, the door was opened, and a woman stood facing him.

And instantly, with a sense of bitter loss and grief, he was sorry he had come. He knew at once that the woman who stood there looking at him with a mistrustful eye was the same woman who had waved to him so many thousand

> What do you think the two women will be like?

---

falter to hesitate in purpose or action	**glint** a tiny bright flash of light	**perplexity** confusion; bewilderment; puzzlement

times. But her face was harsh and pinched and **meager**; the flesh sagged wearily in **sallow** folds, and the small eyes peered at him with timid suspicion and uneasy doubt. All the brave freedom, the warmth and the affection that he had read into her gesture, vanished in the moment that he saw her and heard her unfriendly tongue.

And now his own voice sounded unreal and ghastly to him as he tried to explain his presence, to tell her who he was and the reason he had come. But he faltered on, fighting stubbornly against the horror of regret, confusion, disbelief that surged up in his spirit, drowning all his former joy and making his act of hope and tenderness seem shameful to him.

At length the woman invited him almost unwillingly into the house, and called her daughter in a harsh shrill voice. Then, for a brief agony of time, the man sat in an ugly little parlor, and he tried to talk while the two women stared at him with a dull, bewildered **hostility**, a **sullen**, **timorous** restraint.

And finally, stammering a crude farewell, he departed. He walked away down the path and then along the road toward town, and suddenly he knew that he was an old man. His heart, which had been brave and confident when it looked along the familiar **vista** of the rails, was now sick with doubt and horror as it saw the strange and unsuspected **visage** of an earth which had always been within a stone's throw of him, and which he had never seen or known. And he knew that all the magic of that bright lost way, the vista of that shining line, the imagined corner of that small good universe of hope's desire, was gone forever, could never be got back again.

The engineer's feelings toward the women have been shattered. Why do you think the author chose this way to end the story?

hostility act of war; conflict	**sallow** of a sickly, yellowish color	**visage** appearance
meager having little flesh; thin	**sullen** gloomily silent	**vista** a distant view
	timorous fearful	

The Far and the Near

Thomas Wolfe

Directions Write the answers to these questions using complete sentences.

Comprehension: Identifying Facts

1. At what time does the train pass the little white cottage each day?

2. Who waves to the engineer from the back porch?

3. How many terrible accidents has the engineer seen on the tracks over the twenty years that he has worked for the railroad?

4. What does the engineer resolve to do after he retires?

5. What does the woman look like when she opens the door to the engineer?

6. How does the engineer feel about the woman and her daughter at the beginning of the story?

7. How does the engineer feel just after knocking on the door?

8. How does the older woman call for her daughter?

9. Where do the engineer and the two women talk for a while?

10. How does the engineer feel about the women at the end of the story?

Comprehension: Understanding Main Ideas

11. Describe the life of the train engineer as portrayed by Thomas Wolfe.

12. What kind of personality does the engineer have?

13. How does the author describe the house at the beginning of the story?

14. Explain the meaning of the title of this short story.

15. How had seeing the two women by the house helped the engineer while he had been working?

16. As the engineer walks up to the house, what hints does the author give that something bad will happen?

17. Describe the older woman in this story. In what ways is she unappealing?

18. Why does the engineer feel old after leaving the house?

19. How has the engineer's outlook on life changed by the end of the story?

20. What is it that is "gone forever" in the last line of this story?

Understanding Literature: Protagonist and Antagonist

The protagonist is the hero of a narrative work. The protagonist is the character in a story around whom the action centers. The antagonist is the character who opposes the protagonist. The antagonist is usually the character who represents evil or unhappiness. Review the characters described in Wolfe's short story, "The Far and the Near." Then answer the following questions.

21. Which character would you consider to be the protagonist?

22. Which character is the antagonist?

23. Is there more than one antagonist in this story? If so, who or what?

24. Do you think the protagonist in this story is a strong character? Why or why not?

25. Who wins in this story, the antagonist or the protagonist? Why?

Critical Thinking

26. Why do you think the town and house look so different when the engineer sees them up close?

27. Why do you think the two women seem so friendly from the porch and yet so unfriendly in person?

28. Have you ever expected something to be wonderful, but had it turn out to be a disappointment? Explain your answer.

29. Do you feel sorry for the engineer in this story? At what point did you begin to pity him? Why is he a sad figure by the end of the story?

30. Do you think that the engineer's retirement will be ruined because of this experience? Explain your answer.

Writing on Your Own Write a paragraph explaining how "The Far and the Near" affected you. Answer these questions in your paragraph: What did you learn from the story? Did you like the story's message about life? Was it well written?

Theme for English B
Langston Hughes

Langston Hughes
1902–1967

Literary Terms

free verse poetry that does not have a strict rhyming pattern or regular line length, and uses actual speech patterns for the rhythms of sound

image a word or phrase that appeals to the senses and allows the reader to picture events

rhythm a regular pattern of stressed and unstressed syllables

About the Author

Langston Hughes was a popular African American poet for many years. He was a leader in the Harlem Renaissance in the 1920s. Harlem writers were greatly appreciated at this time. Hughes's house became a meeting place for young African American poets. These writers tried out new forms and styles in their works. Their works expressed African American pride and presented problems African Americans faced because of their race.

Hughes was born in Joplin, Missouri, in 1902. He began writing poetry as a child. While Hughes was working in a Washington hotel, a well-known poet took an interest in his works. The public also began to take an interest. In 1926 his first published book, *The Weary Blues*, led to public readings and travel. By age twenty-seven, Hughes was making a living with his writing.

Later works include novels, plays, and newspaper columns. In 1961, Hughes was elected to the National Institute of Arts and Letters.

About the Selection

"Theme for English B" was written in response to a writing assignment when Hughes was a college student. The poem tells much about the life of a young African American man in New York. It also tells something about the racial problems in America during the 1920s.

This poem is an example of a form of poetry called **free verse**. Unlike many earlier forms of poetry, free verse has no strict rhyming pattern or regular line length. Read this poem aloud to enjoy its **rhythms** of everyday speech. Rhythm is a regular pattern of stressed and unstressed syllables. This poem also uses **images**. An image is a word or phrase that appeals to our senses and allows the readers to picture events.

The City from Greenwich Village, John Sloan

Theme for English B

The instructor said,

> *Go home and write*
> *a page tonight.*
> *And let that page come out of you—*
> 5 *Then, it will be true.*

I wonder if it's that simple?
I am twenty-two, colored, born in Winston-Salem.
I went to school there, then Durham, then here
to this college on the hill above Harlem.
10 I am the only colored student in my class.

What image of life in New York during the 1920s does the poet paint?

The steps from the hill lead down into Harlem,
through a park, then I cross St. Nicholas,
Eighth Avenue, Seventh, and I come to the Y,
the Harlem Branch Y, where I take the elevator
15 up to my room, sit down, and write this page:

It's not easy to know what is true for you or me
at twenty-two, my age. But I guess I'm what
I feel and see and hear, Harlem, I hear you:
hear you, hear me—we two—you, me, talk on this page.
20 (I hear New York, too.) Me—who?
Well, I like to eat, sleep, drink, and be in love.
I like to work, read, learn, and understand life.
I like a pipe for a Christmas present,
or records—Bessie, bop, or Bach.
25 I guess being colored doesn't make me not like
the same things other folks like who are other races.
So will my page be colored that I write?
Being me, it will not be white.
But it will be
30 a part of you, instructor.
You are white—
yet a part of me, as I am a part of you.

That's American.
Sometimes perhaps you don't want to be a part of me.
35 Nor do I often want to be a part of you.
But we are, that's true!
As I learn from you,
I guess you learn from me—
although you're older—and white—
40 and somewhat more free.

This is my page for English B.

Bessie refers to Bessie Smith, who was a great blues singer in the early 1900s. *Bop* is short for bebop, a form of jazz. *Bach* is Johann Sebastian Bach (1685–1750), who is thought by many to be one of the most important composers of classical music.

Directions
Write the answers to these questions using complete sentences.

Comprehension: Identifying Facts

1. Who is talking in the opening lines of this poem?

2. What is the age of the author in this poem?

3. What makes the author different from the others in his class?

Comprehension: Understanding Main Ideas

4. What message does the young poet have for the instructor?

5. How might this selection be considered a free-verse poem?

6. Explain how the introduction and the conclusion of the poem are in agreement.

Understanding Literature: Image

"Theme for English B" is a poem that uses language and images to make the reader understand more about the author. Certain lines of this poem use sense images and emotional impressions. Langston Hughes says, "I feel and see and hear, Harlem . . ." and "(I hear New York, too.)."

7. Do the images in the poem refer to all five senses? Explain your answer.

8. What emotions does the poet feel as he describes each separate place and idea? What emotions does he want the reader to feel?

Critical Thinking

9. Why do you think the poet includes some information about what he likes?

10. In what ways do you think writing this poem fulfilled the assignment?

Writing on Your Own Langston Hughes used images to describe how places—Harlem and New York— were important to him. Write a paragraph using at least two images to explain how a certain place, such as a city, state, building, or park, is important to you.

The Sculptor's Funeral
Willa Cather

Willa Cather

1873–1947

Literary Terms

character a person in a story

setting the place and time in a story

About the Author

Life in America's Midwest was the subject of Willa Cather's many popular writings. Growing up there gave her much knowledge of the people in the Midwest.

Cather was born near Winchester, Virginia, in 1873. Her family moved to a ranch in Nebraska when she was still a child. Schools were far away, so Cather was taught at home. She learned Latin and English literature from her grandmothers. She later attended the University of Nebraska. At college she was a theater critic for the *Lincoln State Journal*. She also began to write poetry and short stories. Cather worked as a reporter after college. She also continued to write short stories.

Cather's first successful novels, published in 1913 and 1918, were about her early life in Nebraska. She won a Pulitzer Prize for *One of Ours* in 1923. Other major works include *O Pioneers!* and *My Antonia*. Cather died in 1947.

About the Selection

"The Sculptor's Funeral" was first published in 1905 in *McClure's Magazine*. This story gives the reader an example of Cather's ability to describe people and places. This story is about **character** and **setting**. A character is a person in a story. The setting is the place and time in a story. The main character, Harvey Merrick, is a famous sculptor. Merrick never appears in the story at all. He has died. His body has been returned to his hometown of Sand City for burial. However, his family and the townspeople never thought of him as a success. Henry Steavens, Merrick's student, and the town's lawyer, Jim Laird, give the reader an understanding of the people of Sand City.

From
The Sculptor's Funeral

The coffin was got out of its rough box and down on the snowy platform. The townspeople drew back enough to make room for it and then formed a closed semicircle about it, looking curiously at the palm leaf which lay across the black cover. No one said anything. The baggage man stood by his truck, waiting to get at the trunks. The engine panted heavily, and the fireman dodged in and out among the wheels with his yellow torch and long oilcan, snapping the spindle boxes. The young Bostonian, one of the dead sculptor's pupils who had come with the body, looked about him helplessly. He turned to the banker, the only one of that black, uneasy, stoop-shouldered group who seemed enough of an individual to be addressed.

"None of Mr. Merrick's brothers are here?" he asked uncertainly.

The man with the red beard for the first time stepped up and joined the others. "No, they have not come yet; the family is scattered. The body will be taken directly to the house." He stooped and took hold of one of the handles of the coffin.

"Take the long hill road up, Thompson, it will be easier on the horses," called the liveryman as the undertaker snapped the door of the hearse and prepared to mount to the driver's seat.

Laird, the red-bearded lawyer, turned again to the stranger. "We didn't know whether there would be anyone with him or not," he explained. "It's a long walk, so you'd better go up in the hack." He pointed to a single battered **conveyance**, but the young man replied stiffly: "Thank you, but I think I will go up with the hearse. If you don't object," turning to the undertaker, "I'll ride with you."

What does this story tell you about the people of Sand City and the life they lead?

A leaf from a palm tree has been placed on the coffin. Since the palm leaf is used as a symbol of victory, it means in this story that Harvey Merrick has been awarded an important decoration for being a famous sculptor.

A *liveryman* is a person who takes care of or works at a livery stable, which is a place where horses and carriages are rented. An *undertaker* is a person whose business is to prepare the dead for burial and to plan funerals. A *hearse* is a vehicle used to carry the dead to the grave.

conveyance a vehicle; a means of transport

They clambered up over the wheels and drove off in the starlight up the long, white hill toward the town. The lamps in the still village were shining from under the low, snow-burdened roofs; and beyond, on every side, the plains reached out into emptiness, peaceful and wide as the soft sky itself, and wrapped in a **tangible**, white silence.

When the hearse backed up to a wooden sidewalk before a naked, weather-beaten frame house, the same **composite**, ill-defined group that had stood upon the station siding was huddled about the gate. The front yard was an icy swamp, and a couple of warped planks, extending from the sidewalk to the door, made a sort of rickety footbridge. The gate hung on one hinge, and was opened wide with difficulty. Steavens, the young stranger, noticed that something black was tied to the knob of the front door.

The grating sound made by the casket, as it was drawn from the hearse, was answered by a scream from the house; the front door was wrenched open, and a tall, **corpulent** woman rushed out bareheaded into the snow and flung herself upon the coffin, shrieking: "My boy, my boy! And this is how you've come home to me!"

As Steavens turned away and closed his eyes with a shudder of unutterable **repulsion**, another woman, also tall, but

composite made up of the same mix of characteristics	**repulsion** intense dislike or disgust
corpulent very fat	**tangible** able to be sensed, especially by touch

flat and **angular**, dressed entirely in black, darted out of the house and caught Mrs. Merrick by the shoulders, crying sharply: "Come, come, mother; you mustn't go on like this!" Her tone changed to one of **obsequious solemnity** as she turned to the banker. "The parlor is ready, Mr. Phelps."

The bearers carried the coffin along the narrow boards, while the undertaker ran ahead with the coffin-rests. They bore it into a large, unheated room that smelled of dampness and disuse and furniture polish, and set it down. . . .

"Take the lid off, Mr. Thompson; let me see my boy's face," wailed the elder woman between her sobs. This time Steavens looked fearfully, almost **beseechingly** into her face, red and swollen under its masses of strong, black, shiny hair. He flushed, dropped his eyes, and then, almost **incredulously**, looked again. There was a kind of power about her face—a kind of brutal handsomeness, even; but it was scarred and furrowed by violence, and so colored and coarsened by fiercer passions that grief seemed never to have laid a gentle finger there. The long nose was **distended** and knobbed at the end, and there were deep lines on either side of it; her heavy black brows almost met across her forehead, her teeth were large and square and set far apart—teeth that could tear. She filled the room; the men were obliterated, seemed tossed about like twigs in an angry water, even Steavens felt himself being drawn into the whirlpool.

The daughter—the tall, raw-boned woman in crêpe, with a mourning comb in her hair which curiously lengthened her long face—sat stiffly upon the sofa, her hands, **conspicuous** for their large knuckles, folded in her lap, her mouth and eyes drawn down, solemnly awaiting the opening of the coffin. Near the door stood a mulatto woman, evidently a servant in the

The black object tied to the doorknob, mentioned on page 266, is probably a ribbon. It is there as a symbol of mourning over Merrick's death.

Here the author gives a detailed description of the elder woman, Merrick's mother. What do you think this woman is like based on what you've learned about her so far?

Crêpe is a light crinkled fabric. *Mulatto* refers to a person of mixed white and black ancestry.

---

angular thin and bony; stiff in character or manner

beseechingly with an anxious, begging manner

conspicuous noticeable; obvious

distended made larger

incredulously with disbelief

obsequious obedient; overly agreeable

solemnity a formal or ceremonial quality

Calico is a cotton or cloth fabric, often patterned.

house, with a timid bearing and an **emaciated** face pitifully sad and gentle. She was weeping silently, the corner of her calico apron lifted to her eyes, occasionally suppressing a long quivering sob. Steavens walked over and stood beside her. . . .

[As he listens to the comments of the people in the room, Steavens realizes that the townspeople had never understood Merrick and becomes aware of the miserable boyhood that the sculptor must have known.]

All this raw, biting ugliness had been the portion of the man whose mind was to become an exhaustless gallery of beautiful impressions—so sensitive that the mere shadow of a poplar leaf flickering against a sunny wall would be etched and held there forever. Surely, if ever a man had the magic word in his fingertips, it was Merrick. Whatever he touched, he revealed its holiest secret; **liberated** it from enchantment and restored it to its **pristine** loveliness. Upon whatever he had come in contact with, he had left a beautiful record of the experience—a sort of **ethereal** signature; a scent, a sound, a color that was his own.

Here the author describes Merrick. What kind of person was he?

Steavens understood now the real tragedy of his master's life; neither love nor wine, as many had **conjectured**; but a blow which had fallen earlier and cut deeper than anything else could have done—a shame not his, and yet so unescapably his, to hide in his heart from his very boyhood. And without—the frontier warfare; the yearning of a boy, cast ashore upon a desert of newness and ugliness and **sordidness**, for all that is **chastened** and old, and noble with traditions.

At eleven o'clock the tall, flat woman in black announced that the watchers were arriving, and asked them to "step into the dining room." As Steavens rose, the lawyer said dryly: "You go on—it'll be a good experience for you. I'm not equal to that crowd tonight; I've had twenty years of them."

How do the things Laird says here hint that something is about to happen?

As Steavens closed the door after him he glanced back at the lawyer, sitting by the coffin in the dim light, with his chin resting on his hand. . . .

chastened pure or decent	**ethereal** heavenly; unworldly; spiritual	**pristine** fresh and innocent
conjecture to guess	**liberate** to free	**sordidness** evil; meanness
emaciated very thin; physically wasted away		

[In the dining room, the townspeople discuss local matters until they are sure that all members of the family have gone to bed. Then, the talk turns once more to the life of the sculptor. The townspeople comment that Harvey Merrick's father spent too much money on his son's education instead of making Harvey stay on the farm and help his family. They add that Harvey was no good at farmwork anyway and would waste time watching sunsets rather than cows.]

Was it possible that these men did not understand, that the palm on the coffin meant nothing to them? The very name of their town would have remained forever buried in the postal guide had it not been now and again mentioned in the world in connection with Harvey Merrick's. He remembered what his master had said to him on the day of his death, after the **congestion** of both lungs had shut off any **probability** of **recovery**, and the sculptor had asked his pupil to send his body home. "It's not a pleasant place to be lying while the world is moving and doing and bettering," he had said with a feeble smile, "but it rather seems as though we ought to go back to the place we came from, in the end. The townspeople will come in for a look at me; and after they have had their say, I shan't have much to fear from the judgment of God!"

The cattleman took up the comment. "Forty's young for a Merrick to cash in; they usually hang on pretty well. Probably he helped it along with whiskey."

"His mother's people were not long lived, and Harvey never had a **robust** constitution," said the minister mildly. He would have liked to say more. He had been the boy's Sunday-school teacher and had been fond of him; but he felt that he was not in a position to speak. His own sons had turned out badly, and it was not a year since one of them had made his last trip home in the express car, shot in a gambling house in the Black Hills.

"Nevertheless, there is no disputin' that Harve frequently looked upon the wine when it was red, also **variegated**, and it shore made an oncommon fool of him," moralized the cattleman.

Merrick's words here mean that he knows the townspeople do not like him and will not say kind things about him at his funeral.

congestion the condition of being clogged	**probability** likelihood **recovery** the act of becoming well again	**robust** healthy **variegated** having different colors

Just then the door leading into the parlor rattled loudly and everyone started involuntarily, looking relieved when only Jim Laird came out. The Grand Army man ducked his head when he saw the spark in his blue, bloodshot eye. They were all afraid of Jim; he was a **drunkard**, but he could twist the law to suit his **client's** needs as no other man in all western Kansas could do, and there were many who tried. The lawyer closed the door behind him, leaned back against it, and folded his arms, cocking his head a little to one side. When he assumed this attitude in the courtroom, ears were always pricked up, as it usually foretold a flood of withering **sarcasm**.

"I've been with you gentlemen before," he began in a dry, even tone, "when you've sat by the coffins of boys born and raised in this town; and, if I remember rightly, you were never any too well satisfied when you checked them up. What's the matter, anyhow? Why is it that **reputable** young men are as scarce as millionaires in Sand City? It might almost seem to a stranger that there was some way something the matter with your **progressive** town. Why did Reuben Sayer, the brightest young lawyer you ever turned out, after he had come home from the university as straight as a die, take to drinking and forge a check and shoot himself? Why did Bill Merrit's son die of the shakes in a saloon in Omaha? Why was Mr. Thomas's son, here, shot in a gambling house? Why did young Adams burn his mill to beat the insurance companies and go to the pen?"

The lawyer paused and unfolded his arms, laying one clenched fist quietly on the table. "I'll tell you why. Because you drummed nothing but money and **knavery** into their ears from the time they wore knickerbockers; because you carped away at them as you've been carping here tonight, holding our friends Phelps and Elder up to them for their models, as our grandfathers held up George Washington and John Adams. But the boys were young, and raw at the business you put them to,

The word *pen* here is a shortened form of *penitentiary,* which is a prison.

Knickerbockers were loose-fitting, short pants gathered at the knee. At this time, such pants were commonly worn by young boys.

client one who pays for the services of another	**knavery** the act of being mischievous or a rascal	**reputable** having a good character or standing
drunkard one who is continuously drunk	**progressive** making use of or interested in new ideas or methods	**sarcasm** the use of bitter statements that tell the opposite of what is true

and how could they match coppers with such artists as Phelps and Elder? You wanted them to be successful rascals; they were only unsuccessful ones—that's all the difference. There was only one boy ever raised in this borderland between **ruffianism** and civilization who didn't come to grief, and you hated Harvey Merrick more for winning out than you hated all the other boys who got under the wheels. Lord, Lord, how you did hate him! Phelps, here, is fond of saying that he could buy and sell us all out any time he's a mind to; but he knew Harve wouldn't have given a tinker's damn for his bank and all his cattlefarms put together; and a lack of appreciation, that way, goes hard with Phelps.

"Old Nimrod thinks Harve drank too much; and this from such as Nimrod and me!

"Brother Elder says Harve was too free with the old man's money—fell short in **filial** consideration, maybe. Well, we can all remember the very tone in which brother Elder swore his own father was a liar, in the county court; and we all know that the old man came out of that partnership with his son as bare as a sheared lamb. But maybe I'm getting personal, and I'd better be driving ahead at what I want to say."

The lawyer paused a moment, squared his heavy shoulders, and went on: "Harvey Merrick and I went to school together, back East. We were dead

filial relating to or befitting a son or daughter

ruffianism behavior that is rough, criminal, or bullying

in earnest, and we wanted you all to be proud of us some day. We meant to be great men. Even I, and I haven't lost my sense of humor, gentlemen, I meant to be a great man. I came back here to practice, and I found you didn't in the least want me to be a great man. You wanted me to be a **shrewd** lawyer—oh, yes! Our veteran here wanted me to get him an increase in **pension**, because he had dyspepsia; Phelps wanted a new county survey that would put the widow Wilson's little bottom farm inside his south line; Elder wanted to lend money at 5 percent a month, and get it collected; and Stark here wanted to wheedle old women up in Vermont into **investing** their **annuities** in real-estate **mortgages** that are not worth the paper they are written on. Oh, you needed me hard enough, and you'll go on needing me!

"Well, I came back here and became the damned **shyster** you wanted me to be. You pretend to have some sort of respect for me; and yet you'll stand up and throw mud at Harvey Merrick, whose soul you couldn't dirty and whose hands you couldn't tie. Oh, you're a **discriminating** lot of Christians! There have been times when the sight of Harvey's name in some Eastern paper has made me hang my head like a whipped dog; and again, times when I liked to think of him off there in the world, away from all this hog wallow, climbing the big, clean upgrade he'd set for himself.

"And we? Now that we've fought and lied and sweated and stolen, and hated as only the disappointed strugglers in a bitter, dead little Western town know how to do, what have we got to show for it? Harvey Merrick wouldn't have given one sunset over your marshes for all you've got put together, and you know it. . . ."

Dyspepsia is indigestion or the condition of having difficulty in digesting something.

The reader is given much information about Laird in this paragraph. Laird was jealous of Merrick, but he was also pleased at Merrick's success. What does this tell you about Laird's character?

annuity a sum of money paid yearly or at some regular period	**invest** to spend money in a way that earns more money	**shrewd** sharply intelligent; cunning; tricky
discriminating showing careful judgments or fine taste	**mortgage** a loan for property	**shyster** one who is dishonest or crooked, especially in practicing law or politics
	pension a fixed sum paid regularly to a person after retirement	

Directions Write the answers to these questions using complete sentences.

Comprehension: Identifying Facts

1. Who goes with the body of Harvey Merrick back to Merrick's hometown of Sand City for burial?

2. What is the meaning of the palm leaf on the coffin?

3. Which family members greet the casket at the house?

4. What had Merrick done for a living?

5. How old is Merrick when he dies?

6. How does Steavens know Merrick?

7. What does Steavens reveal about Merrick's feelings for Sand City?

8. What kind of lawyer is Jim Laird?

9. What bad things do people say about Merrick?

10. What does Laird reveal about the people of Sand City?

Comprehension: Understanding Main Ideas

11. Describe Merrick's mother. What kind of person is she?

12. What information can you gather about Sand City from this story?

13. The author never describes much about Steavens as a person. Why?

14. What bad things does Steavens experience in this story?

15. What kind of relationship does it seem Merrick and Steavens had before Merrick's death?

16. How does the reader know that Merrick was ashamed of his town and his family?

17. Some of the townspeople do not think Merrick was a success. What in this story proves that Merrick was a success?

18. What does Laird reveal about himself toward the end of the story?

19. What kind of message about small towns in America is there in this story?

20. What might be a better title for this story? Why?

Review Continued on Next Page

Understanding Literature: Character

Character is a very important part of a story. The main character is especially important. The main character is usually the one most seen and about whom the story is told. The main character in "The Sculptor's Funeral" is the sculptor, Harvey Merrick, who is dead.

21. How is Merrick still the main character in this story even though he is dead?

22. What kind of person was Merrick? Describe him and his personality as revealed in the story.

23. Aside from Merrick, who else is a main character in this story? Why?

24. Do you think all stories need a main character? Why or why not?

25. How does having a main character add to a story?

Critical Thinking

26. Do you believe that Merrick should have been ashamed of his town? Explain your answer.

27. How do you think young Steavens feels about the town and its people?

28. Explain what you think moves Laird to tell the townspeople what he thinks of them.

29. What do you think is the most memorable setting in this story? Why?

30. Explain a time in your own life when a group of people judged you or someone else unfairly as the people of Sand City judge Harvey Merrick. How did this event make you feel?

Writing on Your Own Choose a character from "The Sculptor's Funeral." Write a paragraph explaining who the character is, what the character is like, and how the character is important in the story. Add whether you liked or disliked the character and explain your opinion.

The Freshest Boy
F. Scott Fitzgerald

F. Scott Fitzgerald
1896–1940

Literary Term

semiautobiography a story based on a person's life written by that person, with some events changed

About the Author

F. Scott Fitzgerald was born in St. Paul, Minnesota, to a family with some wealth. Fitzgerald went to boarding school with students of greater wealth than himself. For this reason, he had trouble fitting in. He later attended Princeton University. Then he joined the army to serve in World War I. He never went overseas. However, he did meet his future wife, Zelda. Later, he worked at an advertising agency in New York. There he began to write seriously. *This Side of Paradise*, published in 1920, was a great success.

The Fitzgeralds became a popular pair, but they lived expensively. Even though Fitzgerald was writing many stories and novels, the couple spent more money than they had. Money problems and the great stock market crash changed their lives for the worse.

Zelda had a mental breakdown in 1930 and went to a mental hospital. Fitzgerald's writing became less popular with the public. Drinking became his escape. He moved to Hollywood but was not well received there. In 1940 he died of a heart attack. Eight years later, Zelda burned to death in a fire at the mental hospital. Today, Fitzgerald is remembered for such major works as *The Great Gatsby* and *Tender Is the Night*.

About the Selection

"The Freshest Boy" is a **semiautobiography**. This is a story based on a person's life written by that person, though some events have been changed. This story describes the rich students that Fitzgerald looked up to in his childhood at a boarding school called St. Regis. Basil, the hero of the story, is not as wealthy as the other boys. He is unpopular. This story describes how Basil reaches an important decision in his life.

From
The Freshest Boy

PART 1

St. Regis School, Eastchester
November 18, 19—

Basil reads a letter that he writes to his mother. Why do you think he does not tell her the truth about life at St. Regis?

"DEAR MOTHER: There is not much to say today, but I thought I would write you about my allowance. All the boys have a bigger allowance than me, because there are a lot of little things I have to get, such as shoe laces, etc. School is still very nice and am having a fine time, but football is over and there is not much to do. I am going to New York this week to see a show. I do not know yet what it will be, but probably the Quacker Girl or little boy Blue as they are both very good. Dr. Bacon is very nice and there's a good phycission in the village. No more now as I have to study Algebra.

"Your Affectionate Son,

"Basil D. Lee."

As he put the letter in its envelope, a **wizened** little boy came into the deserted study hall where he sat and stood staring at him.

"Hello," said Basil, frowning.

"I been looking for you," said the little boy, slowly and **judicially**. "I looked all over—up in your room and out in the gym, and they said you probably might of sneaked off in here."

---

judicially in a manner that judges

wizened small and wrinkled

"What do you want?" Basil demanded.

"Hold your horses, Bossy."

Basil jumped to his feet. The little boy retreated a step.

"Go on, hit me!" he chirped nervously. "Go on, hit me, 'cause I'm just half your size—Bossy."

Basil winced. "You call me that again and I'll spank you."

"No, you won't spank me. Brick Wales said if you ever touched any of us—"

"But I never did touch any of you."

"Didn't you chase a lot of us one day and didn't Brick Wales—"

"Oh, what do you want?" Basil cried in desperation.

"Doctor Bacon wants you. They sent me after you and somebody said maybe you sneaked in here."

Basil dropped his letter in his pocket and walked out—the little boy and his **invective** following him through the door. He traversed a long corridor, muggy with that odor best described as the smell of stale caramels that is so peculiar to boys' schools, ascended a stairs and knocked at an unexceptional but **formidable** door.

Doctor Bacon was at his desk. He was a handsome, redheaded Episcopal clergyman of fifty whose original real interest in boys was now tempered by

formidable having qualities that arouse fear or dread

invective an insult; abusive language

the **flustered cynicism** which is the fate of all headmasters and settles on them like green mould. There were certain **preliminaries** before Basil was asked to sit down—gold-rimmed glasses had to be hoisted up from nowhere by a black cord and fixed on Basil to be sure that he was not an **imposter**; great masses of paper on the desk had to be shuffled through, not in search of anything but as a man nervously shuffles a pack of cards.

"I had a letter from your mother this morning—ah—Basil." The use of his first name had come to startle Basil. No one else in school had yet called him anything but Bossy or Lee. "She feels that your marks have been poor. I believe you have been sent here at a certain amount of—ah—sacrifice and she expects—"

Basil's spirit writhed with shame, not at his poor marks but that his financial **inadequacy** should be so bluntly stated. He knew that he was one of the poorest boys in a rich boys' school.

Perhaps some **dormant** sensibility in Doctor Bacon became aware of his discomfort; he shuffled through the papers once more and began on a new note.

"However, that was not what I sent for you about this afternoon. You applied last week for permission to go to New York on Saturday, to a **matinée**. Mr. Davis tells me that for almost the first time since school opened you will be off bounds tomorrow."

"Yes, sir."

"That is not a good record. However, I would allow you to go to New York if it could be arranged. Unfortunately, no masters are available this Saturday."

Basil's mouth dropped ajar. "Why, I—why, Doctor Bacon, I know two parties that are going. Couldn't I go with one of them?"

Here Doctor Bacon reveals that Basil's family has had to give up a lot by spending much money to send Basil to St. Regis, a private school in which parents pay money for students to attend.

Off bounds refers to being off school grounds. Since school began, Basil had not been allowed off bounds because he was being punished for breaking school rules. What does this tell you about Basil?

cynicism a view that people are encouraged by self-interest; the state of being deeply distrustful of others	**imposter** one who pretends to be someone else	**preliminaries** events occurring before a main event
dormant inactive	**inadequacy** a lacking	
flustered upset	**matinée** a musical or dramatic performance held in the daytime	

Doctor Bacon ran through all his papers quickly. "Unfortunately, one is composed of slightly older boys and the other group made arrangements some weeks ago."

"How about the party that's going to the *Quaker Girl* with Mr. Dunn?"

"It's that party I speak of. They feel that their arrangements are complete and they have purchased seats together."

Suddenly Basil understood. At the look in his eye Doctor Bacon went on hurriedly:

"There's perhaps one thing I can do. Of course there must be several boys in the party so that the expenses of the master can be divided up among all. If you can find two other boys who would like to make up a party, and let me have their names by five o'clock, I'll send Mr. Rooney with you."

"Thank you," Basil said.

Doctor Bacon hesitated. Beneath the cynical **incrustations** of many years an instinct stirred to look into the unusual case of this boy and find out what made him the most **detested** boy in school. Among boys and masters there seemed to exist an **extraordinary** hostility toward him, and though Doctor Bacon had dealt with many sorts of schoolboy crimes, he had neither by himself nor with the aid of trusted sixth-formers been able to lay his hands on its underlying cause. It was probably no single thing, but a combination of things; it was most probably one of those **intangible** questions of personality. Yet he remembered that when he first saw Basil he had considered him unusually **prepossessing**.

He sighed. Sometimes these things worked themselves out. He wasn't one to rush in clumsily. "Let us have a better report to send home next month, Basil."

"Yes, sir."

detested extremely disliked	**incrustation** habits or opinions that have become a deep part of someone or something	**intangible** not able to be perceived or not real
extraordinary beyond what is usual		**prepossessing** tending to please or create a good impression

Basil ran quickly downstairs to the recreation room. It was Wednesday and most of the boys had already gone into the village of Eastchester, whither Basil, who was still on bounds, was forbidden to follow. When he looked at those still scattered about the pool tables and piano, he saw that it was going to be difficult to get anyone to go with him at all. For Basil was quite conscious that he was the most unpopular boy at school.

It had begun almost immediately. One day, less than a **fortnight** after he came, a crowd of the smaller boys, perhaps urged on to it, gathered suddenly around him and began calling him Bossy. Within the next week he had two fights, and both times the crowd was **vehemently** and **eloquently** with the other boy. Soon after, when he was merely shoving **indiscriminately**, like every one else, to get into the dining room, Carver, the captain of the football team, turned about and, seizing him by the back of the neck, held him and dressed him down **savagely**. He joined a group innocently at the piano and was told, "Go on away. We don't want you around."

After a month he began to realize the full extent of his unpopularity. It shocked him. One day after a particularly bitter **humiliation** he went up to his room and cried. He tried to keep out of the way for a while, but it didn't help. He was accused of sneaking off here and there, as if bent on a series of **nefarious** errands. Puzzled and wretched, he looked at his face in the glass, trying to discover there the secret of their dislike—in the expression of his eyes, his smile.

He saw now that in certain ways he had erred at the outset—he had boasted, he had been considered yellow at football, he had pointed out people's mistakes to them, he had shown off his rather extraordinary fund of general

What are the other students at St. Regis like?

| **eloquently** movingly; with very effective words | **humiliation** extreme shame and embarrassment | **nefarious** very wicked or evil |
| **fortnight** a period of two weeks | **indiscriminately** without purpose | **savagely** fiercely
vehemently forcefully |

information in class. But he had tried to do better and couldn't understand his failure to **atone**. It must be too late. He was queered forever.

He had, indeed, become the **scapegoat**, the immediate villain, the sponge which absorbed all **malice** and irritability abroad—just as the most frightened person in a party seems to absorb all the others' fear, seems to be afraid for them all. His situation was not helped by the fact, obvious to all, that the supreme self-confidence with which he had come to St. Regis in September was thoroughly broken. Boys taunted him with **impunity** who would not have dared raise their voices to him several months before.

This trip to New York had come to mean everything to him—**surcease** from the misery of his daily life as well as a glimpse into the long-awaited heaven of romance. Its postponement for week after week due to his sins—he was constantly caught reading after lights, for example, driven by his wretchedness into such **vicarious** escapes from reality— had deepened his longing until it was a burning hunger. It was unbearable that he should not go, and he told over the short list of those whom he might get to accompany him. The possibilities were Fat Gaspar, Treadway, and Bugs Brown. A quick journey to their rooms showed that they had all **availed** themselves of the Wednesday permission to go into Eastchester for the afternoon.

Basil did not hesitate. He had until five o'clock and his only chance was to go after them. It was not the first time he had broken bounds, though the last attempt had ended in disaster and an extension of his confinement. In his room, he put on a heavy sweater—an overcoat was a betrayal of intent—replaced his jacket over it and hid a cap in his back pocket. Then he went downstairs and with an elaborately

Here Basil admits that he has not acted right in the past and it has made him unpopular. He believes that he is unable to correct this problem.

Why is the trip to New York so important to Basil?

atone to make up for offenses or injuries

avail to make use of

impunity freedom from punishment, harm, or loss

malice ill will

scapegoat one that bears the blame for others

surcease a brief rest or break from something

vicarious experienced through imagination

careless whistle struck out across the lawn for the gymnasium. Once there, he stood for a while as if looking in the windows, first the one close to the walk, then one near the corner of the building. From here he moved quickly, but not too quickly, into a grove of lilacs. Then he dashed around the corner, down a long stretch of lawn that was blind from all windows and, parting the strands of a wire fence, crawled through and stood upon the grounds of a neighboring estate. For the moment he was free. He put on his cap against the chilly November wind, and set out along the half-mile road to town.

Eastchester was a suburban farming community, with a small shoe factory. The institutions which **pandered** to the factory workers were the ones **patronized** by the boys—a movie house, a quick-lunch wagon on wheels known as the Dog, and the Bostonian Candy Kitchen. Basil tried the Dog first and happened immediately upon a prospect.

This was Bugs Brown, a **hysterical** boy, subject to fits and strenuously avoided. Years later he became a brilliant lawyer, but at that time he was considered by the boys of St. Regis to be a typical **lunatic** because of his peculiar series of sounds with which he **assuaged** his nervousness all day long.

He **consorted** with boys younger than himself, who were without the **prejudices** of their elders, and was in the company of several when Basil came in.

"Who-ee!" he cried. "Ee-ee-ee!" He put his hand over his mouth and bounced it quickly, making a wah-wah-wah sound. "It's Bossy Lee! It's Bossy Lee! It's Boss-Boss-Boss-Boss-Bossy Lee!"

"Wait a minute, Bugs," said Basil anxiously, half afraid that Bugs would go finally crazy before he could persuade him to

Here Basil sneaks off school grounds to try to find some boys to agree to go to New York with him.

assuage to satisfy; to ease	**lunatic** an insane person	**patronize** to be a regular customer
consort to keep company with	**pander** to offer things that meet the desires of others	**prejudice** a negative view not based on fair reasons or enough information
hysterical very excitable		

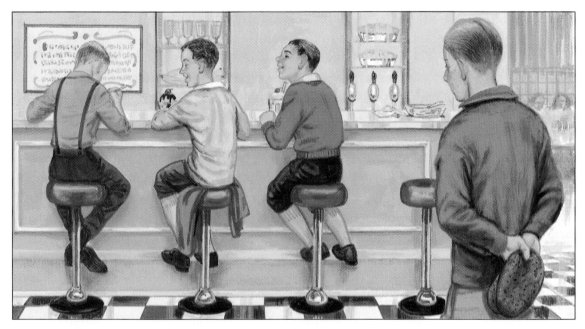

come to town. "Say, Bugs, listen. Don't, Bugs—wait a minute. Can you come up to New York Saturday afternoon?"

"Whee-ee-ee!" cried Bugs to Basil's distress. "Whee-ee-ee!"

"Honestly, Bugs, tell me, can you? We could go up together if you could go."

"I've got to see a doctor," said Bugs, suddenly calm. "He wants to see how crazy I am."

"Can't you have him see about it some other day?" said Basil without humor.

"Whee-ee-ee!" cried Bugs.

"All right then," said Basil hastily. "Have you seen Fat Gaspar in town?"

Bugs was lost in shrill noise, but someone had seen Fat; Basil was directed to the Bostonian Candy Kitchen.

This was a **gaudy** paradise of cheap sugar. Its odor, heavy and sickly and calculated to bring out a sticky sweat upon an adult's palms, hung **suffocatingly** over the whole vicinity and met one like a strong moral **dissuasion** at the door. Inside, beneath a pattern of flies, material as black point lace, a line

dissuasion the act of turning someone away by some means	**gaudy** flashy; dazzling	**suffocatingly** uncomfortably lacking fresh air

of boys sat eating heavy dinners of banana splits, maple nut, and chocolate marshmallow nut sundaes. Basil found Fat Gaspar at a table on the side.

Fat Gaspar was at once Basil's most unlikely and most **ambitious quest**. He was considered a nice fellow—in fact he was so pleasant that he had been courteous to Basil and had spoken to him politely all fall. Basil realized that he was like that to everyone, yet it was just possible that Fat liked him, as people used to in the past, and he was driven desperately to take a chance. But it was undoubtedly a **presumption**, and as he approached the table and saw the stiffened faces which the other two boys turned toward him, Basil's hope **diminished**.

"Say, Fat—" he said, and hesitated. Then he burst forth suddenly. "I'm on bounds, but I ran off because I had to see you. Doctor Bacon told me I could go to New York Saturday if I could get two other boys to go. I asked Bugs Brown and he couldn't go, and I thought I'd ask you."

He broke off, furiously embarrassed, and waited. Suddenly the two boys with Fat burst into a shout of laughter.

"Bugs wasn't crazy enough!"

Fat Gaspar hesitated. He couldn't go to New York Saturday and ordinarily he would have refused without offending. He had nothing against Basil; nor, indeed, against anybody; but boys have only a certain resistance to public opinion and he was influenced by the **contemptuous** laughter of the others.

"I don't want to go," he said indifferently. "Why do you want to ask *me*?"

Then, half in shame, he gave a **deprecatory** little laugh and bent over his ice cream.

"I just thought I'd ask you," said Basil.

Turning quickly away, he went to the counter and in a hollow and unfamiliar voice ordered a strawberry sundae. He ate it mechanically, hearing occasional whispers and snickers

Basil is unsure whether Fat Gaspar will agree to go to New York. Fat is a nice boy, but Basil worries that Fat will not go with him because the other two boys will look down on Fat for agreeing.

Here Fat Gaspar is afraid of being teased by the other boys. What is the result of Fat's fears?

ambitious difficult	**deprecatory** disapproving	**presumption** an action that goes beyond what is right or proper
contemptuous expressing disgust	**diminish** to decrease	**quest** an act of seeking; a pursuit or search

from the table behind. Still in a daze, he started to walk out without paying his check, but the clerk called him back and he was conscious of more **derisive** laughter.

For a moment he hesitated whether to go back to the table and hit one of those boys in the face, but he saw nothing to be gained. They would say the truth—that he had done it because he couldn't get anybody to go to New York. Clenching his fists with **impotent** rage, he walked from the store.

He came immediately upon his third prospect, Treadway. Treadway had entered St. Regis late in the year and had been put in to room with Basil the week before. The fact that Treadway hadn't witnessed his humiliations of the autumn encouraged Basil to behave naturally toward him, and their relations had been, if not **intimate**, at least **tranquil**.

"Hey, Treadway," he cried, still excited from the affair in the Bostonian, "can you come up to New York to a show Saturday afternoon?"

He stopped, realizing that Treadway was in the company of Brick Wales, a boy he had had a fight with and one of his bitterest enemies. Looking from one to the other, Basil saw a look of impatience in Treadway's face and a faraway expression in Brick Wales', and he realized what must have been happening. Treadway, making his way into the life of the school, had just been **enlightened** as to the status of his roommate. Like Fat Gaspar, rather than **acknowledge** himself **eligible** to such an intimate request, he preferred to cut their friendly relations short.

"Not on your life," he said briefly. "So long." The two walked past him into the candy kitchen.

Treadway's response to Basil is mean. Do you think Treadway really means what he says?

Had these slights, so much the bitterer for their lack of passion, been visited upon Basil in September, they would have been unbearable. But since then he had developed a shell of hardness which, while it did not add to his attractiveness,

acknowledge to admit	**enlighten** to be informed	**intimate** close
derisive expressing ridicule		**tranquil** calm
eligible qualifying for	**impotent** helpless; powerless	

spared him certain delicacies of torture. In misery enough, and despair and self-pity, he went the other way along the street for a little distance until he could control the violent **contortions** of his face. Then, taking a roundabout route, he started back to school.

He reached the adjoining estate, intending to go back the way he had come. Half-way through a hedge, he heard footsteps approaching along the sidewalk and stood motionless, fearing the **proximity** of masters. Their voices grew nearer and louder; before he knew it he was listening with horrified fascination:

"—so, after he tried Bugs Brown, the poor nut asked Fat Gaspar to go with him and Fat said, 'What do you ask me for?' It serves him right if he couldn't get anybody at all."

It was the dismal but triumphant voice of Lewis Crum. . . .

Basil is shocked to hear people talk in such a way about him. What does this scene tell you about St. Regis?

PART 2

How does a letter and an overheard conversation affect Basil in New York?

Doctor Bacon, sensing Basil's **predicament** and perhaps the **extremity** of his misery, arranged it that he should go into New York, after all. He went in the company of Mr. Rooney, the football coach and history teacher. At twenty Mr. Rooney had hesitated for some time between joining the police force and having his way paid through a small New England college; in fact he was a hard specimen and Doctor Bacon was planning to get rid of him at Christmas. Mr. Rooney's contempt for Basil was founded on the latter's **ambiguous** and unreliable conduct on the football field during the past season—he had consented to take him to New York for reasons of his own.

Basil sat meekly beside him on the train, glancing past Mr. Rooney's bulky body at the Sound and the fallow fields of Westchester County. Mr. Rooney finished his newspaper,

ambiguous difficult to understand	**extremity** intense degree	**proximity** closeness
contortion a violent twisting	**predicament** a difficult or trying situation	

folded it up and sank into a moody silence. He had eaten a large breakfast and the **exigencies** of time had not allowed him to work if off with exercise. He remembered that Basil was a fresh boy, and it was time he did something fresh and could be called to account. This reproachless silence annoyed him.

"Lee," he said suddenly, with a thinly assumed air of friendly interest, "why don't you get wise to yourself?"

"What sir?" Basil was startled from his excited trance of this morning.

"I said why don't you get wise to yourself?" said Mr. Rooney in a somewhat violent tone. "Do you want to be the butt of the school all your time here?"

"No, I don't," Basil was chilled. Couldn't all this be left behind for just one day?

"You oughtn't to get so fresh all the time. A couple of times in history class I could just about have broken your neck." Basil could think of no appropriate answer. "Then out playing football," continued Mr. Rooney "—you didn't have any nerve. You could play better than a lot of 'em when you wanted, like that day against the Pomfret seconds, but you lost your nerve."

"I shouldn't have tried for the second team," said Basil. "I was too light. I should have stayed on the third."

"You were yellow, that was all the trouble. You ought to get wise to yourself. In class, you're always thinking of something else. If you don't study, you'll never get to college."

"I'm the youngest boy in the fifth form," Basil said rashly.

"You think you're pretty bright, don't you?" He eyed Basil **ferociously**. Then something seemed to occur to him that changed his attitude and they rode for a while in silence. When the train began to run through the thickly clustered communities near New York, he spoke again in a milder voice and with an air of having considered the matter for a long time:

> Basil is called a "fresh boy" in this paragraph. The title of this story, "The Freshest Boy," refers to this paragraph. A fresh boy is a new student who does not fit in or is not liked.

exigency urgency   **ferociously** fiercely

"Lee, I'm going to trust you."

"Yes, sir."

"You go and get some lunch and then go on to your show. I've got some business of my own I got to attend to, and when I've finished I'll try to get to the show. If I can't, I'll anyhow meet you outside."

Basil's heart leaped up. "Yes, sir."

"I don't want you to open your mouth about this at school—I mean, about me doing some business of my own."

"No, sir."

"We'll see if you can keep your mouth shut for once," he said, making it fun. Then he added, on a note of moral sternness, "And no drinks, you understand that?"

"Oh, no, sir!" The idea shocked Basil. He had never tasted a drink, nor even **contemplated** the possibility, save the intangible and nonalcoholic champagne of his café dreams.

On the advice of Mr. Rooney he went for luncheon to the Manhattan Hotel, near the station, where he ordered a club sandwich, French fried potatoes, and a chocolate parfait. Out of the corner of his eye he watched the **nonchalant, debonair, blasé** New Yorkers at neighboring tables, investing them with a romance by which these possible fellow citizens of his from the Middle West lost nothing. School had fallen from him like a burden; it was no more than an unheeded **clamor**, faint and far away. He even delayed opening the letter from the morning's mail which he found in his pocket, because it was addressed to him at school.

He wanted another chocolate parfait, but being **reluctant** to bother the busy waiter any more, he opened the letter and spread it before him instead. It was from his mother:

Mr. Rooney does not want Basil to drink alcohol. Why do you think Mr. Rooney says this?

blasé showing a lack of concern; worldly	**contemplate** to think about	**nonchalant** showing a lack of concern
clamor a loud and steady noise	**debonair** lighthearted	**reluctant** unwilling

"Dear Basil: This is written in great haste, as I didn't want to frighten you by telegraphing. Grandfather is going abroad to take the waters and he wants you and me to come too. The idea is that you'll go to school at Grenoble or Montreux for the rest of the year and learn the languages and we'll be close by. That is, if you want to. I know how you like St. Regis and playing football and baseball, and of course there would be none of that; but on the other hand, it would be a nice change, even if it postponed your entering Yale by an extra year. So, as usual, I want you to do just as you like. We will be leaving home almost as soon as you get this and will come to the Waldorf in New York, where you can come in and see us for a few days, even if you decide to stay. Think it over, dear.

"With love to my dearest boy,

"Mother."

Basil got up from his chair with a dim idea of walking over to the Waldorf and having himself locked up safely until his mother came. Then, **impelled** to some gesture, he raised his voice and in one of his first basso notes called boomingly and without **reticence** for the waiter. No more St. Regis! No more St. Regis! He was almost strangling with happiness.

"Oh, gosh!" he cried to himself. "Oh, golly! Oh, gosh!, Oh, gosh!" No more Doctor Bacon and Mr. Rooney and Brick Wales and Fat Gaspar. No more Bugs Brown and on bounds and being called Bossy. He need no longer hate them, for they were impotent shadows in the stationary world that he was sliding away from, sliding past, waving his hand. "Good-by!" he pitied them. "Good-by!"

It required the **din** of Forty-second Street to sober his **maudlin** joy. With his hand on his purse to guard against the **omnipresent** pickpocket, he moved cautiously toward

"To take the waters" means to visit a health spa or resort. It was believed that bathing in mineral waters was good for one's health.

Why is Basil suddenly happy at this point in the story?

| **din** a loud continued noise | **maudlin** overly emotional | **reticence** restraint; reserve |
| **impel** to move someone or something to action | **omnipresent** present in all places at all times | |

Broadway. What a day! He would tell Mr. Rooney—why, he needn't ever go back! Or perhaps it would be better to go back and let them know what he was going to do, while they went on and on in the dismal, dreary round of school.

He found the theater and entered the lobby with its powdery **feminine** atmosphere of a matinée. As he took out his ticket, his gaze was caught and held by a sculptured **profile** a few feet away. It was that of a well-built blond young man of about twenty with a strong chin and direct gray eyes. Basil's brain spun wildly for a moment and then came to rest upon a name—more than a name—upon a legend, a sign in the sky. What a day! He had never seen the young man before, but from a thousand pictures he knew beyond the possibility of a doubt that it was Ted Fay, the Yale football captain, who had almost single-handed beaten Harvard and Princeton last fall. Basil felt a sort of **exquisite** pain. The profile turned away; the crowd revolved; the hero disappeared. But Basil would know all through the next hours that Ted Fay was here too.

In the rustling, whispering, sweet-smelling darkness of the theater he read the program. It was the show of all shows that he wanted to see, and until the curtain actually rose the program itself had a curious sacredness—a **prototype** of the thing itself. But when the curtain rose it became waste paper to be dropped carelessly to the floor. . . .

Outside again Basil walked up and down, considering. He would give Mr. Rooney half an hour. If, at the end of that time, he had not come out, he would go back to school. After all, Mr. Rooney had laid for him ever since football season— Basil was simply washing his hands of the whole affair, as in a day or so he would wash his hands of school.

He had made several turns up and down, when, glancing up an alley that ran beside the theater his eye was caught by

Why does the author refer to Ted Fay as "the profile"?

exquisite intense	**profile** a human head or face seen in a side view	**prototype** an original model on which something is patterned; a first example that shows the main features of a later type
feminine relating to females		

the sign, Stage Entrance. He could watch the actors come forth.

He waited. Women streamed by him, but those were the days before glorification and he took these drab people for wardrobe women or something. Then suddenly a girl came out and with her a man, and Basil turned and ran a few steps up the street as if afraid they would recognize him—and ran back, breathing as if with a heart attack—for the girl, a **radiant** little beauty of nineteen, was Her and the young man by her side was Ted Fay.

Arm in arm, they walked past him, and **irresistibly** Basil followed. As they walked, she leaned toward Ted Fay in a way that gave them a fascinating air of intimacy. They crossed Broadway and turned into the Knickerbocker Hotel, and twenty feet behind them Basil followed, in time to see them go into a long room set for afternoon tea. They sat at a table for two, spoke vaguely to a waiter, and then, alone at last, bent eagerly toward each other. Basil saw that Ted Fay was holding her gloved hand.

The tea room was separated only by a hedge of potted firs from the main corridor. Basil went along this to a lounge which was almost up against their table and sat down.

Her voice was low and faltering, less certain than it had been in the play, and very sad: "Of course I do, Ted." For a long time, as their conversation continued, she repeated "Of course I do" or "But I do, Ted." Ted Fay's remarks were too low for Basil to hear.

"—says next month, and he won't be put off any more.... I do in a way, Ted. It's hard to explain, but he's done everything for mother and me.... There's no use kidding myself. It was a foolproof part and any girl he gave it to was made right then and there.... He's been awfully thoughtful. He's done everything for me."

Basil's ears were sharpened by the intensity of his emotion; now he could hear Ted Fay's voice too:

irresistibly unable to resist	**radiant** marked by confidence or happiness; glowing

"And you say you love me."

"But don't you see I promised to marry him more than a year ago."

"Tell him the truth—that you love me. Ask him to let you off."

"This isn't musical comedy, Ted."

"That was a mean one," he said bitterly.

"I'm sorry, dear, Ted darling, but you're driving me crazy going on this way. You're making it so hard for me."

"I'm going to leave New Haven, anyhow."

"No, you're not. You're going to stay and play baseball this spring. Why, you're an ideal to all those boys! Why, if you—"

He laughed shortly. "You're a fine one to talk about ideals."

"Why not? I'm living up to my responsibility to Beltzman; you've got to make up your mind just like I have—that we can't have each other."

"Jerry! Think what you're doing! All my life, whenever I hear that waltz—"

Basil got to his feet and hurried down the corridor, through the lobby and out of the hotel. He was in a state of

Ted Fay and the woman are discussing their relationship. How do you know that this discussion is not a pleasant one?

wild emotional confusion. He did not understand all he had heard, but from his **clandestine** glimpse into the privacy of these two, with all the world that his short experience could conceive of at their feet, he had gathered that life for everybody was a struggle, sometimes magnificent from a distance, but always difficult and surprisingly simple and a little sad.

They would go on. Ted Fay would go back to Yale, put her picture in his bureau drawer and knock out home runs with the bases full this spring—at 8:30 the curtain would go up and She would miss something warm and young out of her life, something she had had this afternoon.

It was dark outside and Broadway was a blazing forest fire as Basil walked slowly along toward the point of brightest light. He looked up at the great intersecting planes of radiance with a vague sense of approval and possession. He would see it a lot now, lay his restless heart upon this greater restlessness of a nation—he would come whenever he could get off from school.

But that was all changed—he was going to Europe. Suddenly Basil realized that he wasn't going to Europe. He could not forego the molding of his own **destiny** just to **alleviate** a few months of pain. The conquest of the successive worlds of school, college and New York—why, that was his true dream that he had carried from boyhood into **adolescence**, and because of the jeers of a few boys he had been about to abandon it and run **ignominiously** up a back alley! He shivered violently, like a dog coming out of the water, and **simultaneously** he was reminded of Mr. Rooney.

A few minutes later he walked into the bar, past the quizzical eyes of the bartender and up to the table where Mr. Rooney still sat asleep. Basil shook him gently, then firmly. Mr. Rooney stirred and perceived Basil.

At this point in the story, Basil makes the decision not to leave St. Regis. Why?

adolescence the teen years	**clandestine** secret; hidden	**ignominiously** shamefully
alleviate to relieve; to lessen; to make more bearable	**destiny** a course of events that has already been determined	**simultaneously** at the same time

Mr. Rooney is drunk. Why does his earlier warning about not drinking become important here?

"G'wise to yourself." he muttered drowsily. "G'wise to yourself an' let me alone."

"I am wise to myself," said Basil. "Honest, I am wise to myself, Mr. Rooney. You got to come with me into the washroom and get cleaned up, and then you can sleep on the train again, Mr. Rooney. Come on, Mr. Rooney, please—"

PART 3

Do you think that life will improve for Basil?

It was a long hard time. Basil got on bounds again in December and wasn't free again until March. An **indulgent** mother had given him no habits of work and this was almost beyond the power of anything but life itself to remedy, but he made numberless new starts and failed and tried again.

He made friends with a new boy named Maplewood after Christmas, but they had a silly quarrel; and through the winter term, when a boys' school is shut in with itself and only partly assuaged from its natural savagery by indoor sports, Basil was snubbed and slighted a good deal for his real and imaginary sins, and he was much alone. But on the other hand, there was Ted Fay, and Rose of the Night on the phonograph—"All my life whenever I hear that waltz"—and the remembered lights of New York, and the thought of what he was going to do in football next autumn and the glamorous **mirage** of Yale and the hope of spring in the air.

Fat Gaspar and a few others were nice to him now. Once when he and Fat walked home together by accident from downtown they had a long talk about actresses—a talk that Basil was wise enough not to presume upon afterward. The smaller boys suddenly decided that they approved of him, and a master who had hitherto disliked him put his hand on his shoulder walking to a class one day. They would all forget eventually—maybe during the summer. There would be new fresh boys in September; he would have a clean start next year.

indulgent not strict   **mirage** a dream

One afternoon in February, playing basketball, a great thing happened. He and Brick Wales were at forward on the second team and in the fury of the **scrimmage** the gymnasium echoed with sharp slapping contacts and shrill cries.

"Here yar!"

"Bill! Bill!"

Basil had dribbled the ball down the court and Brick Wales, free, was crying for it.

"Here yar! Lee! Hey! Lee-y!"

Lee-y!

Basil flushed and made a poor pass. He had been called by a nickname. It was a poor **makeshift**, but it was something more than the stark bareness of his **surname** or a term of **derision**. Brick Wales went on playing, unconscious that he had done anything in particular or that he had contributed to the events by which another boy was saved from the army of the bitter, the selfish, . . . and the unhappy. It isn't given to us to know those rare moments when people are wide open and the lightest touch can wither or heal. A moment too late and we can never reach them any more in this world. They will not be cured by our most **efficacious** drugs or slain with our sharpest swords.

Lee-y! It could scarcely be pronounced. But Basil took it to bed with him that night, and thinking of it, holding it to him happily to the last, fell easily to sleep.

What new nickname has Basil been given? Why is this important?

derision ridicule	**makeshift** a crude substitute	**scrimmage** practice play
efficacious effective		**surname** a family name

The Freshest Boy
F. Scott Fitzgerald

Directions Write the answers to these questions using complete sentences.

Comprehension: Identifying Facts

1. Who is the headmaster of St. Regis School?

2. What boys does Basil ask to go to New York?

3. Why do the boys refuse to go with Basil to New York?

4. Who ends up going to New York with Basil?

5. What does Basil do while in New York?

6. What does the letter from Basil's mother tell him?

7. Describe the character of Ted Fay. Why does Basil like him so much?

8. What problem does Ted Fay face?

9. What does Mr. Rooney do while in New York?

10. What happens while playing basketball that makes Basil happy?

Comprehension: Understanding Main Ideas

11. Two letters appear in this story. One is from Basil to his mother and one is from the mother to Basil. Each one tells something important. Reread the information given in each letter. What facts do you learn immediately about Basil from his letter?

12. What facts do you learn about Basil and his mother from her letter?

13. What is Basil trying to hide in his letter to his mother?

14. Many of the students and teachers at St. Regis are not kind people. What evidence is there of this in this story?

15. Explain why it is so important to Basil that he visit New York.

16. Explain why the author includes so much of the story of Ted Fay and the beautiful actress.

17. The turning point for Basil comes when he leaves the hotel after listening to Ted and his girlfriend. What line shows the lesson that he learns from these people? How does this lesson affect his decision about leaving school and going to Europe?

18. Why is Mr. Rooney important in this story?

19. What evidence is there at the end of this story that Basil will succeed at St. Regis?

20. Why is this story titled "The Freshest Boy"?

Understanding Literature: Autobiography and Semiautobiography

An autobiography is the author's story of his or her own life. "The Freshest Boy" is a semiautobiography. It is based on the author's life, but some events have been changed. Reread the life of F. Scott Fitzgerald in the "About the Author" section to see how his own life is part of this story.

21. What is a semiautobiography?

22. How does a semiautobiography differ from an autobiography?

23. What character in this story do you think is Fitzgerald as a child?

24. What problems in this story do you think may have been based on problems Fitzgerald faced in his life?

25. Why do you think an author might want to write about his or her own life?

Critical Thinking

26. How do you think Basil's upbringing, especially his relationship with his mother, has caused some of his problems in making friends?

27. Is it possible for an unpopular student to become accepted? What steps would this student have to take?

28. Basil is the most unpopular student at the school. How is this story realistic?

29. Explain whether you think this story gives you a good idea about life in the early 1900s.

30. Do you believe that Basil will be more popular in the future? Explain your answer.

Writing on Your Own In "The Freshest Boy," the author wrote about events similar to those that took place in his own childhood. Think of an important event in your own life. Write about this event. Choose whether you want to write about it exactly as it happened (autobiography) or with some events, names, or places changed (semiautobiography). Write at least three paragraphs.

Poems
by Robert Frost

Robert Frost
1874–1963

Literary Terms

end rhyme a feature of a poem in which the last words of two lines rhyme with one another

rhyme scheme a pattern of end rhymes in a poem

About the Author

One of America's most popular poets was Robert Frost. He is often called the poet of New England. He was actually born in San Francisco in 1874. His father was a newspaper man and a political figure. When young Frost was ten, his father died. His mother moved the family to New Hampshire.

Frost attended Harvard and Dartmouth College. He did not graduate. He later taught school. His first poem was published in 1894. Most of his poems went unnoticed until 1913. Farming and teaching helped Frost make a living for himself and his new wife, his high school love. The two bought a large farm in New Hampshire. Their life on the farm gave Frost a background for his poetry.

A two-year trip to England brought him success. Back in America, Frost began to speak at colleges and to teach. He gave poetry readings. He received the Pulitzer Prize four times. Frost also received honorary college degrees. In 1960 Congress awarded him a gold medal for his poetry. He died in 1963.

Frost's well-known poems, other than those in this unit, include "Birches," "The Death of the Hired Man," "Stopping by Woods on a Snowy Evening," "The Road Not Taken," and "The Pasture."

About the Selections

The language of Frost's poetry sounds like normal talking. The poems are simple, but the ideas are deep and meaningful. Much of his poetry is about life in the country, the changing seasons, and New England. However, Frost's basic subject is not nature, but the drama of human life.

"A Time to Talk" and "Fire and Ice" each have a **rhyme scheme**. This is a pattern of **end rhymes** in a poem. An end rhyme is a feature of a poem in which the last words of two lines rhyme with one another.

Dodge's Mountain Irises Study, **Connie Hayes**

Mending Wall

Something there is that doesn't love a wall,
That sends the frozen-ground-swell under it,
And spills the upper boulders in the sun;
And makes gaps even two can pass abreast.
5 The work of hunters is another thing:
I have come after them and made repair
Where they have left not one stone on a stone,
But they would have the rabbit out of hiding,
To please the yelping dogs. The gaps I mean,
10 No one has seen them made or heard them made,
But at spring mending-time we find them there.
I let my neighbor know beyond the hill;
And on a day we meet to walk the line
And set the wall between us once again.
15 We keep the wall between us as we go.
To each the boulders that have fallen to each.
And some are loaves and some so nearly balls
We have to use a spell to make them balance:
'Stay where you are until our backs are turned!'

In this poem, two neighbors meet to repair a wall. Are these neighbors alike or different? What is the purpose of a wall?

20 We wear our fingers rough with handling them.
Oh, just another kind of outdoor game,
One on a side. It comes to little more:
There where it is we do not need the wall:
He is all pine and I am apple orchard.
25 My apple trees will never get across
And eat the cones under his pines, I tell him.
He only says, 'Good fences make good neighbors.'
Spring is the mischief in me, and I wonder
If I could put a notion in his head:
30 '*Why* do they make good neighbors? Isn't it
Where there are cows? But here there are no cows.
Before I built a wall I'd ask to know
What I was walling in or walling out,
And to whom I was like to give offense.
35 Something there is that doesn't love a wall,
That wants it down.' I could say **'Elves'** to him,
But it's not elves exactly, and I'd rather
He said it for himself. I see him there
Bringing a stone grasped firmly by the top
40 In each hand, like an old-stone savage armed.
He moves in darkness as it seems to me,
Not of woods only and the shade of trees.
He will not go behind his father's saying,
And he likes having thought of it so well
45 He says again, 'Good fences make good neighbors.'

elf a small often lively creature; a mischievous child

A Time to Talk

When a friend calls to me from the road
And slows his horse to a meaning walk,
I don't stand still and look around
On all the hills I haven't **hoed**,
5 And shout from where I am, 'What is it?'
No, not as there is a time to talk.
I thrust my hoe in the mellow ground,
Blade-end up and five feet tall,
And plod: I go up to the stone wall
10 For a friendly visit.

What is the rhyme
scheme of this poem?
Can you see a pattern?

Fire and Ice

Some say the world will end in fire,
Some say in ice.
3 From what I've tasted of desire
I hold with those who favor fire.
But if it had to perish twice,
6 I think I know enough of hate
To say that for destruction ice
Is also great
9 And would **suffice**.

How is fire like love and
hatred like ice? How
can both be harmful?

hoe to weed or thin with a
hoe, which is a tool with a
thin, flat blade on a long
handle

suffice to meet or satisfy a
need

301

Directions Write the answers to these questions using complete sentences.

Comprehension: Identifying Facts

"Mending Wall"

1. What happens to the wall each year during hunting season and winter?

2. What do the two owners of the wall do each spring?

3. What does the neighbor grow on his land? What does the poet grow on his land?

4. Who says and believes the line "Good fences make good neighbors"?

"A Time to Talk"

5. Who calls to the poet from the road?

6. What is the poet doing when he is interrupted?

7. What kind of visit will the two friends have?

"Fire and Ice"

8. What does the poet suggest will cause the end of the world?

9. Why does the poet "favor fire"?

10. What does the poet "know enough of"?

Comprehension: Understanding Main Ideas

"Mending Wall"

11. Lines 14 and 15 are important for understanding this poem. Explain why.

12. How does the poet feel about the saying "Good fences make good neighbors"?

13. Explain why the setting of this poem is important.

"A Time to Talk"

14. What does this poem suggest about the poet's daily life?

15. From this poem, what can you determine about the personality of the poet?

16. What comment about time and relationships is the poet suggesting?

"Fire and Ice"

17. The poet suggests that love and hate are two destructive forces in life. How does the title "Fire and Ice" represent love and hate?

18. How can hatred be destructive?

19. How can love be destructive?

20. Poems can be humorous, serious, or mysterious. What is the tone of this poem?

Understanding Literature: Rhyme Scheme

A rhyme scheme shows the pattern of rhyming words in a poem. To determine rhyme scheme, look at the last word of the first line of a poem. Label this word *a*. Any words at the end of other lines that rhyme with this word are also labeled *a*. The second rhyme is labeled *b*. The third rhyme is labeled *c*, and so on. For example, if three lines end in rhyming words, the rhyme scheme would be *a, a, a*. If the first and third lines rhyme but the second line does not, the rhyme scheme would be *a, b, a*. If none of the three lines rhyme, the rhyme scheme would be *a, b, c*.

21. Write down the rhyme scheme for "A Time to Talk."

22. Do you notice a pattern? Explain.

23. Write down the rhyme scheme for "Fire and Ice."

24. Do you notice a pattern? Explain.

25. What do you think a regular rhyme scheme adds to a poem?

Critical Thinking

26. Do you agree with the saying "Good fences make good neighbors" as mentioned in "Mending Wall"?

27. What do you think would be another good title for "Mending Wall"? Why?

28. What do you think would be another good title for "A Time to Talk"? Why?

29. Do you agree with the poet's view of life in "A Time to Talk"? Why or why not?

30. What do you think of the poem "Fire and Ice"? How does the poem make you feel?

Writing on Your Own Choose the poem by Robert Frost that you liked best. Write about why you liked the poem, how the poem made you feel, and what new ideas you gained from the poem. Comment on the writing style and the use of rhyme, mood, setting, and imagery.

Impulse
Conrad Aiken

Conrad Aiken

1889–1973

Literary Terms

plot the series of events in a story

setting the place and time in a story

stream of consciousness a technique that develops the plot by allowing the reader to see how and what the characters are thinking

About the Author

Conrad Aiken wrote many award-winning poems, short stories, and novels in his life. His works centered around good and evil. Aiken's interest in the inner workings of the mind make him much like another writer that you have read, Edgar Allan Poe.

Aiken was born in Savannah, Georgia, in 1889. During his childhood, he faced a horrible event. When he was ten, Aiken's father killed his mother and then killed himself. Young Aiken was sent to Massachusetts to live with relatives. He later attended Harvard and graduated in 1912. Then he worked as a newspaper reporter. He spent most of his life living and writing in his home on Cape Cod. A strong sense of New England can be found in his writing.

Many believe that the problems of Aiken's youth added to the dark side of much of his poetry and stories. His characters are constantly looking inside themselves to find answers.

About the Selection

"Impulse" looks at how the human mind works. The main character, Michael Lowes, is a failure in his life. His bills are unpaid, his job is poor, his wife and children are unhappy. Only bridge games with his friends give him a little pleasure. Then one day, Michael's one "impulse" completely changes his life.

This story is an example of **stream of consciousness** writing. This technique allows the reader to see how and what the characters are thinking. It can also help the **plot** develop. Plot is the series of events in a story. Throughout this story, the reader sees into the mind of Michael Lowes and sees events as he sees them. The reader also sees the many **settings** through Michael's eyes. Setting is the place and time in a story.

IMPULSE

Michael Lowes hummed as he shaved, amused by the face he saw—the **pallid**, **asymmetrical** face, with the right eye so much higher than the left, and its eyebrow so peculiarly arched, like a "v" turned upside down. Perhaps this day wouldn't be as bad as the last. In fact, he knew it wouldn't be, and that was why he hummed. This was the biweekly day of escape, when he would stay out for the evening, and play bridge with Hurwitz, Bryant, and Smith. Should he tell Dora at the breakfast table? No, better not. Particularly in view of last night's row about unpaid bills. And there would be more of them, probably, beside his plate. The rent. The coal. The doctor who had attended to the children. Jeez, what a life. Maybe it was time to do a new jump. And Dora was beginning to get restless again—

But he hummed, thinking of the bridge game. Not that he liked Hurwitz or Bryant or Smith—cheap fellows, really—mere pick-up acquaintances. But what could you do about making friends, when you were always hopping about from one place to another, looking for a living, and fate always against you! They were all right enough. Good enough for a little escape, a little party—and Hurwitz always provided good alcohol. Dinner at the Greek's, and then to Smith's room—yes. He would wait till late in the afternoon, and then telephone to Dora as if it had all come up suddenly. Hello, Dora—is that you, old girl? Yes, this is Michael—Smith has asked me to drop in for a hand of bridge—you know—so I'll just have a little snack in town. Home by the last car as usual. Yes. . . . Gooo-bye! . . .

And it all went off perfectly, too. Dora was quiet, at breakfast, but not **hostile**. The pile of bills was there, to be

> What is Michael's impulse? Who is responsible for it?

> Here the word *row* means an argument.

> The author tells much about Michael's life in this first paragraph. What descriptions are given?

asymmetrical not even or well balanced	**hostile** unfriendly	**pallid** pale

sure, but nothing was said about them. And while Dora was busy getting the kids ready for school, he managed to slip out, pretending that he thought it was later than it really was. Pretty neat, that! He hummed again, as he waited for the train. Telooralooraloo. Let the bills wait, damn them! A man couldn't do everything at once, could he, when bad luck hounded him everywhere? And if he could just get a little night off, now and then, a rest and change, a little **diversion**, what was the harm in that?

At half-past four he rang up Dora and broke the news to her. He wouldn't be home till late.

"Are you sure you'll be home at all?" she said, coolly.

That was Dora's idea of a joke. But if he could have foreseen—!

He met the others at the Greek restaurant, began with a couple of araks, which warmed him, then went on to red wine, bad olives, pilaf, and other **obscure** foods; and considerably later they all walked along Boylston Street to Smith's room. It was a cold night, the temperature below twenty, with a fine dry snow sifting the streets. But Smith's room was comfortably warm, he trotted out some gin and the Porto Rican cigars, showed them a new snapshot of Squiggles (his Revere Beach sweetheart), and then they settled down to a nice long cozy game of bridge.

It was during an **intermission**, when they all got up to stretch their legs and renew their drinks, that the talk started—Michael never could remember which one of them it was who had put in the first oar—about impulse. It might have been Hurwitz, who was in many ways the only **intellectual** one of the three, though hardly what you might call a highbrow. He had his queer curiosities, however, and the idea was just such as might occur to him. At any rate, it was he who developed the idea, and with **gusto**.

Here the reader learns that Dora is not happy about Michael's plan to play bridge with his friends.

An *arak* is a Middle Eastern drink. *Pilaf* is a Middle Eastern dish made of seasoned rice and often meat.

diversion something that distracts the mind and amuses	**gusto** enthusiastic enjoyment or appreciation	**intermission** a break
	intellectual well-educated or intelligent	**obscure** relatively unknown

"Sure," he said, "anybody might do it. Have you got impulses? Of course, you got impulses. How many times you think—suppose I do that? And you don't do it, because you know damn well if you do it you'll get arrested. You meet a man you **despise**—you want to spit in his eye. You see a girl you'd like to kiss—you want to kiss her. Or maybe just to squeeze her arm when she stands beside you in the street car. You know what I mean."

"Do I know what you *mean!*" sighed Smith. "I'll tell the world. I'll tell the cock-eyed world! . . ."

"You would," said Bryant. "And so would I."

"It would be easy," said Hurwitz, "to give in to it. You know what I mean? So simple. **Temptation** is too close. That girl you see is too damn good-looking—she stands too near you—you just put out your hand it touches her arm—maybe her leg—why worry? And you think, maybe if she don't like it I can make believe I didn't mean it."

"Like these fellows that slash fur coats with razor blades," said Michael. "Just impulse, in the beginning, and only later a habit."

"Sure. . . . And like these fellows that cut off braids of hair with scissors. They just feel like it and do it. . . . Or stealing."

"Stealing?" said Bryant.

"Sure. Why, I often feel like it. . . . I see a nice little thing right in front of me on a counter—you know, a nice little knife, or necktie, or a box of candy—quick, you put it in your pocket, and then go to the other counter, or the soda fountain for a drink. What would be more human? We all want things. Why not take them? Why not do them? And civilization is only skin-deep. . . ."

"That's right. Skin-deep," said Bryant.

"But if you were caught, by God!" said Smith, opening his eyes wide.

"*Who's* talking about getting caught? . . . *Who's* talking about doing it? It isn't that we do it, it's only that we *want* to

Recall that the title of this story is "Impulse." It is Hurwitz who begins to talk about what this means. An impulse is something that is done without thinking, based on a strong urge. Do you think there is such a thing as an impulse?

How does this paragraph reveal the ways that an impulse can be harmful?

despise to regard as of little worth or purpose	temptation something that causes one to act without the ability to resist

do it. Why, Christ, there's been times when I thought to hell with everything. I'll kiss that woman if it's the last thing I do."

"It might be," said Bryant.

Michael was astonished at this turn of the talk. He had often felt both these impulses. To know that this was a kind of **universal** human **inclination** came over him with something like relief.

Why does Michael feel relieved?

"Of *course*, everybody has those feelings," he said smiling. "I have them myself. . . . But suppose you *did* yield to them?"

"Well, we don't," said Hurwitz.

"I know—but suppose you did?"

Hurwitz shrugged his fat shoulders, **indifferently**.

"Oh, well," he said, "it would be bad business."

"Jesus, yes," said Smith, shuffling the cards.

"Oy," said Bryant.

The game was **resumed**, the glasses were refilled, pipes were lit, watches were looked at. Michael had to think of the last car from Sullivan Square, at eleven-fifty. But also he could not stop thinking of this strange idea. It was amusing. It was fascinating. Here was everyone wanting to steal—toothbrushes, or books—or to **caress** some fascinating stranger of a female in a subway train—the impulse everywhere—why not be a Columbus of the moral world and really do it? . . . He remembered stealing a conch-shell from the drawing room of a neighbor when he was ten—it had been one of the thrills of his life. He had popped it into his sailor blouse and borne it away with perfect **aplomb**. When, later, **suspicion** had been cast upon him, he had smashed the shell in his back yard. And often, when he had been looking at Parker's collection of stamps—the early Americans—

This paragraph is an example of stream of consciousness. The reader sees what Michael is thinking. In this case, Michael is daydreaming of his childhood.

aplomb complete self-confidence or self-assurance	**indifferently** in a way that shows something does not matter	**suspicion** the act of sensing that something is wrong or dangerous; doubt
caress to lightly stroke, rub, or pat	**resume** to return to or to begin again	**universal** recognized by all
inclination a natural way of tending to do something		

The game interrupted his **recollections**, and presently it was time for the usual night-cap. Bryant drove them to Park Street. Michael was a trifle tight, but not enough to be unsteady on his feet. He waved a cheery hand at Bryant and Hurwitz and began to trudge through the snow to the subway entrance. The lights on the snow were very beautiful. The Park Street Church was ringing, with its queer, soft quarter-bells, the half-hour. Plenty of time. Plenty of time. Time enough for a visit to the drugstore, and a hot chocolate—he could see the warm lights of the windows falling on the snowed sidewalk. He zigzagged across the street and entered.

And at once he was seized with a **conviction** that his real reason for entering the drugstore was not to get a hot chocolate—not at all! He was going to steal something. He was going to put the impulse to the test, and see whether (*one*) he could manage it with sufficient skill, and (*two*) whether theft gave him any real satisfaction. The drugstore was crowded with people who had just come from the theatre next door. They pushed three deep round the soda fountain, and the cashier's cage. At the back of the store, in the toilet and **prescription** department, there were not so many, but nevertheless enough to

conviction a strong belief

prescription a medicine ordered by a doctor

recollection a memory

Michael is thinking about stealing something in the drugstore. Why?

give him a fair chance. All the clerks were busy. His hands were in the side pockets of his overcoat—they were deep wide pockets and would serve **admirably**. A quick gesture over a table or counter, the object dropped in—

Oddly enough, he was not in the least excited: perhaps that was because of the gin. On the contrary, he was intensely amused; not to say delighted. He was smiling, as he walked slowly along the right-hand side of the store toward the back; edging his way amongst the people, with first one shoulder forward and then the other, while with a critical and **appraising** eye he examined the wares piled on the counters and on the stands in the middle of the floor. There were some extremely attractive scent-sprays or atomizers—but the dangling bulbs might be troublesome. There were stacks of boxed letter-paper. A basket full of clothes-brushes. Green hot-water bottles. Percolators—too large, and out of the question. A tray of multicolored toothbrushes, bottles of cologne, fountain pens—and then he experienced love at first sight. There could be no question that he had found his chosen victim. He gazed, fascinated, at the delicious object—a deluxe safety-razor set, of heavy gold, in a snakeskin box which was lined with red plush. . . .

Here Michael sees what he wants to steal: a razor set.

It wouldn't do, however, to stare at it too long—one of the clerks might notice. He observed quickly the exact position of the box—which was close to the edge of the glass counter— and prefigured with a quite **precise** mental picture the gesture with which he would **simultaneously** close it and remove it. Forefinger at the back—thumb in front—the box drawn forward and then slipped down toward the pocket—as he thought it out, the muscles in his forearm pleasurably contracted. He continued his slow progress round the store, past the prescription counter, past the candy counter; examined with some show of attention the display of cigarette lighters and blade sharpeners; and then, with a quick

admirably very well; perfectly	**appraising** studying something to determine worth or value	**precise** exact **simultaneously** at the same time

turn, went leisurely back to his victim. Everything was **propitious**. The whole section of counter was clear for the moment—there were neither customers nor clerks. He approached the counter, leaned over it as if to examine some little filigreed "compacts" at the back of the showcase, picking up one of them with his left hand, as he did so. He was thus leaning directly over the box; and it was the simplest thing in the world to clasp it as planned between thumb and forefinger of his other hand, to shut it softly, and to slide it downward to his pocket. It was over in an instant. He continued then for a moment to turn the compact case this way and that in the light, as if to see it sparkle. It sparkled very nicely. Then he put it back on the little pile of cases, turned, and approached the soda fountain—just as Hurwitz had suggested.

He was in the act of pressing forward in the crowd to ask for his hot chocolate when he felt a firm hand close round his elbow. He turned, and looked at a man in a slouch hat and dirty raincoat, with the collar turned up. The man was smiling in a very offensive way.

"I guess you thought that was pretty slick," he said in a low voice which nevertheless managed to **convey** the very **essence** of **venom** and hostility. "You come along with me, mister!"

Michael returned the smile **amiably**, but was a little frightened. His heart began to beat.

"I don't know what you're talking about," he said, still smiling.

"No, of course not!"

The man was walking toward the rear of the store, and was pulling Michael along with him, keeping a **paralyzingly** tight grip on his elbow. Michael was beginning to be angry, but also to be horrified. He thought of wrenching his arm free, but feared it would make a scene. Better not. He

Filigreed means patterned or ornamented.

Michael steals the razor set in this paragraph.

A man has noticed Michael stealing. What do you think will happen to Michael?

amiably agreeably	**paralyzingly** in a manner that makes something powerless	**venom** evil; ill will
convey to express; to explain		
essence a great or concentrated amount	**propitious** favorable; being of good fortune	

permitted himself to be urged **ignominiously** along the shop, through a gate in the rear counter, and into a small room at the back, where a clerk was measuring a yellow liquid into a bottle.

"Will you be so kind as to explain to me what this is all about?" he then said, with what **frigidity** of manner he could muster. But his voice shook a little. The man in the slouch hat paid no attention. He addressed the clerk instead, giving his head a quick backward jerk as he spoke.

"Get the manager in here," he said.

He smiled at Michael, with narrowed eyes, and Michael, hating him, but panic-stricken, smiled foolishly back at him.

"Now, look here—" he said.

But the manager had appeared, and the clerk; and events then happened with revolting and **nauseating** speed. Michael's hand was yanked violently from his pocket, the fatal snakeskin box was pulled out by the detective, and identified by the manager and the clerk. They both looked at Michael with a queer expression, in which astonishment, shame, and **contempt** were mixed with vague curiosity.

"Sure that's ours," said the manager, looking slowly at Michael.

" I saw him **pinch** it," said the detective. "What about it?" He again smiled offensively at Michael. "Anything to say?"

Did Michael really make a bet about stealing something? Why does he say what he says here?

"It was all a joke," said Michael, his face feeling very hot and flushed. "I made a kind of bet with some friends. . . . I can prove it. I can call them up for you."

The three men looked at him in silence, all three of them just faintly smiling, as if **incredulously**.

"Sure you can," said the detective, **urbanely**. "You can prove it in court. . . . Now come along with me, mister."

contempt a feeling of dislike and disgust toward someone or something	**ignominiously** shamefully	**pinch** to steal
	incredulously with disbelief	**urbanely** in a sophisticated, polite way
frigidity a lack of warmth or kindness	**nauseating** causing great disgust	

Michael was astounded at this **appalling** turn of events, but his brain still worked. Perhaps if he were to put it to this fellow as man to man, when they got outside? As he was thinking this, he was firmly conducted through a back door into a dark alley at the rear of the store. It had stopped snowing. A cold wind was blowing. But the world, which had looked so beautiful fifteen minutes before, had now lost its charm. They walked together down the alley in six inches of powdery snow, the detective holding Michael's arm with **affectionate** firmness.

"No use calling the wagon," he said. "We'll walk. It ain't far."

They walked along Tremont Street. And Michael couldn't help, even then, thinking what an extraordinary thing this was! Here were all these good people passing them, and little knowing that he, Michael Lowes, was a thief, a thief by accident, on his way to jail. It seemed so absurd as hardly to be worth speaking of! And suppose they shouldn't believe him? This notion made him shiver. But it wasn't possible— no, it wasn't possible. As soon as he had told his story, and called up Hurwitz and Bryant and Smith, it would all be laughed off. Yes, laughed off.

> Does Michael believe that he has done anything wrong?

He began telling the detective about it: how they had discussed such impulses over a game of bridge. Just a friendly game, and they had joked about it and then, just to see what would happen, he had done it. What was it that made his voice sound so insincere, so hollow? The detective neither slackened his pace nor turned his head. His business-like grimness was alarming. Michael felt that he was paying no attention at all; and, moreover, it occurred to him that this kind of lowbrow official might not even understand such a thing. . . . He decided to try the **sentimental**.

"And good Lord, man, there's my wife waiting for me—!"

"Oh, sure, and the kids too."

"Yes, and the kids!"

---

affectionate careful; kindly; tender

appalling inspiring horror, dismay, or disgust

sentimental emotional or focused on feelings

The detective gave a quick leer over the collar of his dirty raincoat.

"And no Santy Claus *this* year," he said.

Michael saw that it was hopeless. He was wasting his time.

"I can see it's no use talking to you," he said stiffly. "You're so used to dealing with criminals that you think all mankind is criminal, ex post facto."

"Sure."

Arrived at the station, and presented without decorum to the lieutenant at the desk, Michael tried again. Something in the faces of the lieutenant and the sergeant, as he told his story, made it at once apparent that there was going to be trouble. They obviously didn't believe him—not for a moment. But after consultation, they agreed to call up Bryant and Hurwitz and Smith, and to make **inquiries**. The sergeant went off to do this, while Michael sat on a wooden bench. Fifteen minutes passed, during which the clock ticked and the lieutenant wrote slowly in a book, using a blotter very frequently. A clerk had been **dispatched**, also, to look up Michael's record, if any. This gentleman came back first, and reported that there was nothing. The lieutenant scarcely looked up from his book, and went on writing. The first serious blow then fell. The sergeant, reporting, said that he hadn't been able to get Smith (of course—Michael thought—he's off somewhere with Squiggles) but had got Hurwitz and Bryant. Both of them denied that there had been any bet. They both seemed nervous, as far as he could make out over the phone. They said they didn't know Lowes well, were acquaintances of his, and made it clear that they didn't want to be mixed up in anything. Hurwitz had added that he knew Lowes was hard up.

At this, Michael jumped to his feet, feeling as if the blood would burst out of his face.

Ex post facto is a Latin phrase meaning after the fact or done afterward.

Decorum means polite behavior or orderliness.

Why do Hurwitz and Bryant not help out Michael by telling the police about their discussion about impulse?

dispatch to send off on official business	**inquiry** a request for information; an examination of facts

"The damned liars!" he shouted. "The bloody liars! By God—!"

"Take him away," said the lieutenant, lifting his eyebrows, and making a motion with his pen.

Michael lay awake all night in his cell, after talking for five minutes with Dora on the telephone. Something in Dora's cool voice had frightened him more than anything else.

And when Dora came to talk to him the next morning at nine o'clock, his alarm proved to be well-founded. Dora was cold, **detached, deliberate**. She was not at all what he had hoped she might be—sympathetic and helpful. She didn't volunteer to get a lawyer, or in fact to do anything—and when she listened quietly to his story, it seemed to him that she had the appearance of a person listening to a very

deliberate characterized by careful thought; slow or unhurried

detached cool; distant

What kind of person is Dora? Do Dora and Michael seem have a strong marriage?

improbable lie. Again, as he narrated the perfectly simple **episode**—the discussion of "impulse" at the bridge game, the drinks, and the absurd tipsy desire to try a harmless little experiment—again, as when he talked to the store detective, he heard his own voice becoming hollow and insincere. It was exactly as if he knew himself to be guilty. His throat grew dry, he began to falter, to lose his thread, to use the wrong words. When he stopped speaking finally, Dora was silent.

"Well, say something!" he said angrily, after a moment. "Don't just stare at me. I'm not a criminal!"

"I'll get a lawyer for you," she answered, "but that's all I can do."

"Look here, Dora—you don't mean you—"

He looked at her incredulously. It wasn't possible that she really thought him a thief? And suddenly, as he looked at her, he realized how long it was since he had really known this woman. They had drifted apart. She was embittered, that was it—embittered by his non-success. All this time she had slowly been laying up a reserve of resentment. She had resented his inability to make money for the children, the little dishonesties they had had to commit in the matter of unpaid bills, the humiliations of duns, the too-frequent removals from town to town—she had more than once said to him, it was true, that because of all this she had never had any friends—and she had resented, he knew, his gay little parties with Hurwitz and Bryant and Smith, implying a little that they were an **extravagance** which was to say the least **inconsiderate**. Perhaps they *had* been. But was a man to have no **indulgences**? . . .

A *dun* is a demand for payment of a bill.

"Perhaps we had better not go into that," she said.

"Good Lord—you don't believe me!"

"I'll get the lawyer—though I don't know where the fees are to come from. Our bank account is down to seventy-seven dollars. The rent is due a week from today. You've got some

| **episode** a story or a incident | **improbable** unlikely | **indulgence** something that pampers or spoils |
| **extravagance** an expensive event | **inconsiderate** not thinking about or caring for the welfare of others | |

salary coming, of course, but I don't want to touch my own savings, naturally, because the children and I may need them."

Here Dora reveals that she has money saved. Why do you think she is unwilling to use it to help Michael?

To be sure. Perfectly just. Women and children first. Michael thought these things bitterly, but refrained from saying them. He gazed at this queer cold little female with intense curiosity. It was simply extraordinary—simply astonishing. Here she was, seven years his wife, he thought he knew her inside and out, every quirk of her handwriting, **inflection** of voice; her **passion** for strawberries, her ridiculous way of singing; the brown moles on her shoulder, the extreme smallness of her feet and toes, her dislike of silk underwear. Her special voice at the telephone, too—that rather chilly **abruptness**, which had always surprised him, as if she might be a much harder woman than he thought her to be. And the queer **sinuous** cat-like rhythm with which she always combed her hair before the mirror at night, before going to bed—with her head tossing to one side, and one knee advanced to touch the chest of drawers. He knew all these things, which nobody else knew, and nevertheless, now, they amounted to nothing. The woman herself stood before him as **opaque** as a wall.

"Of course," he said, "you'd better keep your own savings." His voice was dull. "And you'll, of course, look up Hurwitz and the others? They'll appear, I'm sure, and it will be the most important evidence. In fact, *the* evidence."

"I'll ring them up, Michael." was all she said, and with that she turned quickly on her heel and went away. . . .

Michael felt doom closing in upon him; his wits went round in circles; he was in a constant sweat. It wasn't possible that he was going to be betrayed? It wasn't possible! He assured himself of this. He walked back and forth, rubbing his hands together, he kept pulling out his watch to see what time it was. Five minutes gone. Another five minutes gone. Damnation, if this lasted too long, this **confounded** business,

abruptness changing without warning	**inflection** a change in pitch or loudness	**passion** an intense feeling or liking
confounded confused; unfortunate	**opaque** stubborn; thick-headed; hard to understand	**sinuous** marked by strong bending movements

Michael's lawyer tells Michael that Hurwitz, Bryant, and Smith do not want to be part of Michael's trial. The men fear that coming to Michael's defense will make them look bad. Michael's lawyer explains that if these men don't tell what they know, Michael will not win in court.

he'd lose his job. If it got into the papers, he might lose it anyway. And suppose it was true that Hurwitz and Bryant had said what they said—maybe they were afraid of losing their jobs too. Maybe that was it! Good God. . . .

This suspicion was confirmed, when, hours later, the lawyer came to see him. He reported that Hurwitz, Bryant, and Smith had all three refused flatly to be mixed up in the business. They were all afraid of the effects of the **publicity**. If **subpoenaed**, they said, they would state that they had known Lowes only a short time, had thought him a little **eccentric**, and knew him to be hard up. Obviously—and the little lawyer picked his teeth with the point of his pencil—they could not be summoned. It would be fatal.

The Judge, not unnaturally perhaps, decided that there was a perfectly clear case. There couldn't be the shadow of a doubt that his man had deliberately stolen an article from the counter of So-and-so's drugstore. The prisoner had stubbornly maintained that it was a result of a kind of bet with some friends, but these friends had refused to give **testimony** in his behalf. Even his wife's testimony—that he had never done such a thing before—had seemed rather half-hearted; and she had admitted, moreover, that Lowes was unsteady, and that they were always living in a state of something like poverty. Prisoner, further, had once or twice jumped his rent and had left behind him in Somerville unpaid debts of considerable size. He was a college man, a man of **exceptional** education and origin, and ought to have known better. His general character might be good enough, but as against all this, here was a perfectly clear case of theft, and a perfectly clear **motive**. The prisoner was sentenced to three months in the house of correction.

Here Michael loses his court case. He will have to go to jail for three months.

eccentric strange; unusual; different	**publicity** gaining public attention	**testimony** an oral explanation of facts in a court by a witness
exceptional better than average	**subpoena** to command one to appear in court	
motive a reason for committing a crime		

By this time, Michael was in a state of complete **stupor**. He sat in the box and stared blankly at Dora who sat very quietly in the second row, as if she were a stranger. She was looking back at him, with her white face turned a little to one side, as if she too had never seen him before, and were wondering what sort of people criminals might be. Human? Subhuman? She lowered her eyes after a moment, and before she had looked up again, Michael had been touched on the arm and led stumbling out of the courtroom. He thought she would of course come to say goodbye to him, but even in this he was mistaken; she left without a word.

And when he did finally hear from her, after a week, it was in a very brief note.

"Michael," it said, "I'm sorry, but I can't bring up the children with a criminal for a father, so I'm taking proceedings for a divorce. This is the last straw. It was bad enough to have you always out of work and to have to slave night and day to keep bread in the children's mouths. But this is too much, to have disgrace into the bargain. As it is, we'll have to move right away, for the schoolchildren have sent Dolly and Mary home crying three times already. I'm sorry, and you know how fond I was of you at the beginning, but you've had your chance. You won't hear from me again. You've always been a good sport, and generous, and I hope you'll make this occasion no exception, and refrain from contesting the divorce. Goodbye—Dora."

Michael held the letter in his hands, unseeing, and tears came into his eyes. He dropped his face against the sheet of notepaper, and rubbed his forehead to and fro across it. . . . Little Dolly! . . . Little Mary! . . . Of course. This was what life was. It was just as meaningless and ridiculous as this; a monstrous joke; a huge injustice. You couldn't trust anybody, not even your wife, not even your best friends. You went on a little **lark**, and they sent you to prison for it, and your friends lied about you, and your wife left you. . . .

Michael's children, Dolly and Mary, are teased at school and sent home crying. The other schoolchildren tease Dolly and Mary because they know that Michael was caught stealing and sent to jail.

Is what happens to Michael really a "huge injustice"?

lark something done for fun or adventure; harmless fun	**stupor** daze; confusion

Contest it? Should he contest the divorce? What was the use? There was the plain fact: that he had been **convicted** for stealing. No one had believed his story of doing it in fun, after a few drinks; the divorce court would be no exception. He dropped the letter to the floor and turned his heel on it, slowly and bitterly. Good riddance—good riddance! Let them all go to hell. He would show them. He would go west, when he came out—get rich, clear his name somehow. . . . But how?

He sat down on the edge of his bed and thought of Chicago. He thought of his childhood there, the Lake Shore Drive, Winnetka, the trip to Niagara Falls with his mother. He could hear the Falls now. He remembered the Fourth of July on the boat; the crowded examination room at college; the time he had broken his leg in baseball, when he was fourteen; and the stamp collection which he had lost at school. He remembered his mother always saying, "Michael, you *must* learn to be orderly"; and the little boy who had died of scarlet fever next door; and the pink conch-shell smashed in the back yard. His whole life seemed to be composed of such **trivial** and **infinitely** charming little episodes as these; and as he thought of them, affectionately and with wonder, he assured himself once more that he had really been a good man. And now, had it all come to an end? It had all come foolishly to an end.

---

convict to find one guilty in a court of law

infinitely never ending

trivial of little worth or importance

Directions Write the answers to these questions using complete sentences.

Comprehension: Identifying Facts

1. What do Michael and Dora Lowes disagree about the night before the story opens?

2. What is the time of year in which this story takes place?

3. What is the topic of conversation during the bridge game?

4. Why does Michael enter the drugstore after the bridge game?

5. What impulse does Michael have in the store?

6. What happens to him because of his impulsive act?

7. What does Michael use as an excuse for what he has done?

8. How does Dora react to what Michael has done?

9. What sentence does Michael receive from the judge?

10. What does Dora tell Michael in the final letter that she sends to him?

Comprehension: Understanding Main Ideas

11. How would you describe the mental state of Michael at the beginning of this story?

12. How does Michael's mental state change at the bridge game and before he steals something?

13. Is Michael a failure in life? Include three examples to support your answer.

14. Why don't the three bridge friends help Michael out?

15. How does the author indicate that Michael does not really consider his three friends to be close?

16. What does impulse mean in this story? Who has impulses?

17. In what ways does Dora seem to be a more responsible person than Michael?

18. Why does Michael keep insisting that he is innocent even though he has been caught stealing?

19. How does Michael feel about life at the end of the story?

20. What is this story's message about stealing?

Review Continued on Next Page

Understanding Literature: Stream of Consciousness and Plot

Conrad Aiken used stream of consciousness in much of his writing. This device allows the reader to observe how and what the characters are thinking. "Impulse" looks into the mind of the main character, Michael Lowes. The use of stream of consciousness can help advance the plot, or the series of events in a story. It also gives the reader insight into the character's mind.

21. What is stream of consciousness?

22. How does stream of consciousness help the reader understand a character better?

23. Which of Michael's thoughts are important to the plot development? Which are important to our understanding of his character?

24. Does Michael's reasoning seem logical to you? Why or why not?

25. Dora is also an important character in the story. Do we see any of her thought processes? Why or why not?

Critical Thinking

26. Do you think another kind of wife might have helped Michael? How? Do you believe that Dora's actions were fair? Why or why not?

27. Do you think "Impulse" might make a good television show or movie? Why or why not?

28. What do you think will happen to Michael after his prison term is up? Do you think that he will change or improve?

29. Do you pity Michael? Do you think the things that happen to him in this story are his own fault? Explain your opinion.

30. Why do you think many human impulses can get people into trouble?

Writing on Your Own Think of one impulse that you have had in the past. Write about the impulse. Explain what it was, how it made you feel, and whether you acted on it. If you did not act on the impulse, explain what you think may have happened if you had acted on it. If you did act on the impulse, explain what happened as a result of your action.

Poems
by Carl Sandburg

Carl Sandburg
1878–1967

Literary Terms

free verse poetry that does not have a strict rhyming pattern or regular line length, and uses actual speech patterns for the rhythms of sound

image a word or phrase that appeals to the senses and allows the reader to picture events

onomatopoeia the use of a word to imitate a sound

About the Author

Carl Sandburg was a biographer, writer of stories for children, and poet. He was born in Galesburg, Illinois, in 1878. His father was a Swedish blacksmith who worked for the railroad. Sandburg attended school until age thirteen. He later joined the army during the Spanish-American War. Then he entered college, but he did not finish. He began to write poetry and worked as a reporter for the *Chicago Daily News*. His first volume of poems was published when he was thirty-eight.

After twenty years of research and writing, Sandburg published one of the most important biographies of this century. *Abraham Lincoln: The War Years* appeared in four volumes and earned him a Pulitzer Prize in 1940. In 1951 he received a Pulitzer Prize for poetry.

In his later years, Sandburg supported himself by reading his poetry and singing. He lived the last years of his life in North Carolina on a farm where he continued to write.

About the Selections

Until Sandburg's time, poetry was mostly from New England. Usually in strict forms, poetry had been read by educated and rich Americans. Sandburg wrote bold poems about farms, prairies, working people, and the city life (especially in Chicago). His **free verse** was realistic. Free verse is poetry that does not have a strict rhyming pattern or regular line length, and uses actual speech patterns for the rhythms of sound.

The following poems are from Sandburg's early years. The use of free verse, **images** (words or phrases that appeal to the senses and allow the reader to picture events), careful word selection, and interesting subject matter all add to his poetry. Notice that "Jazz Fantasia" uses **onomatopoeia**. This is the use of a word to imitate a sound.

Jazz Fantasia

Jazz became popular during the 1920s. This poem describes the sounds and sights of a jazz band and its instruments. What images does this poem make you see? What sounds do you hear?

1   Drum on your drums, batter on your banjos,
    sob on the long cool winding saxophones.
    Go to it, O jazzmen.

4   Sling your knuckles on the bottoms of the happy
    tin pans, let your trombones ooze, and go husha-
    husha-hush with the slippery sandpaper.

    Moan like an autumn wind high in the lonesome treetops,
8   moan soft like you wanted somebody terrible, cry like a
    racing car slipping away from a motorcycle cop, bang-bang!
    you jazzmen, bang altogether drums, traps, banjos,horns, tin
    cans—make two people fight on the top of a stairway and
12 scratch each other's eyes in a clinch tumbling down the stairs.

    Can the rough stuff . . . now a Mississippi steamboat pushes
    up the night river with a hoo-hoo-hoo-oo . . . and the green
    lanterns calling to the high soft stars . . . a red moon rides on
16 the humps of the low river hills . . . go to it,   O jazzmen.

The Jazz Singer, **Charles Demuth**

Cool Tombs

This poem mentions three people in American history: former President Abraham Lincoln; former President and Civil War General Ulysses S. Grant; and Pocahontas, an American Indian woman who was friends with colonists at Jamestown, Virginia, in the early 1600s. What does this poem say about these people?

1   When Abraham Lincoln was shoveled into the tombs, he forgot the **copperheads** and the **assassin** . . . in the dust, in the cool tombs.

4   And Ulysses Grant lost all thought of con men and Wall Street, cash and **collateral** turned ashes . . . in the dust, in the cool tombs.

7   Pocahontas' body, lovely as a poplar, sweet as a red haw in November or a **pawpaw** in May, did she wonder? does she remember? . . . in the dust, in the cool tombs?

10   Take any streetful of people buying clothes and groceries, cheering a hero or throwing **confetti** and blowing tin horns . . . tell me if the lovers are losers . . . tell me if any get
13   more than the lovers . . . in the dust . . . in the cool tombs.

assassin one who commits murder

collateral property that a borrower promises to give up if unable to pay a debt

confetti small bits of brightly colored paper thrown at a celebration

copperhead a person from the North who agreed with the South during the American Civil War

pawpaw a type of tree with fruit and purple flowers

Directions Write the answers to these questions using complete sentences.

Comprehension: Identifying Facts

1. Which musical instruments are mentioned in "Jazz Fantasia"?

2. What historical figures are mentioned in "Cool Tombs"?

3. What do each of these historical figures have in common?

Comprehension: Understanding Main Ideas

4. Explain which words are used to represent the sounds of the instruments in "Jazz Fantasia."

5. Which phrase is repeated in "Jazz Fantasia"? What does it mean?

6. What does the poet mention about both Lincoln and Grant in "Cool Tombs"? How does the question about Pocahontas differ from the other two stanzas? Why?

Understanding Literature: Onomatopoeia

Onomatopoeia is the use of a word to imitate a sound of the thing being written about. Examples of some onomatopoetic words are: *hiss*, *caw*, *moo*, and *clang*. "Jazz Fantasia" has a number of onomatopoetic words used to suggest certain sounds.

7. Identify at least three examples of onomatopoetic words used in "Jazz Fantasia."

8. Think of at least three other words that fit the definition of onomatopoeia. Write your examples on your own paper.

Critical Thinking

9. After reading "Jazz Fantasia," do you get the idea that the poet has an appreciation for music? Explain your answer.

10. Explain what you think "Cool Tombs" is about.

Writing on Your Own Research a famous person in American history by going to the library or using the Internet. Write a poem describing something about this person. Use "Cool Tombs" as a model. Your poem should be at least two stanzas and it should be written in free verse.

Skills Lesson: Onomatopoeia

Have you ever read a word that imitates a sound? For example:

> smack pop crunch bang thump yelp crash clang swish

When read aloud, each word makes a sound that expresses the word's meaning. This is called onomatopoeia. Such words have two purposes: to express the actual meaning of a word and to show how something sounds. The reader gets a clear picture of the action because of the word's meaning and sound.

The following are examples of onomatopoeia from this unit. The first sentence is from "The Far and the Near" by Thomas Wolfe. The second sentence is from "The Sculptor's Funeral" by Willa Cather.

> For a moment the progress of the engine could be marked by heavy bellowing puffs of smoke . . . and finally nothing could be heard but the solid **clacking** tempo of the wheels. . . .

> "Take the long hill road up, Thompson, it will be easier on the horses," called the liveryman as the undertaker **snapped** the door of the hearse and prepared to mount to the driver's seat.

In the first example, *clacking* describes the sound the train wheels make. In the second example, *snapped* tells that the door on the hearse made a snapping sound when shut.

Review

1. What is onomatopoeia?
2. What is unusual about onomatopoetic words?
3. How does onomatopoeia give the reader a clear picture of the action?
4. What onomatopoetic words are used in the examples from "The Far and the Near" and "The Sculptor's Funeral"?
5. Do you think the examples from "The Far and the Near" and "The Sculptor's Funeral" are more effective sentences because of the use of onomatopoeia? Explain.

Writing on Your Own Write three sentences of your own using onomatopoeia in each sentence. Underline each word that is an example of onomatopoeia.

There were many ups and downs in America from 1905 to 1940. World War I, the bloodiest war the world had seen at the time, lasted from 1914 through 1918. Good times followed with the Roaring Twenties. Inventions improved life and people moved to cities in great numbers. However, the stock market crash of 1929 ended those good times and started the Great Depression. It left many people without homes, jobs, and money.

This time in America marked the beginning of modernism in literature. Modernist writers used new ideas and styles to explain the many changes the modern world had created. Writings of this time looked at feelings of being alone and tried to bring society together. Another movement, the Harlem Renaissance, was popular at this time in Harlem, an area in New York City. It focused on African American pride. This was a time when all writers—black and white—could be heard.

Selections

■ "The Far and the Near" is a short story by Thomas Wolfe about a retired train engineer. He visits a woman and her daughter after seeing them only from a distance over the years. He learns that seeing the women up close changes his understanding of them.

■ "Theme for English B" is a poem by Langston Hughes about the poet's struggle as an African American in an all-white college.

■ "The Sculptor's Funeral" is a short story by Willa Cather about the funeral of a famous sculptor in his hometown. The sculptor's student learns that the people in the town do not understand the sculptor's talents.

■ "The Freshest Boy" is a semiautobiographical short story by F. Scott Fitzgerald about a boy at a private school who has trouble fitting in.

■ "Mending Wall," "A Time to Talk," and "Fire and Ice" are poems by Robert Frost about neighbors, friendship, and human emotions.

■ "Impulse" is a short story by Conrad Aiken about one man's impulsive act: stealing.

■ "Cool Tombs" and "Jazz Fantasia" are poems by Carl Sandburg about death and the poet's love for jazz music.

UNIT 5 REVIEW

Directions Write the answers to these questions using complete sentences.

Comprehension: Identifying Facts

1. What years are covered in Unit 5?

2. What were the three main historical events during this time?

3. How did these events affect writers?

4. List five writers who wrote during this time.

5. What is modernism?

Comprehension: Understanding Main Ideas

6. Which selections in this unit focus on how people survive when faced with a crisis in life?

7. Which selections in this unit describe life in good times?

8. Compare and contrast the poetry of Langston Hughes, Robert Frost, and Carl Sandburg. How are their poems alike and different?

9. Describe the plot of "The Far and the Near."

10. Why do the people of Sand City dislike Harvey Merrick in "The Sculptor's Funeral"?

Understanding Literature: Setting and Plot

Many modernist writings in Unit 5 have a strong sense of place and time, or setting. The setting can be very specific: for example, two o'clock in the afternoon or the parlor of the Merrick home in Sand City. The time and place can be very general: for example, an afternoon in February on a farm. In some of the selections in Unit 5, setting is brought into the plot, or the sequence of events in a story or poem. An author may choose to make setting an important part of the plot by placing characters in certain settings. In such cases, the settings are described often in great detail.

11. What are setting and plot?

12. Think of a selection in Unit 5 in which a character goes to a specific place. Explain the importance of setting in this place.

13. Think of another selection in Unit 5 in which a character wants to leave a certain place. Explain the importance of setting in this place.

14. Which setting in Unit 5 did you like best? Why?

15. How did the setting you liked best add to your enjoyment of the story?

Critical Thinking

16. What do the selections in this unit tell you about the time period? Do you think this was a good time to be living in America?

17. Which selection in this unit do you think is the best example of modernist writing? Why?

18. Choose a character from this unit that you liked and one that you disliked. Explain why you liked and disliked these characters.

19. How is the literature in this unit different from what you have read in earlier units? Explain.

20. Langston Hughes was a leader of the Harlem Renaissance in America. His poem "Theme for English B" expresses many ideas behind this movement. Are the ideas in this poem still good ones to live by today? Explain your answer.

Speak and Listen

Choose the poet you liked best from Unit 5 (Langston Hughes, Robert Frost, or Carl Sandburg). Find another poem by this poet at the library. Read the poem to yourself several times. Think of what the poem means to you. Then practice reading the poem aloud. Read the poem to the class when you are confident that you can read it well. Then explain to the class what you think the poem means.

Beyond Words

Think about how setting was important in Unit 5. Then think about a setting from this unit that you can remember clearly. Draw a picture of the setting as you imagine it, paying attention to details from the story. On the back of the picture, write what the setting is and why it was important in the story.

Writing on Your Own

An outline is often helpful when trying to remember the details of a written work. Choose one of the short stories in Unit 5 ("The Far and the Near," "The Sculptor's Funeral," "The Freshest Boy," or "Impulse"). Then write a one-page outline describing the plot of the story you chose. Your outline can list the main idea of each paragraph or it can list each main event in the story.

Test-Taking Tip

If you are asked to compare or contrast things in an essay test, be sure to tell how they are alike and how they are different.

"Violence as a way of achieving racial justice is both impractical and immoral. . . . Violence is not the way."

—Martin Luther King, Jr, *Stride Toward Freedom: The Montgomery Story*, 1958

"Who knows what women can be when they are finally free to become themselves? Who knows what women's intelligence will contribute when it can be nourished without denying love? . . . The time is at hand when the voices of the feminine mystique can no longer drown out the inner voice that is driving women on to become complete."

—Betty Naomi Friedan, *The Feminine Mystique*, 1963

UNIT 6 *Moving Into Modern Times: 1940–1970*

World War II, the postwar period, and many social issues of the 1960s were the main events affecting America from 1940 to 1970. This period of growth challenged Americans to come together as a nation. It also provided many subjects for works of literature.

In this unit, you will learn about the middle of the twentieth century in America and how American literature reflected these times.

World War II, perhaps the most important event of the twentieth century, took place from 1939–1945. It was larger than any war fought before. By the end of the war, over fifty-five million people had been killed, including many Americans. Europe, where most of the fighting had taken place, was left in ruin. Japan, one of America's enemies in the war, suffered from the use of a new weapon: the atomic bomb. The U.S. dropped two atomic bombs on Japanese cities in 1945. The war made America one of the most powerful nations in the world. However, the United States began to face the many responsibilities that being a world power brought.

After the war, the American economy soared. Young people started families, bought homes, and became wealthier.

The United States suddenly had a huge middle class. The growth of business and industry provided new jobs. Transportation and communication developed and became easier to afford. Schools became overcrowded as increasing numbers of American children went to school.

There were many fears during this time. People remembered the grim years of war. Fears of harmful world leaders, communism, and the possibility of a nuclear war grew in the minds of many Americans. The early 1950s brought another conflict, the Korean War. People at this time lost some of their concerns for politics, society, and the economy.

A big change was in the works for the 1960s. The civil rights movement began. This movement tried to increase rights for African Americans

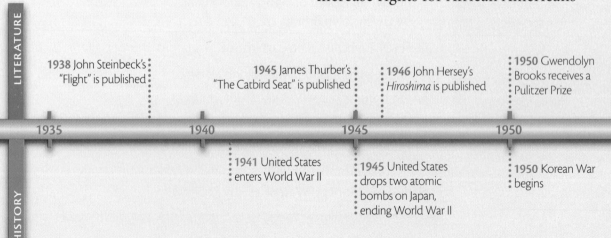

LITERATURE

1938 John Steinbeck's "Flight" is published

1945 James Thurber's "The Catbird Seat" is published

1946 John Hersey's *Hiroshima* is published

1950 Gwendolyn Brooks receives a Pulitzer Prize

1935   1940   1945   1950

1941 United States enters World War II

1945 United States drops two atomic bombs on Japan, ending World War II

1950 Korean War begins

HISTORY

Astronauts landed and walked on the moon for the first time in 1969.

and other groups. People once again became concerned about society. They began to take part in protests for social causes. Women began to gain attention in their search for equality. Americans wanted peace but were suddenly thrust into the Vietnam War. The United states was involved in this war from 1964 to 1973. The war greatly divided the nation.

As a result of events in these years, literature from the 1940s to the late 1960s changed. Some writers wrote of hopelessness, conflict, fears, and challenges. Ernest Hemingway's "The Killers," John Steinbeck's "Flight," and John Hersey's *Hiroshima* are examples of this kind of writing in this unit. Some writers escaped into humor and satire. James Thurber's "The Catbird Seat" is an example of humorous writing in this unit. Other writers described the struggles, losses, and hopes. Authors in this unit representing these causes include Lorraine Hansberry's *To Be Young, Gifted and Black*, Gwendolyn Brooks's "In Honor of David Anderson Brooks, My Father," James Baldwin's *Notes of a Native Son*, Martin Luther King, Jr.'s, *Stride Toward Freedom: The Montgomery Story*, and Robert Hayden's "Monet's 'Waterlilies.'" The hard reality people faced became the subject of many writings.

LITERATURE

1953 Ernest Hemingway receives a Pulitzer Prize

1955 James Baldwin writes *Notes of a Native Son*

1958 Martin Luther King, Jr., publishes *Stride Toward Freedom: The Montgomery Story*

1966 Robert Hayden publishes "Monet's 'Waterlilies'"

1969 Lorraine Hansberry's *To Be Young, Gifted and Black* is published after her death

1955 — 1960 — 1965 — 1970

1955 Martin Luther King, Jr., leads civil rights protest in Montgomery, Alabama

1963 President John F. Kennedy is killed

1965 Vietnam War escalates

1968 Martin Luther King, Jr., is killed

1969 Neil A. Armstrong becomes first American to walk on moon

1970 U.S. census shows 203,302,031 people live in the United States

HISTORY

To Be Young, Gifted and Black
Lorraine Hansberry

Lorraine Hansberry
1930–1964

Literary Terms

autobiography a story about a person's life written by that person

first-person point of view written as if someone is telling the story

narrator one who tells a story

About the Author

To Be Young, Gifted and Black tells the reader much about the author's early years in Chicago where Lorraine Hansberry was born in 1930. She developed an interest in writing at a very early age. Some of Hansberry's early poetry was published by the time she was only twenty-one. A few years later, her play *A Raisin in the Sun*, was running on Broadway. This award-winning play made her the first successful African American woman playwright.

Tragically, at the age of thirty-four, Hansberry died of cancer. Many of her writings were found after her death; her wish was that these works should be published. One note found among her manuscripts said, "If anything should happen . . . someone will complete my thoughts."

About the Selection

The following selection is from *To Be Young, Gifted and Black: Lorraine Hansberry in Her Own Words*. This **autobiography** became both a novel and a play and was published by Hansberry's husband after her death. An autobiography is a story about a person's life written by that person. This autobiography is told in the **first-person point of view**, or as if someone is telling the story. The author is the **narrator**— the person who tells the story.

The conversational tone of this work makes it believable and appealing. Much of the information about the author's early family life is given in the tradition of the very best storytellers. Reading just a few passages makes the reader aware of the struggle, love, and pride that was a part of the author's life during her early years. The place was Chicago, the time was the 1930s, and it was summer.

From To Be Young, Gifted and Black

1   For some time now—I think since I was a child—I have been possessed of the desire to put down the stuff of my life. That is a commonplace impulse, apparently, among persons of **massive** self-interest; sooner or later we all do it. And, I am quite certain, there is only one **internal** quarrel: how much of the truth to tell? How much, how much, how much! It *is* **brutal**, in sober **uncompromising** moments, to reflect on the comedy of concern we all **enact** when it comes to our precious images!

Even so, when such **vanity** as **propels** the writing of such memoirs is examined, certainly one would wish at least to have some boast of social serviceability on one's side.

I shall set down in these pages what shall seem to me to be the truth of my life and essences . . . which are to be found, first of all, on the Southside of Chicago, where I was born. . . .

2   All travelers to my city should ride the elevated trains that race along the back ways of Chicago. The lives you can look into!

I think you could find the tempo of my people on their back porches. The honesty of their living is there in the shabbiness. Scrubbed porches that sag and look their danger. Dirty gray wood steps. And always a line of white and pink clothes scrubbed so well, waving in the dirty wind of the city.

My people are poor. And they are tired. And they are determined to live.

> How does the author describe her neighbors? Her family? Her childhood? How does she make you feel about her world?

> A *memoir* is a person's writing about an event in his or her own life.

---

brutal harsh

enact to act out

internal occurring within

massive a large amount

propel to drive or push forward

uncompromising inflexible; unyielding; not accepting of compromise

vanity great pride in oneself or one's appearance

Our southside is a place apart: each piece of our living is a protest.

3 I was born May 19, 1930, the last of four children. Of love and my parents there is little to be written: their relationship to their children was **utilitarian**. We were fed and housed and dressed and outfitted with more cash than our associates and that was all. We were also vaguely taught certain vague absolutes: that we were better than no one but **infinitely** superior to everyone; that we were the products of the proudest and most mistreated of the races of man; that there was nothing enormously difficult about life; that one *succeeded* as a matter of course.

Life was not a struggle—it was something that one *did*. One won an argument because, if facts gave out, one invented them—with color! The only sinful people in the world were dull people. And, above all, there were two things which were never to be betrayed: the family and the race. But of love, there was nothing ever said.

If we were sick, we were sternly, **impersonally** and carefully nursed and doctored back to health. Fevers, toothaches were attended to with urgency and importance; one always felt *important* in my family. Mother came with a tray to your room with the soup and Vick's salve or gave the enemas in a steaming bathroom. But we were not fondled, any of us—head held to breast, fingers about that head—until we were grown, all of us, and my father died.

At his funeral I at last, in my memory, saw my mother hold her sons that way, and for the first time in her life my sister held me in her arms I think. We were not a loving people: we were **passionate** in our **hostilities** and **affinities**, but the caress embarrassed us.

We have changed little. . . .

> The author says here that family and the African American race were never to be betrayed. What does this tell you about the author's upbringing?

affinities sympathetic relationships; attractions	**impersonally** having no personal connection toward; without feeling	**passionate** having intense feelings toward
hostility an act of war; conflict	**infinitely** in a way that is never ending	**utilitarian** practical; useful

4   Seven years separated the nearest of my brothers and sisters and myself; I wear, I am sure, the **earmarks** of that **familial** station to this day. Little has been written or thought to my knowledge about children who occupy that place: the last born separated by an uncommon length of time from the next youngest. I suspect we are probably a race apart.

   The last born is an object toy which comes in years when brothers and sisters who are seven, ten, twelve years older are old enough to appreciate it rather than poke out its eyes. They do not mind diapering you the first two years, but by the time you are five you are a pest that has to be attended to in the washroom, taken to the movies and "sat with" at night. You are not a person—you are a nuisance who is not particular fun any more. Consequently, you swiftly learn to play alone. . . .

What does this paragraph say about being the youngest child in the author's family?

earmark a distinguishing mark	**familial** of or relating to a family

5 My childhood Southside summers were the ordinary city kind, full of the street games which other rememberers have turned into fine ballets these days, and rhymes that **anticipated** what some people insist on calling modern poetry:

Oh, Mary Mack, Mack, Mack
With the silver buttons, buttons, buttons
All down her back, back, back.
She asked her mother, mother, mother
For fifteen cents, cents, cents
To see the elephant, elephant, elephant
Jump the fence, fence, fence.
Well, he jumped so high, high, high
'Til he touched the sky, sky, sky
And he didn't come back, back, back,
'Til the Fourth of Ju—ly, ly, ly!

I remember skinny little Southside bodies by the fives and tens of us panting the delicious hours away:

"May I?"

And the voice of authority: "Yes, you may—you may take one giant step."

One drew in all one's breath and tightened one's fist and pulled the small body against the heavens, stretching, straining all the muscles in the legs to make—one giant step.

It is a long time. One forgets the reason for the game. (For children's games are always **explicit** in their reasons for being. To play is to win something. Or not to be "it." Or to be high pointer, or outdoer or, sometimes—just the *winner*. But after a time one forgets.)

Why was it important to take a small step, a teeny step, or the most desired of all—one GIANT step?

A giant step to *where*?

6 Evenings were spent mainly on the back porches where screen doors slammed in the darkness with those really very special summertime sounds. And, sometimes, when Chicago

---

anticipate to give advance thought to

explicit expressed without being difficult to understand

nights got too steamy, the whole family got into the car and went to the park and slept out in the open on blankets. Those were, of course, the best times of all because the grownups were **invariably** reminded of having been children in the South and told the best stories then. And it was also cool and sweet to be on the grass and there was usually the scent of freshly cut lemons or melons in the air. Daddy would lie on his back, as fathers must, and explain about how men thought the stars above us came to be and how far away they were.

I never did learn to believe that anything could be as far away as *that*. Especially the stars. . . .

In what ways does this paragraph explain what life was like growing up in Chicago?

7 The man that I remember was an educated soul, though I think now, looking back, that it was as much a matter of the physical bearing of my father as his command of information and of thought that left that impression upon me. I know nothing of the "assurance of kings" and will not use that metaphor on account of it. Suffice it to say that my father's **enduring** image in my mind is that of a man whom kings might have imitated and properly created their own **flattering** descriptions of. A man who always seemed to be doing something brilliant and/or unusual to such an extent that to be doing something brilliant and/or unusual was the way I assumed fathers behaved.

He digested the laws of the State of Illinois and put them into little booklets. He invented complicated pumps and railroad devices. He could talk at length on American history and private enterprise (to which he utterly **subscribed**). And he carried his head in such a way that I was quite certain that there was nothing he was afraid of. Even writing this, how **profoundly** it shocks my inner senses to realize suddenly that *my* father, like all men, must have known *fear*. . . .

Private enterprise is freedom of private business to organize and operate for a profit without unnecessary interference by the government.

enduring lasting	**invariably** constantly	**subscribe** to give support
flattering very favorable	**profoundly** deeply; greatly	

To Be Young, Gifted and Black
Lorraine Hansberry

Directions Write the answers to these questions using complete sentences.

Comprehension: Identifying Facts

1. In what area of Chicago does the author say she grew up?

2. What does the author say riders on the elevated trains will see as they race along the back ways of Chicago?

3. What is the author's date of birth?

4. How many children are in the author's family?

5. Which two things does the author say were never to be betrayed?

6. What does the author remember about her father?

7. What does the author say happened in her family if someone were to become sick?

8. What does the author say happened on some steamy nights in Chicago?

9. What did the author's father do for a living?

10. What thing does the author say her father must have known?

Comprehension: Understanding Main Ideas

11. Reread section one. How does the author set up the story that she is about to relate?

12. What social comment does the author make with this statement: ". . . each piece of our living is a protest"?

13. What attitudes did the Hansberry parents give to their children?

14. How did the author's place in the family influence her personality?

15. How does the author's father seem "bigger than life" in her eyes?

16. How does the author explain her family's attitude toward love?

17. What view toward family does the author express in this selection?

18. What things about Chicago does the author include in this selection?

19. How does the author feel toward her father?

20. How does the author view her childhood?

Understanding Literature: Narrator, Autobiography, and First-Person Point of View

The narrator in a story is the one who tells the story. In the selection *To Be Young, Gifted and Black*, the narrator is the author, Lorraine Hansberry. This autobiography, a story about a person's life written by that person, is told in the first-person point of view. This means that the author is also a character in the story. First person uses the pronoun "I" (or "me" or "my") in relating the facts. In this selection, the author or narrator is recalling events from her own life. The first-person point of view often provides a better insight and more depth into events.

21. Find a sentence from this story that shows the use of first-person point of view. Write down the sentence. Then write why it is first person.

22. How would this story be different if it were told from a point of view other than the first person?

23. Who is the narrator in this story?

24. Why is this selection an autobiography?

25. Why might an autobiography be more effective than a biography— a story about a person written by another person?

Critical Thinking

26. Do you believe that parents should teach their children to be proud? Explain your answer.

27. The author says that "Life was not a struggle—it was something that one *did*." What do you think this means?

28. Why do you think the author wrote this selection?

29. What does this selection have to say about being an African American?

30. How does the author's memories of growing up compare with your own childhood?

Writing on Your Own Write two or three paragraphs about something you remember about growing up. Refer to the Lorraine Hansberry selection for ideas. For example, you may want to write about family life, playing games with friends, or your neighborhood.

The Killers
Ernest Hemingway

Ernest Hemingway
1899–1961

Literary Term

dialogue the conversation among characters in a story

About the Author

Ernest Hemingway was interested in adventure—hunting, fishing, bullfighting, and traveling. This adventure is common in his works.

Born in Oak Park, Illinois, Hemingway was the son of a doctor. When he became older, he worked as a reporter for the *Kansas City Star*. During World War I, he joined a Red Cross unit and served on the front lines in Italy. He was seriously wounded. However, his recovery gave him time to think about the effects of war and other subjects.

After the war, Hemingway went to Paris. He became friends with famous writers and published several important works during the 1920s. He is known for the use of short, direct sentences with few descriptive words. His heroes are tense and unemotional when facing violence. In novels such as *The Sun Also Rises, For Whom the Bell Tolls,* and *A Farewell to Arms,* the heroes are brave and accepting of the harsh world they face.

In 1953, Hemingway received a Pulitzer Prize for *The Old Man and the Sea.* In 1954, he was awarded a Nobel Prize for literature.

About the Selection

"The Killers" is an example of Hemingway's simple writing style. The **dialogue**—the conversation among characters in a story—is short and to the point. "The Killers" takes place in a diner, where two gangsters wait for the arrival of a prizefighter, whom they intend to kill. While the story deals with a planned killing, it is not a story of actual violence.

From The Killers

The door of Henry's lunch-room opened and two men came in. They sat down at the counter.

"What's yours?" George asked them.

"I don't know," one of the men said. "What do you want to eat, Al?"

"I don't know," said Al. "I don't know what I want to eat."

Outside it was getting dark. The street-light came on outside the window. The two men at the counter read the menu. From the other end of the counter Nick Adams watched them. He had been talking to George when they came in.

"I'll have a roast pork tenderloin with applesauce and mashed potatoes," the first man said.

"It isn't ready yet."

"What the hell do you put it on the card for?"

"That's the dinner," George explained. "You can get that at six o'clock."

George looked at the clock on the wall behind the counter.

"It's five o'clock."

"The clock says twenty minutes past five," the second man said.

"It's twenty minutes fast."

"Oh, to hell with the clock," the first man said. "What have you got to eat?"

"I can give you any kind of sandwiches," George said. "You can have ham and eggs, bacon and eggs, liver and bacon, or a steak."

"Give me chicken croquettes with green peas and cream sauce and mashed potatoes."

"That's the dinner."

"Everything we want's the dinner, eh? That's the way you work it."

Several characters appear in this story: the gangsters Al and Max; George, who works at the restaurant; Nick Adams, who is in the restaurant when the gangsters arrive; and the prizefighter, Ole Andreson. What is each character's attitude toward the upcoming murder?

A *tenderloin* is a strip of tender meat.

Croquettes are a small and often rounded mass, usually of minced meat coated with egg and bread crumbs and deep fried.

A *derby hat* is made of felt with a dome-shaped crown and a narrow brim.

"I can give you ham and eggs, bacon and eggs, liver—"

"I'll take ham and eggs," the man called Al said. He wore a derby hat and a black overcoat buttoned across the chest. His face was small and white and he had tight lips. He wore a silk muffler and gloves.

"Give me bacon and eggs," said the other man. He was about the same size as Al. Their faces were different, but they were dressed like twins. Both wore overcoats too tight for them. They sat leaning forward, their elbows on the counter.

"Got anything to drink?" Al asked.

"Silver beer, bevo, ginger-ale," George said.

"I mean you got anything to *drink?*"

"Just those I said."

"This is a hot town," said the other. "What do they call it?"

"Summit."

"Ever hear of it?" Al asked his friend.

"No," said the friend.

"What do you do here nights?" Al asked.

"They eat the dinner," his friend said. "They all come here and eat the big dinner."

"That's right," George said.

"So you think that's right?" Al asked George.

"Sure."

"You're a pretty bright boy, aren't you?"

"Sure," said George.

"Well, you're not," said the other little man. "Is he, Al?"

"He's dumb," said Al. He turned to Nick. "What's your name?"

"Adams."

"Another bright boy," Al said. "Ain't he a bright boy, Max?"

"The town's full of bright boys," Max said.

George put the two platters, one of ham and eggs, the other of bacon and eggs, on the counter. He set down two side-dishes of fried potatoes and closed the wicket into the kitchen.

Wicket refers to a door or an opening through which a cook or waiter can enter the kitchen in a restaurant.

"Which is yours?" he asked Al.

"Don't you remember?"

"Ham and eggs."

"Just a bright boy," Max said. He leaned forward and took the ham and eggs. Both men ate with their gloves on. George watched them eat. . . .

"Hey, bright boy," Max said to Nick. "You go around on the other side of the counter with your boy friend."

"What's the idea?" Nick asked.

"There isn't any idea."

"You better go around, bright boy," Al said. Nick went around behind the counter.

"What's the idea?" George asked.

"None of your damn business," Al said. . . .

[The men continue to talk. Al later asks who is in the kitchen. He takes Nick into the kitchen so that he can keep an eye on both him and the cook.]

"Talk to me, bright boy," Max said. "What do you think's going to happen?"

George did not say anything.

"I'll tell you," Max said. "We're going to kill a Swede. Do you know a big Swede named Ole Andreson?"

"Yes."

"He comes here to eat every night, don't he?"

What are Max and Al like?

"Sometimes he comes here."

"He comes here at six o'clock, don't he?"

"If he comes."

"We know all that, bright boy," Max said. "Talk about something else. Ever go to the movies?"

"Once in a while."

"You ought to go to the movies more. The movies are fine for a bright boy like you."

"What are you going to kill Ole Andreson for? What did he ever do to you?"

"He never had a chance to do anything to us. He never even seen us."

"And he's only going to see us once," Al said from the kitchen.

"What are you going to kill him for, then?" George asked.

"We're killing him for a friend. Just to oblige a friend, bright boy."

"Shut up," said Al from the kitchen. "You talk too . . . much."

"Well, I got to keep bright boy amused. Don't I, bright boy?"

"You talk too damn much," Al said. . . .

George looked up at the clock.

"If anybody comes in you tell them the cook is off, and if they keep after it, you tell them you'll go back and cook yourself. Do you get that, bright boy?"

"All right," George said. "What you going to do with us afterward?"

"That'll depend," Max said. "That's one of those things you never know at the time. . . ."

[The men wait for Ole Andreson to come. At six fifty-five, he still has not come into the diner.]

George said: "Your friend, Ole Andreson, isn't going to come."

"We'll give him ten minutes," Max said.

Max watched the mirror and the clock. The hands of the clock marked seven o'clock, and then five minutes past seven.

"Come on, Al," said Max. "We better go. He's not coming."

Here the gangsters admit they intend to kill Ole Andreson as a favor to someone.

The gangsters say what they say here because they do not want people to come in for the dinner. They do not want people around to witness the murder.

"Better give him five minutes," Al said. . . .

He came out from the kitchen. The cut-off barrels of the shotgun made a slight bulge under the waist of his too tight-fitting overcoat. He straightened his coat with his gloved hands.

"So long, bright boy," he said to George. "You got a lot of luck."

"That's the truth," Max said. "You ought to play the races, bright boy."

The two of them went out the door. George watched them, through the window, pass under the arc-light and cross the street. In their tight overcoats and derby hats they looked like a vaudeville team. . . .

"Listen," George said to Nick. "You better go see Ole Andreson. . . ."

"I'll go see him," Nick said to George. "Where does he live? . . ."

"He lives up at Hirsch's rooming-house," George said to Nick.

"I'll go up there."

Outside the arc-light shone through the bare branches of a tree. Nick walked up the street beside the car-tracks and turned at the next arc-light down a side-street. Three houses up the street was Hirsch's rooming-house. Nick walked up the two steps and pushed the bell. A woman came to the door.

"Is Ole Andreson here?"

"Do you want to see him?"

"Yes, if he's in."

Nick followed the woman up a flight of stairs and back to the end of a corridor. She knocked on the door.

"Who is it?"

"It's somebody to see you, Mr. Andreson," the woman said.

"It's Nick Adams."

"Come in."

Nick opened the door and went into the room. Ole Andreson was lying on the bed with all his clothes on. He had been a heavyweight prizefighter and he was too long for the

Al is hiding a gun under his coat.

Vaudeville refers to a kind of stage entertainment of singing, dancing, or comedy.

Here George tells Nick to warn Ole that the gangsters plan to murder him.

bed. He lay with his head on two pillows. He did not look at Nick.

"What was it?" he asked.

"I was up at Henry's," Nick said, "and two fellows came in . . . and they said they were going to kill you."

It sounded silly when he said it. Ole Andreson said nothing. . . .

"They were going to shoot you when you came in to supper."

Ole Andreson looked at the wall and did not say anything.

"George thought I better come and tell you about it."

"There isn't anything I can do about it," Ole Andreson said.

"I'll tell you what they were like."

"I don't want to know what they were like," Ole Andreson said. He looked at the wall. "Thanks for coming to tell me about it."

"That's all right."

Nick looked at the big man lying on the bed.

"Don't you want me to go and see the police?"

"No," Ole Andreson said. "That wouldn't do any good."

Why do you think Ole does not sound alarmed at what Nick tells him?

"Isn't there something I could do?"

"No. There ain't anything to do."

"Maybe it was just a bluff."

"No. It ain't just a bluff."

Ole Andreson rolled over toward the wall.

"The only thing is," he said, talking toward the wall, "I just can't make up my mind to go out. I been in here all day."

"Couldn't you get out of town?"

"No," Ole Andreson said. "I'm through with all that running around."

He looked at the wall.

"There ain't anything to do now."

"Couldn't you fix it up some way?"

"No. I got in wrong." He talked in the same flat voice. "There ain't anything to do. After a while I'll make up my mind to go out."

"I better go back and see George," Nick said.

"So long," said Ole Andreson. He did not look toward Nick. "Thanks for coming around."

Nick went out. As he shut the door he saw Ole Andreson with all his clothes on, lying on the bed looking at the wall.

"He's been in his room all day," the landlady said downstairs. "I guess he don't feel well. I said to him: 'Mr. Andreson, you ought to go out and take a walk on a nice fall day like this,' but he didn't feel like it."

"He doesn't want to go out."

"I'm sorry he don't feel well," the woman said. "He's an awfully nice man. He was in the ring, you know."

"I know it."

"You'd never know it except from the way his face is," the woman said. They stood talking just inside the street door. "He's just as gentle."

"Well, good-night, Mrs. Hirsch," Nick said. . . .

Nick walked up the dark street to the corner under the arc-light, and then along the car-tracks to Henry's eating-house. George was inside, back of the counter.

"Did you see Ole?"

"Yes," said Nick. "He's in his room and he won't go out. . . ."

Here Ole admits that he has been involved with bad people who want to kill him.

"Did you tell him about it?" George asked.

"Sure. I told him but he knows what it's all about."

"What's he going to do?"

"Nothing."

"They'll kill him."

"I guess they will."

"He must have got mixed up in something in Chicago."

"I guess so," said Nick.

"It's a hell of a thing."

"It's an awful thing," Nick said.

They did not say anything. George reached down for a towel and wiped the counter.

"I wonder what he did?" Nick said.

"Double-crossed somebody. That's what they kill them for."

"I'm going to get out of this town," Nick said.

"Yes," said George. "That's a good thing to do."

"I can't stand to think about him waiting in the room and knowing he's going to get it. It's too damned awful."

"Well," said George, "you better not think about it."

Why do you think Nick wants to leave town?

Directions Write the answers to these questions using complete sentences.

Comprehension: Identifying Facts

1. At what time does George usually begin to serve dinner?

2. What are the two gangsters wearing?

3. What man are the gangsters going to kill?

4. What is their reason for wanting to kill him?

5. At what time do the gangsters leave the diner?

6. Where is Ole Andreson while the men wait for him?

7. Why does Nick go to see Ole?

8. What is Ole doing when Nick goes to see him?

9. What does George think is the reason that the men want to kill Ole?

10. What does Nick say he wants to do at the end of the story?

Comprehension: Understanding Main Ideas

11. Who are Al and Max, and what are these two men like?

12. Why is Nick an important character in this story?

13. Why do Al and Max refer to Nick and George as "bright boys"?

14. What kind of town is Summit?

15. What do the gangsters do to Nick and George?

16. What evidence is there that Ole has run from gangsters before?

17. Why does Ole say that the police will not be able to help him?

18. What kind of man is Ole? Describe him.

19. Why does the author keep referring to time in this story?

20. How does Nick feel about Ole's situation?

Review Continued on Next Page

Understanding Literature: Dialogue

Dialogue is the name given to conversation between or among two or more characters in a narrative. Dialogue can serve several purposes. It can move the story along, tell the reader something more about the characters, help create a mood, or comment on the plot or theme. In "The Killers," the characters tell the reader about their personalities by the way they talk.

21. What purposes does dialogue serve in this story?

22. Describe each of the five characters: Al, Max, George, Nick, and Ole.

23. Describe what you learned about the characters from what they said.

24. Is the dialogue in this story realistic? Why or why not?

25. Do you think dialogue is important in this story? Why or why not?

Critical Thinking

26. Why do you think Ole did not try to run away from the two gangsters?

27. How is this story a good example of the author's simple writing style?

28. Why do you think the author tells the story of the killers but does not describe the actual killing?

29. What might make another good title for this story?

30. What do you think happens to Ole? Explain how you think the story will end.

Writing on Your Own Choose a line of dialogue from "The Killers." Write down the line. Then add three lines of your own dialogue. Try to maintain Hemingway's style of simple dialogue.

John Steinbeck
1902–1968

Literary Terms

animal imagery a literary device that uses animal-like descriptions to tell about a person

setting the time and place in a story

About the Author

John Steinbeck was one of the first major writers to use California as a setting in his writing. His stories described migrant workers, factory workers, and the poor of the west coast.

Steinbeck's early years were spent in Salinas, California. He spent his summers working on local ranches. Later he attended Stanford University for six years but never graduated. In 1925, Steinbeck went to New York to become a writer. He worked on a newspaper, but his love of California was too strong. He returned to California and worked at many jobs while continuing to write.

His sixth novel, *Of Mice and Men*, was published in 1937. It made him famous. However, his most famous novel, *The Grapes of Wrath*, was published in 1939 and received a Pulitzer Prize in 1940. It described farmers and workers who moved to California during the Great Depression.

In 1962 Steinbeck was awarded a Nobel Prize for literature. However, he avoided the attention that surrounded him. Since his death, several of his works have been turned into plays, movies, and television shows.

About the Selection

"Flight" is a short story published in 1938 in a volume called *The Long Valley*. This excerpt is the beginning of that story. It describes the Torres family and especially the nineteen-year-old boy, Pepé. The **setting**, as in most of Steinbeck's works, is California. Setting is the time and place in a story. Notice the **animal imagery** as you read. Animal imagery uses animal-like descriptions to tell about a person.

From *Flight*

At what point does a boy become a man? "I am a man," Pepé declares in this story. Do you agree?

An *aphid* is a kind of small insect that sucks juices from plants.

The word *sterile* here means not having vegetation. *Landward* means toward land.

This paragraph explains that Mr. Torres had been killed by a rattlesnake bite.

A *truant officer* is a person who watches for students who skip school.

About fifteen miles below Monterey, on the wild coast, the Torres family had their farm, a few sloping acres above a cliff that dropped to the brown reefs and to the hissing white waters of the ocean. Behind the farm the stone mountains stood up against the sky. The farm buildings huddled like little clinging aphids on the mountain skirts, crouched low to the ground as though the wind might blow them into the sea. The little shack, the rattling, rotting barn were gray-bitten with sea salt, beaten by the damp wind until they had taken on the color of the granite hills. Two horses, a red cow and a red calf, half a dozen pigs and a flock of lean, multicolored chickens stocked the place. A little corn was raised on the sterile slope, and it grew short and thick under the wind, and all the cobs formed on the landward sides of the stalks.

Mama Torres, a lean, dry woman with ancient eyes, had ruled the farm for ten years, ever since her husband tripped over a stone in the field one day and fell full length on a rattlesnake. When one is bitten on the chest there is not much that can be done.

Mama Torres had three children, two undersized black ones of twelve and fourteen, Emilio and Rosy, whom Mama kept fishing on the rocks below the farm when the sea was kind and when the truant officer was in some distant part of Monterey County. And there was Pepé, the tall smiling son of nineteen, a gentle, **affectionate** boy, but very lazy. Pepé had a tall head, pointed at the top, and from its peak, coarse black

---

affectionate loving

hair grew down like a thatch all around. Over his smiling little eyes Mama cut a straight bang so he could see. Pepé had sharp Indian cheekbones and an eagle nose, but his mouth was as sweet and shapely as a girl's mouth, and his chin was fragile and chiseled. He was loose and gangling, all legs and feet and wrists, and he was very lazy. Mama thought him fine and brave, but she never told him so. She said, "Some lazy cow must have got into thy father's family, else how could I have a son like thee." And she said, "When I carried thee, a sneaking lazy coyote came out of the brush and looked at me one day. That must have made thee so."

Pepé smiled **sheepishly** and stabbed at the ground with his knife to keep the blade sharp and free from rust. It was his inheritance, that knife, his father's knife. The long heavy blade folded back into the black handle. There was a button on the handle. When Pepé pressed the button, the blade leaped out ready for use. The knife was with Pepé always, for it had been his father's knife.

One sunny morning when the sea below the cliff was **glinting** and blue and the white surf creamed on the reef, when even the stone mountains looked kindly, Mama Torres called out the door of the shack, "Pepé, I have a labor for thee."

There was no answer. Mama listened. From behind the barn she heard a burst of laughter. She lifted her full long skirt and walked in the direction of the noise.

Pepé was sitting on the ground with his back against a box. His white teeth glistened. On either side of him stood the two black ones, tense and **expectant.** Fifteen feet away a redwood post was set in the ground. Pepé's right hand lay limply in his lap, and in the palm the big black knife rested. The blade was closed back into the handle. Pepé looked smiling at the sky.

Suddenly Emilio cried, "Ya!"

Pepé's wrist flicked like the head of a snake. The blade seemed to fly open in mid-air, and with a thump the point dug into the redwood post, and the black handle quivered.

expectant waiting for something to happen	**glinting** reflecting light	**sheepishly** timidly, as if embarrassed by a fault

The three burst into excited laughter. Rosy ran to the post and pulled out the knife and brought it back to Pepé. He closed the blade and settled the knife carefully in his **listless** palm again. He grinned self-consciously at the sky.

"Ya!"

The heavy knife lanced out and sunk into the post again. Mama moved forward like a ship and scattered the play.

"All day you do foolish things with the knife, like a toy-baby," she stormed. "Get up on thy huge feet that eat up shoes. Get up!" She took him by one loose shoulder and hoisted at him. Pepé grinned sheepishly and came half-heartedly to his feet. "Look!" Mama cried. "Big lazy, you must catch the horse and put on him thy father's saddle. You must ride to Monterey. The medicine bottle is empty. There is no salt. Go thou now, Peanut! Catch the horse."

A revolution took place in the relaxed figure of Pepé. "To Monterey, me? Alone? Sí, Mama."

She scowled at him. "Do not think, big sheep, that you will buy candy. No, I will give you only enough for the medicine and the salt."

Pepé smiled. "Mama, you will put the hatband on the hat?"

She **relented** then. "Yes, Pepé. You may wear the hatband."

His voice grew **insinuating**, "And the green handkerchief, Mama?"

"Yes, if you go quickly and return with no trouble, the silk green handkerchief will go. If you make sure to take off the handkerchief when you eat so no spot may fall on it. . . ."

"Sí, Mama. I will be careful. I am a man."

"Thou? A man? Thou art a peanut."

He went into the rickety barn and brought out a rope, and he walked **agilely** enough up the hill to catch the horse.

When he was ready and mounted before the door, mounted on his father's saddle that was so old that the oaken frame showed through torn leather in many places, then

Notice the animal imagery in this paragraph. Mama calls Pepé "big sheep."

agilely with quick, graceful motion	**listless** having no desire to act	**relent** to become less severe; to let up
insinuating distrusting; doubting		

Mama brought out the round black hat with the tooled
leather band, and she reached up and knotted the green silk
handkerchief about his neck. Pepé's blue denim coat was
much darker than his jeans, for it had been washed much less
often.

Mama handed up the big medicine bottle and the silver
coins. "That for the medicine," she said, "and that for the salt.
That for a candle to burn for the papa. That for dulces for the
little ones. Our friend Mrs. Rodriguez will give you dinner
and maybe a bed for the night. When you go to the church
say only ten Paternosters and only twenty-five Ave Marias.
Oh! I know, big coyote. You would sit there flapping your
mouth over Aves all day while you looked at the candles and
the holy pictures. That is not good devotion to stare at the
pretty things."

The black hat, covering the high pointed head and black
thatched hair of Pepé, gave him dignity and age. He sat the
rangy horse well. Mama thought how handsome he was, dark
and lean and tall. "I would not send thee now alone, thou

Dulces means candy or
sweets.

Paternosters and *Ave
Marias* are prayers.

little one, except for the medicine," she said softly. "It is not good to have no medicine, for who knows when the toothache will come, or the sadness of the stomach. These things are."

"Adios, Mama," Pepé cried. "I will come back soon. You may send me often alone. I am a man."

"Thou art a foolish chicken."

He straightened his shoulders, flipped the reins against the horse's shoulder and rode away. He turned once and saw that they still watched him, Emilio and Rosy and Mama. Pepé grinned with pride and gladness and lifted the tough buckskin horse to a trot.

When he had dropped out of sight over a little dip in the road, Mama turned to the black ones, but she spoke to herself. "He is nearly a man now," she said. "It will be a nice thing to have a man in the house again." Her eyes sharpened on the children. "Go to the rocks now. The tide is going out. There will be abalones to be found." She put the iron hooks into their hands and saw them down the steep trail to the reefs. She brought the smooth stone metate to the doorway and sat grinding her corn to flour and looking occasionally at the road over which Pepé had gone. The noonday came and then the afternoon, when the little ones beat the abalones on a rock to make them tender and Mama patted the tortillas to make them thin. They ate their dinner as the red sun was plunging down toward the ocean. They sat on the doorsteps and watched the big white moon come over the mountain tops.

Mama said, "He is now at the house of our friend Mrs. Rodriguez. She will give him nice things to eat and maybe a present."

Emilio said, "Some day I too will ride to Monterey for medicine. Did Pepé come to be a man today?"

Mama said wisely, "A boy gets to be a man when a man is needed. Remember this thing. I have known boys forty years old because there was no need for a man."

Soon afterwards they retired, Mama in her big oak bed on one side of the room, Emilio and Rosy in their boxes full of straw and sheepskins on the other side of the room.

An *abalone* is a shellfish that clings to rocks and can be used for food.

A *metate* is a stone used to grind grains, such as corn.

The moon went over the sky and the surf roared on the rocks. The roosters crowed the first call. The surf **subsided** to a whispering **surge** against the reef. The moon dropped toward the sea. The roosters crowed again.

The moon was near down to the water when Pepé rode on a winded horse to his home flat. His dog bounced out and circled the horse yelping with pleasure. Pepé slid off the saddle to the ground. The weathered little shack was silver in the moonlight and the square shadow of it was black to the north and east. Against the east the piling mountains were misty with light; their tops melted into the sky.

Pepé walked wearily up the three steps and into the house. It was dark inside. There was a rustle in the corner.

Mama cried out from her bed. "Who comes? Pepé, is it thou?"

"Sí, Mama."

"Did you get the medicine?"

"Sí, Mama."

"Well, go to sleep, then. I thought you would be sleeping at the house of Mrs. Rodriguez." Pepé stood silently in the dark room. "Why do you stand there, Pepé? Did you drink wine?"

"Sí, Mama."

"Well, go to bed then and sleep out the wine."

His voice was tired and patient, but very firm. "Light the candle, Mama. I must go away into the mountains."

"What is this, Pepé? You are crazy." Mama struck a sulphur match and held the little blue burr until the flame spread up the stick. She set light to the candle on the floor beside her bed. "Now, Pepé, what is this you say?" She looked anxiously into his face.

He was changed. The fragile quality seemed to have gone from his chin. His mouth was less full than it had been, the lines of the lips were straighter, but in his eyes the greatest change had taken place. There was no laughter in them any

---

subside to settle; to become less active

surge a swelling, rolling, or sweeping forward

more, nor any bashfulness. They were sharp and bright and purposeful.

He told her in a tired **monotone**, told her everything just as it had happened. A few people came into the kitchen of Mrs. Rodriguez. There was wine to drink. Pepé drank wine. The little quarrel—the man started toward Pepé and then the knife—it went almost by itself. It flew, it darted before Pepé knew it. As he talked, Mama's face grew stern, and it seemed to grow more lean. Pepé finished. "I am a man now, Mama. The man said names to me I could not allow."

Pepé explains here that he has killed a man with his knife.

Mama nodded. "Yes, thou art a man, my poor little Pepé. Thou art a man. I have seen it coming on thee. I have watched you throwing the knife into the post, and I have been afraid." For a moment her face had softened, but now it grew stern again. "Come! We must get you ready. Go. Awaken Emilio and Rosy. Go quickly."

Pepé stepped over to the corner where his brother and sister slept among the sheepskins. He leaned down and shook them gently. "Come, Rosy! Come, Emilio! The mama says you must arise."

The little black ones sat up and rubbed their eyes in the candlelight. Mama was out of bed now, her long black skirt over her nightgown. "Emilio," she cried. "Go up and catch the other horse for Pepé. Quickly now! Quickly." Emilio put his legs in his overalls and stumbled sleepily out the door.

"You heard no one behind you on the road?" Mama demanded.

"No, Mama. I listened carefully. No one was on the road."

Mama darted like a bird about the room. From a nail on the wall she took a canvas water bag and threw it on the floor. She stripped a blanket from her bed and rolled it into a tight tube and tied the ends with string. From a box beside the stove she lifted a flour sack half full of black stringy jerky. "Your father's black coat, Pepé. Here, put it on."

monotone spoken without a varying pitch or key

Pepé stood in the middle of the floor watching her activity. She reached behind the door and brought out the rifle, a long 38-56, worn shiny the whole length of the barrel. Pepé took it from her and held it in the crook of his elbow. Mama brought a little leather bag and counted the cartridges into his hand. "Only ten left," she warned. "You must not waste them." Emilio put his head in the door. "Qui' st 'l caballo, Mama."

Qui' st 'l caballo means here is the horse.

"Put on the saddle from the other horse. Tie on the blanket. Here, tie the jerky to the saddle horn."

Still Pepé stood silently watching his mother's frantic activity. His chin looked hard, and his sweet mouth was drawn and thin. His little eyes followed Mama about the room almost suspiciously.

Rosy asked softly, "Where goes Pepé?"

Mama's eyes were fierce. "Pepé goes on a journey. Pepé is a man now. He has a man's thing to do."

Pepé straightened his shoulders. His mouth changed until he looked very much like Mama.

At last the preparation was finished. The loaded horse stood outside the door. The water bag dripped a line of moisture down the bay shoulder.

The moonlight was being thinned by the dawn and the big white moon was near down to the sea. The family stood by the shack. Mama **confronted** Pepé. "Look, my son! Do not stop until it is dark again. Do not sleep even though you are tired. Take care of the horse in order that he may not stop of weariness. Remember to be careful with the bullets—there are only ten. Do not fill thy stomach with jerky or it will make thee sick. Eat a little jerky and fill thy stomach with grass. When thou comest to the high mountains, if thou seest any of the dark watching men, go not near to them nor try to speak to them. And forget not thy prayers." She put her lean hands on Pepé's shoulders, stood on her toes and kissed him formally on both cheeks, and Pepé kissed her on both cheeks.

Is Mama a good mother? Why or why not?

confront to meet face-to-face

Then he went to Emilio and Rosy and kissed both of their cheeks. . . .

Pepé pulled himself into the saddle. "I am a man," he said.

It was the first dawn when he rode up the hill toward the little canyon which let a trail into the mountains. Moonlight and daylight fought with each other, and the two warring qualities made it difficult to see. Before Pepé had gone a hundred yards, the outlines of his figure were misty; and long before he entered the canyon, he had become a gray, indefinite shadow.

Mama stood stiffly in front of her doorstep, and on either side of her stood Emilio and Rosy. They cast **furtive** glances at Mama now and then.

When the gray shape of Pepé melted into the hillside and disappeared, Mama relaxed. She began the high, whining keen of the death wail. "Our beautiful— our brave," she cried. "Our protector, our son is gone." Emilio and Rosy moaned beside her. "Our beautiful— our brave, he is gone." It was the formal wail. It rose to a high piercing whine and subsided to a moan. Mama raised it three times and then she turned and went into the house and shut the door.

Emilio and Rosy stood wondering in the dawn. They heard Mama whimpering in the house. They went out to sit on the cliff above the ocean. They touched shoulders. "When did Pepé come to be a man?" Emilio asked.

furtive secret; sly

"Last night," said Rosy. "Last night in Monterey." The ocean clouds turned red with the sun that was behind the mountains.

"We will have no breakfast," said Emilio. "Mama will not want to cook." Rosy did not answer him. "Where is Pepé gone?" he asked.

Rosy looked around at him. She drew her knowledge from the quiet air. "He has gone on a journey. He will never come back."

"Is he dead? Do you think he is dead?"

Rosy looked back at the ocean again. A little steamer, drawing a line of smoke, sat on the edge of the horizon. "He is not dead," Rosy explained. "Not yet...."

Directions Write the answers to these questions using complete sentences.

Comprehension: Identifying Facts

1. Where does the Torres family live?

2. What animals does the Torres family have on their farm?

3. What had happened to Pepé's father?

4. What item had Pepé inherited from his father?

5. Why does Pepé have to visit the city?

6. What are the names of the two younger children?

7. What happens to Pepé at the house of Mrs. Rodriguez?

8. After returning from the city, where does Pepé say he must go?

9. What things does Mama give Pepé for his journey?

10. What is the last advice that Mama gives to Pepé before he goes away?

Comprehension: Understanding Main Ideas

11. Explain how the setting of this story is important. How does the setting help readers understand the Torres family?

12. Why had Mama never let Pepé go into town alone before?

13. What changes take place in the character of Pepé?

14. Explain the meaning of this statement that Mama says in this story: "A boy gets to be a man when a man is needed."

15. In what ways is Pepé not a responsible person?

16. What evidence is there that Mama believes that Pepé has become a man?

17. How does Mama explain to the two younger children what has happened to Pepé? Is she shielding the children from what really happened? Explain.

18. How do the younger children react to Pepé's leaving?

19. What evidence is there that Mama had been afraid Pepé would get in trouble someday?

20. Why is this story titled "Flight"? What does this title mean?

Understanding Literature: Animal Imagery

Animal imagery is important in "Flight." For example, Mama Torres calls her son a "foolish chicken." This and other names express how Mama feels toward Pepé and add to the interest of the story. They also convey a loving aspect of Mama's character.

21. Find three other animal images mentioned in this story.

22. Explain what each example from question 21 means.

23. What do you learn about Mama by reading these images?

24. What do you learn about Pepé by reading these images?

25. How do these images add to the story?

Critical Thinking

26. Why do you think the author pays so much attention to the knife and to Pepé's skill at throwing it? Did you guess that the knife would eventually cause trouble for Pepé? Explain.

27. Do you think Mama was right to send Pepé away in the night? Explain your answer.

28. Do you think that Pepé acts in an adult way at the Rodriguez house?

29. Do you believe that Pepé will ever return home? Explain your answer.

30. Do you agree with Pepé when he says that he is a man? Why or why not?

Writing on Your Own Pretend you are a newspaper reporter writing an article for a California newspaper about what happened with Pepé at the Rodriguez house. Write the article based on the facts given in this story. Create your own details to make the article complete. Remember to answer these questions: Who was involved? What happened? When did it happen? Where did it happen? Why did it happen? How did it happen?

In Honor of David Anderson Brooks, My Father Gwendolyn Brooks

Gwendolyn Brooks
1917–

About the Author

Many people feel that poet Gwendolyn Brooks is good at making events in her own life interesting to others. Her natural style offers views of simple events in a creative way. Her poetry has been in many magazines, newspapers, and books.

Brooks was born in Kansas. However, she spent almost all of her life in Chicago. Her family encouraged her to write. At thirteen, one of her poems was published in a magazine. She also sent poems to a Chicago newspaper. After graduating from Wilson Junior College, Brooks worked in publishing. She became a successful poet. She married Henry Blakely in 1939, and they had two children.

In 1950, Brooks was awarded a Pulitzer Prize for *Annie Allen*. She received other awards for her works, including Poet Laureate of Illinois. She has tried to help other writers. African American poets once published a collection of their works, called *To Gwen With Love*, to thank her for her support.

About the Selection

Poets often write about other people in their poems. Sometimes people in a poem are not real; sometimes they are. This selection is written about the poet's father. The poet helps the reader to understand some important facts about his life and his death.

Notice that this poem has a **rhyme scheme**. This is a pattern of end rhymes in a poem. This poem is also a **requiem**. A requiem is a prayer for the dead or something written in honor of the dead.

In Honor of
David Anderson Brooks,
My Father

July 30, 1883 – November 21, 1959

A dryness is upon the house
My father loved and tended.
Beyond his firm and **sculptured** door
4   His light and lease have ended.

He walks the valleys, now—replies
To sun and wind forever.
No more the cramping chamber's chill,
8   No more the **hindering** fever.

Now out upon the wide clean air
My father's soul revives,
All innocent of self-interest
12   And the fear that strikes and strives.

He who was Goodness, Gentleness,
And Dignity is free,
Translates to public Love
16   Old private Charity.

What does this poem tell you about David Anderson Brooks? What does it tell you about the poet's relationship with her father?

hindering hampering; blocking or slowing progress

sculptured carved; decorated with markings or carvings

In Honor of David Anderson Brooks, My Father Gwendolyn Brooks

Directions Write the answers to these questions using complete sentences.

Comprehension: Identifying Facts

1. How many stanzas are included in this poem?

2. What personality traits does the author remember about her father?

3. Notice the subtitle that is included with this poem. What age was the poet's father when he died?

Comprehension: Understanding Main Ideas

4. What opposites do you see in this poem?

5. List the emotions that you believe the author is feeling as she wrote this poem. Explain your answer.

6. Certain lines indicate that the author believes in an afterlife. Which lines in this poem show that belief?

Understanding Literature: Rhyme Scheme and Requiem

The rhyme scheme is a pattern sometimes found in poetry in which lines end in rhyming words. In a rhyme scheme, letters are used to indicate the rhymes found in each line. Suppose that you have a stanza with four lines. Depending on the rhyming words used,

different patterns are possible. If lines 1 and 2 and lines 3 and 4 rhyme, the pattern would be described as *a, a, b, b*. If lines 1 and 3 and lines 2 and 4 rhyme, the pattern would be *a, b, a, b*. If lines 2 and 4 rhyme, but lines 1 and 3 do not, the pattern would be *a, b, c, b*.

Requiem comes from a Latin word meaning "rest" or "quiet." A requiem is a prayer for the dead or a work that has been written in honor of the dead.

7. What rhyme scheme is used in the first stanza of this poem?

8. Read the poem "In Honor of David Anderson Brooks, My Father" again. Explain why this poem could be called a requiem.

Critical Thinking

9. Do you think that the author fears death? Why or why not?

10. Do you think that David Anderson Brooks was a good father? Why or why not?

> **Writing on Your Own** Think of an idea for a poem. It can be a poem about a relative, as Gwendolyn Brooks's poem is. It can also be about a place, idea, or thing. Then write the poem in at least two stanzas with four lines per stanza, and with the rhyme scheme *a, b, a, b*.

The Catbird Seat
James Thurber

James Thurber
1894–1961

Literary Terms

metaphor a figure of speech that makes a comparison

simile a figure of speech that makes a comparison using the words *like* or *as*

theme the main idea of a literary work

Thurber's self-portrait above shows his cartoon style.

About the Author

James Thurber was perhaps one of the greatest humorous writers of modern times. He was also a cartoonist. His favorite **theme**—the main idea of a literary work—was a dazed man struggling in a complex world. Male characters were weak, but the women were strong.

Thurber was born in Columbus, Ohio, in 1894. He attended Ohio State University (which he claimed has never been the same since), but did not graduate. He was a clerk during World War I. Later he became a newspaper reporter in Paris, New York, and Ohio. He wrote humorous articles for *The New Yorker* magazine and was hired as a staff writer in 1927.

Thurber was an unusual-looking man. He was tall and thin. He was a great wit. He often tricked people on the telephone by using a different voice. He eventually quit working full time for the magazine, but he continued to write articles. When Thurber visited his friends at the magazine, he often left doodles of people and animals on their desks. This doodling was the start of his life as a cartoonist.

Unfortunately, in his later years, Thurber went blind. His works became more sad and painful. Thurber died in 1961.

About the Selection

Thurber liked to use the theme of the battle of the sexes. The little man, daydreaming his life away, and the determined strong woman make up a humorous clashing. "The Catbird Seat" is a story of such a pair. The mild office clerk, Mr. Erwin Martin, is threatened by a loud, pushy woman, Mrs. Ulgine Barrows. Mr. Martin's precious filing system is being threatened. Is there any way for him to protect it?

Watch for **similes** and **metaphors** in this selection. A simile is a comparison that uses the words *like* or *as*. A metaphor is a figure of speech that makes a comparison. Both add to the humor in this story.

The Catbird Seat

The main character in this story, Mr. Martin, has a hidden personality. On the outside he is plain, calm, and likable. What is he like on the inside? How does this affect his actions?

What is Mr. Martin planning to do to Mrs. Barrows?

Mr. Martin bought the pack of Camels on Monday night in the most crowded cigar store on Broadway. It was theater time and seven or eight men were buying cigarettes. The clerk didn't even glance at Mr. Martin, who put the pack in his overcoat pocket and went out. If any of the staff at F & S had seen him buy the cigarettes, they would have been astonished, for it was generally known that Mr. Martin did not smoke, and never had. No one saw him.

It was just a week to the day since Mr. Martin had decided to rub out Mrs. Ulgine Barrows. The term "rub out" pleased him because it suggested nothing more than the correction of an error—in this case an error of Mr. Fitweiler. Mr. Martin had spent each night of the past week working out his plan and examining it. As he walked home now he went over it again. For the hundredth time he resented the element of **imprecision**, the margin of guesswork that entered into the business. The project as he had worked it out was casual and bold, the risks were considerable. Something might go wrong anywhere along the line. And therein lay the cunning of his scheme. No one would ever see in it the cautious, painstaking hand of Erwin Martin, head of the filing department at F & S, of whom Mr. Fitweiler had once said, "Man is **fallible** but Martin isn't." No one would see his hand, that is, unless it were caught in the act.

Sitting in his apartment, drinking a glass of milk, Mr. Martin reviewed his case against Mrs. Ulgine Barrows, as he had every night for seven nights. He began at the beginning. Her quacking voice and braying laugh had first **profaned** the halls of F & S on March 7, 1941 (Mr. Martin had a head for

---

fallible able to make mistakes

imprecision not exact

profane to treat with disrespect or abuse

dates). Old Roberts, the personnel chief, had introduced her as the newly appointed special advisor to the president of the firm, Mr. Fitweiler. The woman had **appalled** Mr. Martin instantly, but he hadn't shown it. He had given her his dry hand, a look of **studious** concentration, and a faint smile. "Well," she said, looking at the papers on his desk, "are you lifting the oxcart out of the ditch?" As Mr. Martin recalled that moment, over his milk, he squirmed slightly. He must keep his mind on her crimes as a special advisor, not on her **peccadillos** as a personality. This he found difficult to do, in spite of entering an objection and sustaining it. The faults of the woman as a woman kept chattering on in his mind like an unruly witness. She had, for almost two years now, baited him. In the halls, in the elevator, even in his own office, into which she romped now and then like a circus horse, she was constantly shouting these silly questions at him. "Are you

appall to overcome with shock or surprise	**peccadillo** a slight offense	**studious** earnest; relating to study

Why does Mrs. Barrows ask Mr. Martin these questions?

This paragraph explains what some of Mrs. Barrows's sayings mean and where they came from. She learned the sayings by listening to broadcasts of Dodger baseball games. Notice that "sitting in the catbird seat" means being in a good situation.

This paragraph shows a humorous side of Mr. Martin. He is holding a court case for Mrs. Barrows in his head.

lifting the oxcart out of the ditch? Are you tearing up the pea patch? Are you hollering down the rain barrel? Are you scraping around the bottom of the pickle barrel? Are you sitting in the catbird seat?"

It was Joey Hart, one of Mr. Martin's two assistants, who had explained what the gibberish meant. "She must be a Dodger fan," he had said. "Red Barber announces the Dodger games over the radio and he uses those expressions—picked 'em up down South." Joey had gone on to explain one or two. "Tearing up the pea patch" meant going on a **rampage**; "sitting in the catbird seat" meant sitting pretty, like a batter with three balls and no strikes on him. Mr. Martin dismissed all this with an effort. It had been annoying, it had driven him near to distraction, but he was too solid a man to be moved to murder by anything so childish. It was fortunate, he reflected as he passed on to the important charges against Mrs. Barrows, that he had stood up under it so well. He had maintained always an outward appearance of polite **tolerance**. "Why, I even believe you like the woman," Miss Paird, his other assistant, had once said to him. He had simply smiled.

A gavel rapped in Mr. Martin's mind and the case proper was resumed. Mrs. Ulgine Barrows stood charged with willful, **blatant**, and **persistent** attempts to destroy the efficiency and system of F & S. It was **competent**, material, and **relevant** to review her **advent** and rise to power. Mr. Martin had got the story from Miss Paird, who seemed always able to find things out. According to her, Mrs. Barrows had met Mr. Fitweiler at a party, where she had rescued him from the embraces of a powerfully built drunken man who had mistaken the president of F & S for a famous retired Middle Western football coach. She had led him to a sofa and somehow worked upon him a monstrous magic. The aging

advent coming into being or use	**persistent** continuing without regard to opposition or failure	**relevant** the condition of being appropriate
blatant done on purpose	**rampage** a course of violent or reckless actions	**tolerance** the ability to withstand pain or hardship
competent acceptable; suitable		

gentleman had jumped to the conclusion there and then that this was a woman of **singular** attainments, equipped to bring out the best in him and in the firm. A week later he had introduced her into F & S as his special advisor. On that day confusion got its foot in the door. After Miss Tyson, Mr. Brundage, and Mr. Bartlett had been fired and Mr. Munson had taken his hat and stalked out, mailing his resignation later, old Roberts had been emboldened to speak to Mr. Fitweiler. He mentioned that Mr. Munson's department had been "a little **disrupted**" and hadn't they perhaps better resume the old system there? Mr. Fitweiler had said certainly not. He had the greatest faith in Mrs. Barrows's ideas. "They require a little seasoning, a little seasoning, is all," he had added. Mr. Roberts had given it up. Mr. Martin reviewed in detail all the changes wrought by Mrs. Barrows. She had begun chipping at the cornices of the firm's edifice and now she was swinging at the foundation stones with a pickaxe.

A *cornice* is the very top piece, often overhanging, of a building. An *edifice* is a large building. The last sentence in this paragraph is a metaphor. Mrs. Barrows's changes to the company are being compared humorously to the destruction of the office building with a pickaxe.

    Mr. Martin came now, in his summing up, to the afternoon of Monday, November 2, 1942—just one week ago. On that day, at 3 P.M., Mrs. Barrows had bounced into his office. "Boo!" she had yelled. "Are you scraping around the bottom of the pickle barrel?" Mr. Martin had looked at her from under his green eyeshade, saying nothing. She had begun to wander about the office, taking it in with her great, popping eyes. "Do you really need *all* these filing cabinets?" she had demanded suddenly. Mr. Martin's heart had jumped. "Each of these files," he had said, keeping his voice even, "plays an **indispensable** part in the system of F & S." She had brayed at him, "Well, don't tear up the pea patch!" and gone to the door. From there she had bawled, "But you sure have got a lot of fine scrap in here!" Mr. Martin could no longer doubt that the finger was on his beloved department. Her pickaxe was on the upswing, poised for the first blow. It had not come yet; he had received no blue memo from the enchanted Mr. Fitweiler bearing **nonsensical** instructions

disrupted thrown into disorder	**indispensable** unable to do without	**nonsensical** not making sense
		singular excellent

Here the true cause of Mr. Martin's hatred toward Mrs. Barrows is revealed. She wants to change his precious filing system. The court case inside his head ends here with him deciding on the death penalty for Mrs. Barrows.

deriving from the **obscene** woman. But there was no doubt in Mr. Martin's mind that one would be forthcoming. He must act quickly. Already a precious week had gone by. Mr. Martin stood up in his living room, still holding his milk glass. "Gentlemen of the jury," he said to himself, "I demand the death penalty for this horrible person."

The next day Mr. Martin followed his routine, as usual. He polished his glasses more often and once sharpened an already sharp pencil, but not even Miss Paird noticed. Only once did he catch sight of his victim; she swept past him in the hall with a **patronizing** "Hi!" At five-thirty he walked home, as usual, and had a glass of milk, as usual. He had never drunk anything stronger in his life—unless you could count ginger ale. The late Sam Schlosser, the S of F & S, had praised Mr. Martin at a staff meeting several years before for his **temperate** habits. "Our most efficient worker neither drinks nor smokes," he had said. "The results speak for themselves." Mr. Fitweiler had sat by, nodding approval.

Mr. Martin was still thinking about that red-letter day as he walked over to the Schrafft's on Fifth Avenue near Forty-sixth Street. He got there, as he always did, at eight o'clock. He finished his dinner and the **financial** page of the *Sun* at a quarter to nine, as he always did. It was his custom after dinner to take a walk. This time he walked down Fifth Avenue at a casual pace. His gloved hands felt moist and warm, his forehead cold. He transferred the Camels from his overcoat to a jacket pocket. He wondered, as he did so, if they did not represent an unnecessary note of strain. Mrs. Barrows smoked only Luckies. It was his idea to puff a few puffs on a Camel (after the rubbing-out), stub it out in the ashtray holding her lipstick-stained Luckies, and thus drag a small red herring across the trail. Perhaps it was not a good idea. It would take time. He might even choke, too loudly.

A *red herring* is something that distracts attention from the real issue. The term comes from the old practice of drawing red herring across a trail to confuse hunting dogs.

derive to come from	**obscene** disgusting; offensive	**temperate** keeping or held within limits; moderate
financial related to money	**patronizing** in a way that suggests one is superior	

Mr. Martin had never seen the house on West Twelfth Street where Mrs. Barrows lived, but he had a clear enough picture of it. Fortunately, she had bragged to everybody about her ducky first-floor apartment in the perfectly darling three-story red-brick. There would be no doorman or other attendants; just the **tenants** of the second and third floors. As he walked along, Mr. Martin realized that he would get there before nine-thirty. He had considered walking north on Fifth Avenue from Schrafft's to a point from which it would take him until ten o'clock to reach the house. At that hour people were less likely to be coming in or going out. But the **procedure** would have made an awkward loop in the straight thread of his casualness, and he had abandoned it. It was impossible to figure when people would be entering or leaving the house, anyway. There was a great risk at any hour. If he ran into anybody, he would simply have to place the rubbing-out of Ulgine Barrows in the inactive file forever. The same thing would hold true if there were someone in her apartment. In that case he would just say that he had been passing by, recognized her charming house and thought to drop in.

What do you think Mr. Martin will do to Mrs. Barrows?

It was eighteen minutes after nine when Mr. Martin turned into Twelfth Street. A man passed him, and a man and a woman, talking. There was no one within fifty paces when he came to the house, halfway down the block. He was up the steps in the small vestibule in no time, pressing the bell under the card that said "Mrs. Ulgine Barrows." When the clicking in the lock started, he jumped forward against the door. He got inside fast, closing the door behind him. A bulb in a lantern hung from the hall ceiling on a chain seemed to give a monstrously bright light. There was nobody on the stair, which went up ahead of him along the left wall. A door opened down the hall in the wall on the right. He went toward it swiftly, on tiptoe.

A *vestibule* is a passage, lobby, or a small room between the outer door and the inside of a building.

"Well, for God's sake, look who's here!" bawled Mrs. Barrows, and her braying laugh rang out like the report of a

procedure the planned way of completing a task

tenant one who lives in an apartment building

Notice the many similes in this paragraph: "like the report of a shotgun," "like a football tackle," "as jumpy as a goat," and "as white as a sheet." How do they add to the humor in this story?

A *toddy* is a hot drink consisting of liquor, water, sugar, and spices.

Here Mr. Martin is looking for a weapon to use to murder Mrs. Barrows.

An *andiron* is a metal support for firewood used in a fireplace, often used in pairs.

A *highball* is an alcoholic drink of water or carbonated liquid mixed with a liquor such as whiskey and served in a tall glass.

shotgun. He pushed past her like a football tackle, bumping her. "Hey, quit shoving!" she said, closing the door behind them. They were in her living room, which seemed to Mr. Martin to be lighted by a hundred lamps. "What's after you?" she said. "You're as jumpy as a goat." He found he was unable to speak. His heart was wheezing in his throat. "I—yes," he finally brought out. She was jabbering and laughing as she started to help him off with his coat. "No, no," he said. "I'll put it here." He took it off and put it on a chair near the door. "Your hat and gloves, too," she said. "You're in a lady's house." He put his hat on top of the coat. Mrs. Barrows seemed larger than he had thought. He kept his gloves on. "I was passing by," he said. "I recognized—is there anyone here?" She laughed louder than ever. "No, " she said, "we're all alone. You're as white as a sheet, you funny man. Whatever *has* come over you? I'll mix you a toddy." She started toward a door across the room. "Scotch-and-soda be all right? But say, you don't drink, do you?" She turned and gave him her amused look. Mr. Martin pulled himself together. "Scotch-and-soda will be all right," he heard himself say. He could hear her laughing in the kitchen.

Mr. Martin looked quickly around the living room for the weapon. He had counted on finding one there. There were andirons and a poker and something in a corner that looked like an Indian club. None of them would do. It couldn't be that way. He began to pace around. He came to a desk. On it lay a metal paper knife with an **ornate** handle. Would it be sharp enough? He reached for it and knocked over a small brass jar. Stamps spilled out of it and it fell to the floor with a clatter. "Hey," Mrs. Barrows yelled from the kitchen, "are you tearing up the pea patch?" Mr. Martin gave a strange laugh. Picking up the knife, he tried its point against his left wrist. It was blunt. It wouldn't do.

When Mrs. Barrows reappeared, carrying two highballs, Mr. Martin, standing there with his gloves on, became **acutely** conscious of the fantasy he had wrought. Cigarettes in his

acutely sharply; intensely

ornate overly decorated

pocket, a drink prepared for him—it was all too grossly **improbable**. It was more than that; it was impossible. Somewhere in the back of his mind a vague idea stirred, sprouted. "For heaven's sake, take off those gloves," said Mrs. Barrows. "I always wear them in the house," said Mr. Martin. The idea began to bloom, strange and wonderful. She put the glasses on a coffee table in front of a sofa and sat on the sofa. "Come over here, you odd little man," she said. Mr. Martin went over and sat beside her. It was difficult getting a cigarette out of the pack of Camels, but he managed it. She held a match for him laughing. "Well," she said, handing him his drink, "this is perfectly marvelous. You with a drink and a cigarette."

Mr. Martin puffed, not too awkwardly, and took a gulp of the highball. "I drink and smoke all the time," he said. He clinked his glass against hers. "Here's nuts to that old windbag, Fitweiler," he said, and gulped again. The stuff tasted awful, but he made no **grimace**. "Really, Mr. Martin," she said, her voice and posture changing, "you are insulting our employer." Mrs. Barrows was now all special advisor to the president. "I am preparing a bomb," said Mr. Martin, "which will blow the old goat higher than hell." He had only had a little of

grimace an expression of disgust on a person's face

improbable not likely

379

the drink, which was not strong. It couldn't be that. "Do you take dope or something?" Mrs. Barrows asked coldly. "Heroin," said Mr. Martin. "I'll be coked to the gills when I bump that old buzzard off." "Mr. Martin!" she shouted, getting to her feet. "That will be all of that. You must go at once." Mr. Martin took another swallow of his drink. He tapped his cigarette out in the ashtray and put the pack of Camels on the coffee table. Then he got up. She stood glaring at him. He walked over and put on his hat and coat. "Not a word about this," he said, and laid an index finger against his lips. All Mrs. Barrows could bring out was "Really!" Mr. Martin put his hand on the doorknob. "I'm sitting in the catbird seat," he said. He stuck his tongue out at her and left. Nobody saw him go.

Mr. Martin got to his apartment, walking, well before eleven. No one saw him go in. He had two glasses of milk after brushing his teeth, and he felt **elated**. It wasn't tipsiness, because he hadn't been tipsy. Anyway, the walk had worn off all effects of the whiskey. He got in bed and read a magazine for a while. He was asleep before midnight.

Mr. Martin got to the office at eight-thirty the next morning, as usual. At a quarter to nine, Ulgine Barrows, who had never before arrived at work before ten, swept into his office. "I'm reporting to Mr. Fitweiler now!" she shouted. "If he turns you over to the police, it's no more than you deserve!" Mr. Martin gave her a look of shocked surprise. "I beg your pardon?" he said. Mrs. Barrows snorted and bounced out of the room, leaving Miss Paird and Joey staring after her. "What's the matter with that old devil now?" asked Miss Paird. "I have no idea," said Mr. Martin, resuming his work. The other two looked at him and then at each other. Miss Paird got up and went out. She walked slowly past the closed door of Mr. Fitweiler's office. Mrs. Barrows was yelling inside, but she was not braying. Miss Paird could not hear what the woman was saying. She went back to her desk.

Why do you think Mr. Martin does and says these things in this paragraph? Was this what you expected would happen?

Do you think Mr. Fitweiler will believe what Mrs. Barrows tells him about Mr. Martin?

elated filled with joy

Forty-five minutes later, Mrs. Barrows left the president's office and went into her own, shutting the door. It wasn't until half an hour later that Mr. Fitweiler sent for Mr. Martin. The head of the filing department, neat, quiet, **attentive**, stood in front of the old man's desk. Mr. Fitweiler was pale and nervous. He took his glasses off and twiddled them. He made a small, bruffing sound in his throat. "Martin," he said, "you have been with us more than twenty years." "Twenty-two, sir," said Mr. Martin. "In that time," pursued the president, "your work and your—uh—manner have been **exemplary**." "I trust so, sir," said Mr. Martin. "I have understood, Martin," said Mr. Fitweiler, "that you have never taken a drink or smoked." "That is correct, sir," said Mr. Martin. "Ah, yes." Mr. Fitweiler polished his glasses. "You may describe what you did after leaving the office yesterday, Martin," he said. Mr. Martin allowed less than a second for his bewildered pause. "Certainly, sir," he said. "I walked home. Then I went to Schrafft's for dinner. Afterward I walked home again. I went to bed early, sir, and read a magazine for a while. I was asleep before eleven." "Ah, yes," said Mr. Fitweiler again. He was silent for a moment, searching for the proper words to say to the head of the filing department. "Mrs. Barrows," he said finally, "Mrs. Barrows has worked hard, Martin, very hard. It grieves me to report that she has suffered a severe breakdown. It has taken the form of a persecution complex accompanied by distressing **hallucinations**." "I am very sorry, sir," said Mr. Martin. "Mrs. Barrows is under the **delusion**," continued Mr. Fitweiler, "that you visited her last evening and behaved yourself in an—uh—unseemly manner." He raised his hand to silence Mr. Martin's little pained outcry. "It is the nature of these psychological diseases," Mr. Fitweiler said, "to fix upon the least likely and most innocent party as the— uh—source of persecution. These matters are not for the lay mind to grasp, Martin. I've just had my psychiatrist, Dr. Fitch,

Here the author reveals that Mr. Fitweiler does not believe Mrs. Barrows's story. He thinks she is crazy, because he thinks Mr. Martin would never act in such a way.

attentive paying careful attention; alert	**exemplary** serving as a good example	**hallucination** a completely mistaken vision or perception
delusion a false belief		

on the phone. He would not, of course, commit himself, but he made enough generalizations to **substantiate** my suspicions. I suggested to Mrs. Barrows, when she had completed her—uh—story to me this morning, that she visit Dr. Fitch, for I suspected a condition at once. She flew, I regret to say, into a rage, and demanded—uh—requested that I call you on the carpet. You may not know, Martin, but Mrs. Barrows had planned a reorganization of your department—subject to my approval, of course, subject to my approval. This brought you, rather than anyone else, to her mind—but again that is a **phenomenon** for Dr. Fitch and not for us. So, Martin, I am afraid Mrs. Barrows's usefulness here is at an end." "I am dreadfully sorry, sir," said Mr. Martin.

Mr. Fitweiler plans to fire Mrs. Barrows.

It was at this point that the door to the office blew open with the suddenness of a gas-main explosion and Mrs. Barrows **catapulted** through it. "Is the little rat denying it?" she screamed. "He can't get away with that!" Mr. Martin got up and moved **discreetly** to a point beside Mr. Fitweiler's chair. "You drank and smoked at my apartment," she bawled at Mr. Martin, "and you know it! You called Mr. Fitweiler an old windbag and said you were going to blow him up when you got coked to the gills on your heroin!" She stopped yelling to catch her breath and a new glint came into her popping eyes. "If you weren't such a drab, ordinary little man," she said, "I'd think you'd planned it all. Sticking your tongue out, saying you were sitting in the catbird seat, because you thought no one would believe me when I told it! My God, it's really too perfect!" She brayed loudly and **hysterically**, and the fury was on her again. She glared at Mr. Fitweiler. "Can't you see how he has tricked us, you old fool? Can't you see his little game?" But Mr. Fitweiler had been **surreptitiously** pressing all the buttons under the top of his

How is Mr. Martin in "the catbird seat" at this point in the story?

catapult to throw or launch; to move with great force	**hysterically** showing a very high level of emotion	**substantiate** to confirm
discreetly acting in a quiet, unnoticed manner	**phenomenon** a rare or unusual event	**surreptitiously** secretly

desk and employees of F & S began pouring into the room. "Stockton," said Mr. Fitweiler, "you and Fishbein will take Mrs. Barrows to her home. Mrs. Powell, you will go with them." Stockton, who had played a little football in high school, blocked Mrs. Barrows as she made for Mr. Martin. It took him and Fishbein together to force her out of the door into the hall, crowded with stenographers and office boys. She was still screaming **imprecations** at Mr. Martin, tangled and **contradictory** imprecations. The hubbub finally died out down the corridor.

A *stenographer* is a person employed to take notes or to write in shorthand.

"I regret that this has happened," said Mr. Fitweiler. "I shall ask you to dismiss it from your mind, Martin." "Yes, sir," said Mr. Martin, **anticipating** his chief's "That will be all" by moving to the door. "I will dismiss it." He went out and shut the door, and his step was light and quick in the hall. When he entered his department he had slowed down to his customary gait, and he walked quietly across the room to the W20 file, wearing a look of studious concentration.

| **anticipate** to predict or expect what will happen | **contradictory** going against what was previously said | **imprecation** a curse; swearing |

The Catbird Seat
James Thurber

Directions Write the answers to these questions using complete sentences.

Comprehension: Identifying Facts

1. What does Erwin Martin do at F & S?

2. What does Ulgine Barrows do at F & S?

3. How do others view Mr. Martin as a person?

4. What evidence is there that people at F & S do not like Mrs. Barrows?

5. What does Mr. Martin fear about Mrs. Barrows?

6. What does Mr. Martin plan to do to Mrs. Barrows at the beginning of the story?

7. What does Mr. Martin search for in Mrs. Barrows's apartment?

8. What does Mr. Martin end up doing in Mrs. Barrows's apartment?

9. How does Mr. Fitweiler react to the story Mrs. Barrows tells the next day at work?

10. What happens to Mrs. Barrows at the end of the story?

Comprehension: Understanding Main Ideas

11. Why is Mr. Martin an odd character?

12. Why is Mrs. Barrows not very likable?

13. In what unusual way does Mr. Martin consider whether he should murder Mrs. Barrows?

14. Does it seem as if Mrs. Barrows deserves her position at F & S? Explain.

15. In what ways does Mr. Martin act out of character at Mrs. Barrows's apartment? Why does he act like this?

16. How does Mrs. Barrows react to Mr. Martin's strange actions at her apartment? What does this reveal about her character?

17. What does Mr. Fitweiler believe has happened to Mrs. Barrows at the end of the story?

18. How does Mr. Martin react to what happens to Mrs. Barrows?

19. One of Mr. Martin's assistants explains the expression "sitting in the catbird seat." What does this mean? Where did it come from? How is it a good name for this story?

20. At which point in the story did you realize that this was not a serious murder mystery?

Understanding Literature: Humor

Many types of humor exist in writing. Humor can be found in exaggerated situations or characters, regional dialect, plays on words, odd behavior, sharp and mean comments, criticism of society, quick jokes, or slow and easy plot development. Thurber uses many of these to make "The Catbird Seat" a very funny story.

21. How does Thurber use humor in this story?

22. Does Thurber's humor work in this story? Why or why not?

23. How might this have been a very different story if it were written without humor?

24. Which part of this story was the most humorous to you? Why?

25. Mr. Martin and Mrs. Barrows are in many ways average people. How does the author make these characters funny?

Critical Thinking

26. This story takes place in 1941 and 1942. Explain how a character such as Mr. Martin might react to the changes that have occurred in the workplace since that time.

27. Do you feel sorry for any of the characters in this story? Why or why not?

28. Who do you think has won this particular war between the sexes? Why?

29. Do you think anyone will ever find out what Mr. Martin did? Explain.

30. Do you think Mrs. Barrows will try to do anything to get back at Mr. Martin? Explain.

Writing on Your Own Write a humorous short story of your own about a real or imagined event. Use some of the techniques Thurber used in "The Catbird Seat," such as funny characters, odd behavior, or unexpected events.

Hiroshima
John Hersey

John Hersey
1914–1993

Literary Terms

fiction writing that is imaginative and designed to entertain

historical fiction writing that draws on factual events of history

novel fiction that is book-length and has more plot and character details than a short story

third-person point of view a point of view that refers to characters as "he" or "she" and expresses some characters' thoughts

About the Author

John Hersey was a novelist who used actual events from history as the subject of most of his works. This is called **historical fiction**. The events of World War II and after the war were tied into his first works. He studied at Yale and Cambridge and later became a journalist. The reporter's writing style and a good eye for detail are clear in his **fiction**. Fiction is writing that is imaginative and designed to entertain.

Hersey was born in 1914, in Tientsin, China. His parents were American missionaries. The family returned to the United States in 1925. Hersey spent much of his life writing fiction and teaching at Yale University. He won the Pulitzer Prize in 1945 for another war story, *A Bell for Adano*. *Hiroshima* was first published in 1946.

About the Selection

"At exactly fifteen minutes past eight in the morning, on August 6, 1945, Japanese time. . ." These are the first words of the historical **novel**, *Hiroshima*. A novel is fiction that is book-length and has more plot and character details than a short story. *Hiroshima* dramatically and clearly tells of the effect of the first atomic bomb. It destroyed 4.7 miles of the city of Hiroshima, Japan. The United States dropped a second bomb on another Japanese city, Nagasaki, three days later, to bring an end to World War II. On August 14, 1945, Japan surrendered.

Hiroshima looks at the lives of people who survived to tell their stories of the morning the atomic bomb was dropped. This selection opens Chapter 2. The characters have been introduced already. The reaction to the atomic bomb's destruction is beginning. This selection looks at the frightening events of August 6, 1945.

Notice that this story is told in the **third-person point of view**. This point of view refers to characters as "he" or "she" and expresses some characters' thoughts.

From Hiroshima

Chapter 2 The Fire

Immediately after the explosion, the Reverend Mr. Kiyoshi Tanimoto, having run wildly out of the Matsui estate and having looked in wonderment at the bloody soldiers at the mouth of the dugout they had been digging, attached himself sympathetically to an old lady who was walking along in a daze, holding her head with her left hand, supporting a small boy of three or four on her back with her right, and crying, "I'm hurt! I'm hurt! I'm hurt!" Mr. Tanimoto transferred the child to his own back and led the woman by the hand down the street, which was darkened by what seemed to be a local column of dust. He took the woman to a grammar school not far away that had previously been **designated** for use as a **temporary** hospital in case of emergency. By this **solicitous** behavior, Mr. Tanimoto at once got rid of his terror. At the school, he was much surprised to see glass all over the floor and fifty or sixty injured people already waiting to be treated. He reflected that, although the all-clear had sounded and he had heard no planes, several bombs must have been dropped. He thought of a hillock in the rayon man's garden from which he could get a view of the whole of Koi—of the whole of Hiroshima, for that matter—and he ran back up to the estate.

How does this selection make you feel about what happened in Hiroshima?

The mushroom cloud pictured below is the explosion of the atomic bomb over Hiroshima.

designate to set apart for a certain purpose

temporary lasting for only a short or set time

solicitous protective

From the mound, Mr. Tanimoto saw an astonishing **panorama**. Not just a patch of Koi, as he had expected, but as much of Hiroshima as he could see through the clouded air was giving off a thick, dreadful miasma. Clumps of smoke, near and far, had begun to push up through the general dust. He wondered how such extensive damage could have been dealt out of a silent sky; even a few planes, far up, would have been **audible**. Houses nearby were burning, and when huge drops of water the size of marbles began to fall, he half thought that they must be coming from the hoses of firemen fighting the blazes. (They were actually drops of condensed moisture falling from the **turbulent** tower of dust, heat, and fission fragments that had already risen miles into the sky above Hiroshima.)

Mr. Tanimoto turned away from the sight when he heard Mr. Matsuo call out to ask whether he was all right. Mr. Matsuo had been safely cushioned within the falling house by the bedding stored in the front hall and had worked his way out. Mr. Tanimoto scarcely answered. He had thought of his wife and baby, his church, his home, his **parishioners**, all of them down in that awful murk. Once more he began to run in fear—toward the city.

A *miasma* is a heavy fog.

The word *fission* refers to the splitting of atoms resulting in the release of large amounts of energy. The atomic bomb dropped on Hiroshima used this fission process.

What does this paragraph tell about the destruction the atomic bomb caused?

This picture shows the destruction of Hiroshima after the bombing.

audible able to be heard

panorama a complete view of an area in every direction

parishioner a member of a church community

turbulent causing great unrest or disturbance

Directions Write the answers to these questions using complete sentences.

Comprehension: Identifying Facts

1. Who is the main character of this selection?

2. What does he see, hear, and feel when he surveys the city?

3. How had Mr. Matsuo been protected during the blast?

Comprehension: Understanding Main Ideas

4. Explain the huge drops of water that begin to fall.

5. Why is Mr. Tanimoto surprised that the sky has no planes in it?

6. Why does he begin to run to the city?

Understanding Literature: Point of View

The point of view is the perspective from which a story is told. A character can tell the story from the first-person point of view, which means that the pronoun "I" will be used frequently. "I saw the woman and the small boy." A story may also be told in the third-person point of view by a narrator who is not involved in the story at all. "He saw the woman and the small boy." The "he" and "she" pronouns will be used frequently.

7. In which point of view is *Hiroshima* told?

8. How does the reader find out what the characters think and feel? Could another character have observed this? Explain your answer.

Critical Thinking

9. Is "The Fire" a good title for this chapter of the book? Why or why not? What might be another chapter title?

10. What do you think happened to Mr. Tanimoto's family?

Writing on Your Own Write a paragraph of at least five sentences telling some part of Mr. Tanimoto's story. Change the point of view to first person so that it appears that you are the central character. Use the pronoun "I" to relate some of these events.

Notes of a Native Son
James Baldwin

James Baldwin

1924–1987

Literary Terms

autobiography a story about a person's life written by that person

essay a kind of writing that deals with one main subject and states facts and opinions to support the author's beliefs

About the Author

James Baldwin's honest and powerful works have made him an important modern writer. The carefully crafted language, strong sentence structure, and deep insights into people are Baldwin's strong points.

Baldwin was born in New York City in 1924. He was raised in Harlem. His stepfather was a preacher who wanted Baldwin to become one, too. This large family did not provide much time or quiet for Baldwin's two favorite activities, reading and writing. However, he managed to do both.

Baldwin left a preaching career after only three years. He wrote, worked, and lived in Greenwich Village. His first novel, completed at age twenty-two, was not a success. He eventually moved to Paris, France, and wrote several of his best works, including *Go Tell It on the Mountain* and *Notes of a Native Son.*

About the Selection

Notes of a Native Son is a collection of **essays** written in 1955 during Baldwin's first stay in Paris. An essay is a kind of writing that deals with one main subject and states facts and opinions to support the author's beliefs. This selection from that work is an **autobiography**. An autobiography is a story about a person's life written by that person. Many of the author's comments about being an African American reflect the problems and attitudes during the 1950s. Baldwin was one of the first great modern African American authors. Many of these writers did not really become successful until the next decade. During that period, the 1960s, African American literature became more popular.

From Notes of a Native Son

I was born in Harlem thirty-one years ago. I began plotting novels at about the time I learned to read. The story of my childhood is the usual **bleak fantasy**, and we can dismiss it with the **restrained** observation that I certainly would not consider living it again. In those days my mother was given to the **exasperating** and mysterious habit of having babies. As they were born, I took them over with one hand and held a book with the other. The children probably suffered, though they have since been kind enough to deny it, and in this way I read *Uncle Tom's Cabin* and *A Tale of Two Cities* over and over and over again; in this way, in fact, I read just about everything I could get my hands on—except the Bible, probably because it was the only book I was encouraged to read. I must also confess that I wrote—a great deal—and my first professional triumph, in any case, the first effort of mine to be seen in print, occurred at the age of twelve or thereabouts, when a short story I had written about the Spanish revolution won some sort of prize in an extremely short-lived church newspaper. I remember the story was **censored** by the lady editor, though I don't remember why, and I was outraged.

Also wrote plays, and songs, for one of which I received a letter of congratulations from Mayor La Guardia, and poetry, about which the less said, the better. My mother was delighted

How did James Baldwin's early life affect his personal development and his career?

Uncle Tom's Cabin by Harriet Beecher Stowe was an important antislavery novel. *A Tale of Two Cities* was a popular novel by British author Charles Dickens.

bleak grim; lacking in warmth, life, or kindliness

exasperating very annoying

censor to change something because it could be displeasing to others

fantasy a daydream or imaginary story

restrain to hold back; to keep under control

Seventh Avenue and 125th Street, Harlem, 1953.

A fellowship is a sum of money an organization offers to a person for advanced study, such as research or writing.

by all these goings-on, but my father wasn't; he wanted me to be a preacher. When I was fourteen I became a preacher, and when I was seventeen I stopped. Very shortly thereafter I left home. For God knows how long I struggled with the world of **commerce** and industry—I guess they would say they struggled with *me*—and when I was about twenty-one I had enough done of a novel to get a Saxton Fellowship. When I was twenty-two the fellowship was over, the novel turned out to be unsalable, and I started waiting on tables in a Village restaurant and writing book reviews—mostly, as it turned out, about the Negro problem, concerning which the color of my skin made me automatically an expert. Did another book, in company with photographer Theodore Pelatowski, about the storefront churches in Harlem. This book met exactly the same fate as my

commerce business

first—fellowship, but no sale. (It was a Rosenwald Fellowship.) By the time I was twenty-four I had decided to stop reviewing books about the Negro problem—which, by this time, was only slightly less horrible in print than it was in life—and I packed my bags and went to France, where I finished, God knows how, *Go Tell It on the Mountain*. . . .

One of the difficulties about being a Negro writer (and this is not special pleading, since I don't mean to suggest that he has it worse than anybody else) is that the Negro problem is written about so widely. The bookshelves groan under the weight of information, and everyone therefore considers himself informed. And this information, furthermore, operates usually (generally, popularly) to **reinforce traditional** attitudes. Of traditional attitudes there are only two—For or Against— and I, personally, find it difficult to say which attitude has caused me the most pain. I am speaking as a writer; from a social point of view I am perfectly aware that the change from ill-will to good-will, however motivated, however imperfect, however expressed, is better than no change at all.

But it is part of the business of the writer—as I see it—to examine attitudes, to go beneath the surface, to tap the source. From this point of view the Negro problem is nearly **inaccessible**. It is not only written about so widely; it is written about so badly. It is quite possible to say that the price a Negro pays for becoming **articulate** is to find himself, at length, with nothing to be articulate about. . . .

I know, in any case, that the most crucial time in my own development came when I was forced to recognize that I was a kind of **bastard** of the West; when I followed the line of my past I did not find myself in Europe but in Africa. And this meant that in some subtle way, in a really **profound** way, I brought to Shakespeare, Bach, Rembrandt, to the stones of

> What does the author say in this paragraph about being an African American writer?

articulate able to express oneself clearly and effectively	**inaccessible** not able to be looked at or considered	**reinforce** to strengthen; to support
bastard a person of unknown origin	**profound** very deep; intense	**traditional** the accepted or usual way of doing things

Paris, to the cathedral at Chartres, and to the Empire State Building, a special attitude. These were not really my creations, they did not contain my history; I might search in them in vain forever for any reflection of myself. I was an **interloper**; this was not my **heritage**. At the same time I had no other heritage which I could possibly hope to use—I had certainly been unfitted for the jungle or the tribe. I would have to appropriate these white centuries, I would have to make them mine—I would have to accept my special attitude, my special place in this scheme—otherwise I would have no place in *any* scheme. What was the most difficult was the fact that I was forced to admit something I had always hidden from myself, which the American Negro has had to hide from himself as the price of his public progress; that I hated and feared white people. This did not mean that I loved black people; on the contrary, I despised them, possibly because they failed to produce Rembrandt. In effect, I hated and feared the world. And this meant, not only that I thus gave the world an altogether murderous power over me, but also that in such a self-destroying **limbo** I could never hope to write.

One writes out of one thing only—one's own experience. Everything depends on how **relentlessly** one forces from this experience the last drop, sweet or bitter, it can possibly give. This is the only real concern of the artist, to recreate out of the disorder of life that order which is art. The difficulty then, for me, of being a Negro writer was the fact that I was, in effect, prohibited from examining my own experience too closely by the tremendous demands and the very real dangers of my social situation. . . .

About my interests: I don't know if I have any, unless the **morbid** desire to own a sixteen-millimeter camera and make experimental movies can be so classified. Otherwise, I love to

The author admits here that at one point in his life, he hated both white and black people. How did this affect him?

The author explains here that one must write about one's own experiences. He admits that he was prevented from looking at his own experiences because of his race.

heritage one's racial or social background	**limbo** a state of uncertainty	**relentlessly** attempting to achieve something without giving up
interloper a person who interferes or intrudes on the rights of others	**morbid** gloomy or unpleasant	

eat and drink—it's my **melancholy conviction** that I've scarcely ever had enough to eat (this is because it's *impossible* to eat enough if you're worried about the next meal)—and I love to argue with people who do not disagree with me too profoundly, and I love to laugh. I do *not* like bohemia, or bohemians, I do not like people whose principal aim is pleasure, and I do not like people who are *earnest* about anything. I don't like people who like me because I'm a Negro; neither do I like people who find in the same accident grounds for **contempt**. I love America more than any other country in the world, and, exactly for this reason, I insist on the right to criticize her **perpetually**. I think all theories are suspect, that the finest principles may have to be modified, or may even be **pulverized** by the demands of life, and that one must find, therefore, one's own moral center and move through the world hoping that this center will guide one aright. I consider that I have many responsibilities, but none greater than this: to last, as Hemingway says, and get my work done.

I want to be an honest man and a good writer.

Bohemia refers to a community of people who live an unusual life.

Do you agree that Americans have the right to criticize their country?

contempt the act of despising; a lack of respect	**melancholy** causing or tending to cause sadness	**pulverize** to crush; to grind into small pieces
conviction a strong belief	**perpetually** all the time; continually	

Directions Write the answers to these questions using complete sentences.

Comprehension: Identifying Facts

1. How old was James Baldwin at the time of this writing?

2. What does Baldwin say he held in the other hand while one hand held a baby?

3. At about what age does Baldwin remember winning his first writing prize?

4. At what age did Baldwin become a preacher? When did he quit?

5. Where did Baldwin finish writing *Go Tell It on the Mountain*?

6. At what age did Baldwin go to Paris, France?

7. What does Baldwin say is the only thing a writer writes about?

8. What interests does Baldwin say he has?

9. What kinds of people does Baldwin say that he does not like?

10. At the end of this essay, what two things does Baldwin say he wants to be?

Comprehension: Understanding Main Ideas

11. What information does Baldwin provide that explains why he became a writer?

12. What evidence is there that Baldwin had a large family?

13. What kind of experiences does Baldwin say he had in the working world?

14. Which two attitudes does Baldwin claim are reinforced in all the information about the "Negro problem"?

15. Why does Baldwin say the "Negro problem" is "nearly inaccessible"?

16. Explain what Baldwin believes is the "business of the writer."

17. Who does Baldwin admit to having hatred for in this selection?

18. How does Baldwin express that he felt out of place in America?

19. Baldwin writes that he loves America, yet must "insist on the right to criticize her." Explain what is meant by this comment.

20. What personality traits of Baldwin's are presented at the end of this selection?

Understanding Literature: Essay and Autobiography

An essay is a kind of writing that deals with one main subject and states facts and opinions to support the author's beliefs. Some essays are autobiographies, or writings in which authors write about themselves. An essay is also written in paragraph form. It may argue or analyze a certain situation.

21. Why are these paragraphs from *Notes of a Native Son* an essay?

22. What is the main subject of this essay?

23. What are some other subjects in this essay?

24. Why is this essay also an autobiography?

25. From whose point of view is this essay?

Critical Thinking

26. Baldwin describes life for African Americans during the 1950s. How do you think society has changed for African Americans since that time? Explain your answer.

27. Do you think Baldwin had a difficult life? Why or why not?

28. Do you agree with Baldwin's views on "theories" as mentioned near the end of this selection?

29. Do you think Baldwin seems like an educated man? Explain your answer.

30. Do you think you would have liked to meet Baldwin based on what you have just read? Why or why not?

Writing on Your Own Baldwin ends this selection with this sentence: "I want to be an honest man and a good writer." Think about what you would like to accomplish in life. Narrow your goals to a few simple ideas. Then put these ideas into a single sentence as Baldwin did.

Stride Toward Freedom: The Montgomery Story
Martin Luther King, Jr.

Martin Luther King, Jr.

1929–1968

Literary Term

essay a kind of writing that deals with one main subject and states facts and opinions to support the author's beliefs

About the Author

Perhaps no other American has done more for civil rights than Martin Luther King, Jr. His powerful speeches, strong leadership, and nonviolent protests did much to strengthen African American rights in the 1950s and 1960s.

King was born in Atlanta, Georgia, in 1929. Both his father and his grandfather were Baptist preachers. Following their lead, King himself became a Baptist preacher. Receiving degrees from Morehouse College, Crozer Theological Seminary, and Boston University, King was well educated.

King's civil-rights work began in 1955. He and an African American woman named Rosa Parks successfully protested segregation on buses in Montgomery, Alabama. King led similar protests in Birmingham, Alabama. He is most famous for joining other civil-rights leaders on a march toward Washington, D.C., in 1963. There he gave his famous "I Have a Dream" speech to over 200,000 people.

Unfortunately, King's life and work were cut short when he was shot and killed on April 4, 1968. He left behind his many successes, including a Nobel Peace Prize, many moving speeches, and several important writings such as *Stride Toward Freedom: The Montgomery Story.* He also greatly increased the bond between black and white Americans. In 1986, Congress made the third Monday in January a national holiday in his name.

About the Selection

Many people today remember King as a great public speaker. He was also a talented writer. *Stride Toward Freedom: The Montgomery Story* was published in 1958. This book is an **essay** because it deals with one main subject and states facts and opinions to support the author's beliefs. This and other books by King provide an understanding of his beliefs on civil rights and protest. The following selection talks about three ways people deal with being treated poorly.

From Stride Toward Freedom: The Montgomery Story

Oppressed people deal with their oppression in three characteristic ways. One way is **acquiescence**: the oppressed resign themselves to their doom. They **tacitly** adjust themselves to oppression and thereby become conditioned to it. . . .

There is such a thing as the freedom of exhaustion. Some people are so worn down by the yoke of oppression that they give up. A few years ago in the slum areas of Atlanta, a Negro guitarist used to sing almost daily: "Been down so long that down don't bother me." This is the type of negative freedom and resignation that often engulfs the life of the oppressed.

But this is not the way out. To accept passively an unjust system is to cooperate with that system; thereby the oppressed become as evil as the oppressor. Noncooperation with evil is as much a moral **obligation** as is cooperation with good. The oppressed must never allow the conscience of the oppressor to slumber. Religion reminds every man that he is his brother's keeper. To accept injustice or **segregation** passively is to say to the oppressor that his actions are morally right. It is a way of allowing his conscience to fall asleep. At this moment the oppressed fails to be his brother's keeper. So acquiescence—while often the easier way—is not the moral way. It is the way of the coward. The Negro cannot win the respect of his oppressor by acquiescing; he merely increases the oppressor's arrogance and **contempt**. Acquiescence is interpreted as proof of the Negro's **inferiority**. The Negro

According to Martin Luther King, Jr., what are the three ways that people deal with oppression?

What does the guitarist's song mean?

The first way people deal with oppression is *acquiescence*. This means that people accept their oppression. Why does the author not like acquiescence?

acquiescence the act of accepting or giving in to authority	**inferiority** the state of feeling or being less important than others	**oppressed** crushed or held back by an abuse of power or authority	**tacitly** expressed without words
contempt a feeling of dislike and disgust toward someone or something	**obligation** a duty or responsibility	**segregation** the act of separating people by race, ethnic group, or social class	

cannot win the respect of the white people of the South or the peoples of the world if he is willing to sell the future of his children for his personal and immediate comfort and safety.

A second way that oppressed people sometimes deal with oppression is to resort to physical violence and corroding hatred. Violence often brings about momentary results. Nations have frequently won their independence in battle. But in spite of **temporary** victories, violence never brings **permanent** peace. It solves no social problem; it merely creates new and more complicated ones.

Violence as a way of achieving racial justice is both impractical and immoral. It is impractical because it is a descending spiral ending in destruction for all. The old law of an eye for an eye leaves everybody blind. It is immoral because it seeks to humiliate the opponent rather than win his understanding; it seeks to **annihilate** rather than to convert. Violence is immoral because it thrives on hatred rather than love. It destroys community and makes brotherhood impossible. It leaves society in **monologue** rather than **dialogue**. Violence ends by defeating itself. It creates bitterness in the survivors and **brutality** in the destroyers. . . .

If the American Negro and other victims of oppression succumb to the temptation of using violence in the struggle for freedom, future generations will be the recipients of a desolate night of bitterness, and our chief **legacy** to them will be an endless reign of meaningless chaos. Violence is not the way.

The third way open to oppressed people in their quest for freedom is the way of nonviolent resistance. . . . The nonviolent resister agrees with the person who acquiesces that one should not be physically aggressive toward his

---

The second way people deal with oppression is with violence. *What does the author think about this way?*

The author believes that violence destroys communication. After violence has occurred, people talk, but no one listens. This is a monologue. The author prefers a dialogue, in which communication is shared.

The third way people deal with oppression is nonviolent resistance. *Why does the author prefer this way over the first two?*

---

annihilate to destroy

brutality a harsh or violent act

dialogue the act of two or more people communicating

legacy something given to a later generation by an ancestor

monologue the act of one person speaking

permanent lasting forever

temporary lasting for only a short or set time

Martin Luther King, Jr., (above) was considered to be an excellent speaker.

opponent, but he balances the equation by agreeing with the person of violence that evil must be resisted. He avoids the nonresistance of the former and the violent resistance of the latter. With nonviolent resistance, no individual or group need submit to any wrong, nor need anyone resort to violence in order to right a wrong.

It seems to me that this is the method that must guide the actions of the Negro in the present crisis in race relations.

Through nonviolent resistance the Negro will be able to rise to the noble height of opposing the unjust system while loving the **perpetrators** of the system. The Negro must work passionately and **unrelentingly** for full **stature** as a citizen, but he must not use inferior methods to gain it. He must never come to terms with falsehood, **malice**, hate, or destruction.

Nonviolent resistance makes it possible for the Negro to remain in the South and struggle for his rights. The Negro's problem will not be solved by running away. He cannot listen to the glib suggestion of those who would urge him to migrate en masse to other sections of the country. By grasping his great opportunity in the South, he can make a lasting contribution to the moral strength of the nation and set a **sublime** example of courage for generations yet unborn.

En masse means *as a whole.*

By nonviolent resistance, the Negro can also enlist all men of goodwill in his struggle for equality. The problem is not a purely racial one, with Negroes set against whites. In the end, it is not a struggle between people at all but a tension between justice and injustice. Nonviolent resistance is not aimed against oppressors but against oppression. Under its banner, consciences, not racial groups, are enlisted.

If the Negro is to achieve the goal of integration, he must organize himself into a militant and nonviolent mass movement. All three elements are **indispensable**. The movement for equality and justice can only be a success if it has both a mass and militant character; the barriers to be overcome require both. Nonviolence is an **imperative** in order to bring about ultimate community. . . .

imperative very necessary	**perpetrator** one who commits an act that goes against rules or laws	**sublime** lofty; grand
indispensable very necessary		**unrelentingly** not letting up or weakening
malice ill will	**stature** position or standing	

Stride Toward Freedom: The Montgomery Story Martin Luther King, Jr.

Directions Write the answers to these questions using complete sentences.

Comprehension: Identifying Facts

1. What main group of people is this essay discussing?

2. What is acquiescence?

3. According to the author, what are the problems with acquiescence?

4. What are the problems with violent resistance?

5. How is violence "impractical" and "immoral"?

6. How does violence affect communication?

7. What is nonviolent resistance?

8. How is nonviolent resistance a good way to deal with oppression?

9. Who is nonviolent resistance aimed at?

10. How are African Americans to achieve integration?

Comprehension: Understanding Main Ideas

11. What reasons does the author give to explain why people choose acquiescence?

12. Why does the author say that acquiescence is just as bad as being the oppressor?

13. How does acquiescence make one inferior, or less important?

14. What is the author's opinion of war?

15. What does violence do to future generations?

16. How does nonviolent resistance prevent violence?

17. How does the author think nonviolent resistance will help African Americans in the South?

18. How does nonviolent resistance relate to justice and injustice according to the author?

19. What does the author believe is very necessary to bring about a good community?

20. How are acquiescence, violence, and nonviolent resistance related?

Review Continued on Next Page

Understanding Literature: Essay

An essay is a kind of writing that deals with one main subject and states facts and opinions to support the author's beliefs. *Stride Toward Freedom: The Montgomery Story* is an essay that shows good organization. It is divided into three mains ideas. Within each part are several points that the author communicates. Because this essay is so well organized, it is called a formal essay.

21. Why is this selection an essay?

22. What are the three main ideas of this essay?

23. What are some other less important ideas in this essay?

24. What is the tone of this essay?

25. Is Martin Luther King, Jr., convincing in this essay? Why or why not?

Critical Thinking

26. Do you agree that simply putting up with oppression is not a good way to handle the problem? Explain.

27. What problems do you think a violent society causes? Do you think that King would agree with you?

28. Do you think it is practical for people to be nonviolent when protesting? Why do you think nonviolence is necessary when protesting?

29. This essay was first published in 1958. Do you think King's ideas still apply today? Explain.

30. What part of this essay do you agree with the most? Why?

Writing on Your Own Write at least three paragraphs about how you think violence affects society and how violence might be stopped. Use Martin Luther King's essay to support the ideas in your own writing.

Monet's "Waterlilies"
Robert Hayden

Robert Hayden
1913–1980

About the Author

Robert Earl Hayden was born in Detroit, Michigan, in 1913. He began publishing poetry in 1940. Much of his poetry is thought to be quiet and loving. However, some of it shows the harsh realities of modern life.

Hayden received many awards for his work. He was elected to the National Academy of American Poets and has written several collections of poetry. He was coeditor of *A Source Book of Afro-American Literature*. He was a professor of English at Fisk University and Writer in Residence at the University of Michigan. He died in 1980.

Literary Terms

mood the feeling that writing creates

simile a figure of speech that makes a comparison using the words *like* or *as*

About the Selection

"Monet's 'Waterlilies'" is a short poem that shows how the poet escaped the troubles of the times by going to a museum to see a peaceful painting, Monet's "Waterlilies." Claude Monet was a French painter who used light and color to paint many lovely scenes.

The United States in 1966 was caught up in difficulties at home and in other countries. America was becoming more involved in the Vietnam War, and thousands of American soldiers were being killed. Many Americans began to protest the war. News of the war was sent through Saigon, the capital of South Vietnam, by the American government. Civil-rights issues in the 1960s also began to explode. Peaceful protests for equality for African Americans sometimes turned violent. Selma, Alabama, was the site of a 1965 protest in which police killed two protesters.

This poem mixes horrifying events with the simple pleasures of life. **Similes** add to the **mood** of this poem. A simile is a comparison that uses the words *like* or *as*. Mood is the feeling that writing creates.

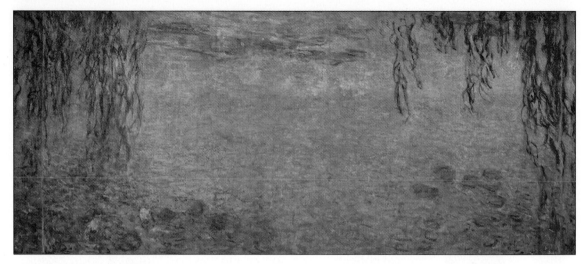

Waterlilies: The Morning No. 2, (central detail), Claude Monet

Notice the simile in the second line. The poet compares the news of war and protest to poisoning the air like nuclear fallout—radioactive particles that fall to the earth after a nuclear explosion. What does this tell you about the mood of this poem?

Monet's "Waterlilies"

Today as the news from Selma and Saigon
poisons the air like fallout,
3   I come again to see
the **serene** great picture that I love.
Here space and time exist in light
6   the eye like the eye of faith believes.
        The seen, the known
dissolve in **iridescence**, become
9   **illusive** flesh of light
        that was not, was, forever is.

O light beheld as through **refracting** tears.
12   Here is the **aura** of that world
        each of us has lost.
Here is the shadow of its joy.

aura an atmosphere or energy surrounding something	**iridescence** a shiny rainbow-like play of color
illusive difficult to tell whether something is real	**refracting** altering; changing
	serene calm; peaceful

Directions Write the answers to these questions using complete sentences.

Comprehension: Identifying Facts

1. What cities are mentioned in this poem?

2. What is the poet looking at?

3. Which lines refer to the way the poet sees the world?

Comprehension: Understanding Main Ideas

4. Why does the poet use the word "poisons" in line two?

5. Explain the emotion in line 11.

6. What does the poet believe is lost?

Understanding Literature: Mood

Mood is the feeling that writing creates. Love, anger, sadness, loss, and peacefulness are common moods in poetry. The mood in "Monet's 'Waterlilies'" is very important to the poem's meaning.

7. What is the mood of "Monet's 'Waterlilies'"?

8. How does the mood make the meaning of this poem more clear?

Critical Thinking

9. How could looking at a peaceful, beautiful painting help someone who is troubled by world or personal events?

10. What things do you do to escape from a difficult event in your life? How does it help?

Writing on Your Own Write a paragraph explaining how some event in your life can "poison" your air. How do troubles invade your peaceful feelings?

Skills Lesson Dialogue

In a literary work, when a character speaks to another character or characters, it is called dialogue. Most fictional stories use dialogue. Its purpose is to tell the story, to give more information about a character, or to set a mood. Another purpose is to keep the reader interested. The reader can enjoy humorous, surprising, or interesting things a character says.

Learn to recognize dialogue by looking for two things: quotation marks and a phrase telling that someone is speaking. For example:

"Have you seen my dog?" asked Nancy.

In this example, the words inside the quotation marks show what Nancy says. The phrase *asked Nancy* tells the reader that Nancy is speaking. Sometimes, there is no phrase to tell the reader who said the dialogue. The reader has to decide which character is speaking.

Authors in this unit used dialogue differently. In the next column is dialogue from Ernest Hemingway's "The Killers." Notice that Hemingway's use of short dialogue makes it seem very simple and real.

"I wonder what he did?" Nick said.

"Double-crossed somebody. That's what they kill them for."

The next example is from "The Catbird Seat" by James Thurber. The dialogue in this story is often very funny. This dialogue is from Mrs. Barrows.

"Is the little rat denying it?" she screamed.

Review

1. What is dialogue?

2. What is the purpose of dialogue?

3. What two things tell the reader that dialogue is being used?

4. How is Hemingway's dialogue realistic?

5. How would you describe Thurber's dialogue?

Writing on Your Own Write your own dialogue between two characters that you make up. Write at least three dialogue sentences per character. Be sure to use quotation marks.

UNIT 6 SUMMARY

You have completed studying the works in Unit 6. This unit covers the years from 1940 to 1970. Some of the most important events of the twentieth century were written about and discussed in this unit.

World War II brought changes to the entire world from 1939 to 1945. The postwar period brought about a comfortable life for most Americans who bought homes, found jobs, and raised children. Two other wars—the Korean War and the Vietnam War— would follow World War II in the 1950s and 1960s. The 1960s brought years of unrest as Americans had to deal with war and struggles for equality. Violence was common during the last years of this decade.

Literature changed along with the times. Many of the writers whose works appear in this unit dealt with the harsh realities of the times in their writings.

Selections

- *To Be Young, Gifted and Black* is Lorraine Hansberry's autobiography. It discusses her childhood in Chicago and her family.

- "The Killers" is a short story by Ernest Hemingway about two gangsters who plan to kill a Swedish boxer.

- "Flight" is a short story by John Steinbeck about a young man who gets into trouble while in town and must flee his family.

- "In Honor of David Anderson Brooks, My Father" is a poem by Gwendolyn Brooks honoring her father after his death.

- "The Catbird Seat" is a humorous short story by James Thurber about an odd man's plot to rid a coworker who threatens his harmony at work.

- *Hiroshima* by John Hersey is a historical novel about the terror an atomic bomb causes after being dropped on Hiroshima, Japan.

- *Notes of a Native Son* is James Baldwin's autobiography. The selection discusses his life as an African American writer.

- *Stride Toward Freedom: The Montgomery Story* is an essay by Martin Luther King, Jr., about the three ways people deal with oppression.

- "Monet's 'Waterlilies'" is a poem by Robert Hayden about the peace the poet feels in a troubled world after looking at a work of art.

UNIT 6 REVIEW

Directions Write the answers to these questions using complete sentences.

Comprehension: Identifying Facts

1. What major event occurred during the earlier years of the period that is covered in Unit 6?

2. What increases began during the years after World War II?

3. What war began during the early 1950s?

4. Name at least one famous person who was killed during the 1960s.

5. What conflict divided the nation during the 1960s?

Comprehension: Understanding Main Ideas

6. Explain how American life during the years covered in this unit was different from life in America today.

7. Explain how the civil rights movement gained strength during this period.

8. Explain how the selection *To Be Young, Gifted and Black* is an example of an autobiography.

9. Compare "The Killers" by Ernest Hemingway and "Flight" by John Steinbeck. How are these authors' writing styles similar?

10. What is Martin Luther King's *Stride Toward Freedom: The Montgomery Story* about? What three main ideas are presented in this selection?

Understanding Literature: Mood

Unit 6 covers a period that saw great social change. The works in this unit represent those changes. These selections include poetry, short stories, essays, poems, novels, and autobiographies. The works range from serious to humorous and represent many moods. Mood is the feeling that writing creates. The plot, characters, themes, and language add to the mood. A mood might be suspenseful or scary, gloomy or witty, serious or light-hearted, positive or negative, warm or critical, hopeful or tragic. The mood is usually established early in the piece. Generally, the mood is carried throughout a work. However, some stories can start out humorously and end unhappily.

11. What is mood?

12. Why is mood important in literature?

13. What is the mood of "In Honor of David Anderson Brooks, My Father" by Gwendolyn Brooks?

14. What is the mood of "The Catbird Seat" by James Thurber?

15. What is the mood of *Hiroshima* by John Hersey?

Critical Thinking

16. Do you think James Baldwin did a good job of expressing his attitude toward life in *Notes of a Native Son*? Why or why not?

17. How does "Monet's 'Waterlilies'" express some of the problems of the 1960s?

18. One theme of this unit is civil rights. Do you think the problems with civil rights that were expressed in this unit are still problems today? Why or why not?

19. Which writer in this unit gave you the best picture of life in the twentieth century? Explain your answer.

20. Identify your favorite writer and selection from this unit. Explain the reasons for your selection.

Speak and Listen

Choose one selection from Unit 6. Write a paragraph describing how you felt about this particular work. Read your prepared comments several times, then present them to the class.

Beyond Words

Choose a selection from Unit 6. Create an illustrated book jacket for this work. Include the name of the work, the author, and an interesting and eye-catching illustration.

Writing on Your Own

Two selections from this unit, *Notes of a Native Son* and *To Be Young, Gifted and Black* are autobiographies. Think of a time in your own life that was important. Write a short chapter of your own autobiography telling about this event. Use the two autobiographies in this unit to get an idea of the kind of information and subjects to include. Once you have finished, reread what you have written, checking for mistakes or things to add.

Test-Taking Tip

Try to answer all questions as completely as possible. When asked to explain your answer, do so in complete sentences.

"History, despite its
wrenching pain,
Cannot be unlived, and
if faced
With courage, need not
be lived again."

—Maya Angelou, "On the
Pulse of Morning," read at
President Bill Clinton's
inauguration, 1993

"It is easy to start a
prose poem, but not to
make it a work of art."

—Robert Bly, *Selected Poems*,
"The Prose Poem as an
Evolving Form," 1986

Contemporary American Literature:
1971–Present

You have learned that the United States has a very rich history. The last thirty years in America continued this tradition. During these years, the United States became involved in world affairs perhaps more than ever before. America continued to be a major world power. With this power came both struggles and successes.

The current period in literature is called contemporary literature. In this unit, you will study contemporary literature and learn more about recent events in American history.

The final thirty years of the twentieth century saw many historical, political, and social events.

Political problems took place in the 1970s. President Richard Nixon helped bring the United States out of the Vietnam War by 1973, but he soon faced another problem. It was discovered that he had taken part in a cover-up of an illegal act during the 1972 election. As a result, he resigned in 1974. This event was called the Watergate scandal. It was the first time in American history that a President had resigned. Gerald Ford then took office. The nation's 200th birthday in 1976 brought a new beginning. A new President, Jimmy Carter, brought the nation through the remainder of the 1970s.

In the 1980s, Americans experienced a growth of jobs, education, and wealth under the leadership of President Ronald Reagan. Millions of Americans worked to find answers to problems for people who were homeless, jobless, uneducated, or ill. Women became better educated and entered the workforce. In 1981, President Reagan appointed the first female justice of the Supreme Court, Sandra Day O'Connor.

Many world problems affected America in the 1990s. The United States became involved in the Persian Gulf War under President George Bush. American and United Nations forces freed the nation of Kuwait from an invasion by Iraq, another Middle Eastern country. Problems continued in the Middle East and elsewhere when President Clinton took office in 1993. American troops were sent to troubled spots such as Somalia, Bosnia-Herzegovina, and Haiti. Despite these foreign problems, Americans made huge advances in the 1990s. The economy reached an all-time high, while unemployment was very

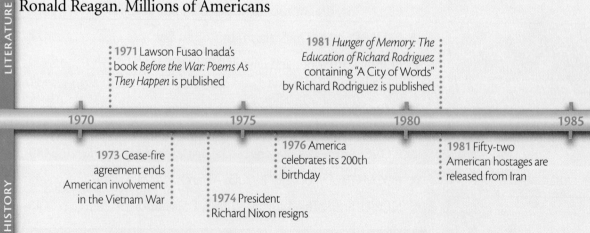

LITERATURE

1971 Lawson Fusao Inada's book *Before the War: Poems As They Happen* is published

1981 *Hunger of Memory: The Education of Richard Rodriguez* containing "A City of Words" by Richard Rodriguez is published

1970   1975   1980   1985

1973 Cease-fire agreement ends American involvement in the Vietnam War

1974 President Richard Nixon resigns

1976 America celebrates its 200th birthday

1981 Fifty-two American hostages are released from Iran

HISTORY

low. Computers and other advances became important.

As the new century begins in the United States, Americans face many new challenges. American leaders must work with world leaders to solve the problems of a large population. Civil rights, the economy, and the environment will continue to be important topics.

Current or recent literature is called contemporary literature. The contemporary writers in this unit speak about many themes. Some of these works—"morning mirror" by Lucille Clifton, "My Father and Myself Facing the Sun" by Lawson Fusao Inada, "Passports to Understanding" by Maya Angelou, and *The Hundred Secret Senses* by Amy Tan—take a look at relationships. The poems "my dream about the poet" by Lucille Clifton and

Maya Angelou (above) read her poem "On the Pulse of Morning" at President Bill Clinton's inauguration in 1993.

"The Starfish" by Robert Bly examine creativity and nature. Other selections—"A City of Words" by Richard Rodriguez, "Papi Working" by Julia Alvarez, and *The Antelope Wife* by Louise Erdrich—paint a picture of life today.

The American experience is richer because of the voices of many writers. Ethnic literature has given all Americans new points of view.

LITERATURE

1987 Lucille Clifton's *Next: New Poems* containing "morning mirror" and "my dream about the poet" is published

1992 Robert Bly's *What Have I Ever Lost by Dying?: Collected Prose Poems* containing "The Starfish" is published

1993 *Wouldn't Take Nothing for My Journey Now* containing "Passports to Understanding" by Maya Angelou is published

1995 Amy Tan's *The Hundred Secret Senses* is published

1995 *The Other Side/El Otro Lado* containing "Papi Working" by Julia Alvarez is published

1998 *The Antelope Wife* by Louise Erdrich is published

1985   1990   1995   2000

HISTORY

1986 Space shuttle *Challenger* explodes after launch, killing all seven crew members

1990 U.S. census shows 248,709,873 people live in the United States

1991 American and United Nations forces defeat Iran in the Persian Gulf War

1995 Car bomb explodes and kills 169 people in Oklahoma City

1997 *Pathfinder* lands on Mars

A City of Words
Richard Rodriguez

Richard Rodriguez

1944–

Literary Terms

conflict the struggle that the protagonist faces in a story

protagonist the main character in a story around whom most of the action centers

About the Author

Richard Rodriguez was born in San Francisco, California, to Mexican parents. He spoke mostly Spanish until he went to school. Like many Hispanic Americans, Rodriguez experienced life in two cultures.

Rodriguez attended Stanford and Columbia Universities. He did graduate work at the Warburg Institute in London and at the University of California at Berkeley. His essays have appeared in *American Scholar*, *College English*, and *Change*.

Many of his writings take a close look at the importance of Spanish and English in his life. *Hunger of Memory: The Education of Richard Rodriguez*, a book about his education, was published in 1981. The book won the Christopher Award a year later. The following selection from that book tells how Rodriguez struggled with the guilt of losing his ability to speak Spanish. Rodriguez helps the reader to see his world through his eyes.

About the Selection

The following autobiographical selection was taken from *Hunger of Memory: The Education of Richard Rodriguez*. In this book, the author discusses the experience of growing up in California. Like many Americans of various ethnic backgrounds, the writer grew up with two languages and two cultures. He became so good at speaking English that speaking Spanish became difficult. His parents and grandparents looked down on him for his poor Spanish. This selection describes the author's view of this problem. The problem is the source of the **conflict** in this selection. Conflict is the struggle that the **protagonist** faces in a story. The protagonist is the main character in a story around whom most of the action centers.

A City of Words

I grew up victim to a **disabling** confusion. As I grew **fluent** in English, I no longer could speak Spanish with confidence. I continued to understand spoken Spanish. And in high school, I learned how to read and write Spanish. But for many years I could not pronounce it. A powerful guilt blocked my spoken words; an essential glue was missing whenever I'd try to connect words to form sentences. I would be unable to break a barrier of sound, to speak freely. I would speak, or try to speak, Spanish, and I would manage to utter halting, hiccuping sounds that betrayed my unease.

When relatives and Spanish-speaking friends of my parents came to the house, my brother and sisters seemed **reticent** to use Spanish, but at least they managed to say a few necessary words before being excused. I never managed so gracefully. I was cursed with guilt. Each time I'd hear myself addressed in Spanish, I would be unable to respond with any success. I'd know the words I wanted to say, but I couldn't manage to say them. I would try to speak, but everything I said seemed to me horribly **anglicized**. My mouth would not form the words right. My jaw would tremble. After a phrase or two, I'd cough up a warm and silvery sound. And stop.

It surprised my listeners to hear me. They'd lower their heads, better to grasp what I was trying to say. They would repeat their questions in gentle, **affectionate** voices. But by then I would answer in English. No, no, they would say, we want you to speak to us in Spanish. ("... *en español*"). But I couldn't do it. *Pocho* then they called me. Sometimes playfully, teasingly, using the tender **diminutive**—*mi pochito*.

> How does the author learn to live with two languages and two cultures in this selection?

> The author explains here that he felt guilty for being unable to speak Spanish. Why do you think he felt this way?

affectionate loving; tender	**diminutive** a familiarly known word or name	**fluent** able to speak a language very well
anglicized made like English; changed to English usage	**disabling** weakening	**reticent** unwilling

Sometimes not so playfully, mockingly, *Pocho*. (A Spanish dictionary defines the word as an adjective meaning "colorless" or "bland." But I heard it as a noun, naming the Mexican-American who, in becoming an American, forgets his native society.) "*¡Pocho!*" the lady in the Mexican food store muttered, shaking her head. I looked up to the counter where red and green peppers were strung like Christmas tree lights and saw the frowning face of the stranger. My mother laughed somewhere behind me. (She said that her children didn't want to practice "our Spanish" after they started going to school.) My mother's smiling voice made me suspect that the lady who faced me was not really angry at me. But, searching her face, I couldn't find the hint of a smile.

Embarrassed, my parents would regularly need to explain their children's inability to speak flowing Spanish during those years. My mother met the wrath of her brother, her only brother, when he came up from Mexico one summer with his family. He saw his nieces and nephews for the very first time. After listening to me, he looked away and said what a disgrace it was that I couldn't speak Spanish, "*su proprio idioma.*" He made that remark to my mother; I noticed, however, that he stared at my father.

I clearly remember one other visitor from those years. A longtime friend of my father's from San Francisco would come to stay with us for several days in late August. He took great interest in me after he realized that I couldn't answer his questions in Spanish. He would grab me as I started to leave the kitchen. He would ask me something. Usually he wouldn't bother to wait for my mumbled response. Knowingly, he'd murmur: "*¿Ay Pocho, Pocho, adónde vas?*" And he would press his thumbs into the upper part of my arms, making me squirm with currents of pain. Dumbly, I'd stand there, waiting for his wife to notice us, for her to call him off with a **benign** smile. I'd giggle, hoping to **deflate** the tension between us, pretending that I hadn't seen the glittering scorn in his glance.

Why do people look down on the author's inability to speak Spanish?

Su propio idioma means *your real language.*

Adónde vas means *where are you going?*

How do you think the author felt after being treated this way by the friend from San Francisco?

benign gentle; kind	**deflate** to reduce; to lessen

I remember that man now, but seek no revenge in this telling. I **recount** such incidents only because they suggest the fierce power Spanish had for many people I met at home; the way Spanish was associated with closeness. Most of those people who called me a *pocho* could have spoken English to me. But they would not. They seemed to think that Spanish was the only language we could use, that Spanish alone permitted our close association. (Such persons are **vulnerable** always to the ghetto merchant and the politician who have learned the value of speaking their clients' family language to gain immediate trust.) For my part, I felt that I had somehow committed a sin of betrayal by learning English. But betrayal against whom? Not against visitors to the house exactly. No, I felt that I had betrayed my immediate family. I *knew* that my parents had encouraged me to learn English. I *knew* that I had turned to English only with angry **reluctance**. But once I spoke English with ease, I came to *feel* guilty. (This guilt defied **logic**.) I felt that I had shattered the **intimate** bond that had once held the family close. This original sin against my family told whenever anyone addressed me in Spanish and I responded, **confounded**.

But even during those years of guilt, I was coming to sense certain **consoling** truths about the language and intimacy. I remember playing with a friend in the backyard one day, when my grandmother appeared at the window. Her face was stern with suspicion when she saw the boy (the *gringo*) I was with. In Spanish she called out to me, sounding the whistle of her ancient breath. My companion looked up and watched her intently as she lowered the window and moved, still visible, behind the light curtain, watching us both. He wanted to know what she had said. I started to tell him, to say—to

This paragraph explains the conflict in this selection. The author felt guilty for speaking English instead of Spanish. He explains that he felt guilty because his people used Spanish as a way to bond with one another. By speaking English, he thought that he had destroyed his bond with his family.

Gringo means *foreigner* or *American*.

confounded confused	**logic** reason; something that makes sense	**reluctance** unwillingness
consoling comforting		
intimate marked by very close association or contact; very personal or private	**recount** to explain; to tell	**vulnerable** open to attack or harm; able to be hurt

translate her Spanish words into English. The problem was, however, that though I knew how to translate exactly what she had told me, I realized that any translation would **distort** the deepest meaning of her message: It had been directed only to me. This message of intimacy could never be translated because it was not *in* the words she had used but passed *through* them. So any translation would have seemed wrong; her words would have been stripped of an essential meaning. Finally, I decided not to tell my friend anything. I told him that I didn't hear all she had said.

This **insight** unfolded in time. Making more and more friends outside my house, I began to distinguish intimate voices speaking through *English*. I'd listen at times to a close friend's **confidential** tone or secretive whisper. Even more remarkable were those instances when, for no special reason apparently, I'd become conscious of the fact that my companion was speaking only to me. I'd marvel just hearing his voice. It was a stunning event: to be able to break through his words, to be able to hear this voice of the other, to realize that it was directed only to me. After such moments of intimacy outside the house, I began to

confidential private	**insight** understanding; the act of forming an understanding about the nature of something
distort to twist or change the true meaning of something	

420

trust hearing intimacy conveyed through my family's English. Voices at home at last **punctured** sad confusion. I'd hear myself addressed as an intimate at home once again. Such moments were never as **raucous** with sound as past times had been when we had had "private" Spanish to use. (Our English-sounding house was never to be as noisy as our Spanish-speaking house had been.) Intimate moments were usually soft moments of sound. My mother was in the dining room while I did my homework nearby. And she looked over at me. Smiled. Said something—her words said nothing very important. But her voice sounded to tell me (*We are together*) I was her son.

(Richard!)

Intimacy thus continued at home; intimacy was not stilled by English. It is true that I would never forget the great change of my life, the **diminished** occasions of intimacy. But there would also be times when I sensed the deepest truth about language and intimacy: *Intimacy is not created by a particular language; it is created by intimates.* The great change in my life was not **linguistic** but social. If, after becoming a successful student, I no longer heard intimate voices as often as I had earlier, it was not because I spoke English rather than Spanish. It was because I used public language for most of the day. I moved easily at last, a citizen in a crowded city of words.

This paragraph explains how the author got through the conflict in this story. He explains that he learned to appreciate intimacy in people, not in the words they spoke.

---

diminished made less; decreasing

linguistic relating to languages or speech

puncture to put a hole in

raucous very loud, noisy, or disorderly

Directions Write the answers to these questions using complete sentences.

Comprehension: Identifying Facts

1. What problem does the author describe in this selection?

2. How does the author say he sounded when, as a boy, he tried to speak Spanish?

3. What word (meaning colorless or bland) does the author say his relatives called him?

4. How well could the author's brother and sisters speak Spanish?

5. What people does the author remember in this story?

6. How does the author say his relatives reacted to his being unable to speak Spanish?

7. How does the author say he felt about not being able to speak Spanish?

8. What happens with the author and his friend in the backyard?

9. What does the author remember about doing his homework?

10. What kind of "great change" does the author say occurred in his life?

Comprehension: Understanding Main Ideas

11. What does the author seem to think about being called *Pocho* as a child?

12. Besides the author, who suffers from the author's inability to speak Spanish?

13. Why was it so important to the author's friends and relatives that he speak Spanish?

14. In what ways does the author show his lack of confidence as a child?

15. What bond does the author say he felt he lost by not speaking Spanish?

16. Why does the author say that he could not translate his grandmother's words the day he played with his friend in the yard?

17. What does the word *intimacy* mean to the author?

18. How does the author believe intimacy can be reached?

19. What conclusion does the author reach about language?

20. What "social" change does the author achieve at the end of the selection?

Understanding Literature: Conflict and Protagonist

The conflict in a story is the struggle the protagonist, or main character, faces. Although many kinds of conflict exist, two types are represented in "A City of Words." One type describes the conflict among the various characters. The other describes a character's inner conflict.

21. What conflict is there between the author and his parents?

22. What conflict is there between the author and his other relatives?

23. What inner conflict does the author have?

24. How does the author resolve his inner conflict?

25. How can conflict make a reader interested in a story?

Critical Thinking

26. Would you be angry if your relatives treated you like the author's relatives treated him? Explain your answer.

27. Do you think you would have felt the guilt the author felt if you were in his situation? Explain.

28. Do you think the author's family and friends acted appropriately toward him? Explain.

29. Do you think it is important for people to use their native language? Why or why not?

30. How does this selection make you feel about people who must live with two languages and cultures?

Writing on Your Own Think of an inner conflict in your own life that is similar to Richard Rodriguez's inner conflict with language. Write a paragraph explaining this conflict. Write how this conflict made you feel and how you resolved it.

Poems
by Lucille Clifton

Lucille Clifton

1936–

Literary Terms

free verse poetry that does not have a strict rhyming pattern or regular line length, and uses actual speech patterns for the rhythms of sound

style an author's way of writing

About the Author

Lucille Clifton was born in New York in 1936. She began working to help her family at an early age. Books and words were the center of her life, however. Even as a child, she loved to tell stories. She later attended college and helped form a theater group. She married in 1958 and had six children.

When Clifton was thirty-three, one of her poems won a contest. The prize was a reading in New York, where an editor for Random House was in the audience. Clifton's first work, "Good Times," was published about a year later. Since then, her poetry about poverty, homelessness, unfair treatment of blacks in Africa, and the humor and tragedy of life have brought her success. She has twice been nominated for the Pulitzer Prize in poetry. She also served as the poet laureate of Maryland from 1979 to 1985.

About the Selections

Clifton's two poems that follow tell about the author and her view of life. The author sees and feels many emotions, but she focuses mostly on joy. Many readers find her poetry emotional and creative. Read these poems carefully so that you too can appreciate the quality of these poems written in **free verse**. This kind of poetry has no strict rhyming pattern or regular line length, and uses actual speech patterns for the rhythms of sound. In addition to the free verse, notice that Clifton's poems do not use uppercase letters to begin sentences or lines. This is the author's particular **style** of writing poetry. Style is an author's way of writing.

morning mirror

my mother her sad eyes worn as bark
faces me in the mirror. my mother
whose only sin was dying, whose only
4 enemy was time, frowns in the glass.
once again she has surprised me
in an echo of her life but
my mother refuses to be reflected;
8 thelma whose only strength was love,
warns away the **glint** of likeness,
the woman is loosened in the mirror and
thelma lucille begins her day.

Whose face does the poet see in the mirror?

my dream about the poet

a man.
i think it is a man.
sits down with wood.
4 i think he's holding wood.
he carves.
he is making a world
he says
8 as his fingers cut citizens
trees and things
which he **perceives** to be a world
but someone says that is
12 only a poem.
he laughs.
i think he is laughing.

What do the poet and the man in the dream have in common?

glint a glimmer; a trace

perceive to see; to observe; to become aware through the senses

Directions Write the answers to these questions using complete sentences.

Comprehension: Identifying Facts

1. In "morning mirror," what was the mother's only sin?

2. Who is actually looking into the mirror in "morning mirror"?

3. In "my dream about the poet," what three things does the poet see the man carve in her dream?

Comprehension: Understanding Main Ideas

4. How is the poet like her mother in "morning mirror"?

5. In "my dream about the poet," who might the poet be seeing as "a man" in this poem?

6. Why do you think the poet used the line "only a poem" in "my dream about the poet"?

Understanding Literature: Style

Usually, poetry is written using standard English. At times, though, poets do not follow rules of grammar or punctuation.

Lucille Clifton does not use punctuation in a normal way and does not capitalize letters that should be capitalized. Authors do this to create a special style in their writing.

7. In what ways does Clifton's poetry not follow standard English?

8. Why do you think that she may have chosen to write without following standard English?

Critical Thinking

9. Name three emotions that the poet suggests in these two poems.

10. Which of Clifton's two poems do you prefer? Explain your choice.

Writing on Your Own Rewrite one of these poems using standard English. Make sure each sentence is a complete thought and has a subject (doer) and a predicate (action or verb). Add any punctuation and capitalize letters that begin sentences. Compare your version to the original. Do you get the same effect from your version?

The Starfish
Robert Bly

Robert Bly
1926–

Literary Terms

imagery the use of words that appeal to the senses

metaphor a figure of speech that makes a comparison without using *like* or *as*

prose written language that is not verse

prose poem an open form of poetry that is written as prose rather than as traditional poetry

simile a figure of speech that makes a comparison using *like* or *as*

About the Author

Robert Bly is a native of Minnesota and has lived there most of his life. He graduated from Harvard. He had originally majored in math. He decided to support himself and his family by writing poetry, translating poems, and giving poetry readings. He began a poetry magazine in 1958. He took up many causes in the 1960s and 1970s, especially protests against the Vietnam War.

About the Selection

"The Starfish" is a **prose poem** from Bly's book *What Have I Ever Lost by Dying?: Collected Prose Poems*. A prose poem is an open form of poetry that is written as **prose** rather than as traditional poetry. Prose is written language that is not verse. Prose poems use **imagery** and figures of speech such as **similes** and **metaphors**. Imagery is the use of words that appeal to the senses. A simile is a figure of speech that makes a comparison using *like* or *as*. A metaphor is a figure of speech that makes a comparison without using *like* or *as*. These devices attempt to create a picture for the reader. Bly's observations are made clear through his particular use of language.

Bly directs the reader's attention to objects or events and how they relate to the human world. Some of his other poems deal with objects such as an ant hill, an amethyst, and a mushroom. To each he brings a new vision and understanding. Bly comments, "I have learned also to accept the fantasy that often appears toward the end of the poem."

The Starfish

How is this prose poem different from traditional poetry? How is it similar?

It is low tide. Fog. I have climbed down the cliffs from Pierce Ranch to the tide pools. Now the **ecstasy** of the low tide, kneeling down, alone. In six inches of clear water I notice a purple starfish—with nineteen arms! It is a delicate purple, the color of old carbon paper, or an attic dress . . . at the webs between the arms sometimes a more intense sunset red glows through. The fingers are relaxed . . . some curled up at the tips . . . with delicate rods . . . apparently globes on top of each, as at world's fairs, waving about. The starfish slowly moves up the groin of the rock . . . then back down . . . many of its arms rolled up now, lazily, like a puppy on its back. One arm is especially active and curves up over its own body as if a dinosaur were looking behind him.

This first paragraph uses a simile: "like a puppy on its back." Do you see any other similes in this prose poem?

How slowly and evenly it moves! The starfish is a glacier, going sixty miles a year! It moves over the pink rock, by means I cannot see . . . and into marvelously floating delicate brown weeds. It is about the size of the bottom of a pail. When I reach out to it, it tightens and then slowly relaxes. . . . I take an arm and quickly lift. The underside is a pale tan. . . . Gradually, as I watch, thousands of tiny tubes begin rising from all over the underside . . . hundreds in the mouth, hundreds along the nineteen underarms . . . all looking . . . feeling . . . like a man looking for a woman . . . tiny heads blindly feeling for a rock and finding only air. A purple rim runs along the underside of every arm, with paler tubes. Probably its moving-feet.

The second sentence in this paragraph is a metaphor. The poet compares the starfish to a glacier. Notice that the comparison does not use *like* or *as*.

I put him back in. He unfolds—I had forgotten how purple he was—and slides down into his rock groin, the snaillike feelers waving as if nothing had happened, and nothing has.

The poet uses colors to create imagery in this prose poem. This last paragraph refers to the starfish's purple color. What other imagery do you see in this selection?

ecstasy intense joy or delight; a state of overwhelming emotion; a trance-like state

Directions Write the answers to these questions using complete sentences.

Comprehension: Identifying Facts

1. Where is the poet as he observes the starfish?

2. What does the poet do to the starfish?

3. What does the poet conclude has happened?

Comprehension: Understanding Main Ideas

4. What animals does the poet refer to when describing the starfish's arms? Why?

5. What does the poet realize the starfish's tiny tubes are blindly feeling for? To what does he compare this?

6. What colors seem important to the poet when describing the starfish?

Understanding Literature: Prose Poem, Simile, Metaphor, and Imagery

A prose poem is an open form of poetry that is written as prose rather than in the form of traditional poetry. You probably noticed that "The Starfish" looks much more like prose than poetry.

However, the selection is still a poem for several reasons. The words and sentence structure are very poetic. Certain literary devices common in poetry, such as simile, metaphor, and imagery, can be found in this poem. These devices combine with the prose form to make an interesting new literary form.

7. Why is "The Starfish" a prose poem? How is it more like a poem than prose?

8. Identify at least one of each of these devices in Bly's poem: simile, metaphor, and imagery.

Critical Thinking

9. How has the poet observed almost magical details of a starfish? Cite examples.

10. What do you think is important about the final three words of this prose poem?

Writing on Your Own Write your own prose poem in which you use your observation skills to make a statement about a thing, such as an ant, a rose, a windowpane, or a tree stump. These are all subjects that Robert Bly has written about in other prose poems.

My Father and Myself Facing the Sun
Lawson Fusao Inada

Lawson Fusao Inada
1938–

Literary Terms

allusion something referring to a historical event, a person, a place, or a work of literature

free verse poetry that does not have a strict rhyming pattern or regular line length, and uses actual speech patterns for the rhythms of sound

image a word or phrase that appeals to the senses and allows the reader to picture events

metaphor a figure of speech that makes a comparison without using *like* or *as*

About the Author

Born in 1938 in Fresno, California, Lawson Fusao Inada is a Sansei, or a third-generation Japanese American. During World War II, many Japanese Americans in the United States were moved to places called internment camps. Americans feared Japanese Americans because the United States was fighting Japan in the war. Inada grew up in internment camps in California, Arkansas, and Colorado. He later studied at Fresno State College, the University of Iowa, and the University of Oregon.

Inada has published poetry, given readings, and held seminars on multicultural education. He also has received an Excellence in Teaching Award from the Oregon State Board of Higher Education. One of his first successful books was *Before the War: Poems As They Happen*, published in 1971.

About the Selection

"My Father and Myself Facing the Sun" is a poem of place, generations, heritage, and time. All of these are important to the meaning of this poem. As the title suggests, this poem is a simple story of a man and his father. The men—like all fathers and sons—are similar and different.

Images are words or phrases that appeal to the senses and allow the reader to picture events. In this poem, the images used are original and unusual. Look for these images as you read the poem. This poem also uses **metaphors**. A metaphor is a figure of speech that makes a comparison without using *like* or *as*. Another technique the author uses is **allusion**. Allusion is referring to a historical event, a person, a place, or a work of literature. Like many contemporary poems, this poem is written in **free verse**. Free verse is poetry that does not have a strict rhyming pattern or regular line length, and uses actual speech patterns for the rhythms of sound.

My Father and Myself Facing the Sun

How are the father and son in this poem alike? How are they different?

We are both strong, dark, bright men,
though perhaps you might not notice,
finding two figures flat against the **landscape**
4 like the shadowed backs of mountains.

Which would not be far from wrong,
for though we both have on western clothes
and he is seated on a yellow spool
8 of emptied and forgotten telephone cable
and I **recline** on a green aluminum lounge,

Hiroshima is a Japanese city on which the United States dropped an atomic bomb in August of 1945 in an effort to end World War II. Over 92,000 people were killed. This is an example of an allusion because the author is referring to a historical event.

we are both facing into the August sun
as **august** as Hiroshima and the coming of autumn.

12 There are differences, however, if you care
to discover, coming close, respectfully.
You must discover the landscape as you go.

Come. It is in the eyes, the face, the way
16 we would greet you stumbling as you arrive.
He is much the smooth, grass-brown slopes
reaching knee-high around you as you walk;
I am the cracks of cliffs and gulleys,
20 pieces of secret deep in the back of the eye.

This stanza has several metaphors. The author compares himself and his father to certain landscapes.

But he is still my father, and I his son.
After a while, there is time to go fishing,
both of us squatting on rocks in the dusk,
24 leaving peaks and treeline responsible for light.
There is a lake below, which both of us
acknowledge, by facing, forward, like the sun.

acknowledge to take notice of	**landscape** the landforms of an area; a scene	**recline** to lean backwards
august awe-inspiring		

Ripples of fish, moon, **luminous** insects.
28 Frogs, owls, crickets at their sound.
Deer, raccoon, badger come down to drink.

Notice the images in this stanza. What do you picture when reading this?

At the water's edge, the children are fishing,
casting shadows from the enormous shoreline.
32 Everything functions in the function of summer.

And gradually, and not by chance, the action
stops, the children hush back among rocks
and also watch, with nothing to capture but dust.

36 There are four of us, together among others.

And I am not at all certain what all this means
if they mean anything, but feel with all my being
that I must write this down, if I write anything.

40 My father, his son, his grandsons, strong, **serene**.

Night, night, night, before the following morning.

luminous giving off or reflecting a glowing light

serene calm; tranquil

My Father and Myself Facing the Sun
Lawson Fusao Inada

Directions Write the answers to these questions using complete sentences.

Comprehension: Identifying Facts

1. What words are used to describe the father and the son in the first two stanzas?

2. What month of the year is mentioned? What historical event is mentioned in connection with this month?

3. What time of day is it at the end of the poem?

Comprehension: Understanding Main Ideas

4. In what way does the author describe the differences between himself and his father?

5. What do the descriptive landscape lines mean in terms of personality differences?

6. Who are the children who are fishing with the father and son? Why do you think the poet does not describe them in more detail?

Understanding Literature: Metaphor

A metaphor is an example of figurative language that makes a comparison between two things. Remember that metaphors do not use the words *like* or *as* in the comparison. Calling someone a star is an example of a metaphor. People—like stars—can be bright, shining, and noticeable. Metaphors provide symbolic images in a literary work. The metaphors in "My Father and Myself Facing the Sun" are many and varied. Explore the poem once again.

7. Look for metaphors in the poem. In particular, notice the metaphors in lines 17–20. Why do you think the author chose to use the language he did?

8. Is the poem strengthened or weakened by these images? Explain your answer.

Critical Thinking

9. What do you think happens to make the action of fishing stop in line 34?

10. How do you feel about the line ". . . I must write this down, if I write anything"? What does this line mean?

Writing on Your Own Study how Inada used metaphors to describe himself and his father in "My Father and Myself Facing the Sun." Write two or three metaphors that describe you as a person. Be creative in coming up with unusual descriptions.

Passports to Understanding
Maya Angelou

Maya Angelou
1928–

Literary Term

personal essay a kind of writing that explores the author's opinion of a topic in a light and often entertaining way

About the Author

Maya Angelou was born Marguerite Johnson in St. Louis, Missouri, in 1928. She was raised in Arkansas and California. She became a singer and dancer in the 1950s. At thirty, Angelou began to write for a newspaper. She met writers and civil-rights leaders who encouraged her to continue to write and speak.

Angelou published her first book, an autobiography called *I Know Why the Caged Bird Sings*, in 1970. Its success allowed her to publish more books and to begin to publish poetry. Her moving poems have become contemporary American classics. She has also written plays and screenplays, and most recently, essays.

In 1993, Angelou was granted a huge national audience when President Bill Clinton invited her to read a poem at his inauguration. The poem she wrote for this event was titled "On the Pulse of Morning."

Angelou is a Reynolds Professor at Wake Forest University. She has received several honorary degrees.

About the Selection

Angelou's collection of essays, *Wouldn't Take Nothing for My Journey Now*, was published in 1993. The following selection, "Passports to Understanding," is the second essay in the book. It is a **personal essay**. A personal essay is a kind of writing that explores the author's opinion of a topic in a light and often entertaining way. This essay's title and the book's title speak to the content. In these essays, Angelou reviews her life, offering advice and encouragement to her new and faithful readers. "Passports to Understanding" offers straightforward advice about learning to appreciate people all over the world.

Passports to Understanding

What is the main idea of this personal essay? Why does the author value travel?

Human beings are more alike than unalike, and what is true anywhere is true everywhere, yet I encourage travel to as many destinations as possible for the sake of education as well as pleasure.

It is necessary, especially for Americans, to see other lands and experience other cultures. The American, living in this vast country and able to **traverse** three thousand miles east to west using the same language, needs to hear languages as they **collide** in Europe, Africa, and Asia.

A tourist, browsing in a Paris shop, eating in an Italian *ristorante*, or idling along a Hong Kong street, will encounter three or four languages as she **negotiates** the buying of a blouse, the paying of a check, or the choosing of a trinket. I do not mean to suggest that simply overhearing a foreign tongue adds to one's understanding of that language. I do know,

What does the author think about language?

however, that being exposed to the existence of other languages increases the **perception** that the world is populated by people who not only speak differently from oneself but whose **cultures** and **philosophies** are other than one's own.

Perhaps travel cannot prevent **bigotry**, but by demonstrating that all peoples cry, laugh, eat, worry, and die, it can introduce the idea that if we try to understand each other, we may even become friends.

bigotry prejudice; the lack or absence of respect or under-standing of differences in other people	**culture** the customs, beliefs, behaviors, and traits of a certain group of people	**philosophy** the values, beliefs, attitudes, and concepts of a person or group
collide to come together with solid or direct impact; to clash	**negotiate** to make a deal	**traverse** to go or travel across or over
	perception an awareness of an idea or concept	

A world traveler might see the Great Wall of China (above left), an open-air café in Paris, France (above right), or native people of Central America (below left) or Africa (below right).

437

Directions Write the answers to these questions using complete sentences.

Comprehension: Identifying Facts

1. What advice does Maya Angelou give at the beginning of the selection?

2. What places does she mention visiting?

3. What does she say that all people do?

Comprehension: Understanding Main Ideas

4. Why does the author believe that Americans living in a vast country three thousand miles wide especially need to be reminded to see other lands?

5. What does she say a tourist will learn while browsing, idling, or eating in another country?

6. What conclusion does Angelou draw?

Understanding Literature: Formal and Personal Essays

You have read several essays in this textbook. Most of the essays were formal essays with a formal structure and a serious tone. "Passports to Understanding" is a personal essay. It explores the author's opinion on travel in a light and entertaining way. Notice that the author's tone is very conversational. This is common in personal essays.

7. What is a formal essay?

8. What is a personal essay?

Critical Thinking

9. Explain the author's opinion in this essay.

10. Do you agree with the author's opinion? Why or why not?

Writing on Your Own Write a paragraph to expand upon the ideas expressed in paragraphs one, two, and three in "Passports to Understanding." Use personal knowledge to identify some cultures and philosophies that are different from yours. Be specific. Write in the conversational tone Angelou used.

Amy Tan
1952–

Literary Terms

character a person in a story

characterization the way a writer develops characters by revealing personality traits

dialect a regional variety of language

dialogue the conversation among characters in a story

novel fiction that is book-length and has more plot and character details than a short story

About the Author

Today's literature has many voices. Asian American women make up an important group in contemporary literature. Amy Tan is perhaps the most noted Asian American writer. Her works have been a success because her writing gives a very real view of the Asian experience in the United States.

Tan was born in Oakland, California, in 1952. Her parents were born in China but moved to America. They had been forced to leave three daughters in China when they came to the United States. This loss and the deaths of Tan's father and brother had a big impact on Tan's writing.

Tan and her mother moved to Switzerland where Tan received her high school education. She returned to the United States and studied English at San Jose State University. Her hobby of writing soon turned into a career with her first book, *The Joy Luck Club*, which was published in 1989. It was a great success.

About the Selection

The passage included here is a chapter from the first pages of Tan's **novel**, *The Hundred Secret Senses*. A novel is fiction that is book-length and has more plot and character details than a short story. This selection examines the lives of two half sisters, American-born Olivia and her Chinese-born half sister, Kwan.

The **characters**—the people in the story—are introduced early in the novel. The author uses **characterization** to show the reader what the characters are like. The selection provided here uses **dialogue** and **dialect** to set the stage for the events that unfold over thirty years. Dialogue is the conversation among characters in a story. Dialect is a regional variety of language. Words and sentences show the reader how someone sounds when speaking.

From The Hundred Secret Senses

The Girl With the Yin Eyes

Notice that this dialogue is an example of dialect. The author uses language that clearly shows how the characters talk. How does Kwan sound?

My sister Kwan believes she has yin eyes. She sees those who have died and now **dwell** in the World of Yin, ghosts who leave the mists just to visit her kitchen on Balboa Street in San Francisco.

"Libby-ah," she'll say to me. "Guess who I see yesterday, you guess." And I don't have to guess that she's talking about someone dead.

Actually, Kwan is my half sister, but I'm not supposed to mention that publicly. That would be an insult, as if she deserved only fifty percent of the love from our family. But just to set the **genetic** record straight, Kwan and I share a father, only that. She was born in China. My brothers, Kevin and Tommy, and I were born in San Francisco after my father, Jack Yee, **immigrated** here and married our mother, Louise Kenfield.

Mom calls herself "American mixed grill, a bit of everything white, fatty, and fried." She was born in Moscow, Idaho, where she was a champion baton twirler and once won a county fair prize for growing a **deformed** potato that had the **profile** of Jimmy Durante. She told me she dreamed she'd

Jimmy Durante was a famous comedian.

deformed shaped oddly; twisted	**genetic** related to the study of genes—the "blueprints" that show the makeup of a person	**immigrate** to come and live in a country where one was not born
dwell to live		**profile** a human head or face seen in a side view

one day grow up to be different—thin, **exotic**, and noble like Luise Rainer, who won an Oscar playing O-lan in *The Good Earth*. When Mom moved to San Francisco and became a Kelly girl instead, she did the next-best thing. She married our father. Mom thinks that her marrying out of the Anglo race makes her a **liberal**. "When Jack and I met," she still tells people, "there were laws against mixed marriages. We broke the law for love." She neglects to mention that those laws didn't apply in California.

The word *Anglo* refers to a white person of the United States.

None of us, including my mom, met Kwan until she was eighteen. In fact, Mom didn't even know Kwan *existed* until shortly before my father died of renal failure. I was not quite four when he passed away. But I still remember moments with him. Falling down a curly slide into his arms. **Dredging** the wading pool for pennies he had tossed in. And the last day I saw him in the hospital, hearing what he said that scared me for years.

Kevin, who was five, was there. Tommy was just a baby, so he was in the waiting room with my mom's cousin, Betty Dupree—we had to call her Aunt Betty—who had moved out from Idaho as well. I was sitting on a sticky vinyl chair, eating a bowl of strawberry Jell-O cubes that my father had given me from his lunch tray. He was propped up in bed, breathing hard. Mom would cry one minute, then act

dredging digging; gathering; scooping

exotic not native to the place where one is found; mysterious

liberal one who is open-minded or does things that are not typical or established

cheerful. I tried to figure out what was wrong. The next thing I remember, my father was whispering and Mom leaned in close to listen. Her mouth opened wide and wider. Then her head turned sharply toward me, all twisted with horror. And I was terror-struck. How did he know? How did Daddy find out I flushed my turtles, Slowpoke and Fastpoke, down the toilet that morning? I had wanted to see what they looked like without their coats on, and ended up pulling off their heads.

"Your daughter?" I heard my mom say. "Bring her back?" And I was sure that he had just told her to bring me to the pound, which is what he did to our dog Buttons after she chewed up the sofa. What I recall after that is a jumble: the bowl of Jell-O crashing to the floor, Mom staring at a photo, Kevin grabbing it and laughing, then me seeing this tiny black-and-white snapshot of a skinny baby with patchy hair. At some point, I heard my mother shouting: "Olivia, don't argue, you have to leave now." And I was crying, "But I'll be good."

Soon after that, my mother announced: "Daddy's left us." She also told us she was going to bring Daddy's other little girl from China to live in our house. She didn't say she was sending me to the pound, but I still cried, believing everything was vaguely connected—the headless turtles whirling down the toilet, my father abandoning us, the other girl who was coming soon to take my place. I was scared of Kwan before I ever met her. . . .

This paragraph explains a misunderstanding the narrator has. She thinks that her father is mad at her, but he is not. He simply wants his wife to bring back Kwan, his daughter from China, to the United States.

Why is the narrator scared of Kwan?

Directions Write the answers to these questions using complete sentences.

Comprehension: Identifying Facts

1. Where does Kwan live?

2. Who are the members of the family in the story?

3. Describe the mother's background.

4. How old is Kwan when she meets the family?

5. Why is Olivia at the hospital?

6. Who is Aunt Betty?

7. What does Olivia fear about her father?

8. What feelings does Olivia have toward Kwan?

9. What country did Kwan come from?

10. How is it clear in this story that Olivia is upset?

Comprehension: Understanding Main Ideas

11. How is Kwan different from Olivia?

12. What is the "World of Yin" and why does Kwan believe she has "yin eyes"?

13. Why does Kwan think that she sees ghosts?

14. What kind of marriage does it seem Olivia's mother and father have?

15. Why does Olivia fear that her father is mad at her?

16. Why does Olivia fear that she will be sent to the pound?

17. In what ways is Olivia a realistic four-year-old?

18. Why does Olivia fear Kwan even though she had never met her before?

19. Who is the main character in this story?

20. How is dialect used in this story?

Review Continued on Next Page

Understanding Literature: Dialogue

One way writers can reveal information about characters is by what they say and how they say it. This selection uses dialogue from Kwan and Olivia's mother. The reader can learn much about the characters through this dialogue.

21. What can the reader learn about Kwan from paragraph two?

22. Explain how this description by Olivia's mom adds to her mom's character: "American mixed grill, a bit of everything white, fatty, and fried."

23. What does the dialogue "Olivia, don't argue, you have to leave now." mean in this story?

24. How does Olivia become confused by the conversation she overhears between her father and her mother?

25. Why is it reasonable that Olivia fears that the quote "Bring her back" applies to her?

Critical Thinking

26. Why do you think that Amy Tan does not fully develop the character of the father?

27. Why do you think the father reveals his secret when he does?

28. How do you think Olivia's mother feels when she learns that her husband has a Chinese child?

29. Do you think the dialect in this story is realistic? Why or why not?

30. Did you find this selection humorous or sad? Explain your answer.

Writing on Your Own Write a short dialogue between two family members from an imaginary family. Create the two characters and develop lines for each. Try to create a sense of who the characters are as you write the dialogue. Be sure to use quotation marks around the spoken words. Remember, these characters are your invention. Be imaginative. Do *not* use your own family for this exercise.

Papi Working
Julia Alvarez

Julia Alvarez
1950–

About the Author

Julia Alvarez was born in New York in 1950. She was raised until the age of ten in the Dominican Republic, an island nation in the Caribbean Sea near Cuba. She later attended and graduated from Vermont's Middlebury College and received her masters in fine arts in 1985. She is currently an English professor at Middlebury College.

A novelist and poet, Alvarez first wrote stories for class assignments. She often wrote of her life in the Dominican Republic. Alvarez's writing engages the reader with the mix and interplay of two languages—English and Spanish.

Literary Terms

free verse poetry that does not have a strict rhyming pattern or regular line length, and uses actual speech patterns for the rhythms of sound

imagery the use of words that appeal to the senses

About the Selection

The following selection, "Papi Working," is a poem from the collection *The Other Side/El Otro Lado*. The many characteristics of Alvarez's popular fiction are found in this collection. These poems look at the experiences of new immigrants in the United States as remembered by Alvarez.

"Papi Working" shows the coming together of two languages and two cultures. The importance of hearing Spanish for recent immigrants is explained in this poem. The poet uses Spanish words in several key places in this poem. Notice also the **imagery** in this poem. Imagery is the use of words that appeal to the senses. This poem is written in **free verse**. This is poetry that does not have a strict rhyming pattern or regular line length, and uses actual speech patterns for the rhythms of sound.

Papi Working

The long day spent listening
to homesick hearts,
the tick tock of the clock—
4 the way Americans mark time,
long hours, long days.
Often they came only to hear him
say *nada* in their mother tongue.
8 *I found nothing wrong.*
To dole out *jarabe* for the children's coughs,
convince the *doña* to stay off that leg.

In his white *saco* Mami ironed out,
12 smoothing the tired wrinkles
till he was young again,
he spent his days, long days,
tending to the ills of immigrants,
16 his own heart heavy with what was gone,
this new country like a pill
that slowly kills but keeps you
from worse deaths.
20 *What was to be done?*

They came to hear him say
nada in their mother tongue.

Notice the many Spanish words in this poem. *Nada* means *nothing; jarabe* is *syrup; doña* means *lady;* and *saco* is a *jacket.* How does the use of Spanish and the imagery add to the effectiveness of this poem?

Papi Working
Julia Alvarez

Directions Write the answers to these questions using complete sentences.

Comprehension: Identifying Facts

1. What does Papi do for a living?

2. Who is introduced in stanza two?

3. What do the people want to hear?

Comprehension: Understanding Main Ideas

4. Does it seem like the immigrants who go to see Papi are doing well in America? Explain.

5. What is the mother tongue?

6. Why do the immigrants want to hear the mother tongue?

Understanding Literature: Hispanic Literature

Julia Alvarez is one of the many writers who enrich traditional American literature with the experiences of Hispanic Americans. Her ability to mix English with Spanish in the same poem, even the same line, expands our understanding. Language is enriched as English-speaking Americans learn new words and add them to American English.

7. If you did not speak Spanish and were not told what the Spanish words in this poem mean, do you think you would have had trouble understanding the poem? Why or why not?

8. Why do you think that Hispanic literature has become popular in recent years?

Critical Thinking

9. What do you think made Papi come to America? Why was his heart heavy?

10. Based on what you learned in this poem and on your own experiences, what do you think are some problems that immigrants face?

Writing on Your Own Think of some of the ways Spanish language has already been added to English. Write an informative paragraph identifying several traditions, foods, or names that were Hispanic that have become a part of America today.

Louise Erdrich
1954–

Literary Terms

mood the feeling that writing creates

novel fiction that is book-length with more plot and character details than a short story

simile a figure of speech that makes a comparison using the words *like* or *as*

style an author's way of writing

About the Author

Poet and novelist Louise Erdrich is a mixed-blood member of the Turtle Mountain Band of Chippewa. She was born in 1954 in Little Falls, Minnesota. She grew up in North Dakota. Erdrich graduated from Dartmouth College in 1976 and received a degree in creative writing from Johns Hopkins University in 1979. She worked for *The Circle*, an American Indian newspaper of the Boston Indian Council. She has also written textbooks.

Erdrich's father, a teacher with the Bureau of Indian Affairs, gave Erdrich a nickel for each story she wrote as a child. As an adult, she has since written several successful poems, short stories, and novels. Several of her works have earned awards. Some of her best-known titles include *The Beet Queen, Love Medicine*, and *Jacklight*.

About the Selection

This selection is from Erdrich's sixth **novel**, *The Antelope Wife*. A novel is fiction that is book-length with more plot and character details than a short story. *The Antelope Wife* connects history, legends, and myths of American Indians with contemporary American Indian life. The characters are drawn from earlier novels. This selection, "Miss Peace McKnight," is from the first chapter of the novel, which introduces the reader to each character.

Erdrich's **style** is very real. Style is an author's way of writing. She uses many **similes** in this selection. Simile is a figure of speech that makes a comparison using the words *like* or *as*. Her style also captures the **mood**—the feeling that writing creates—of sadness, gloom, and magic of the Indian reservations.

FROM
THE ANTELOPE WIFE

MISS PEACE MCKNIGHT

Family duty was deeply planted in Miss Peace McKnight, also the knowledge that if she did not nobody else would—do the duty, that is, of seeing to the future of the McKnights. Her father's Aberdeen button-cart business failed after he ran out of dead sheep—his own, whose bones he cleverly thought to use after a spring disaster. He sawed buttons with an instrument **devised** of **soldered** steel, ground them to a luster with a polisher of fine sand glued to cloth, made holes with a bore and punch that he had self-invented. It was the absence, then, of sheep **carcasses** that forced his daughter to do battle with the spirit of ignorance.

Peace McKnight. She was sturdily made as a captain's chair, yet drew water with graceful wrists and ran dancing across the rutted road on curved white ankles. Hale, Scots, full-breasted as a pouter pigeon, and dusted all over like an egg with freckles, wavy brown-black hair secured with her father's gift—three pins of carved bone—she came to the Great Plains with enough education to apply for and win a teaching certificate.

Her class was piddling at first, all near grown, too. Three **consumptive** Swedish sisters not long for life, one boy **abrupt** and full of anger. A German. Even though she spoke plainly and slowly as humanly possible, her students fixed her with stares of tongueless **suspicion** and were incapable of following a single direction. She had to start from the beginning, teach the alphabet, the numbers, and had just reached the letter *v*, the word *cat*, subtraction, which they were naturally better at than addition, when she noticed someone standing at the back of her classroom. Quietly alert, observant, she had been there for some time. The girl stepped forward from the darkness.

abrupt rude; blunt	**devise** to create	**suspicion** uncertainty; doubt
carcass a dead body	**soldered** joined together by the melting of a metal called solder	
consumptive sickly		

What is the author's writing style like?

This paragraph explains that Peace McKnight's father uses sheep bones to make buttons for a living. However, this business fails because there are no more sheep bones. What does this tell you about Peace McKnight's family life?

Notice the similes in the second paragraph. Peace McKnight is compared to a captain's chair, a pouter pigeon, and an egg using the words *like* and *as*.

Contemporary American Literature Unit 7 **449**

She had roan coppery skin and wore a necklace of bright indigo beads. She was slender, with a **pliable** long waist, graceful neck, and she was about six years old.

Miss McKnight blushed pink-gold with interest. She was charmed, first by the confidence of the child's smile and next by her immediate assumption of a place to sit, study, organize herself, and at last by her listening intelligence. The girl, though silent, had a hungry, curious quality. Miss McKnight had a teaching gift to match it. Although they were fourteen years apart, they became, **inevitably**, friends.

Then sisters. Until fall, Miss McKnight slept in the school cloakroom and bathed in the river nearby. Once the river iced over at the edges, an argument developed among the few and far between **homesteads** as to which had enough room and who could afford her. No one. Matilda Roy stepped in and pestered her father, known as a strange and **reclusive** fellow, until he gave in and agreed that the new teacher could share the small trunk bed he had made for his daughter, so long as she helped with the poultry.

Mainly, they raised guinea fowl that Scranton Roy had bought from a Polish widow. The speckled purple-black vulturine birds were half wild, clever. Matilda's task was to spy on, hunt down, and follow the hens to their hidden nests. The girls, for Peace McKnight was half girl around Matilda, laughed at the birds' tricks and hid to catch them. Fat, speckled, furious with shrill guinea pride, they acted as house watchdogs and scolded in the oak trees. Then from the pole shed where they wintered. In lard from a neighbor's pig, Scranton Roy fried strips of late squash, dried sand-dune morels, inky caps, field and oyster mushrooms, crushed acorns, the guinea eggs. He baked sweet bannock, dribbled on it wild aster honey aged in the hole of an oak, dark and **pungent** as mead.

The small sod and plank house was whitewashed inside and the deep sills of small bold windows held geraniums and started seeds. . . .

What is the mood of this selection?

The author is describing different foods here. A *morel* is a kind of fungus that can be eaten. A *bannock* is a flat bread or biscuit made with oatmeal or barley meal. *Mead* is a dark-colored drink made of water, honey, malt, and yeast.

homestead the home and surrounding land of a family	**inevitably** unable to be avoided; certain to happen at some point	**pungent** having a sharp or biting odor
	pliable able to bend freely	**reclusive** tending to withdraw from others

The Antelope Wife
Louise Erdrich

Directions Write the answers to these questions using complete sentences.

Comprehension: Identifying Facts

1. What does Peace McKnight look like?

2. What does Peace do for a living?

3. Where does Peace live at first?

Comprehension: Understanding Main Ideas

4. What does Peace like most about little Matilda Roy?

5. How do Matilda and Peace learn to enjoy raising fowl?

6. What kind of life do teachers like Peace lead?

Understanding Literature: Style and Mood

An author's way of writing is called style. Part of Louise Erdrich's style is to use a varied sentence structure. This makes her writing more interesting. Not all sentences in the selection about Peace McKnight are complete. Erdrich purposely arranged the length of her sentences to help create mood, or the feeling that writing creates. Some sentences are quite long and connected with several dashes and commas. A few are not true sentences at all; they are just a few words that end with a period.

7. Cite two examples from this selection of sentences with just two words.

8. Explain why you think Erdrich may have used simple sentences at times, then longer and more complex sentences at other times.

Critical Thinking

9. What would you miss most about your life today if you lived like Peace McKnight? Explain your answer.

10. What do you think happens to Peace? To Matilda?

Writing on Your Own There are two full descriptions in this selection, one of Peace and one of Matilda. Reread these paragraphs and note the information that is given and the picture that you form in your head. Using this style, write a paragraph describing yourself or a family member. Write only three or four sentences, but include as much detail as you can.

Imagery

Have you ever read something and then pictured in your mind what you just read? In literature, this is called imagery. It is the use of words that appeal to the senses. Imagery can affect our sense of sight, smell, sound, taste, and touch. Following is an example.

> The oak tree's old, dead branches clattered together in the wind.

This example appeals to the reader's sense of sight and sound. Most likely, when reading the sentence, you pictured what an old oak tree looks like and you heard in your mind the sound of branches knocking together. Imagery adds to writing because it allows the reader to experience things mentally by reading only a few simple words.

Following is an example of imagery from "The Starfish" by Robert Bly.

> I had forgotten how purple he was . . . the snaillike feelers waving as if nothing had happened. . . .

Bly appeals to the reader's sense of sight in this example. He describes the starfish as being purple and having tiny feelers.

This example is from Julia Alvarez's poem "Papi Working."

> . . . to homesick hearts, the tick tock of the clock . . .

"Tick tock" appeals to the sense of sound. It tells the reader how the clock sounds.

Review

1. What is imagery?
2. What senses does imagery appeal to?
3. How does imagery add to writing?
4. What sense is appealed to in the example from "The Starfish"?
5. What sense is appealed to in the example from "Papi Working"?

Writing on Your Own Write five sentences of your own using imagery to describe a person, place, or thing. Appeal to all five senses in your sentences.

UNIT 7 SUMMARY

American history and literature have been rounded out by the works in this unit. The 400 years of literature in this book come together in the last thirty years of the twentieth century, from 1971 to the present. The changes that have taken place in America have been huge. Political problems, fast growth, and world problems were main events during this time. Yet, compared to many other countries, the United States is still a new nation. A promising, yet most likely difficult, future awaits.

Life and literature in contemporary America show the excitement of our fast-paced world. During this time, many voices have shaped American literature. Richard Rodriguez, Lucille Clifton, Robert Bly, Lawson Fusao Inada, Maya Angelou, Amy Tan, Julia Alvarez, and Louise Erdrich are the contemporary authors in this unit. Whatever is in the future for American literature, it will be improved by the voices of the many people who make up America today and will help to create the America of tomorrow.

Selections

- "A City of Words" is a selection from an autobiography by Richard Rodriguez.

- "morning mirror" and "my dream about the poet" are poems by Lucille Clifton that express her views on her mother and creativity.

- "The Starfish" is a prose poem by Robert Bly about an unusual starfish that the poet sees in a tide pool.

- "My Father and Myself Facing the Sun" by Lawson Fusao Inada is a poem comparing the poet's father with himself.

- "Passports to Understanding" is a personal essay by Maya Angelou about the many benefits travel can bring.

- The selection from *The Hundred Secret Senses*, a novel by Amy Tan, describes a young girl's fears and her father's death.

- "Papi Working" by Julia Alvarez is a poem describing the poet's father, who cares for Hispanic immigrants.

- The selection from *The Antelope Wife*, a novel by Louise Erdrich, describes a young teacher named Peace McKnight and gives a short view of her life in the Midwest.

UNIT 7 REVIEW

Directions Write the answers to these questions using complete sentences.

Comprehension: Identifying Facts

1. What years are covered in Unit 7?

2. What changes occurred in America under President Reagan?

3. What changes occurred in America under President Clinton?

4. What is contemporary literature?

5. List three writers whose works are included in this unit.

Comprehension: Understanding Main Ideas

6. Compare "A City of Words" by Richard Rodriguez to "Passports to Understanding" by Maya Angelou.

7. What are some differences between Robert Bly's "The Starfish" and the poetry in this unit?

8. What is a novel?

9. What is Lawson Fusao Inada's poem "My Father and Myself Facing the Sun" about?

10. Explain how the works of ethnic writers have added to American literature.

Understanding Literature: Contemporary Literature

Modern American writing includes works by Asian Americans, Hispanic Americans, American Indians, and African Americans. An awareness of these various cultures and heritages makes every American richer.

Contemporary literature includes some new forms of writing. Prose poetry is an open form of poetry that is written as prose rather than poetry. Contemporary poetry has become different from traditional poetry. Free verse—poetry that does not have a strict rhyming pattern or regular line length—is very common today. Some poets use little or no punctuation and no capital letters. The novel—fiction that is book-length with more plot and character details than a short story—has become the most common form of literature.

11. How are contemporary works different from earlier works?

12. What is prose poetry? Whose prose poetry appears in this unit?

13. What is free verse?

14. Whose novels appear in this unit?

15. Why do you think novels have become so popular today?

Critical Thinking

16. Identify your favorite work in Unit 7. Explain your choice.

17. Which selection in this unit do you think is the best example of contemporary literature? Why?

18. Why do you think contemporary poets like to use free verse? Explain.

19. Do you think that contemporary literature does a good job of including all of America's voices? Why or why not?

20. What do you think will be the most popular kind of literature in the future? Explain your prediction.

Speak and Listen

Practice debating with another student about the impact of television on literature. One student should take the position that television will be the literature of the future. The other student should take the position that television can never take the place of literature. Use facts, statistics, and reasoning to support your position. Then present your debate to the class. Choose another student to be timekeeper. Limit the debate to five minutes per person. After the debate is over, find out how many students agree with each debater.

Beyond Words

America is often described as a "melting pot." This is a place where people of various ethnic backgrounds, social classes, languages, religions, and cultures come together. Make a collage—a collection of pictures taken from magazines or newspapers. Look for pictures in which America is shown to be a melting pot. Arrange your pictures in an artistic and attractive way. If you wish, title your collage.

Writing on Your Own

Write your own piece of contemporary literature. Choose one of the following genres: poem, prose poem, personal essay, or autobiography. Answer this question in your writing: *What is it like to be living in the United States today?* Go back and review the selections in Unit 7 to see how the writers in this unit wrote their literature. If you plan to write a poem, consider using free verse or other contemporary styles.

Test-Taking Tip

After you have completed a test, reread each question and answer. Ask yourself: *Have I answered the question that was asked? Have I answered it completely?*

Correcting Common Writing Mistakes

1. Make subjects and verbs agree
- Singular subjects must have singular verbs.
- Plural subjects must have plural verbs.
- Compound subjects must have plural verbs.

2. Make pronouns agree with antecedents
- In gender:
  - Replace the name of a male person with a masculine pronoun.
  - Replace the name of a female person with a feminine pronoun.
  - Replace singular names with *it* or *its.*
  - Replace plural names with *they, them,* or *their.*
- In number:
  - Make the pronoun singular if its antecedent is singular.
  - Make the pronoun plural if its antecedent is plural.

3. Capitalize proper nouns and proper adjectives
- Capitalize proper nouns.
- Capitalize the first word of any sentence or title.
- Capitalize the names of languages.
- Capitalize the pronoun *I.*
- Capitalize all proper adjectives.

4. Use correct verb tenses
- Action verbs tell what someone did.
- State-of-being verbs express the condition of the subject.
- Helping verbs help the main verb express tense, or time.
  - Use one main verb in a verb phrase.
  - Use helping verbs in a verb phrase.
  - Use the main verb last in a verb phrase.

- Make sure the verb tenses are logical.
- Use the same verb tenses if the actions occurred at the same time.
- Use different verb tenses if the actions occurred at different times.

5. Use and spell verb forms correctly
- Form the past tense of a regular verb by adding *-ed* or *-d.*
- Use the past participle to form the past perfect tenses.

6. Use and spell possessives and plurals correctly
- Use a possessive noun to show ownership or a relationship between two things.
- Make a singular noun possessive by adding an apostrophe (') and the letter *s.*
- Make a plural noun possessive by adding only an apostrophe.
- Add both an apostrophe and the letter s if the plural noun does not end in an *s.*

7. Avoid run-on sentences
- Begin sentences with a capital letter.
- End each sentence with a period, question mark, or exclamation point.
- Do not end a sentence or separate two sentences with a comma.
- Use a comma plus a conjunction to connect two complete ideas.

8. Avoid sentence fragments
- Make sure each sentence has a subject and a verb that express a complete idea.
- Use a subject and a predicate.
- Do not capitalize the first word of a phrase that does not begin a new idea.

Paragraphs

The Three Parts of a Paragraph

1. The topic sentence

The topic sentence states the main idea in a paragraph. It is usually the first sentence of a paragraph. It lets the reader know what your paragraph is going to be about. The topic sentence should get the reader's attention. It should make the reader want to read the rest of your paragraph.

Ask yourself these questions to help you write your topic sentence:

- What is the purpose of my paragraph?
- What is the main point I want to make?
- Why am I writing this paragraph?
- What will this paragraph be about?

2. The body

The body of a paragraph is the group of sentences that tell more about your main idea. It supports the point of view of your topic sentence. The body can include:

- Facts
- Details
- Explanations
- Reasons
- Examples
- Illustrations

3. The conclusion or summary

The last sentence of a paragraph is a conclusion or a summary. A conclusion is a judgment. It is based on the facts that you presented in your paragraph. Your conclusion must make sense.

A summary is a statement that briefly repeats the main ideas of your paragraph. It repeats your idea or ideas in slightly different words. It does not add new information.

The Purposes of a Paragraph

Every paragraph has one of five purposes. The five purposes are:

1. To give information or facts

Facts are included in all three parts of a paragraph. You may gather facts by reading, listening, or observing.

2. To explain your ideas

You may use this kind of paragraph to:

- Make something clear
- Help someone understand an idea
- Give the meaning of something
- Give reasons for something

3. To ask for information

In this kind of paragraph, make your questions clear and specific. That way, you get specific answers.

4. To persuade

This kind of paragraph helps you to convince someone to act or believe a certain way. You must be sure of what you are saying. Then you can persuade someone.

5. To tell a story

The story you tell in this kind of paragraph can be imaginary or true. A true story should follow the order in which things happened.

Checklist for Proofreading and Revising

✔ **Use this checklist to proofread and revise your papers.**

Check your paper
- ❏ Do I have a meaningful title?
- ❏ Do I have a conclusion or a summary at the end?

Check your paragraphs
- ❏ Do I start every paragraph on a new line?
- ❏ Is the first line of every paragraph indented?
- ❏ Does my first sentence (topic sentence) in every paragraph explain the main idea of my paragraph? Does it attract my reader's attention well?
- ❏ Do sentences in the middle of my paragraphs support the main idea?
- ❏ Do I include facts, details, explanations, reasons, examples, or illustrations to support my main idea?
- ❏ Do I need to take out any sentences that do not relate to my main idea?

Check your sentences
- ❏ Do I capitalize the first word of every sentence?
- ❏ Do I end every sentence with the correct punctuation mark?
- ❏ Do I express a complete idea in every sentence?
- ❏ Do my pronouns all have clear antecedents?
- ❏ Do I have any run-on sentences that I need to correct?
- ❏ Can I improve my sentences?

- ❏ Can I add adjectives, adverbs, or prepositional phrases?
- ❏ Can I combine short, related ideas into longer, more varied sentences?

Check your verbs
- ❏ Do I have a subject and a verb in every sentence?
- ❏ Do my subject and verb agree in every sentence?
- ❏ Is my verb tense logical in every sentence?
- ❏ Is my verb tense consistent in every sentence?
- ❏ Are my irregular verbs correct?

Check your punctuation and capitalization
- ❏ Did I capitalize all my proper nouns and proper adjectives?
- ❏ Did I capitalize and punctuate all my direct quotations correctly?
- ❏ Did I use a comma to separate words in a series?

Check your spelling
- ❏ Did I choose the correct spelling for each homonym?
- ❏ Did I use an apostrophe only in contractions and possessive nouns?
- ❏ Did I spell every plural noun correctly?
- ❏ Did I spell all words with *ie* or *ei* correctly?
- ❏ Did I drop the silent *e* before adding an ending beginning with a vowel?
- ❏ Did I double the final consonant before adding an ending?

Planning and Writing Reports

Plan the report
- Choose a broad subject you would like to explore.
- Select a topic in that subject area.
- Find out how much information is in the library about your topic.
- Limit your topic so that you have enough information to write a complete report.
- Write a title for your report.
- List your subtopics, or the parts of your larger topic.

Find information
- Go to the library to find information on your topic.
- Look in the library catalog for books that have useful information.
- Check almanacs, encyclopedias, atlases, or other sources in the library reference section.
- Check *The Reader's Guide to Periodical Literature* for magazines with information you could use.
- Take notes on the information you find.
- Use index cards.
- Start each card with this information about the source you find facts in:
  - authors' names
  - book or article and magazine title
  - page numbers
  - volume numbers
  - date of publication
- Copy all the information that you may need.
- Copy any quotations exactly as they are printed.
- Use a different card for each source.

Get organized
- Put your note cards in order by topic and subtopic.
- Do not use notes that may not fit anywhere.
- List your main topics.
- Choose an order that seems suitable for your topics.
- Write a final topic outline.

Write your report
- Write your report using note cards and an outline.
- Begin your report with a topic paragraph that states the main idea.
- Use your own words to write the ideas you found in your sources (paraphrase).
- Write an author's exact words if you use direct quotations.
- Name the author or source of any direct quotations you use.
- Repeat your main ideas in a summary paragraph at the end.
- Proofread your report.
- Revise and rewrite it as needed.
- Include a title page at the front of your report.

Prepare a bibliography
- Use the bibliographic information on your note cards.
- Put your cards in alphabetical order.
- Include a blank page after your bibliography.

Handbook of Literary Terms

A

act the separate sections of a play

action what goes on in a story

alliteration the repetition of initial consonant sounds

allusion something referring to a historical event, a person, a place, or a work of literature

almanac a calendar and date book

anecdote a short, funny story

animal imagery a literary device that uses animal-like descriptions to tell about a person

antagonist a person or thing in the story struggling against the main character

aphorism a wise and clever saying

assonance the repetition of vowel sounds

autobiography a story about a person's life written by that person

B

ballad a simple song that often uses a refrain and sometimes uses rhyme and is passed from person to person

biography a person's life story told by someone else

blank verse unrhymed iambic pentameter

by-line a line in a news article that tells who wrote it

C

character a person in a story

characterization the way a writer develops characters by revealing personality traits

chorus a group of actors who comment on and explain the action in a play

classical drama the rules that define the form of a play

climax an event that triggers the comic or tragic ending of a play

column a regularly appearing article in a periodical

comedy a play with a nontragic ending

coming-of-age story a story that tells how a young person matures

conflict a struggle the main character of a story has

connotation images or emotions connected to a word

consonance the repetition of consonant sounds usually within the context of several words

contemporary current or recent literature

couplet a rhyming pair

D

denouement the resolution to a story

detective story a story in which the main character solves a crime

dialect a regional variety of language

Handbook of Literary Terms

dialogue the conversation among characters in a story; the words that characters in a play speak

diary a record of personal events, thoughts, or private feelings

drama a play

dramatic monologue a poem in which a character talks to the reader

E

editorial a news writer's personal opinion about an event or topic

elegy a poem that mourns someone's death

end rhyme a feature of a poem or song in which the last words of two lines rhyme with one another

epic a long story written in verse

essay a written work that shows a writer's opinions on some basic or current issue

exaggeration a use of words to make something seem worse than it is; stretching the truth to a great extent

excerpt a short passage from a longer piece of writing

expressionistic drama a play that may seem realistic but that changes some elements for dramatic effect

F

fable a short story or poem with a moral, often with animals who act like humans

fantasy stories in which wizards and other creatures participate

feature story a news story that analyzes the effect and importance of an event

fiction writing that is imaginative and designed to entertain

figurative language language that makes a comparison and is not meant to be taken literally

first person written as if someone is telling the story

flashback a look into the past at some point in a story

folktale a story that has been handed down from one generation to another

free verse poetry that does not have a strict rhyming pattern or regular line length, and uses actual speech patterns for the rhythms of sound

G

genre a kind of literature

ghost writer someone paid to write a person's autobiography and let that person take the credit

H

haiku a Japanese poetry form, made of seventeen unrhymed syllables

Harlem Renaissance a literary movement within modern literature that focuses on African American pride

historical fiction writing that draws on factual events of history

humor literature created to be funny

humorist someone who writes funny works

hyperbole a gross exaggeration

I

iambic pentameter five two-beat sounds in a line of poetry

image a word or phrase that appeals to the senses and allows the reader to picture events

imagery pictures created by words; the use of words that appeal to the senses

immediate news stories on TV and in newspapers as the event happens

Internet a worldwide network of computers that speak a common language

irony the use of words that seem to say one thing but mean the opposite

J

joke a short story that ends with a punchline

journal writing that records a writer's first impressions about a subject

journalism the gathering and communicating of news to the public

L

legend a traditional story that was at one time told orally and was handed down from one generation to another

letter impressions and feelings written to a specific person

limerick a humorous five-line poem

local color a kind of writing that reflects the way people speak, dress, and behave, and the customs popular in certain places

lullaby a soothing song or poem sung to a baby

M

metaphor a figure of speech that says one thing *is* another; a figure of speech that makes a comparison

modernism a literary movement in the twentieth century that focuses on trying to explain the many changes of the modern world

monologue a longer story told in person

mood the feeling that writing creates

moral a message in a story

myth a story that explains how some things in the natural world came to be

N

narrator the teller of a story

naturalism a literary movement that focuses on the survival of the fittest against nature and features characters as being helpless against events that are beyond human control and understanding

neoclassical recent plays written in the classical form

news cycle the length of time between the publishing of a news item and an update or reaction to the item

news story the first reports of an event; mainly covers the bare facts

nonfiction writing about real people and events

novel fiction that is book-length and has more plot and character details than a short story

O

onomatopoeia the use of a word to imitate a sound

P

pamphlet a short printed essay about a specific problem; it has no cover or has a paper cover

parody an exaggerated look at a situation

pen name a false name used for writing

personal essay a kind of writing that explores the author's opinion of a topic in a light and often entertaining way

personification giving human characteristics to a nonhuman object

persuasive meant to influence

playwright the author of a play

plot the series of events in a story

poem a short piece of literature that usually has rhythm and paints powerful or beautiful impressions with words

point of view the position from which the author or storyteller tells the story

proclamation letters about important events meant to be read aloud

prop piece of equipment used on-stage during a play

prose written language that is not verse

prose poem an open form of poetry that is written as prose rather than as traditional poetry

protagonist the main character in a story

pun humorous use of words or phrases

R

realism a literary movement in which authors write about life as it is, not as they wish it to be

realistic drama a play that tells a story just as it might happen in real life

refrain the repetition of words or phrases to create mood or emphasis

regionalism a word or phrase that comes from a particular area

requiem a prayer for the dead; a work that has been written in honor of the dead

rhyme words with the same vowel and ending sounds

rhyme scheme a pattern of end rhymes in a poem

rhythm a regular pattern of stressed and unstressed syllables

rising action the buildup of excitement in a story

romanticism a literary movement marked by the excitement of learning, the sense of hopefulness, the spirit of individual freedom, strong morals, deeply personal thoughts, emotional sincerity, an interest in nature, and an interest in the unusual and the original

routine a longer story that a storyteller uses over and over in a live performance

S

sarcasm a heavy, sometimes mean-spirited kind of irony

satire humorous writing that makes fun of foolishness or evil

"sci-fi" a kind of science fiction that predicts what the future might be like

science fiction a type of literature that deals with people, places, and events that could not happen in our reality

semiautobiography a story based on a person's life written by that person, with some events changed

sequence the order of events in a literary work

setting the time and place in a story

short story a brief prose narrative

sidebar research and analysis of a news story

simile a figure of speech that makes a comparison using the words *like* or *as*

sketch a brief writing that often runs from subject to subject and is often humorous

sonnet a fourteen-line poem divided into four sections, in iambic pentameter

speech a written work meant to be read aloud

spiritual a religious and emotional song developed among enslaved Africans in the South during the middle of the 1800s

stanza a group of lines that forms a unit and often has the same rhythm and rhyme pattern

stereotype a simplified idea about another person

stream of consciousness a writing technique that develops the plot by allowing the reader to see how and what the characters are thinking

style an author's way of writing

subtitle a second, less important title under the first that gives more information about the writing

surrealism a writing style that is meant to be understood by a reader's subconscious

symbol a person, place, or thing that represents an idea or thought

symbolism the larger meaning of a person, place, or object

T

theme the main idea of a literary work

third person a point of view that refers to characters as "he" or "she" and expresses some characters' thoughts

tone the attitude an author takes toward a subject

tragedy a play in which the main character is destroyed

transcendentalism a literary movement in which the spiritual world has greater value than the material world and the individual is of great importance

turning point a story about an experience that changes a literary character's life

V

verse word patterns that follow definite rhythm and rhyme

villanelle a nineteen-line poem with several repeating rhymes

W

Web site material that a newspaper puts on the Internet for the public to read

aberration a belief that goes against what is common or normal, 196

abode a home, 73

abominable quite disagreeable or unpleasant, 208

abrupt characterized by changing without warning; rude; blunt, 187, 449

abruptly without warning, 226

abruptness changing without warning, 317

acclamation applause; a loud, eager expression of approval, 98

accost to speak to in an intense, harsh way, 97

acknowledge to admit; to take notice of, 285, 432

acquiesce to accept, 212

acquiescence the act of accepting or giving in to authority, 399

acute sharp and severe, 236

acutely sharply; intensely, 378

adherent one who follows or supports something, 29

admirably very well; perfectly, 310

admonition a gentle warning, 69, 198

adolescence the teen years, 293

advent coming into being or use, 374

adversity a state of misfortune, 14

affectionate careful; kindly; tender; loving, 313, 356, 417

affinities sympathetic relationships; attractions, 338

affirm to state positively, 13, 136

aggressively forcefully, 223

agilely with quick, graceful motion, 358

agitate to bother, 130

agitatedly being upset, 204

agitation movement; the act of disturbing something, 232

agony extreme pain of mind or body, 216

allay to calm or reduce, 52

alleviate to relieve; to lessen; to make more bearable, 293

allusion hints or hinting, 42

ambiguous difficult to understand, 286

ambitious having desire to achieve a goal; difficult, 100, 284

amiably agreeably, 311

anatomy the physical makeup of a living thing, 103, 200

anglicized made like English; changed to English usage, 417

anguish extreme pain or distress, 150

angular thin and bony; stiff in character or manner, 267

annihilate to destroy, 400

annuity a sum of money paid yearly or at some regular period, 272

anomalous unusual, 53

anticipate to give advance thought to; to predict or expect what will happen, 340, 383

anticipation an expectation that something will happen, 241

apathetically with little or no emotion, 237

apathy a lack of feeling or emotion, 99

aplomb complete self-confidence or self-assurance, 308

appall to overcome with shock or surprise, 373

appalling inspiring horror, dismay, or disgust, 313

apparition a ghost, 46

appeasingly in a way that calms or gives in, 240

appendage a smaller part that sticks out from something larger, 224

appraising studying something to determine worth or value, 310

apprehension understanding; fear, 196, 224

apprentice one who works for a professional for a certain period of time to learn the professional's art or trade, 163

approbation approval; praise, 136

apropos to the purpose; at the right time, 195

archfiend a chief demon or devil, especially Satan, 53

ardor intensity, 103

articulate able to express oneself clearly and effectively, 393

assassin one who commits murder, 326

assent to agree; agreement, 137, 190

assert to state positively, 240

assertion the act of stating positively or standing up for, 155

assimilate to make similar, 89

assuage to lessen; to satisfy; to ease, 150, 282

asymmetrical not even or well balanced, 305

atone to make up for offenses or injuries, 281

atrocity a horrifying event, 43

attentive paying careful attention; alert, 381

attribute to connect; to explain by indicating a cause, 29, 46

audible able to be heard, 388

august awe-inspiring, 432

aura an atmosphere or energy surrounding something, 406

auroral referring to arches of light that appear in the upper atmosphere of a planet's polar regions, 73

avail to make use of, 281

aversion dislike, 48

barbarian one who is not thought to be civilized, 14

barbarously harshly or cruelly, 187

bastard a person of unknown origin, 393

beguile to deceive or trick, 150

bemoan to express deep grief, 93

beneficent kind; charitable, 212

benevolent marked by goodwill; marked by doing good, 155

benign gentle; kind, 418

bequeath to give or leave by will, 211

bereavement the feeling of loss, especially in the death of a loved one, 150

Glossary

beseech to beg,144

beseechingly with an anxious, begging manner, 267

bestow to give as a gift, 69

bewitching attractive in a mysterious way, 90

bigotry prejudice; the lack or absence of respect or understanding of differences in other people, 436

blasé showing a lack of concern; worldly, 288

blatant done on purpose, 374

bleak grim; lacking in warmth, life, or kindliness, 391

blissful happy, 51

blithely happily and with little thought, 101

boisterously noisily; loudly, 97

bosom the human chest, often thought of as the seat of emotions, 51

bravado a show of bravery, 52

brazen made of brass, 82

broker an agent who handles sales and purchases for other people, 144

brutal unfeeling; cruel; harsh, 337

brutality a harsh or violent act, 400

buoyancy a tendency to float in liquid, 76

buxom healthily plump, 87

calculate to figure out, often by use of mathematics, 225

capacious containing or able to contain a great deal, 29

capitulate to surrender; to yield, 102

carcass a dead body, 237, 449

caress a light stroking, rubbing, or patting, 229, 308

catapult to throw or launch; to move with great force, 382

celestial supreme; heavenly, 24

censor to change something because it could be displeasing to others, 391

cessation stopping, 216

chastened pure or decent, 268

chide to scold, 241

chiding scolding, 90

chimera something made up by the mind; a dream, 48

chink a small opening between the logs of a cabin, 73

circulation the orderly movement of blood through the body, 230

circumscribe to define clearly, 100

circumstance condition, 134

civility courtesy; politeness, 110

clamor a loud and steady noise, 288

clandestine secret; hidden, 293

client one who pays for the services of another, 270

coerce to force, 213

collateral property that a borrower promises to give up if unable to pay a debt, 326

collide to come together with solid or direct impact; to clash, 436

comber a long, curling wave of the sea, 213

commerce business, 392

compel to drive or urge forcefully, 226

competent acceptable; suitable, 374

complaisant willing to please, 88

comport to behave; to act according to what is expected, 28

composite made up of several parts; made up of the same mix of characteristics, 200, 266

conception idea, 240

confetti small bits of brightly colored paper thrown at a celebration, 326

confidential private, 420

confiscate to take, 93

conflagration a large fire; a conflict or war; a terrible fire, 45, 233

confounded confused; unfortunate, 317, 419

confront to meet face-to-face, 363

congestion the condition of being clogged, 269

congregation a group of people gathered for worship, 144

conjectural guessed at or unproven, 222

conjecture to guess, 268

conjointly combined, 53

conjurer a magician, 84

consequence result, 197

consign to give someone over to the control of another, 53

consolation comfort, 150

consoling comforting, 419

consort to keep company with, 282

conspicuous obvious; noticeable, 163, 267

constitute to make up or form, 47

constituted made up; set up, 153

consume to use up, 228

consummate to complete, 44

consumption the wasting away of the body caused by tuberculosis, 100

consumptive sickly, 449

contemplate to think about, 163, 198, 288

contemporaries people of the same or nearly the same age, 69

contempt deep dislike or scorn; a feeling of dislike and disgust toward someone or something; the act of despising; a lack of respect, 190, 312, 395, 399

contemptuous expressing disgust, 284

contemptuously in an uncaring or hateful manner, 49

contending struggling or contesting, 31

contortion a violent twisting, 286

contradict to go against, 70, 153

contradictory going against what was previously said, 383

contritely regretfully, 206

contrivance an artificial arrangement, 205

conventicle a meeting; a secret meeting, 75

conventional ordinary; commonplace, 69

converge to come together, 254

convey to express; to explain, 311

Glossary

conveyance a vehicle; a means of transport, 265

convict to find one guilty in a court of law, 320

conviction a strong belief; an opinion, 153, 309, 395

copperhead a person from the North who agreed with the South during the American Civil War, 326

coquetry flirting, 90

cordial tending to revive or cheer, 85

cornice the very top piece of a building, often overhanging, 110

corpulent very fat, 266

countenance facial expression, 30

covet to wish for heavily, 57

criticism judgment by others, 164

crystalline clear or sparkling, 206

cultivation growth, 70

culture the customs, beliefs, behaviors, and traits of a certain group of people, 436

cumulative combined, 70

curtsy to show respect by a slight lowering of the body with bended knees, 88

cynical deeply distrustful, 194

cynicism a view that people are encouraged by self-interest; being deeply distrustful, 278

damnation the act of being sent to hell, 53

debauch an act that goes against morals, such as heavy drinking, 44

debonair lighthearted, 288

deception a trick, 84

decrepit old, 86

deem to think or judge; to consider, 83

deferential respectful, 88

deficiency lack, 99

deflate to reduce; to lessen, 418

deformed shaped oddly; twisted, 440

deign to do something in a snobbish way, 28

dejection sadness, 73, 188

deliberate characterized by careful thought; slow or unhurried, 315

deliberately slowly; without hurrying, 253

deliberation a discussion for or against a certain idea, 31

delirium wild excitement, 92

delusion a false belief about the self, others, or objects, 87, 381

demoniacal possessed or influenced by a devil or an evil spirit, 50

deprecatory disapproving, 284

depressed saddened, 224

depression the lowering of activity, 200

deprivation loss or removal, 153

deprive to take something away, 198

derision ridicule, 295

derisive expressing ridicule, 285

derive to come from, 376

designate to set apart for a certain purpose, 387

desolate lacking inhabitants, 14, 199

despise to regard as of little worth or purpose, 307

destiny a course of events that has already been determined, 293

destitution extreme poverty, 130

detached cool; distant, 315

detested hated; extremely disliked, 51, 279

devise to invent; to create, 225, 449

diabolical devilish; relating to the devil, 195

dialogue a discussion; the act of two or more people communicating, 132, 400

diffuse to scatter or spread freely, 85

diminish to decrease, 284

diminished made less; decreasing, 421

diminutive a familiarly known word or name, 417

din a loud continued noise, 289

direful dreadful, 196

disabling weakening, 417

discern to detect with the eyes, 201

discharge to take off; to remove or let go, 162

disclosure the act of making something known, 136

disconsolate dejected; downcast; cheerless, 165

discreetly acting in a quiet, unnoticed manner, 382

discriminating showing careful judgments or fine taste, 272

disdainfully proudly, 102

disengage to break loose, 90

disentanglement the act of freeing something from being tangled, 210

disjointed lacking order; hard to understand, 189

dispatch to send off on official business, 314

disregard to pay no attention to, 140

disrupted thrown into disorder, 375

dissever to separate, 58

dissuasion the act of turning someone away by some means, 283

distended made larger, 267

distinction worthiness; a special honor, 163

distort to twist or change the true meaning of something, 420

divers various, 80

diversion something that distracts the mind and amuses, 306

docility the quality of being easy to control; tameness, 41

doggedly stubbornly, 191

dolefully sadly, 92

dormant inactive, 278

dotage a state of mental decay or decrease in alertness, 86

draught a drink, 87

dredging digging; gathering; scooping, 441

drowse to be drowsy or tired, 160

drunkard one who is continuously drunk, 161, 270

dunderpate a stupid person; a dunce, 28

dwell to live, 440

earmark a distinguishing mark, 339

Glossary

ebb to fall from a higher to a lower level, 231

ebony a kind of hard, dark wood, 82

eccentric strange; unusual; different, 318

eccentricity an odd or abnormal behavior, 83

ecstasy intense joy or delight; a state of overwhelming emotion; a trance-like state, 428

efface to erase, wipe away, or rub out, 89

effervescent bubbling, 85

efficacious effective, 295

elated marked by high spirits; filled with joy, 138, 380

elf a small often lively creature; a mischievous child, 300

eligible qualifying for, 285

eloquently movingly; with very effective words, 280

emaciated very thin; physically wasted away, 268

embrace a hug, 90

eminent famous, 69

emphatic forceful; attracting special attention, 192

enact to act out, 337

endear to cause to be loved, 48

endeavor to strive to reach or achieve something, 154

enduring lasting, 341

enlighten to be informed, 285

ensue to follow, 236

entanglement the state of being tangled, 230

entreat to plead, 103

entreaty a plea, 144

episode a story or incident, 316

equivocal uncertain, 44

espouse to take up and support as a cause, 99

essence a great or concentrated amount, 311

esteem to regard, 24

eternal lasting forever, 156

eternity endless life; the everlasting, 110

ethereal heavenly; unworldly; spiritual, 268

ethics principles guiding a person or group; the study of good and bad, 191

eventide evening, 173

evince to reveal, 31

evolve to develop; to become, 235

exalt to raise in rank, power, or character, 163

exasperate to excite into anger, 49

exasperating very annoying, 391

exceptional better than average, 318

excruciating causing great pain, 235

excursion a short trip, 74

exemplary serving as a good example, 381

exhilaration the feeling of being excited, 87

exigency urgency, 287

exotic not native to the place where one is found; mysterious, 441

expanse a great extent of something spread out, 190

expectant waiting for something to happen, 357

expectation something that is expected, 153

expedient a solution to a problem, 50

expel to force out, 224

explicit expressed without being difficult to understand, 340

expostulation discussion, 144

expound to explain, 41

exquisite intense, 290

extemporaneous done on the spur of the moment, 70

extraordinary unusual; beyond what is usual, 255, 279

extravagance an expensive event, 316

extremity intense degree; a limb of the body, 89, 231, 286

exuberant joyously unrestrained, 89

exude to ooze out, 73

exult to be extremely joyful, 53

facilitate to help bring about; to make easier, 162

fallible able to make mistakes, 372

falter to hesitate in purpose or action, 256

familial of or relating to a family, 339

fancy imagination; a liking formed by chance rather than reason, 123

fantasy a daydream or imaginary story, 391

felicitous very well suited; pleasant or delightful, 100

felicity a state of happiness, 52

feminine relating to females, 290

ferociously fiercely, 287

fervent marked by intense feeling, 123

festooned decorated, 81

fidelity loyalty or devotion, 42

filial relating to or befitting a son or daughter, 271

financial related to money, 376

firmament sky; heavens, 30

flagon a bottle or flask, often used for wine, 103

flattering very favorable, 341

flounder to struggle to move or get proper footing, 227

fluent able to speak a language very well, 417

flustered upset, 278

foemen enemies, 107

foliage leaves, flowers, and branches, 83

forbore avoided, 51

forenoon late morning, 133

formidable causing fear or dread; having qualities that arouse fear or dread, 199, 277

formulae a set form of words for use in a ceremony, 217

formulate to organize into a statement, 198

fortitude strength of mind, 25

fortnight a period of two weeks, 280

fragmentary incomplete, 206

franchise a right given to people, especially the right to vote, 153

frigidity a lack of warmth or kindness, 312

fugitive a person who is fleeing or trying to escape, 136

fundamental main or basic, 154

furtive secret; sly, 364

gait a manner of walking, 226

gaudy flashy; having tasteless design; dazzling, 160, 283

genetic related to the study of genes—the "blueprints" that show the makeup of a person, 440

gentry members of the ruling or upper class, 80

gilded giving the false appearance of gold, 162

gilding a thin coating of gold; something that gives an attractive but often false appearance, 123

gilt gold, or looking like gold, 82

girded bound up, 135

glint a tiny bright flash of light; a glimmer; a trace, 256, 425

glinting reflecting light, 357

gossamer light or unimportant, 42

grandeur grandness; greatness; magnificence, 29, 162, 254

grimace an expression of disgust on a person's face, 379

grotesque horrible; not natural; strange, 206

gusto enthusiastic enjoyment or appreciation, 306

guttural coming from the throat, 31

habitually done out of habit, 46

haggard having a worn-out appearance, 206

hallow to be made sacred or holy, 173

hallucination a completely mistaken vision or perception, 381

haste swiftness, 110

heather a flowering plant that grows on a moor, 111

heritage one's racial or social background, 394

hewn cut, 31

hindering hampering; blocking or slowing progress, 369

hobgoblin an imaginary fear; something that causes fear, 70

hoe to weed or thin with a hoe, which is a tool with a thin, flat blade on a long handle, 301

homage respect, 103

homestead the home and surrounding land of a family, 450

hostile unfriendly, 305

hostilities violent acts, 216

hostility an act of war; violent actions, 257, 338

humiliation extreme shame and embarrassment; the act of being reduced to a lower position in one's own eyes or the eyes' of others, 280

hysterical very excitable, 282

hysterically showing a very high level of emotion, 382

ignominiously shamefully, 293, 312

illusive difficult to tell whether something is real, 406

imbibe to take in; to drink, 84

immigrate to come and live in a country where one was not born, 440

immortal unable to be killed, 45

immortality the quality or state of living forever, 111, 222

impel to move someone or something to action, 289

impending about to occur, 197

imperative very necessary, 230, 402

imperceptible unable to be sensed or imagined, 49, 233

impersonal not personal, 209

impersonally having no personal connection toward; without feeling, 338

impetuous marked by force of movement or action, 195

impious lacking proper respect for God; lacking proper respect, 24, 203

implacable unable to be changed or resisted, 214

imposter one who pretends to be someone else, 278

impotent helpless; incapable of restraining oneself, 101, 285

imprecation a curse; swearing, 383

imprecision not exact, 372

impregnated filled with, 85

improbable unlikely, 316, 379

impudently in a manner marked by boldness or cockiness, 197

impunity freedom from punishment, harm, or loss, 281

impute to claim as a cause, 86

inaccessible not able to be looked at or considered, 393

inadequacy a lacking, 278

inaudibly not able to be heard, 99

incentive something that excites someone into action, 154

inclination a natural way of tending to do something, 44, 308

incompetency the inability to act due to a lack of needed skills or qualities, 198

inconsiderate not thinking about or caring for the welfare of others, 316

incredulously with disbelief 267, 312

incrustation habits or opinions that have become a deep part of someone or something, 279

incumbent resting on, 49

indifference the state of feeling no concern or interest about anything, 188

indifferently in a way that shows something does not matter, 308

indiscriminately without purpose, 280

indispensable unable to do without; very necessary, 375, 402

indivisible unable to be separated, 44

indulge to take pleasure in or yield to the desire of, 208

indulgence something that pampers or spoils, 316

Glossary

indulgent not strict, 294

inevitable unable to be avoided, 25

inevitably unable to be avoided; certain to happen at some point, 450

infallible unable to make errors, 30

infamous having a reputation of the worst kind, 80

infamy evil reputation brought on by a shocking event, 47

inferiority being of lower status or of less importance; the state of feeling or being less important than others, 155, 399

infidel one who has no religious beliefs, 25

infinitely never ending, 320, 338

infirmity being feeble or frail; old, 89

inflection a change in pitch or loudness, 317

ingenuity the ability to invent or to be clever, 30

ingenuously innocently; with childlike simplicity, 195

inimitable unable to be copied, 97

innumerable too many to be numbered, 200

inquiry a question; a request for information; an examination of facts, 52, 314

inscription something written or engraved, 86

inscrutability an inability to be easily found out or understood, 52

insight understanding; the act of forming an understanding about the nature of something, 420

insinuating distrusting; doubting, 358

instrumentality the use of something, 43

insufferable difficult to bear, 49

insular of, relating to, or being an island, 76

insulated kept from transferring heat, 76

intangible not able to be perceived; not real, 221, 279

intellectual well-educated or intelligent, 306

intemperance regular drinking of large amounts of alcohol, 43

interloper a person who interferes or intrudes on the rights of others, 394

intermingled mixed in, 88

intermission a break, 306

internal occurring within, 337

intervene to come between, 228

intervening occurring between two things, 76

intimacy very close friendship or contact, 229

intimate a person's very close friend; marked by very close association or contact; very personal or private, 49, 285, 419

intrude to force in or upon without permission, 163

intuitively naturally, 99

invariably constantly, 140, 187, 341

invective an insult; abusive language, 277

invest to spend money in a way that earns more money, 272

investment money spent in a way that earns more money; doing something in order to receive something in return, 20

invincible unable to be defeated, 28

iridescence a shiny rainbow-like play of color, 406

irresistibly unable to resist, 291

irrevocable unable to be taken back, 44

jamb the upright pieces forming the sides of the opening for a door, 146

jeopardize to expose to danger or risk, 45

judicially in a manner that judges, 276

knavery the act of being mischievous or a rascal, 270

landscape the landforms of an area; a scene, 432

lapse to slip away gradually, 164

lark something done for fun or adventure; harmless fun, 319

lavished wasted, 93

legacy something given to a later generation by an ancestor, 400

liberal one who is open-minded or does things that are not typical or established, 441

liberate to free, 268

limbo a state of uncertainty, 394

linguistic relating to languages or speech, 421

listless having no desire to act, 358

listlessly without interest, energy, or spirit, 204

loathing extreme disgust, 47

logic reason; something that makes sense, 419

lope the way in which a horse moves forward, 170

luminous giving off or reflecting a glowing light, 433

lunatic an insane person, 282

luring tempting; attracting with a hint of pleasure, 255

magnitude great size, 29, 138

maim to batter, mangle, or harm seriously, 208

makeshift a crude substitute, 295

malevolence the state of being cruel or evil, 43

malice ill will, 281, 402

manifest to display or make obvious, 155

manifold many times; a great deal, 17

manipulation the act of working with the hands to complete a task, 235

martial warlike; related to war or military life, 25

massive forming or consisting of a large mass; a large amount, 253, 337

matinée a musical or dramatic performance held in the daytime, 278

maudlin overly emotional, 289

Glossary

meager having little flesh; thin, 257

meditate to think deeply, 222

melancholy very sad, 130, 395

mendicant a beggar, 80

methodically performed with a certain method or order, 234

mincingly in a delicate way, 237

mingle to mix together, 107, 130

minstrel one of a group of performers giving a program of melodies, jokes, and skits, 160

mirage the appearance of water that is not really there, caused by the bending or reflection of rays of light; a dream, 76, 294

mirthfully gladly, 89

miseries things that cause one to suffer, 13

mishap bad luck or misfortune; an unfortunate accident, 254

moderate calm, 145

momentary from time to time, 98

monologue the act of one person speaking, 400

monotone spoken without a varying pitch or key, 362

monotonously varying very little, 225

moor a wide area of open land, often high but poorly drained, 111

morbid gloomy or unpleasant, 394

morsel a small piece of food, 130

mortgage a loan for property, 272

mortifying shameful, 97

motive a reason for committing a crime, 318

motley made up of a varied mixture, 193

mottled full of spots or blotches, 30

multitude a great number, 14

muse to become absorbed in thought, 98

myriad a great number, 209

mystic mysterious, 188

nauseating causing great disgust, 312

nefarious very wicked or evil, 280

negotiate to make a deal, 436

nocturnal of, relating to, or occurring in the night, 75

nonchalant showing a lack of concern, 288

nonsensical not making sense, 375

notoriously generally known and talked of, 163

nourishing providing energy from food, 69

nourishment energy from food, 131

nucleus a central point, group, or mass; the center; the core, 83, 236

obligation a duty or responsibility, 200, 399

obscene disgusting; offensive, 376

obscure relatively unknown, 80, 306

obsequious obedient; overly agreeable, 267

obstreperous marked by loud noise, 200

odious deserving hatred, 48

ominous forbidding or alarming, 145, 192

omnipresent present in all places at all times, 289

opaque stubborn; thick-headed; hard to understand, 317

oppressed crushed or held back by an abuse of power or authority, 399

oppressive overpowering, 238

opprobrious disrespectful, 197

optimism the state of believing in the best possible outcome, 191

oration formal speech, 188

ornate overly decorated, 378

outskirts an area away from the center or near a border, 253

pallid pale, 305

pallor paleness; lack of color, especially in the face, 213

pander to offer things that meet the desires of others, 282

panorama a complete view of an area in every direction, 388

paralyze powerless; unable to move, 254

paralyzingly in a manner that makes something powerless, 311

parched very dry; very thirsty, 107

parishioner a member of a church community, 388

parley to speak to one another, 136

partiality fondness, 42, 164

particle a very small piece, 227

passion an intense feeling or liking, 317

passionate having intense feelings toward, 90, 338

pathos something in an experience that brings on a feeling of pity, 208

patronize to be a regular customer, 282

patronizing in a way that suggests one is superior, 376

pawpaw a type of tree with fruit and purple flowers, 326

peccadillo a slight offense, 373

pension a fixed sum paid regularly to a person after retirement, 272

pensioned paid a regular, fixed sum following retirement, 255

perceive to see; to observe; to become aware through the senses, 425

perception an awareness of an idea or concept, 436

peremptorily sternly; with a sense of urgency or command, 237

periodically from time to time, 217

permanent lasting forever, 400

perpendicular being at a right angle to a given line or plane, 213

perpetrator one who commits an act that goes against rules or laws, 402

perpetually all the time; continually, 395

perplexing complicated; very puzzling or confusing, 130

perplexity confusion; bewilderment; puzzlement, 256

persevere to continue in the face of difficulties, 17

persist to go on in spite of opposition, 240

Glossary

persistent continuing without regard to opposition or failure, 374

personification something meant to represent a person or a human form, 208

pertinacity stubbornness, 48

pestilence disease; something that is destructive, 48

petty small or minor, 31

phantasm a spirit or ghost, 41

phenomenon a rare or unusual event, 216, 382

philosophy the study of values, beliefs, attitudes, and concepts; the values, beliefs, attitudes, and concepts of a person or group, 436

phosphorescence a lasting light without heat, 206

picturesque charming or quaint in appearance, 189

pilgrimage a journey to a sacred place, 93

pinch to steal, 312

pittance a small amount, 132

plagiarize to copy someone else's writing, 93

plausible reasonable, 212

pliable able to bend freely, 450

plight a difficult situation, 209

poignant emotionally moving, touching, or painful, 238

portraiture a drawing, 46

precarious dangerous; depending on chance events, 132

precise exact, 310

predicament a difficult or trying situation, 286

prejudice a negative view not based on fair reasons or enough information, 282

preliminaries events occurring before a main event, 278

preliminary coming before something else, 211

premises a building or part of a building, 52

prepossessing tending to please or create a good impression, 279

preposterous against nature, reason, or common sense, 198

prescription a medicine ordered by a doctor, 309

presentiment a feeling that something is about to happen, 138

presumption an attitude or belief based on a rude sense of self importance; an action that goes beyond what is right or proper, 101, 284

pretence a feeling or an action that is not sincere, 25

pristine fresh and innocent, 268

probability likelihood, 269

probable very likely, 189

procedure the planned way of completing a task, 377

procure to obtain, 42

prodigious unusual; causing amazement or wonder, 161

prodigy a highly talented child, 100

profane to treat with disrespect or abuse, 372

profile a human head or face seen in a side view, 290, 440

profound complete; very deep; intense, 188, 393

profoundly deeply; greatly, 341

progressive making use of or interested in new ideas or methods, 270

projectile a self-propelling weapon; a missile, 207

projection a part that sticks out, 50

propel to drive or push forward, 337

propitious favorable; being of good fortune, 311

propound to offer, 29

propriety following socially acceptable rules of acting and speaking, 28

prototype an original model on which something is patterned; a first example that shows the main features of a later type, 290

protruding sticking out, 223

providence help from God, 69, 140, 164

provoked excited into anger, 134

proximity closeness, 286

publicity gaining public attention, 318

pulverize to crush; to grind into small pieces, 395

puncture to put a hole in, 421

pungent having a sharp or biting odor, 450

quaff to drink deeply, 89

quench to cause to lose heat or warmth; to relieve or satisfy with liquid, 17

quest an act of seeking; a pursuit or search, 284

rabble the lowest class of people; a mob, 103

rabid going to extreme lengths, 52

radiance brightness; a glow, 99

radiant marked by confidence or happiness; glowing, 291

rampage a course of violent or reckless actions, 374

raucous very loud, noisy, or disorderly, 421

rebuke to turn back or keep down, 99

recede to move back or away, 253

recline to lean backwards, 432

reclusive tending to withdraw from others, 450

recognition the act of understanding or realizing something, 194

recoil to fall back under pressure; to shrink, 231

recollection a memory, 139, 309

recompense a reward or compensation; an equivalent or return for something done, 17

recount to explain; to tell, 419

recovery the act of becoming well again, 269

refracting altering; changing, 406

refrain to keep oneself from doing, 150

reinforce to strengthen; to support, 393

reiterate to state or do over again, 225

Glossary

rejuvenescent causing a return of youthfulness, 85

relapse a slip or fall to a previous worse state, 98

relent to become less severe; to let up, 358

relentlessly attempting to achieve something without giving up, 394

relevant the condition of being appropriate, 374

relinquish to give up, 25

reluctance unwillingness, 211, 419

reluctant unwilling, 288

render to give up; to make, 238

renowned famous, 28, 164

repentance the act of turning away from sin or feeling regret, 86

repose rest, 211

reposing resting, 47

repulsion intense dislike or disgust, 266

reputable having a good character or standing, 270

respite rest, 210

restrain to hold back; to keep under control, 391

resume to return to or to begin again, 308

reticence restraint; reserve, 289

reticent unwilling, 417

reverberation an echo, 53

robust healthy, 269

roseate rose colored, 210

ruddy reddish in color, 97

ruffianism behavior that is rough, criminal, or bullying, 271

sagacious wise; keen, 41

sallow of a sickly, yellowish color, 257

sanitary relating to health, 155

sarcasm the use of bitter statements that tell the opposite of what is true, 270

satisfactory good enough, 135

saturated filled completely with something, 73

savagely fiercely, 280

scapegoat one that bears the blame for others, 281

scatheless unharmed; uninjured, 197

sceptic one who doubts, 85

scrimmage practice play, 295

scruple a hesitation to do something because it is wrong, 43

scrutiny a searching look or close watch, 191

sculptured carved; decorated with markings or carvings, 369

seclusion the act of being alone or away from others, 80

sedentary doing much sitting or not moving, 30

segregation the act of separating people by race, ethnic group, or social class, 399

sentimental emotional or focused on feelings, 313

serenade to sing or play music, often outdoors at night to court a loved one, 74

serene calm; peaceful; tranquil, 406, 433

serenely calmly, 193

sheepishly timidly, as if embarrassed by a fault, 357

shrewd sharply intelligent; cunning; tricky, 272

shyster one who is dishonest or crooked, especially in practicing law or politics, 272

simper to smile in a silly manner, 88

simultaneously at the same time, 214, 293, 310

singe to burn slightly, 229

singular unique; excellent, 188, 375

sinister suggesting a feeling of fear; evil, 191

sinuous marked by strong bending movements, 317

smatterer one who speaks about something but has a limited understanding of the topic, 28

smite to strike sharply, 134

solace relief; comfort, 14

soldered joined together by the melting of a metal called solder, 449

solemnity a formal or ceremonial quality, 267

solicit to approach with a request; to ask for, 41

solicitous protective, 387

solitary single, 131

solitude the state of being alone or isolated, 173

somber dark colored, 173

sorcery magic, 255

sordidness evil; meanness, 268

spasmodically with muscles jerking violently and uncontrollably, 236

speculatively in a manner marked by curiosity, 223

speculator a person who assumes business risks in hopes of gain; one who buys or sells in the hopes of profiting from market changes, 144

splenetic full of feelings of anger or ill will, 102

stature position or standing, 402

stealthily slowly and secretly, 75

stigma a mark of shame, 83, 153

studious earnest; relating to study, 373

stupefied groggy; amazed, 47

stupor daze; confusion, 319

subdue to conquer; to bring under control, 224

sublime lofty; grand, 402

subpoena to command one to appear in court, 318

subscribe to give support, 341

subside to settle; to become less active, 361

substantial firmly constructed; large, 74

substantiate to confirm, 382

subtle difficult to understand or detect, 193, 221

succinctly without wasting words, 41

succor to aid or help, 14

succumb to yield to superior strength, force, or desire, 49

suffice to meet or satisfy a need, 301

suffocatingly uncomfortably lacking fresh air, 283

suffusion a blush, 86

sullen gloomily silent, 257

supplicant begging, 208

surcease a brief rest or break from something, 281

surge a sudden rush; a swelling, rolling, or sweeping forward, 234, 361

surmise to guess or imagine, 110

surmount to get to the top of, 188

surname a family name or nickname, 29, 295

surpass to become better, greater, or stronger than, 198

surreptitiously secretly, 382

suspicion the act of sensing that something is wrong or dangerous; doubt; uncertainty, 308, 449

sustain to give support or relief, 14

sustenance enough food or drink to keep the body strong, 131

tacitly expressed without words, 399

tangible able to be sensed, especially by touch, 208, 266

tarn a small, steep-banked mountain lake or pool, 75

tarnished dulled or destroyed in luster by air, dust, or dirt, 82

tarry to delay, 145

tedious tiresome; boring, 13

teeming filled to overflowing, 146

temperament attitude; personality, 43

temperamental of or relating to how one thinks or behaves, 224

temperate keeping or held within limits; moderate, 376

tempo the rate or motion of an activity; pace, 253

temporary lasting for only a short or set time, 387, 400

temptation something that causes one to act without the ability to resist, 307

tenant one who lives in an apartment building, 377

tender to offer, 150

terrestrial of or relating to the earth, 74

testimony an oral explanation of facts in a court by a witness, 318

thitherward toward that place, 82

throng a crowd of people, 97

timidity a lack of courage or self-confidence, 140

timorous fearful, 257

tinctured having a quality of, 42

tinged having a slight amount of shading of color, 76

tippet a shoulder cape, often with hanging ends, 110

tolerance the ability to withstand pain or hardship, 374

traditional the accepted or usual way of doing things, 393

tragedy a terrible event, 190, 254

tranquil calm, 164, 285

tranquilly calmly, 31

transfix to be held motionless, 102

transient passing very quickly, 92, 160

transpire to take place, 217

traverse to go or travel across or over, 436

treacherous dangerous, 234

trellised supported on a frame of latticework, 145

tremulous nervous, 86

trivial of little worth or importance, 165, 320

tulle a sheer net used for veils, 110

tumultuous violent; marked by noisy movement, 190

turbulent causing great unrest or disturbance, 388

turmoil extreme confusion or rapid movement, 199

tyranny unjust governmental control, 24

uncanny peculiar; unnatural, 191

unceremoniously not formally, 97

uncompromising inflexible; unyielding; not accepting of compromise, 337

uncongenial unsuited; unagreeable in nature, taste, or outlook, 42

undulation a wave-like appearance, 221

unfathomable not capable of being understood, 44

universal recognized by all, 308

unlamented without grief, sorrow, or regret, 25

unrelentingly not letting up or weakening, 402

unwonted unusual, 224

urbanely in a sophisticated, polite way, 312

utilitarian practical; useful, 338

vanity great pride in oneself or one's appearance, 337

variegated having different colors, 269

veer to change direction or course, 196

vehemently forcefully, 280

venerable old and respected, 80

venom evil; ill will, 311

veracious truthful; honest, 83

vestige a trace; a tiny bit, 102

vexed irritated; annoyed, 134

vicarious experienced through imagination, 281

virtue a good quality or trait, 85

visage face; appearance, 82, 257

vista a distant view, 257

vital full of life, 145

vogue popularity, 88

vulnerable open to attack or harm; able to be hurt, 419

waif a stray person, 197

wan dim, 189

wildering wandering, 123

wistfully longingly, 191

wistfulness the state of being full of longing, 234

wizened small and wrinkled, 276

yearn to long for, 229

Index of Authors and Titles

Index of Authors and Titles

Index of Titles by Genre

Index of Titles by Genre

Index of Fine Art

Index

Index

Index

Index

Index

Index

Index

Acknowledgments

Acknowledgment is made for permission to reprint or record the following copyrighted material.

Page 110: "Because I could not stop for Death" is reprinted by permission of the publishers and the Trustees of Amherst College from *The Poems of Emily Dickinson*, Thomas H. Johnson, ed., Cambridge, Mass.: The Belknap Press of Harvard University Press, Copyright © 1951, 1955, 1979, 1983 by the President and Fellows of Harvard College.

Pages 248, 324: (Print) "Jazz Fantasia" from *Smoke and Steel* by Carl Sandburg, copyright 1920 by Harcourt Brace & Company and renewed 1948 by Carl Sandburg, reprinted by permission of the publisher. (Audio) "Jazz Fantasia" from *Smoke and Steel* by Carl Sandburg, copyright 1920 by Harcourt Brace & Company and renewed 1948 by Carl Sandburg, reproduced by permission of the publisher.

Page 248: From "I, Too" in *Collected Poems* by Langston Hughes. Copyright © 1994 by the Estate of Langston Hughes. Reprinted by permission of Alfred A. Knopf, Inc.

Pages 253–57: (Print) "The Far and the Near" is reprinted with the permission of Scribner, a Division of Simon & Schuster from *From Death to Morning* by Thomas Wolfe. Copyright 1935 by Charles Scribner's Sons; copyright renewed © 1963 by Paul Gitlin. (Audio) "The Far and the Near" from *From Death to Morning* by Thomas Wolfe. © 1935 by Paul Gitlin, Administrator, C.T.A. of the Estate of Thomas Wolfe. Permission granted by the Estate of Thomas Wolfe.

Pages 261–62: "Theme for English B" from *Collected Poems* by Langston Hughes. Copyright © 1994 by the Estate of Langston Hughes. Reprinted by permission of Alfred A. Knopf, Inc., and Harold Ober Associates Incorporated.

Pages 276–95: "The Freshest Boy" is excerpted with permission of Scribner, a Division of Simon & Schuster, and Harold Ober Associates, Inc., from *Taps at Reveille* by F. Scott Fitzgerald. Copyright 1928 by The Curtis Publishing Company. Copyright renewed © 1956 by Frances Scott Fitzgerald Lanahan.

Pages 299–300: "Mending Wall" from *The Poetry of Robert Frost*, edited by Edward Connery Lathem, Copyright 1944, 1951, © 1958 by Robert Frost. © 1967 by Lesley Frost Ballantine. Copyright 1916, 1923, 1930, 1939, © 1969 by Henry Holt & Company. Reprinted by permission of Henry Holt and Company, Inc.

Page 301: "A Time to Talk" from *The Poetry of Robert Frost*, edited by Edward Connery Lathem, Copyright 1944, 1951, © 1958 by Robert Frost. © 1967 by Lesley Frost Ballantine. Copyright 1916, 1923, 1930, 1939, © 1969 by Henry Holt & Company. Reprinted by permission of Henry Holt and Company, Inc.

Page 301: "Fire and Ice" from *The Poetry of Robert Frost*, edited by Edward Connery Lathem, Copyright 1944, 1951, © 1958 by Robert Frost. © 1967 by Lesley Frost Ballantine. Copyright 1916, 1923, 1930, 1939, © 1969 by Henry Holt & Company. Reprinted by permission of Henry Holt and Company, Inc.

Pages 305–20: "Impulse" from *The Collected Short Stories of Conrad Aiken* by Conrad Aiken. Copyright © 1933 by Conrad Aiken. Copyright renewed © 1961 by Conrad Aiken. Reprinted by permission of Brandt & Brandt Literary Agents, Inc.

Page 326: (Print) "Cool Tombs" from *Cornhuskers* by Carl Sandburg, copyright 1918 by Holt, Rinehart and Winston and renewed 1946 by Carl Sandburg, reprinted by permission of the publisher. (Audio) "Cool Tombs" from *Cornhuskers* by Carl Sandburg, copyright 1918 by Holt, Rinehart and Winston and renewed 1946 by Carol Sandburg, reproduced by permission of the publisher.

Pages 332, 399–402: (Print) From *Stride Toward Freedom: The Montgomery Story* by Martin Luther King, Jr. Reprinted by arrangement with The Heirs to the Estate of Martin Luther King, Jr., c/o Writers House, Inc. as agent for the proprietor. Copyright 1958 by Martin Luther King, Jr., copyright renewed © 1986 by Coretta Scott King. (Audio) From *Stride Toward Freedom: The Montgomery Story* by Martin Luther King, Jr. License granted by Intellectual Properties Management, Atlanta, Georgia, as exclusive licensor of the King Estate. Copyright 1958 by Martin Luther King, Jr., copyright renewed © 1986 by Coretta Scott King.

Pages 337–41: (Print) Reprinted with the permission of Simon & Schuster from *To Be Young, Gifted and Black: Lorraine Hansberry in Her Own Words* adapted by Robert Nemiroff. Copyright © 1969 by Robert Nemiroff and Robert Nemiroff as executor of the Estate of Lorraine Hansberry. (Audio) From *To Be Young, Gifted and Black: Lorraine Hansberry in Her Own Words* by Lorraine Hansberry, adapted by Robert Nemiroff. Copyright © 1969 by Robert Nemiroff and Robert Nemiroff as Executor of the Estate of Lorraine Hansberry. Reproduced by permission of William Morris Agency, Inc. on behalf of the Author.

Pages 345–52: (Print) "The Killers" is reprinted with permission of Scribner, a Division of Simon & Schuster, from *Men Without Women* by Ernest Hemingway. Copyright 1927 by Charles Scribner's Sons. Copyright renewed 1955 by Ernest Hemingway. (Audio) "The Killers" from *Men Without Women* by Ernest Hemingway, 1927. © Hemingway Foreign Rights Trust. Reproduced with permission.

Pages 356–65: "Flight" from *The Long Valley* by John Steinbeck. Copyright 1938, renewed © 1966 by John Steinbeck. Used by permission of Viking Penguin, a division of Penguin Putnam, Inc.

Page 369: "In Honor of David Anderson Brooks, My Father" from *Blacks* by Gwendolyn Brooks. © 1991. By permission of the author.

Pages 372–83: "The Catbird Seat" from *The Thurber Carnival*, by James Thurber. Copyright © 1945 James Thurber. Copyright © renewed 1973 by Helen Thurber and Rosemary A. Thurber. Reprinted by arrangement with Rosemary A. Thurber and the Barbara Hogenson Agency.

Pages 387–88: From *Hiroshima* by John Hersey. Copyright 1946 and renewed 1974 by John Hersey. Reprinted by permission of Alfred A. Knopf, Inc.

Pages 391–95: "Autobiographical Notes" from *Notes of a Native Son* by James Baldwin © 1955, renewed 1983, by James Baldwin. Reprinted by permission of Beacon Press, Boston.

Page 406: "Monet's 'Waterlilies'" by Robert Hayden. Copyright © by Robert Hayden. Reprinted by permission of Liveright Publishing Corporation.

Page 412: From "The Prose Poem as an Evolving Form" in *Selected Poems* by Robert Bly. Copyright © 1986 by Robert Bly. Reprinted by permission of HarperCollins Publishers.

Acknowledgments

Page 412: "On the Pulse of Morning" from *Collected Poems by Maya Angelou* by Maya Angelou. Copyright © 1993 by Maya Angelou. Reprinted by permission of Random House, Inc.

Pages 417–21: "A City of Words" from *Hunger of Memory* by Richard Rodriguez. Reprinted by permission of David R. Godine, Publisher, Inc. Copyright © 1982 by Richard Rodriguez.

Page 425: Lucille Clifton: "morning mirror" copyright © 1987 by Lucille Clifton. Reprinted from *Next: New Poems* with the permission of BOA Editions, Ltd. 260 East Ave., Rochester, NY 14604.

Page 425: Lucille Clifton: "my dream about the poet" copyright © 1987 by Lucille

Clifton. Reprinted from *Next: New Poems* with the permission of BOA Editions, Ltd. 260 East Ave., Rochester, NY 14604.

Page 428: "The Starfish" from *What Have I Ever Lost by Dying?: Collected Prose Poems* by Robert Bly. Copyright © 1992 by Robert Bly. Reprinted by permission of HarperCollins Publishers.

Pages 432–33: "My Father and Myself Facing the Sun" by Lawson Fusao Inada. Reprinted by permission of the author.

Page 436: "Passports to Understanding" from *Wouldn't Take Nothing for My Journey Now* by Maya Angelou. Copyright © 1993 by Maya Angelou. Reprinted by permission of Random House, Inc.

Pages 440–42: From *A Hundred Secret Senses* by Amy Tan. Copyright © 1995 by Amy Tan. Reprinted by permission of G. P. Putnam's, a division of Penguin Putnam, Inc.

Page 446: "Papi Working" from *The Other Side/El Otro Lado* by Julia Alvarez. Published by Dutton, a division of Penguin USA. Reprinted by permission of Susan Bergholz Literary Services, New York. All rights reserved.

Pages 449–50: "Miss Peace McKnight" in *The Antelope Wife* by Louise Erdrich. Copyright © 1998 by Louise Erdrich. Reprinted by permission of HarperFlamingo.

Images   Page viii, David Young-Wolff/PhotoEdit; p. 6 (top), Tony Freeman/PhotoEdit; p. 6 (bottom), Myrleen Ferguson Cate/PhotoEdit; p. 8, The Granger Collection; p. 11, The Granger Collection; p. 12 (top), The Granger Collection; p. 12 (bottom), Judy King; p. 13, The Granger Collection; p. 16, Judy King; p. 17, The Granger Collection; p. 19, The Granger Collection; p. 20, The Granger Collection; p. 21, Brown Brothers; p. 23, The Granger Collection; p. 24, The Granger Collection; p. 27, The Granger Collection; p. 30, Jeff Spackman; p. 34, Judy King; p. 35, Sandy Rabinowitz; p. 37, Judy King; p. 38, Diana Magnuson; pp. 40, 56, SuperStock; pp. 42, 45, 51, Carole Katchen; p. 57, David David Gallery, Philadelphia/SuperStock; p. 64, The Granger Collection; p. 67, Judy King; p. 68, The Granger Collection; p. 72, The Granger Collection; p. 73, The Granger Collection; p. 75, Corbis; p. 79, Stock Montage/SuperStock; pp. 81, 84, 91, Cindy Spencer; p. 96, 106, The Granger Collection; p. 98, David David Gallery, Philadelphia/SuperStock; p. 102, Musee d'Art Moderne de la Ville de Paris, France/Giraudon, Paris/SuperStock; p. 107, The Granger Collection; p. 109, Brown Brothers; p. 110, Christie's Images/SuperStock; p. 111, Kay Shaw Photography; p. 118, Private Collection/Bridgeman Art Library, London/SuperStock; p. 121, The Granger Collection; p. 122, Corbis; p. 123, The Granger Collection; p. 125, Corbis; p. 126, The Granger Collection; p. 127, Christie's Images/SuperStock; p. 129, Photographs and Prints Division, Schomberg Center for Research in Black Culture, The New York Public Library, Astor, Lenox, and Tilden Foundations; pp. 131, 139, Keinyo White; p. 133, Judy King; p. 143, The Granger Collection; p. 144, Corbis-Bettmann; p. 146, Corbis; p. 149, The Granger Collection; p. 150, Brown Brothers; p. 152, Corbis; p. 154, The Granger Collection; p. 156, Photographs and Prints Division, Schomberg Center for Research in Black Culture, The New York Public Library, Astor, Lenox, and Tilden Foundations; p. 159, SuperStock; p. 161, Corbis-Bettmann; p. 165, Judy King; p. 168, Judy King; p. 170, The Granger Collection; p. 172 (top left), Brown Brothers; p. 172 (bottom right), Judy King; p. 173, © Allan Kearney/ENP Images; p. 175, Judy King; p. 176, Sandra Bierman; p. 182, © Sterling and Francine Clark Art Institute, Williamstown, Massachusetts; p. 185, photo by South Dakota Tourism; p. 186, Corbis; pp. 189, 194–95, 201, 207, 214, Guy Porfirio/John Edwards Illustration; p. 220, Brown Brothers; pp. 222, 227, 232, 241, Guy Porfirio/John Edwards Illustration; p. 248, SuperStock, Inc., Collection, Jacksonville/Gil Mayers/SuperStock; p. 251, Culver Pictures; p. 252, The Granger Collection; p. 255, David Fischer/John Edwards Illustration; p. 260, Brown Brothers; p. 261, John Sloan, *The City from Greenwich Village*, Gift of Helen Farr Sloan, © 1998 Board of Trustees, National Gallery of Art, Washington, D.C.; p. 264, Brown Brothers; pp. 266, 271, Yoshi Miyake; p. 275, Brown Brothers; pp. 277, 283, 292, Karen Tafoya/John Edwards Illustration; p. 298, Brown Brothers; p. 299, Connie Hayes; p. 301, SuperStock; p. 304, Culver Pictures; pp. 309, 315, Steve Moore; p. 323, Brown Brothers; p. 325, Christie's Images/SuperStock; p. 326, SuperStock; p. 332, UPI/Corbis-Bettmann; p. 335, Bettmann; p. 336, UPI/Corbis-Bettmann; p. 339, Corbis; p. 344, Brown Brothers; pp. 347, 350, Joel Iskowitz; p. 355, Brown Brothers; pp. 359, 364, Pamela Johnson; p. 368, The Granger Collection; p. 369, 1998 PhotoDisc; p. 371 (top), UPI/Corbis-Bettmann; p. 371 (bottom), The Granger Collection; pp. 373, 379, Benrei Huang; p. 386, © Rollie McKenna; p. 387, UPI/Corbis-Bettmann; p. 388, UPI/Corbis-Bettmann; p. 390, Corbis; p. 392, UPI/Corbis-Bettmann; p. 398, SuperStock; p. 401, Corbis-Bettmann; p. 405, PACH/Corbis-Bettmann; p. 406, Giraudon/Art Resource, NY; p. 412, Gallery Contemporanea, Jacksonville/SuperStock; p. 415, Dennis Brack/Black Star; p. 416, courtesy of David R. Godine, Publishers, Inc.; p. 420, Sandy Rabinowitz; p. 424, courtesy of St. Mary's College of Maryland, St. Mary's City, Maryland; p. 427, Jerry Bauer; p. 429, © Gerry Ellis/ENP Images; p. 431, © Bill McClain; p. 433, © Gerry Ellis/ENP Images; p. 435, © Jim Stratford/Black Star; p. 437 (top left), Jeff Greenberg/PhotoEdit; p. 437 (top right), Bill Bachman/PhotoEdit; p. 437 (bottom left), Jackie Grove/PhotoEdit; p. 437 (bottom right), Alan Oddie/PhotoEdit; p. 439, © 1995 Robert Foothorap; p. 441, Robert Roth; p. 445, © Daniel Cima; p. 446, Judy King; p. 448, © Miriam Berkley Photography.

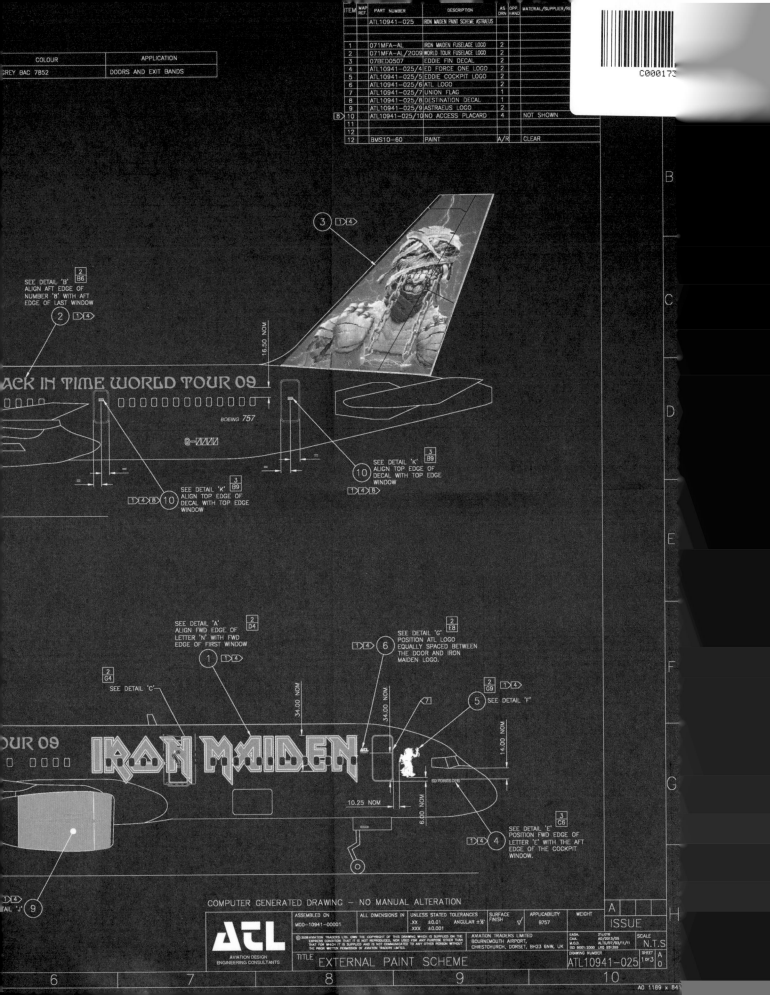

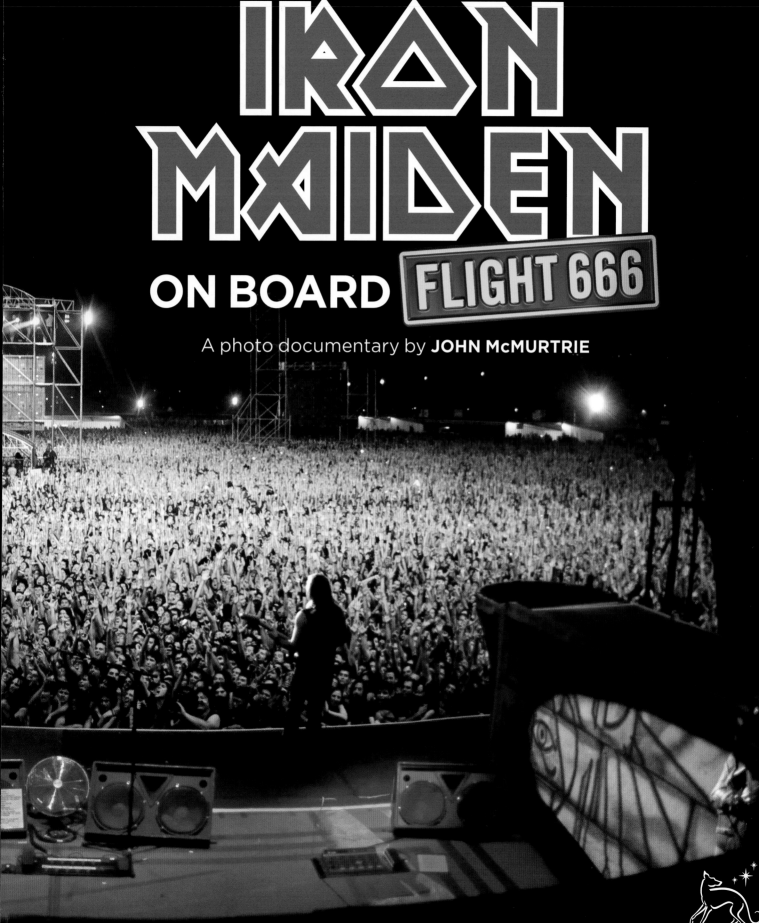

IRON MAIDEN

ON BOARD FLIGHT 666

A photo documentary by **JOHN McMURTRIE**

CONTENTS

Foreword by **BRUCE DICKINSON** 6
Introduction by **JOHN McMURTRIE** 9

FOREWORD BY **BRUCE DICKINSON**

The idea of ED FORCE ONE, a flying tour bus with band, crew and equipment on the same aircraft, came to me when I was a solo artist. We flew around America in a very old, low and slow piston engined Piper Navajo, six of us and a drum kit precariously lashed to the insides. Fast forward 10 years. After two years flying the band on the "Bruce Goose" a Cessna 421 seven seater, I ended up flying 757s and 737s for Astraeus Airlines and had moved to the Captain's seat. I asked our then Director of Flight Operations, John Mahon, what it would take to secure equipment down the back of a 757 instead of passenger seats. Being Irish, John reflected back to his days as a loader on DC-3 Dakotas flying nightfreight newspapers in and out of Dublin. "Ahh just a big 9G Cargo Net...that should do it...." It turned out to be a bit more complicated than that.

〉〉〉〉〉〉

I had just mooted the idea to IRON MAIDEN Manager Rod Smallwood – the advantages were several. Essentially the globe would be reduced to the equivalent of a North American tour. The delays and costs associated with freight, customs and inconvenient airline schedules would be circumvented and territories which hitherto had been deemed "uneconomical" for the band to tour, could now be included. Mr Mercator and every schoolboy's map of the world went out the window and we bought ourselves a large globe. The next question was, which way round to go? Conventional wisdom said that it is better to go west around the world as this way you gain time. Being essentially unconventional, I disagreed. The prevailing winds would save 10% of time and

fuel if we went eastbound – a considerable sum – but even more compelling was time and jet lag. On a 6 or 8 week tour, jet lag would be more or less continuous. The crucial factor was to adjust our bodies so that we were alert at 9pm local time every day – stage time. The range and distances we would cover meant that the maximum time change over any 2 days would be 5 hours – ie we would arrive at 10pm our time, and in fact it would be 3am local. So...after a couple of beers we go to bed at 1am (our time) as the sun rises locally!! Waking up after a solid 8 hours rest at 10 o'clock (our time) but... oh dear 3pm local...what on earth is going on? By 9pm locally our bodies are thinking "OK 4pm in the afternoon. I could cope with running round and doing a gig..." Conversely, trying to do the same thing eastbound (New York for example) we would be wide awake at 6am and at 9pm our bodies would be telling us to go to sleep. The next hurdle was to persuade agents and promoters to think outside of their comfort zone..."Mumbai to Perth? You can't do that! You'd need a time machine..." and of course that's exactly what ED FORCE ONE is – a time machine.

〉〉〉〉〉〉

The 757 is one of Mr Boeing's most elegant creations. It has the lines of a bird of prey, an extraordinary conjoining of engineering and aesthetics. Talk to most pilots and ask if they would like to fly a 757 and most likely a gleam would appear in their eye. The 757 though is no spring chicken. The last one came off the production line in 2005, and many question why Boeing don't still make them. Simply, there is no replacement for a 757 in the world except another

757. It is more than half British; it's wing was a British design that flew on the Hawker Siddeley Trident and its two Rolls-Royce RB211E4 engines provide a massive thrust to weight ratio. At full thrust on a lightly laden aircraft, ED FORCE ONE is climbing at over 7000 feet per minute, more than 60 miles an hour vertically – there are jet fighters that can't do that. It will then cruise at 80% of the speed of sound for almost 8 hours and still land with international standard fuel reserves. When you are on holiday in your airbus or 737 and land, bear in mind that a 757 can land in half that distance, and when your 737 or airbus is stuck on the ground because of weather, a 757 can often go almost unrestricted. The 757 is a beast. And the number of this beast is ED FORCE ONE.

)))))

Earlier there was talk of newspapers and netting for securing our freight on ED FORCE ONE. If only it were possible. ED FORCE ONE was a groundbreaking enterprise. Technically, operationally and politically. Let's start with the politics. ED FORCE ONE coincided with a new regime governing all aviation in Europe – E.A.S.A. We would be the first modification to an aircraft to be fully approved by the new regulator, so we had to expect rigorous auditing and forensic attention to detail. Technically our "cargo net" had morphed into an entirely different set of rules. New rules dictated that all cargo had to be secured in a totally fireproof compartment. The whole idea that made ED FORCE ONE viable was that we could change it from 221 passengers to our combi-format and back again – how could we achieve a "fireproof containment vessel" and

still not destroy the passenger cabin? Lastly there were many operational changes to plan and train for. We would be flying across The Andes, landing in Quito at very high elevations, as well as Bogota which all required special simulator training. The loading and unloading of ED FORCE ONE would be very specific and require special procedures, especially with regard to distribution of fuel. Finally the Cabin Crew would all have to be trained in the new format and in the new locations of emergency equipment. Whilst all Astraeus Cabin Crew provide a terrific service, people often have no idea how rigorously they are trained to provide their primary function – which is safety.

)))))

To facilitate all of this required more than 6 months of intense planning and some very fraught moments. Gradually the obstacles were overcome and it was a painstaking process inching towards our certification goal rather than leaping out of our baths like Archimedes and crying "Eureka!" There were comedic moments. The test day for the fireproof bags came. These bags sit atop the steel plates in the former passenger cabin at the rear of ED FORCE ONE. The idea was that in the event of the cargo catching fire, it would be unable to breach the material and as an aside, any smoke would be cleared and not contaminate the passenger cabin. So far so good, and the day of testing arrived. Solemn "Men From The Ministry" stood around a forlorn-looking fireproof bag on a freezing winter's day as engineers and firemen attempted to sustain a fire in it. Alas, the bag was so effective that any fire was almost immediately extinguished. This was unsatisfactory, so the bag

was subjected finally to a hail of Molotov cocktails in an effort to damage it. After 2 hours the men in suits departed, apparently satisfied. The outside of the bag moreover, never even became warm. They returned later, to embark on the enjoyable pursuit of lobbing smoke bombs into the back of the airliner in the hope of asphyxiating its occupants in the forward cabins. Mr Boeing's Smoke Clearance System worked as advertised, and the project was a go! As the reality sank in that we were going to do this after all, the media buzz started. The ED FORCE ONE name itself came from particularly inspired fans responding to a naming competition on the Maiden website and seized the imagination. The Powerslave-inspired livery of the 'Somewhere Back In Time World Tour' looked sensational on paper and was simply awesome in the flesh. Indeed, I was worried that The Final Frontier livery would not live up to its predecessor. Silly me. The media event that was ED FORCE ONE followed us round the world. Never mind being a rock 'n' roll band, our arrival was almost Presidential in many countries, making primetime news locally as well as CNN, Sky, Fox and ABC news globally.

〉〉〉〉〉〉

So what is it like to Captain ED FORCE ONE? Well, first of all I'm one of 3 pilots on board as well as 2 engineers and 4 cabin crew, plus a ground handling coordinator and a loadmaster. I fly typically around 30% of the flights. The rest of the time I am available as a back-up in the event of sickness or incapacitation (as happened on the way from Mumbai to Perth when food poisoning struck a crew member). Sadly this meant I was never able to sample Nicko's vintage wine selection in flight. On the other hand, I always arrived at the destination without a hangover! As Captain I'm responsible for everything that goes on aboard the aircraft, even if the mistake is someone else's! I have a great team to work with and to get the best out of people I believe in speaking openly about concerns and keeping information free-flowing between us all. The Captain's job is as much about management as it is about flying. Now that may not sound romantic, but it's actually very rewarding to identify and solve problems...before they become problems. It's an old adage but the saying 'A Captain using his knowledge and experience to ensure he never has to use his knowledge and experience' is especially applicable to unusual situations like ED FORCE ONE. As for the experience of flying, well this is too short an article to go on about it in length, except to say that I wrote a song about it. I played it to lots of my Airline chums and got a pretty decent thumbs-up. So the lyrics to 'Coming Home' are as close as I can get to the experience other than inviting you up there alongside me to share the experience. On a last point of interest, if you are curious as to what countries you can cover with the span of your hand at 41,000 feet – Belgium sprang to mind. One dark night with Brussels spread below like fluorescent yellow brain coral.... If that conjures up an image, terrific. If not, that's what this book is for. John McMurtrie captured in pictures all things I've probably forgotten and then some. Here it all is; in fact, if it's not in here, it probably never happened! Have fun out there... tailwinds and happy landings to you all!

Bruce Dickinson

INTRODUCTION BY **JOHN MCMURTRIE**

I will never forget the feeling at London Stansted Airport in 2008 as ED FORCE ONE throttled back and we thundered down the runway for the very first time. Everyone had the same look on their face. A combination of excitement, trepidation and down right terror. As the airport whizzed past my window I remember worrying if I had packed all my photographic gear. Lenses, camera bodies, batteries, laptop, hard drives. There was no way I had left anything behind, because we had been preparing for this for the last few months. I then tried to rationalise what we were about to do.

We are going on an adventure and the lead singer of IRON MAIDEN is at the controls!

Apparently Bruce knows what he is doing up front, he's passed all the relevant exams and they made him a captain. Are they mad? We are talking about the 'Bruce Bullet', the one who screams across the stage, tells crazy stories in the bar and drives cars way too fast! As we reach the end of the runway and ED FORCE ONE lifts into the air it dawns on me how historic this all is. Travelling twice around the world on board a customised Boeing 757 piloted by the lead singer of a heavy metal band. IRON MAIDEN have never done things by halves and have constantly taken things to a higher level. This big adventure is no exception and it's 30,000 feet higher! I am no stranger to touring, having worked as a music photographer for the last 2 decades. I have been on the road with bands many times before, on buses and the odd

private jet, but to embark on a journey this ambitious is something else; it is staggering.

It turns out Bruce knows exactly what he is doing. He has been flying now for 20 years, 10 of those on commercial jets and has accumulated over 7000 flying hours. We are in safe hands.

This book isn't just a snapshot of a band at their peak but a journal of 6 individuals who simply want to play to their fans in every corner of the globe and how they achieved it. My part as the photographer is to capture that journey as it unfolds. One hundred percent of the photographs in this book are moments as they happened. Not 'set-ups' or 'photo calls', just IRON MAIDEN being honest and doing what they do. Sometimes, even I struggled to keep up with the band's movements on a day to day basis. One minute we are flying, and then the next, Janick is out sight seeing, Steve is playing football, Adrian tennis, Dave and Nicko golfing and Bruce could be out doing one of a thousand activities! But what is guaranteed every night when IRON MAIDEN step out on stage, is a spectacular show with energy and passion. As a photographer you couldn't ask for a better subject to shoot.

I liken touring with IRON MAIDEN to that of a white knuckle ride at a theme park. You spend most of the time screaming and holding on for dear life. But when it comes to an end you just want to do it again, again, again!

John McMurtrie

IRON MAIDEN MASCOT 'EDDIE'

BRUCE DICKINSON

NICKO McBRAIN

STEVE HARRIS

ADRIAN SMITH

JANICK GERS

DAVE MURRAY

The newly decorated tail fin of ED FORCE ONE pokes out of a busy hangar on an airfield in Hampshire. Inside, the Boeing 757 is being inspected by Bruce as the modifications are completed. Trucks arrive for a dry run of loading and unloading the plane.

Will the elaborate stage set, all of IRON MAIDEN's instruments plus the complex sound equipment, fit in the customised plane?

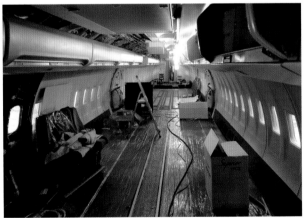

Flight cases are stacked up on pallets and a single fork-lift truck begins the slow process of loading the cargo bays. After several hours of careful manoeuvring, 12 tonnes of equipment has been loaded. It fits! It will be another month before ED FORCE ONE is finally ready for its maiden voyage.

On a cold Christmas Eve in 2007 ED FORCE ONE leaves the hangar and takes off for Gatwick Airport, England. The aircraft now has to be approved for transit by the European aviation authorities.

SOMEWHERE BACK IN TIME WORLD TOUR 2008

FEATURING HIGHLIGHTS FROM THE FIRST LEG ON BOARD ED FORCE ONE

FEBRUARY 2008
1ST MUMBAI, INDIA
4TH PERTH, AUSTRALIA
6TH MELBOURNE, AUSTRALIA
7TH MELBOURNE, AUSTRALIA
9TH SYDNEY, AUSTRALIA
10TH SYDNEY, AUSTRALIA
12TH BRISBANE, AUSTRALIA
15TH YOKOHAMA, JAPAN
16TH TOKYO, JAPAN
19TH LOS ANGELES, CA, USA
21ST GUADALAJARA, MEXICO
22ND MONTERREY, MEXICO

24TH MEXICO CITY, MEXICO
26TH SAN JOSE, COSTA RICA
28TH BOGOTA, COLOMBIA

MARCH 2008
2ND SAO PAULO, BRAZIL
4TH CURITIBA, BRAZIL
5TH PORTO ALEGRE, BRAZIL
7TH BUENOS AIRES, ARGENTINA
9TH SANTIAGO, CHILE
12TH SAN JUAN, PUERTO RICO
14TH NEW JERSEY, NJ, USA
16TH TORONTO, CANADA

7:30am: Dawn breaks at Stansted airport as the final pre-flight checks take place. Only hours earlier at 2am the Aviation Authority finally gave ED FORCE ONE permission to travel fully loaded with cargo and passengers. The aircraft has passed the stringent safety checks but only just in the nick of time. The remaining cargo can now be loaded, the band and crew begin boarding. ABOVE: Bruce and co-pilot John Haile check the flight plans as the remaining members of IRON MAIDEN arrive and see the customised aircraft for the very first time. RIGHT & BELOW: Adrian Smith, Dave Murray and Manager Rod Smallwood step aboard. Nicko receives a last minute delivery of fine wines, much to his approval.

ABOVE: Captain Bruce Dickinson welcomes everyone on board Flight 666 and promises that it will be a very exciting journey.

LEFT: All baggage loaded and Bruce gets the thumbs up from ground crew that ED FORCE ONE is ready to depart. Months of planning have led to this moment in time and Flight 666 departs London, Stansted airport at 09:58am, destination Mumbai, India.

Flying via Baku to refuel, ED FORCE ONE touches down in Mumbai at 2am. Although it is early there are many fans within the airport to welcome the band and even more outside. RIGHT: The following day Steve, Dave and Janick sample the sights, sounds and smells of Bombay, stopping at several temples and at the Gateway to India. After a few hours of sightseeing, the band party are whisked back to the hotel for a press conference with India's enthusiastic media.

1ST FEBRUARY 2008. Finally, after months of preparation, it is show day. RIGHT: The band arrive for a rare sound check and a production rehearsal.

TOP LEFT: Although the stage is made from unconventional materials (bamboo and wooden planks) everyone is very satisfied with arrangements.

OPPOSITE LEFT: The word is given to open the doors to the mass of fans outside.

BELOW: IRON MAIDEN take to the stage at 8.30pm for the very first show of the Somewhere Back in Time World Tour.

1ST FEBRUARY 2008. Bandra Kurla Complex, Mumbai, India.

7am: After 12 hours of travelling, IRON MAIDEN arrive in Australia to a heartfelt welcome on their first visit since 1992. A longer than anticipated refuel in Jakarta has resulted in touch down being 5 hours later than expected. BELOW: The weary fans who have waited all night are rewarded for their patience as the band sign autographs and pose for photos.

4TH FEBRUARY 2008.
TOP LEFT: The pyrotechnic team arrive at the Burswood Dome to rehearse the many explosions and fire effects for the Australian shows. Due to strict aviation regulations travelling with pyrotechnics on board ED FORCE ONE is prohibited. The Pyro team will travel independently to each venue.

LEFT: Bruce in the dressing room, Perth.

BELOW: All members of the band are present to run through all the Pyro cues to avoid incineration during the show. The band then take time to pose with Eddie.

4TH FEBRUARY 2008. Burswood Dome, Perth, Australia.

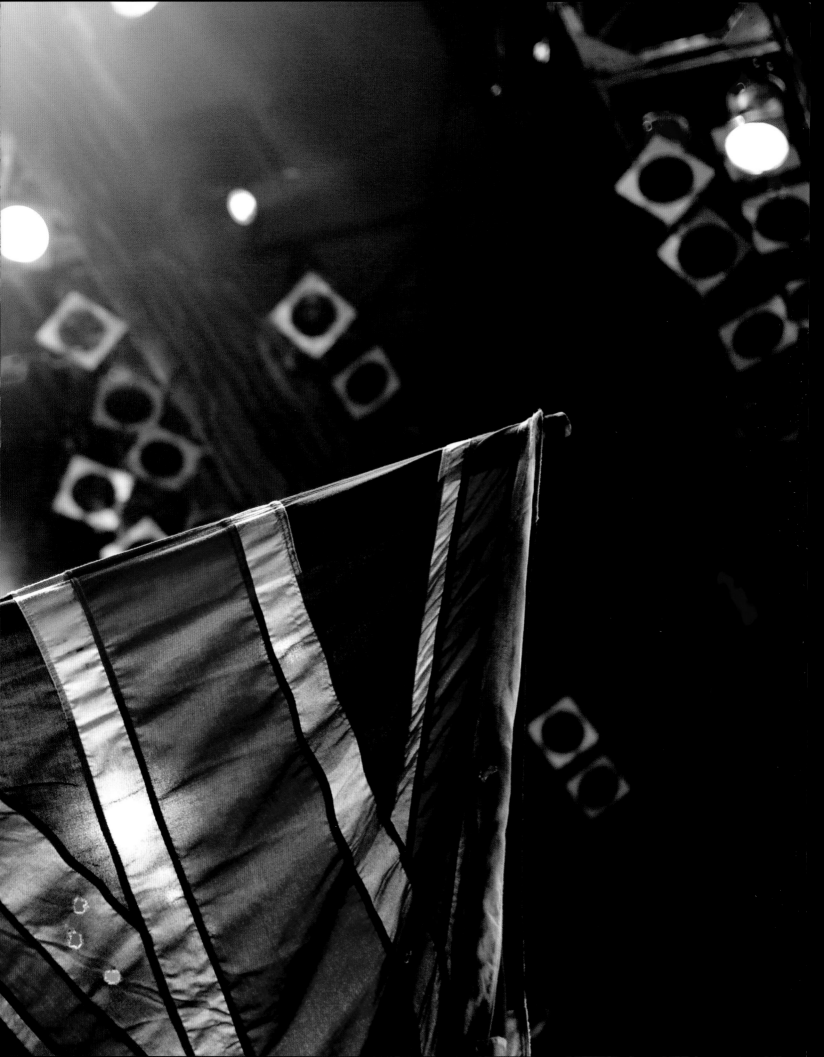

Janick and Bruce make their way to the stage for the first of two sold out shows in Melbourne.

8TH FEBRUARY 2008. Steve Harris, Sydney Harbour, Australia.

9TH FEBRUARY 2008. Acer Arena, Sydney, Australia.

9TH FEBRUARY 2008. Acer Arena, Sydney, Australia.

11TH FEBRUARY 2008, SYDNEY. Janick is searched before boarding ED FORCE ONE for the short flight to Brisbane.

ED FORCE ONE arrives in Brisbane

ABOVE: To celebrate Dickie Bell's impending retirement a crew shot is hastily arranged on stage at the Brisbane Entertainment Centre. A framed picture of the crew will be presented to Dickie in Tokyo.

LEFT: Dickie Bell has been IRON MAIDEN's production manager since 1981 and is credited for keeping the show on the road for all those years. This is his third retirement and he is insistent that this time it is for good. Some say he rules with a rod of Iron; whatever you do, 'take your hands out of your pockets!'

Bruce shows off his DIY haircut.

Steve en route to the stage.

ABOVE: Steve Harris by the 'Thunder Gate', Sensoji Temple, Tokyo.

RIGHT: Dickie Bell walks Adrian Smith to the stage at Tokyo's Messe Hall. After 27 years of dedicated service, this will be the last time Dickie tours with Maiden. Or will it?

Messe Arena, Tokyo. IRON MAIDEN take to the stage at 7:30pm. It is normal for concerts in Japan to start early. What is not customary are venues without seats. The crowd and IRON MAIDEN both benefit from this.

Flight 666 takes off at 1pm Sunday from Tokyo to Los Angeles. Flying via Alaska for United States immigration and a fuel stop. TOP: Bruce takes over the controls for the 5 hour night flight, crossing the International Date line en route to Los Angeles. BOTTOM: Steve Harris, Alaska. On arrival in LA the local time is now 9.30am – some 3 and a half hours back in time and it is still Sunday. Manager Rod Smallwood has a 48 hour birthday.

In honour of the LA Lakers' former home ground, Eddie walks out in front of a capacity crowd sporting the team's colours.

19TH FEBRUARY 2008. The Forum, Los Angeles, CA, USA.

Nicko, backstage warm up.

Adrian honours Mexico.

ABOVE: Janick and Nicko at the Pyramid of the sun.

Close to Mexico City the band visit the pyramids of Teotihuacan. These impressive structures celebrate the sun and the moon and are believed to date back over 2000 years. The surrounding ancient city was populated by over 200,000 people who mysteriously disappeared. Legend has it that inside the pyramids human sacrifice was regularly performed to ensure the sun would continue to rise.

RIGHT: A local guide conducts an ancient ceremony to bless the group and Nicko reciprocates with a prayer of goodwill.

Janick and Nicko are then led deep down into the core of the pyramid under the Altar of Death where, according to local legend, 30,000 people were sacrificed in one day to the Sun God.

23RD FEBRUARY 2008. On arrival in Mexico City the band attend a press conference in the hotel.

ABOVE: The group are led through a staff passageway, past the kitchens and through a single door where the media are waiting.

24TH FEBRUARY 2008. Over 55,000 people are packed into a sold out Foro Sol Stadium, Mexico's National Baseball Stadium.

The crowd is deafening throughout and as a sign of acknowledgement Bruce pauses and lets them sing on.

MEXICO CITY AIRPORT 25 FEBRUARY 2008

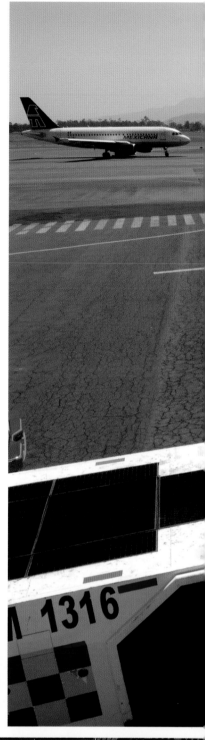

On departure, an important piece of paperwork goes astray by the local Airport authority leading to a real 'Mexican Stand Off'.
FAR RIGHT: Relief Pilot Ivan is ordered by air traffic control to abort take-off and return the aircraft to the gate. ED FORCE ONE powers down on the taxi way between the runway and the terminal, preventing any plane access to or from the terminal. A major delay now would jeopardise tomorrow's show in Costa Rica.

A precarious situation develops between flight crew and the authorities. Tensions begin to rise and language difficulties add to the drama.

LEFT: Captain John Mahon finally receives the 'important' flight documentation allowing ED FORCE ONE to depart. Flight 666 takes off 90 minutes late, Mexico City airport re-opens and ED FORCE ONE touches down in San Jose in time for the stage equipment to clear customs.

All tickets for the show sold out over 3 months ago and the excitement in San Jose builds. To relax before the show, Nicko sets off for a round of golf. Having only played one hole, a golf ball fires past, striking Nicko on the left forearm; causing a possible fracture. Medics attend to the arm as bruising appears and it begins to swell. Nicko rests the arm, covers it with an ice pack and a call is made to the production office at the venue, warning Nicko has been injured.

The crew await news as Nicko is taken to hospital and the swollen arm is x-rayed.

A capacity crowd at the Estadio Ricardo Saprissa stadium.

ABOVE: One hour before show time Nicko arrives. The arm is not fractured and although painful, Nicko is able to play the show.

IRON MAIDEN smash the record in Costa Rica for the biggest crowd attendance ever for a music event in this country.

The scene in Bogota airport is complete chaos as the members of IRON MAIDEN make their way into the terminal. It is unclear which way to turn as the band are led through one check point after another. Finally they are led into the President's private immigration area where the military and police all want autographs. A dozen police outriders escort the band through the city and around the Simon Bolivar Park where mile upon mile of tents line the road. Fans started queuing for the show over a week ago. This is Maiden's first visit to Bogota and by show day there are 45,000 people waiting to welcome them.

ABOVE: The crowd unveil a 100 foot Maiden Colombian flag which stretches out over the audience.

Two bars into 'The Number Of The Beast' the Maiden crew smell electrical burning and Bruce struggles to clear his throat on stage. The crew investigate and discover a cloud of tear gas is blowing across the venue from the outside park. This along with water cannons are being used by the militia to deter the many fans without tickets trying to break into the sold out show.

IRON MAIDEN play on and the tear gas clears.

ABOVE: The day before a sold out show at the 40,000 capacity Palmiers Stadium, Steve meets up with his team mates from IRON MAIDEN FC at the Sao Paulo Atletico sports ground. Based in the East End of London, the team have flown out to play a squad hastily pulled together of ex Corinthians, members of Sepultura and music execs. Within the first 15 minutes, Maiden FC are 2 goals ahead. After a full 90 minutes of play in blistering heat the final score is IRON MAIDEN 8 – BRAZIL 0.

RIGHT: Band Manager **Rod Smallwood** lends his support.

2ND MARCH 2008.
ABOVE: IRON MAIDEN win the football but the crowd in Sao Paulo claim victory for being the loudest and the most enthusiastic of the tour so far.

LEFT: Bruce draped in a Brazilian flag stops the show as a chant of 'Ole Ole Ole' erupts from the stadium.

4TH MARCH 2008. The military police hold back fans as the band arrive at Curitiba Airport.

RIGHT: Bruce powers down ED FORCE ONE and jumps aboard the people carrier that is transporting the band to their hotel.

ABOVE: As the vehicle drives onto the perimeter road, crowds flood out from the main terminal and give chase. Police outriders clear a path through the airport gates and the vehicle exits onto the streets of Buenos Aires.

With the crowds left behind, everyone relaxes and enjoys a few minutes of temporary calm until the cavalcade turns the last corner towards the hotel. Although extra security have been drafted in, the vehicle is suddenly surrounded by hordes of fans. It is virtually impossible to enter the hotel. The band are weary after a long day of travel but are still in good spirits and acknowledge the fans as they are escorted into the hotel.

The security withdraw and secure the doors as the high spirited crowd surges forward singing 'Run To The Hills'.

LEFT: The hotel manager, fearing the glass may shatter any moment, moves all guests to a safe distance and pleads for calm.

RIGHT: From either side of ED FORCE ONE, the snow capped peaks of the Andes can be seen stretching out as far as the horizon. Almost everyone on board is taking in the view.

On the ground fans have been gathering for several hours and as Bruce taxis ED FORCE ONE to its stand it is clear that this arrival is going to be a lively one. BELOW: All along the perimeter fence there are masses of fans waving flags and chanting "Maiden". As the band are quickly escorted through Immigration the legions of fans move along the outer walls and pause at every window desperate to get a glimpse.

This continues all the way through the terminal until everyone is bundled into vehicles and escorted away from the chaos. The hotel is no different and security advise entry via the underground staff entrance to avoid a repeat of Buenos Aires.

ABOVE: Once inside the hotel the band have a very brief break and are then whisked in front of Chile's media for a press conference. Outside, the hotel is surrounded by cheering fans.

LEFT: Later that evening the band relax for a meal and sample Chile's fine wines with predictable results.

ABOVE: High above Santiago on the edge of the Andes, Steve Harris shows the Flight 666 film crew, Kevin, Martin, Sam and Scot, exactly what they can do with their sound equipment.

RIGHT: As the film crew attempt a piece to camera, Steve notices something orange with 8 legs moving closer. The Tarantula spider crosses the road with a little help from Steve.

LEFT: Steve and Nicko make their way to the stage in Santiago.

9TH MARCH 2008. Pista Atletica, Santiago, Chile.

9TH MARCH 2008. Pista Atletica, Santiago, Chile.

ABOVE: Day of show and the entire stage set has been built, lighting and sound rigs in place but no power. The Maiden sound rig requires UK 220 volts and the brand new San Juan Coliseum can only offer US 110 volts. Technical details for the show were sent months in advance and an essential transformer is not supplied. As the venue staff search Puerto Rico for a transformer electricians try and resolve the problem. It is looking very likely the show will have to be cancelled. 12,000 people are waiting patiently outside for the doors to open. FAR RIGHT: At 6.15pm, Rod Smallwood films a piece to camera in front of the IRON MAIDEN stage set. If the show is cancelled, the film will be given to the local TV news so the fans get an explanation – it would not be possible to reschedule. RIGHT: The Maiden road crew can do nothing but continue to await news. As the venue prepares to cancel, the electricians 'hotwire' the generator giving a stable 220 volt current. It works and the doors open.

The stage gets power and IRON MAIDEN take to the stage on time.

Laura Ingle from Fox News interviews Nicko in flight.

Dave Murray leaves the dressing room in New Jersey.

14TH MARCH 2008. Izod Center, New Jersey, USA.

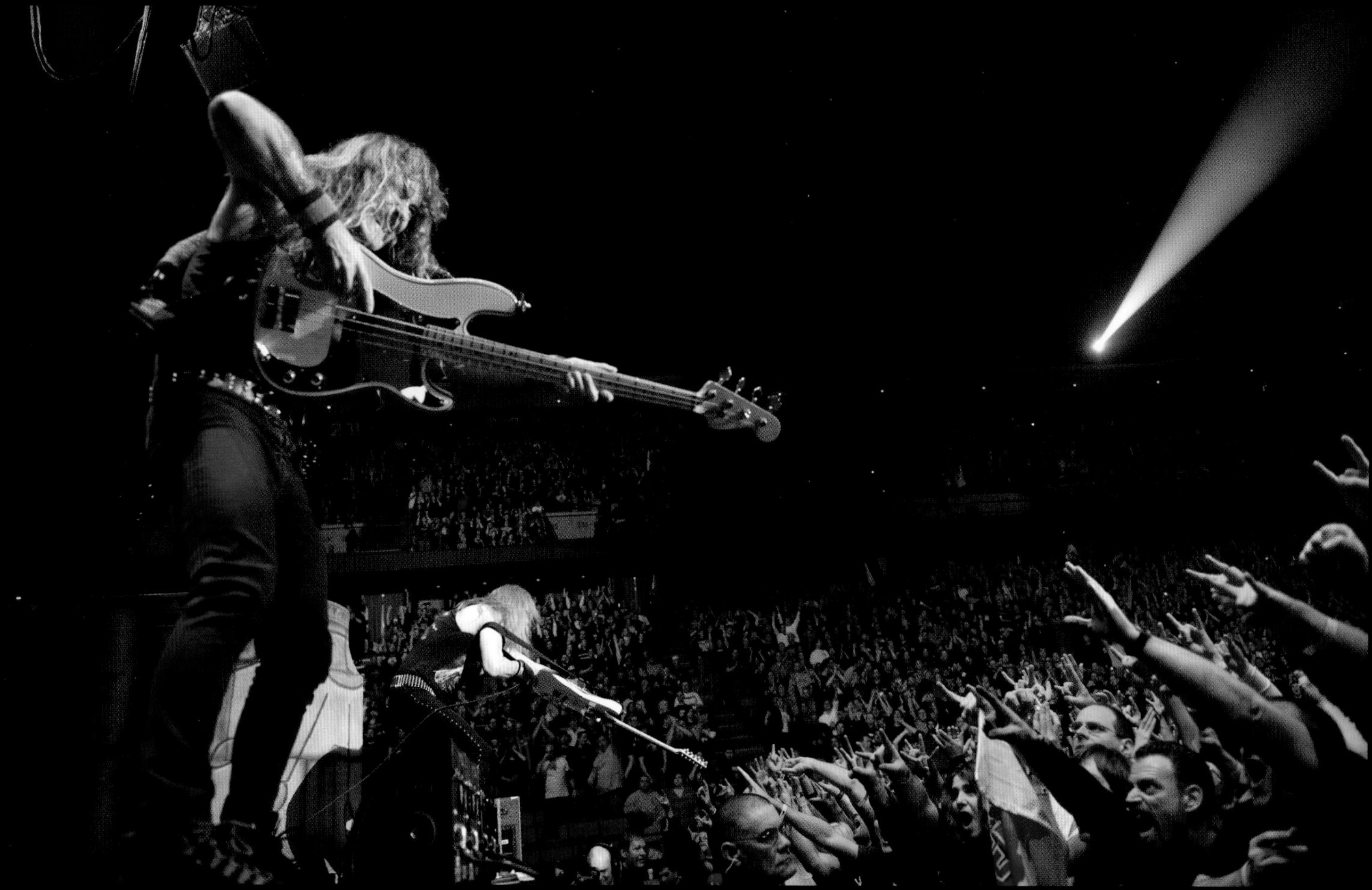

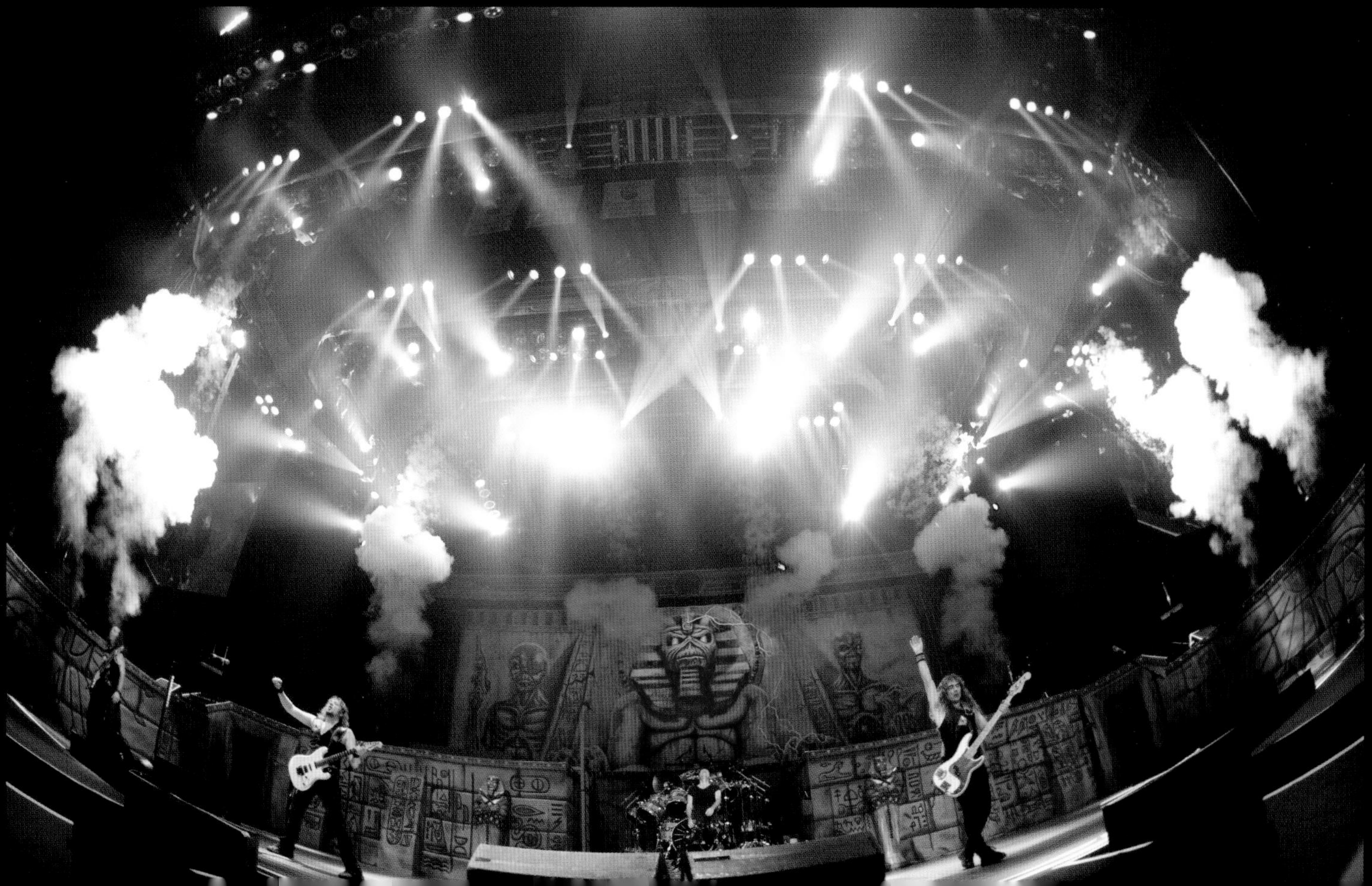

Travelling over 50,000 miles across 5 continents, 23 shows in only 45 days and playing to nearly 500,000 fans, the first leg of this successful tour comes to a close in Toronto. It is a world first for any band to tour in this way and everyone backstage is in a joyous mood as IRON MAIDEN take to the stage.

Onstage, Bruce thanks the Killer Krew and everyone involved with ED FORCE ONE for all their hard work.

The very next day the band board ED FORCE ONE and head home to Stansted, London. Job done!

BOTTOM LEFT: An exhausted but happy crew prepare for the final flight.

BELOW: Jeremy Smith from ROCK-IT CARGO loads the band's precious freight for the very last time on this tour.

SOMEWHERE BACK IN TIME WORLD TOUR 2008

FEATURING HIGHLIGHTS FROM THE SECOND LEG ACROSS NORTH AMERICA

MAY 2008
21ST SAN ANTONIO, TX, USA
22ND HOUSTON, TX, USA
25TH ALBUQUERQUE, NM, USA
26TH PHOENIX, AZ, USA
28TH CONCORD, CA, USA
30TH LOS ANGELES, CA, USA
31ST LOS ANGELES, CA, USA

JUNE 2008
2ND SEATTLE, WA, USA
3RD VANCOUVER, BC, CANADA

5TH CALGARY, AB, CANADA
6TH EDMONTON, AB, CANADA
8TH REGINA, SK, CANADA
9TH WINNIPEG, SK, CANADA
11TH ROSEMONT IL, USA
12TH CUYAHOGA FALLS, OH, USA
14TH HOLMDEL, NJ, USA
15TH NEW YORK, NY, USA
17TH CAMDEN, NJ, USA
18TH COLUMBIA, MD, USA
20TH MANSFIELD, MA, USA
21ST MONTREAL, QC, CANADA

22ND MAY 2008. Woodlands, Houston, Texas, USA.

25TH MAY 2008. Journal Pavilion, Albuquerque, New Mexico, USA.

SOMEWHERE BACK IN TIME
WORLD TOUR 2008

FEATURING HIGHLIGHTS FROM THE THIRD LEG ACROSS EUROPE

JUNE 2008
27TH BOLOGNA, ITALY
29TH DESSEL, BELGIUM

JULY 2008
1ST PARIS, FRANCE
2ND PARIS, FRANCE
5TH TWICKENHAM, LONDON, UK
9TH LISBON, PORTUGAL
11TH MERIDA, SPAIN
16TH STOCKHOLM, SWEDEN
18TH HELSINKI, FINLAND
19TH TAMPERE, FINLAND
22ND TRONDHEIM, NORWAY
24TH OSLO, NORWAY

26TH GOTHENBURG, SWEDEN
27TH HORSENS, DENMARK
31ST WACKEN FESTIVAL, GERMANY

AUGUST 2008
2ND ATHENS, GREECE
4TH BUCHAREST, ROMANIA
7TH WARSAW, POLAND
8TH PRAGUE, CZECH REP
10TH SPLIT, CROATIA
12TH BUDAPEST, HUNGARY
14TH BASEL, SWITZERLAND
16TH ASSEN, NETHERLANDS
19TH MOSCOW, RUSSIA

ABOVE: Earlier in the day Janick surveys the giant stadium.

RIGHT: The band prepare to go on stage at the home of English rugby.

LEFT: Maiden security chief, Jeff Weir, arrives to escort the band up to the stage.

IRON MAIDEN make a triumphant return to the UK playing to 50,000 fans at Twickenham stadium.

5TH JULY 2008. Twickenham Stadium, London, England.

RIGHT:
Steve and Janick before walking out in front of 57,000 people at Ullevi stadium in Gothenburg.

This is the second time Maiden have sold out the National Stadium and Gothenburg is transformed into 'Maidenville' by the hordes of devoted Swedish fans.

26TH JULY 2008. Ullevi Stadium, Gothenburg, Sweden.

SOMEWHERE BACK IN TIME WORLD TOUR 2009

FEATURING HIGHLIGHTS FROM THE FOURTH LEG ON BOARD ED FORCE ONE

FEBRUARY 2009
10TH BELGRADE, SERBIA
13TH DUBAI, UAE
15TH BANGALORE, INDIA
20TH AUCKLAND, NEW ZEALAND
22ND CHRISTCHURCH, NEW ZEALAND
25TH MONTERREY, MEXICO
26TH GUADALAJARA, MEXICO
28TH MEXICO CITY, MEXICO

MARCH 2009
3RD SAN JOSE, COSTA RICA
5TH CARACAS, VENEZUELA
7TH BOGOTA, COLOMBIA

10TH QUITO, ECUADOR
12TH MANAUS, BRAZIL
14TH RIO DE JANEIRO, BRAZIL
15TH SAO PAULO, BRAZIL
18TH BELO HORIZONTE, BRAZIL
20TH BRASILIA, BRAZIL
22ND SANTIAGO, CHILE
26TH LIMA, PERU
28TH BUENOS AIRES, ARGENTINA
31ST RECIFE, BRAZIL

APRIL 2009
2ND FT LAUDERDALE, FLORIDA, USA

Guitars, drums, staging, drapes, sound & lighting desks, backline and Eddie all have to be loaded into ED FORCE ONE's customised cargo bay after each show. Everything has to be loaded on to specially designed flight pallets, covered in a protective fire blanket and securely strapped down before each flight. The entire process takes up to 6 hours and another 3 to unload.

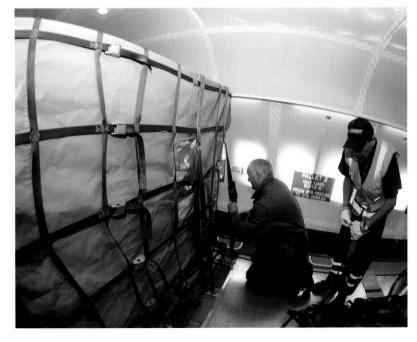

To keep ED FORCE ONE in the air, two engineers travel with the touring party to carry out routine maintenance after each and every flight. Any defects on the aircraft noted by the Flight Crew can be attended to before the next departure.

It is rare for a major music act to visit Quito and unprecedented for a stage show as ambitious as IRON MAIDEN's to drop in. At 9200ft above sea level it is one of the highest cities in the world. Maiden arrive 2 days before show day in order to acclimatise to the altitude. On the streets surrounding the airport over 1500 fans are desperate to get closer to Maiden. The first attempt to drive out is aborted after advice from the military, who are struggling to secure the perimeter. Maiden finally escape by sending the Killer Krew to an alternative gate as a decoy. At the hotel, police link arms to hold back the enthusiastic crowd that is growing ever larger. Fans unfurl a large banner welcoming Maiden to Ecuador. High on a distant hill on the outskirts of the city massive letters spell out 'Maiden'.

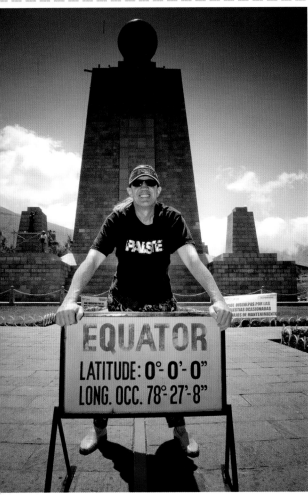

FAR LEFT: Nicko at the Equator. 0-0-0 Latitude – this is the middle of the world.

ABOVE: Nicko hits a golf ball from the Northern hemisphere into the Southern hemisphere.

LEFT: Steve Harris high above Quito city.

BELOW: Bruce challenges Ecuador's Olympic team to a series of duels.

Situated at the basin of the Amazon and deep in the rain forest, Maiden are invited on a boat to see where the Amazon river begins.

ABOVE: The cruise leaves the quay in beautiful sunshine which soon fades as threatening black clouds move in and the rain pours. The River Solimões, a dark clear water, meets the muddy Rio Negre creating a stark line in the water.

FAR RIGHT: Janick and Nicko stand in the rain at the confluence.

LEFT: Adrian Smith hangs on as the boat turns around to return to Manaus.

BELOW: Nicko McBrain, 12th March 2009, Sambodrome Stadium, Manaus, Brazil.

ABOVE: ED FORCE ONE touches down in Rio for the premiere of the movie 'FLIGHT 666'.

RIGHT: The band arrive at the prestigious Cine Odeon to rapturous applause and a media frenzy begins.

ABOVE: The band line up in front of the world's press.

LEFT: Bruce introduces the movie to the audience before discreetly leaving the theatre.

The movie receives critical acclaim and goes on to win 'Best Music Documentary' at the South By South West Music awards in Texas and a Juno award (Canadian equivalent of a Grammy) for Best Music DVD.

Despite torrential rain hindering the stage build the previous day, the show in Rio is faultless.

Flight 666 from Rio is put back to 2pm to allow Bruce a full night of sleep after the previous night's show. Without this rest period, strict aviation rules would prohibit Bruce piloting that day. The Killer Krew travel by road overnight and start the set build at 7am at the renowned Formula 1 racing circuit Interlagos.

As the band prepare to take to the stage at 8pm there are still 20,000 excited ticket holders queuing outside. The band and Manager Rod Smallwood, insist it would not be appropriate to start the show and delay the stage time. To avoid the crowd getting restless, Rod Smallwood makes an announcement from the stage to rapturous applause. By 9pm there are 70,000 people inside the stadium chanting "Maiden" and the band go on. The reaction from the crowd is euphoric.

LEFT: The day after the show Bruce rides a helicopter back to the Interlagos track and takes control of a supercharged Porsche 911. After several hair raising laps around the circuit (one with a terrified journalist from *The Times* newspaper), Bruce challenges the attending media to a Go-Kart race on the training circuit. 25 brutally fast laps around the 'mini-Interlagos' track later and Bruce comes in first place, winning a gold watch that runs backwards in time.

LEFT: Following a morning of racing cars, Bruce fences Brazil's finest athletes for the next 3 hours!

17TH MARCH 2009. Sao Paulo, Brazil.

High above the stage set riggers secure the massive light show

Santiago 2008 sold out instantly and the demand for tickets was unprecedented. As promised Maiden return, but this time with the full stage show flown down by air freight from Sao Paulo. To avoid any disappointment the Club Hipico Racecourse has double the capacity of 2008.

RIGHT: Bruce relaxes backstage before stepping out in front of 60,000+ in Chile.

BELOW: As Maiden take to the stage, a small minority jump over the barriers and refuse to move. Security attempt to clear them without success and the Carabineros, Chile's much revered riot police, step into the pit area with full armour and batons. Fortunately just the sight of the Carabineros is enough to move the offenders away without the use of force. The show continues without incident.

26TH MARCH 2009. Lima, Peru. Steve Harris walks through the players tunnel of the Estadio Nacional en route to the stage.

1ST APRIL 2009. ED FORCE ONE band and crew take time for a group photo on a fuel stop in Barbados.

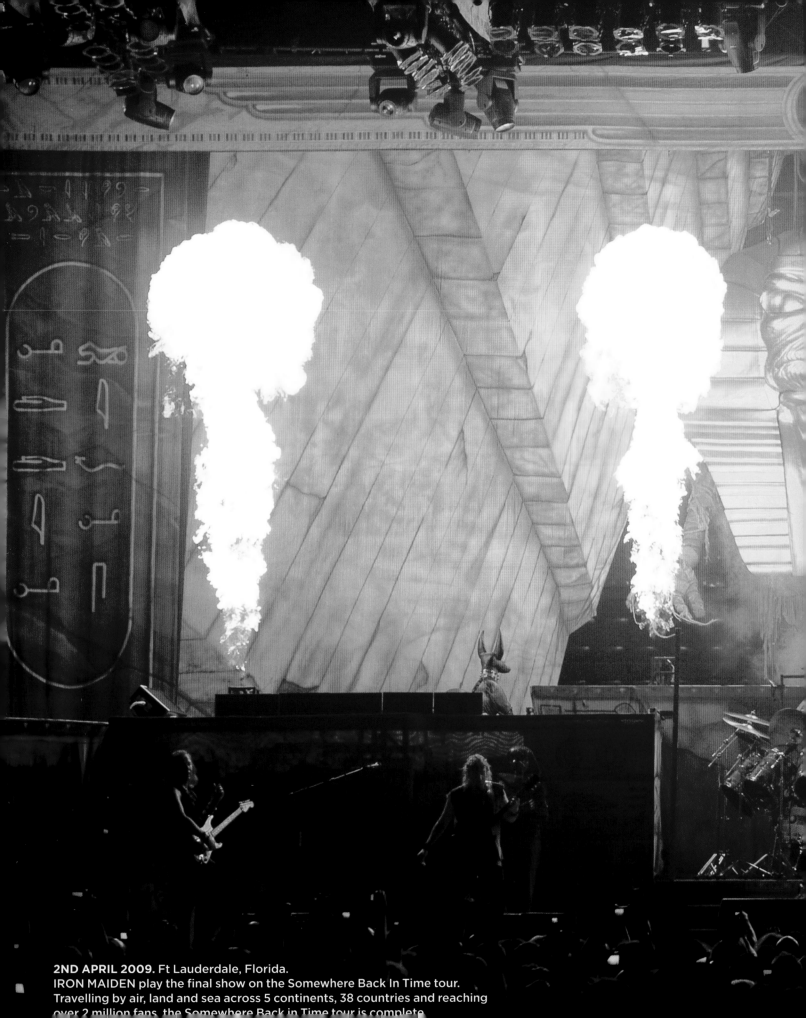

2ND APRIL 2009. Ft Lauderdale, Florida.
IRON MAIDEN play the final show on the Somewhere Back In Time tour.
Travelling by air, land and sea across 5 continents, 38 countries and reaching
over 2 million fans, the Somewhere Back in Time tour is complete.

THE KILLER KREW

Tour Manager: Ian Day

Tour Manager: Steve Gadd

Production Manager: Patrick Ledwith

Lighting Designer: Rob Coleman

Production Coordinator: Zeb Minto

Monitor Engineer: Steve 'Gonzo' Smith

Stage Manager: Bill Conte

FOH Sound Engineer: Doug Hall

Guitar Techs: Colin Price, Justin Garrick, Sean Brady & Michael Kenney (& keyboards).

Drum Tech: Charlie Charlesworth

Sound Tech: Ian 'Squid' Walsh

Set Carpenters: Paul Stratford, Ashley Groom, Philip Stewart & Griff Dickinson

Sound System Tech: Mike Hackman

Lighting Chief: Antti Saari

Video Director: Andy Matthews

Wardrobe: Natasha De Sampayo

Head of Security: Jeffrey Weir

Masseuse/Security: Peter Lokrantz

Video Tech: Nicholas Birtwistle

Production Assistant: Kerry Harris

THE FINAL FRONTIER WORLD TOUR 2010

FEATURING HIGHLIGHTS FROM NORTH AMERICA AND EUROPE

JUNE 2010
9TH DALLAS, TX, USA
11TH HOUSTON, TX, USA
12TH SAN ANTONIO, TX, USA
14TH DENVER, CO, USA
16TH ALBUQUERQUE, NM, USA
17TH PHOENIX, AZ, USA
19TH SAN BERNARDINO, CA, USA
20TH CONCORD, CA, USA
22ND AUBURN, WA, USA
24TH VANCOUVER, BC, CANADA
26TH EDMONTON, AB, CANADA
27TH CALGARY, AB, CANADA
29TH SASKATOON, SK, CANADA
30TH WINNIPEG, MB, CANADA

JULY 2010
3RD TORONTO, ON, CANADA
6TH OTTAWA, ON, CANADA
7TH MONTREAL, QC, CANADA
9TH QUEBEC CITY, CANADA

11TH HOLMDEL, NJ, USA
12TH NEW YORK, NY, USA
14TH PITTSBURGH, PA, USA
15TH CLEVELAND, OH, USA
17TH DETROIT, MI, USA
18TH CHICAGO, IL, USA
20TH WASHINGTON D.C., USA

30TH DUBLIN, IRELAND

AUGUST 2010
1ST KNEBWORTH, UK
5TH WACKEN, GERMANY
7TH STOCKHOLM, SWEDEN
8TH PORI, FINLAND
11TH BERGEN, NORWAY
14TH BUDAPEST, HUNGARY
15TH TRANSYLVANIA, ROMANIA
17TH UDINE, ITALY
19TH HASSELT, BELGIUM
21ST VALENCIA, SPAIN

In a rehearsal studio in Ft Lauderdale IRON MAIDEN run through the set list for The Final Frontier 2010 tour.

WICKERMAN
GHOST OF THE NAVIGATOR
BRIGHTER THAN 1000 SUNS
ELDORADO
DANCE OF DEATH/PASCHENDALE
BENJAMIN BREEG
THESE COLOURS DON'T RUN
BLOOD BROTHERS
WILDEST DREAMS
NO MORE LIES
BRAVE NEW WORLD
FEAR OF THE DARK
IRON MAIDEN

NUMBER OF THE BEAST
HALLOWED BE THY NAME
RUNNING FREE.

The tour kicks off in Dallas in 4 days' time. The production team and set designers (Hangman) are there already, building the new stage set in anticipation of the band's arrival.

ABOVE: Bruce Dickinson arrives at the venue to inspect the new stage set.

ABOVE RIGHT: The Final Frontier Eddie is unveiled.

RIGHT: Soundcheck in Dallas.

Production rehearsals continue for a second day and go on until late at night. This leg of the tour will use trucks and tour buses to transport the show and crew across North America. The band will travel to each city using a Gulf Stream Jet and Bruce will occasionally use the 'Bruce Goose' (a 7 seated twin prop aircraft) to get to shows.

US Navy Commander 'Patton' Thurman and Major Marc 'Monkey' Mulkey take Bruce and Rod to
'Carswell Field' Naval base to inspect the F/A 18 Hornets up close and try out the flight simulators.

In celebration of the band's soon to be released studio album *The Final Frontier*, IRON MAIDEN are invited on a VIP tour of NASA Houston.

ABOVE & RIGHT: The band are shown around Space Shuttle and the International Space Station training unit by esteemed astronaut Mike Massimino.

BELOW MIDDLE: Mike gives the band a personal tour of NASA, recounting his own first hand experiences in space.

BELOW: Nicko on the Space Shuttle lavatory.

ABOVE: The band are then taken into the live NASA Mission Control Center.

ABOVE LEFT: Janick and Dave take in the atmosphere of the historic moon landings operations room.

ABOVE: Nicko and Rod on the hot phone.

The tour continues into the evening and Bruce, Nicko, Dave and Janick are offered the chance to fly the Space Shuttle flight simulator (an experience that is normally reserved for astronauts only). Everyone is strapped tightly into the flight seats and the cockpit is tilted back to simulate a real launch. Bruce is at the controls first, blasting off with the entire cockpit shaking. The cockpit rolls over and the trainer informs Bruce he is travelling at 17,000mph. The booster rockets are ejected and out of the windows the world fades further away. After entering orbit Bruce re-enters the earth's atmosphere and takes full control, gliding the Space Shuttle home successfully using a projected guidance system. Everyone takes a turn blasting off and the engineer congratulates Nicko for a 'text book' landing.

Tres Amigos. The Alamo, San Antonio, Texas.

12TH JUNE 2010. San Antonio, Texas.

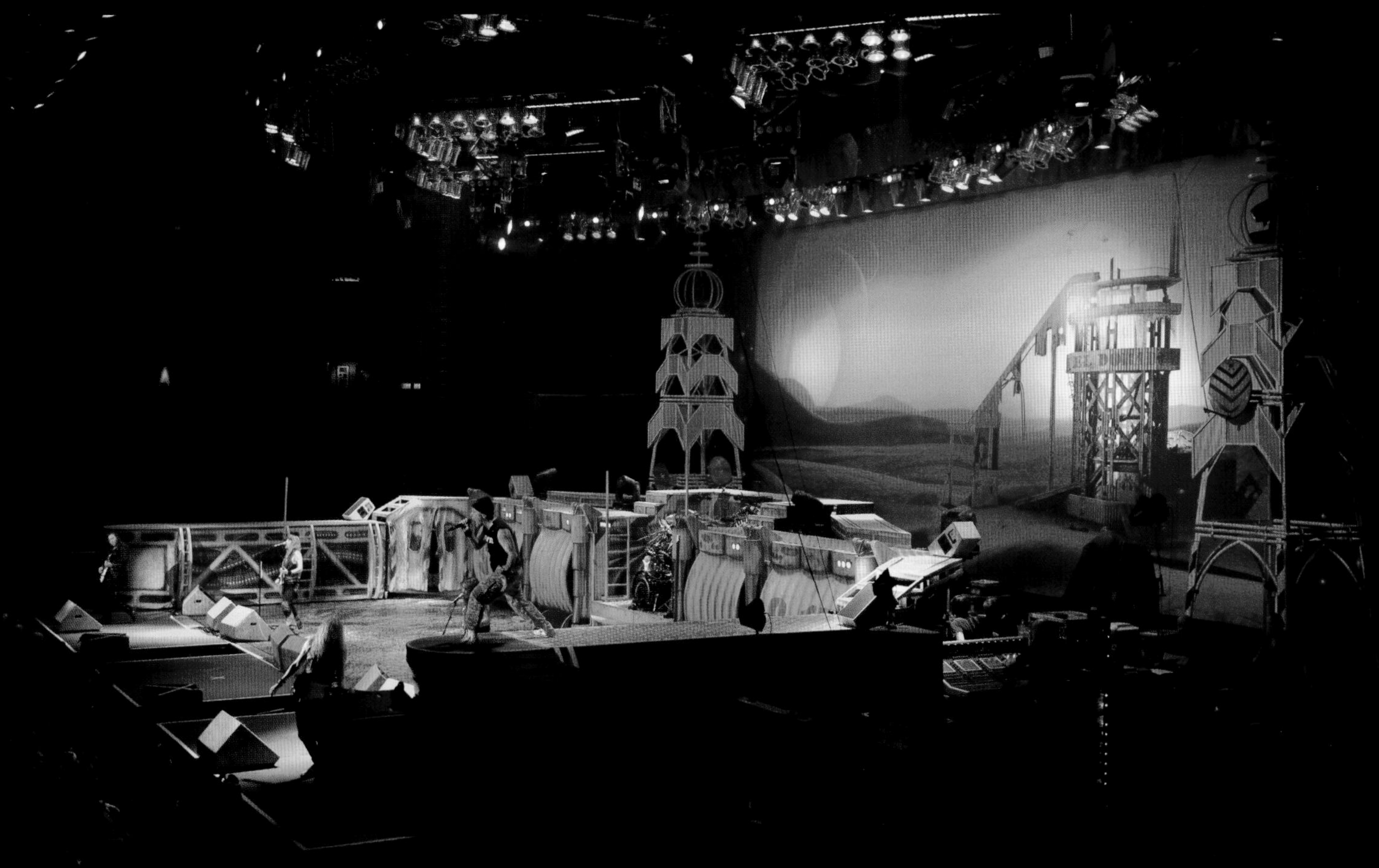

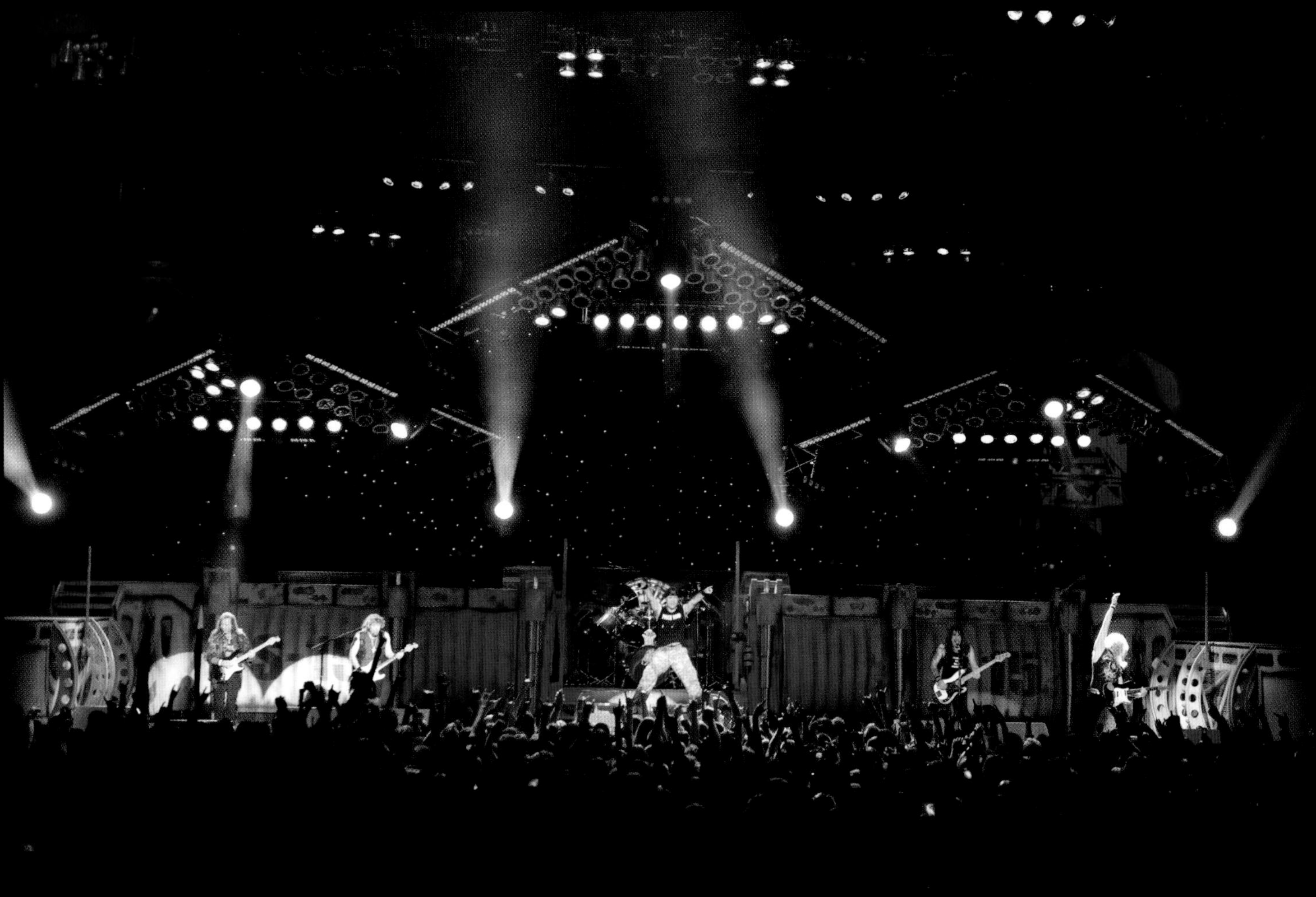

17TH JUNE 2010. Phoenix, Arizona.

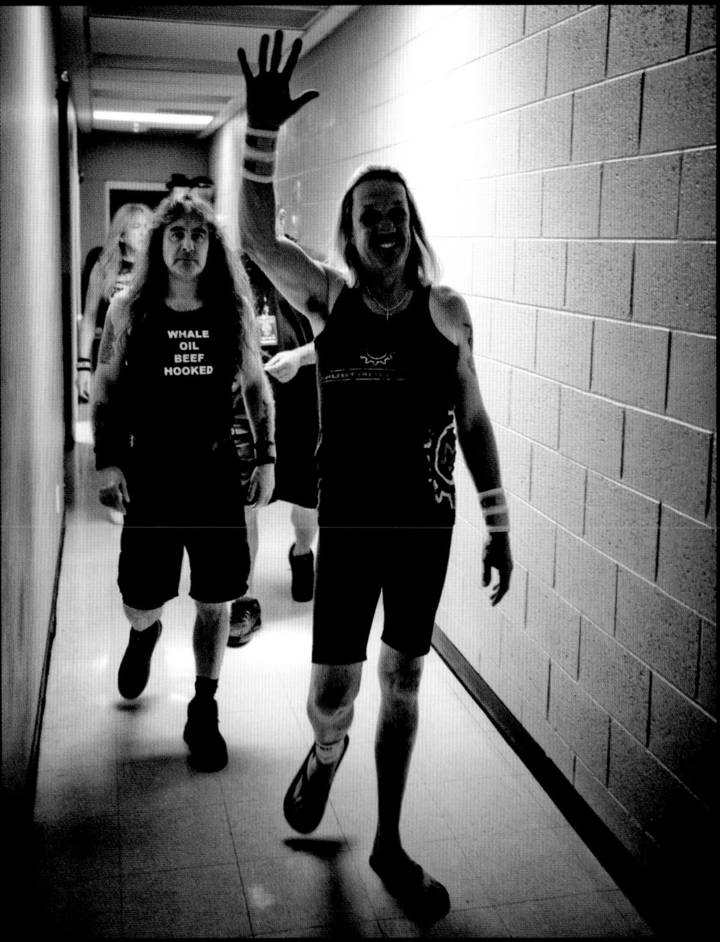

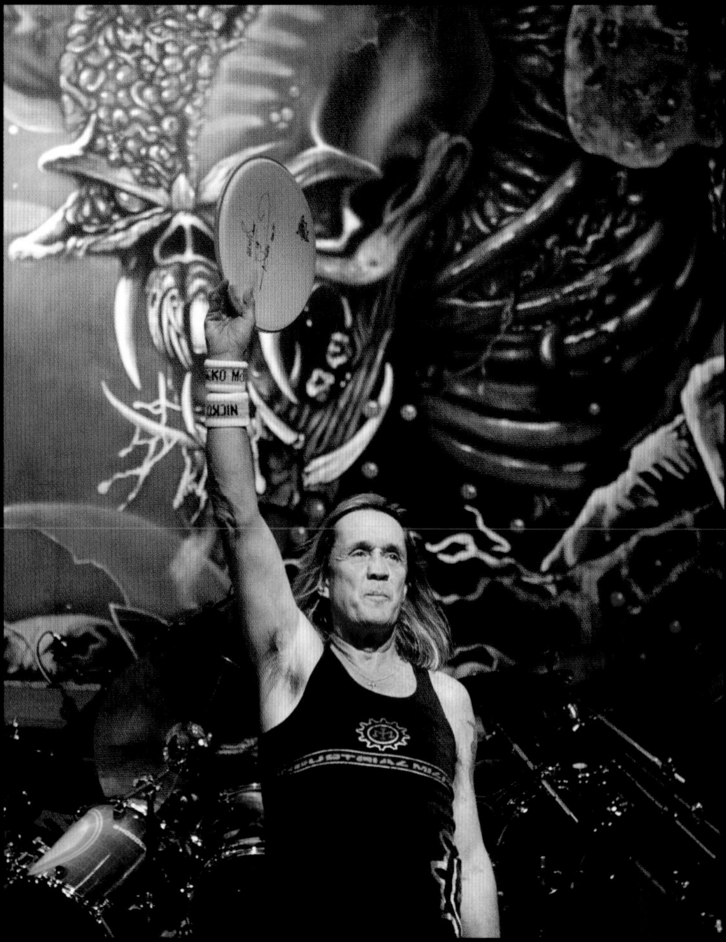

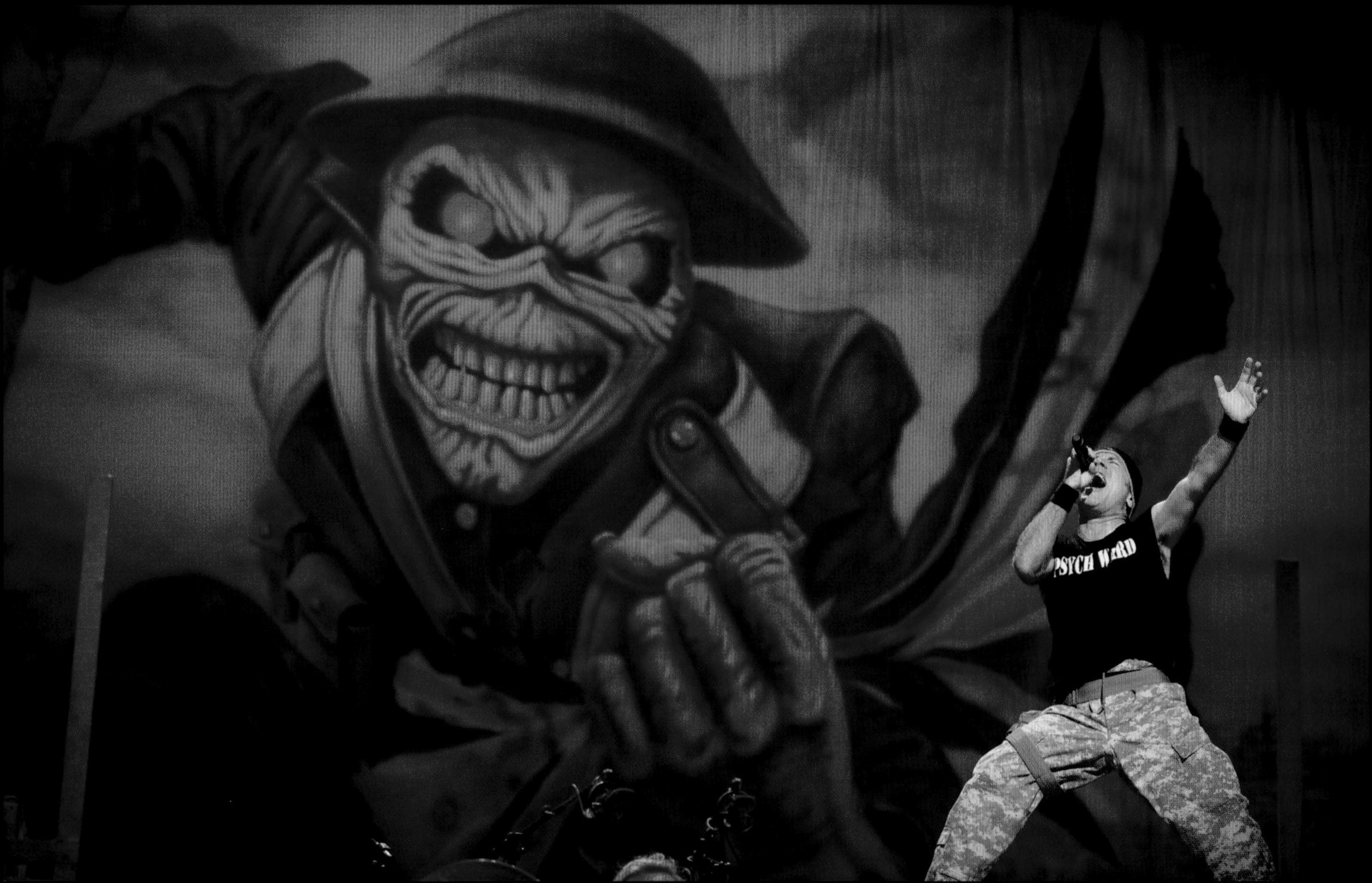

TOP LEFT: THE 'Bruce Goose' is fuelled up at a Santa Monica Airfield.

TOP RIGHT: For fun, Bruce races the band party to Concord; flying out of Santa Monica an hour earlier than the rest of the band in their Gulf Stream Jet.

ABOVE: Bruce lands 20 minutes ahead of the group much to the band's amusement.

24TH JUNE 2010. Vancouver, Canada.

1ST AUGUST 2010. Sonisphere Festival, Knebworth, England.

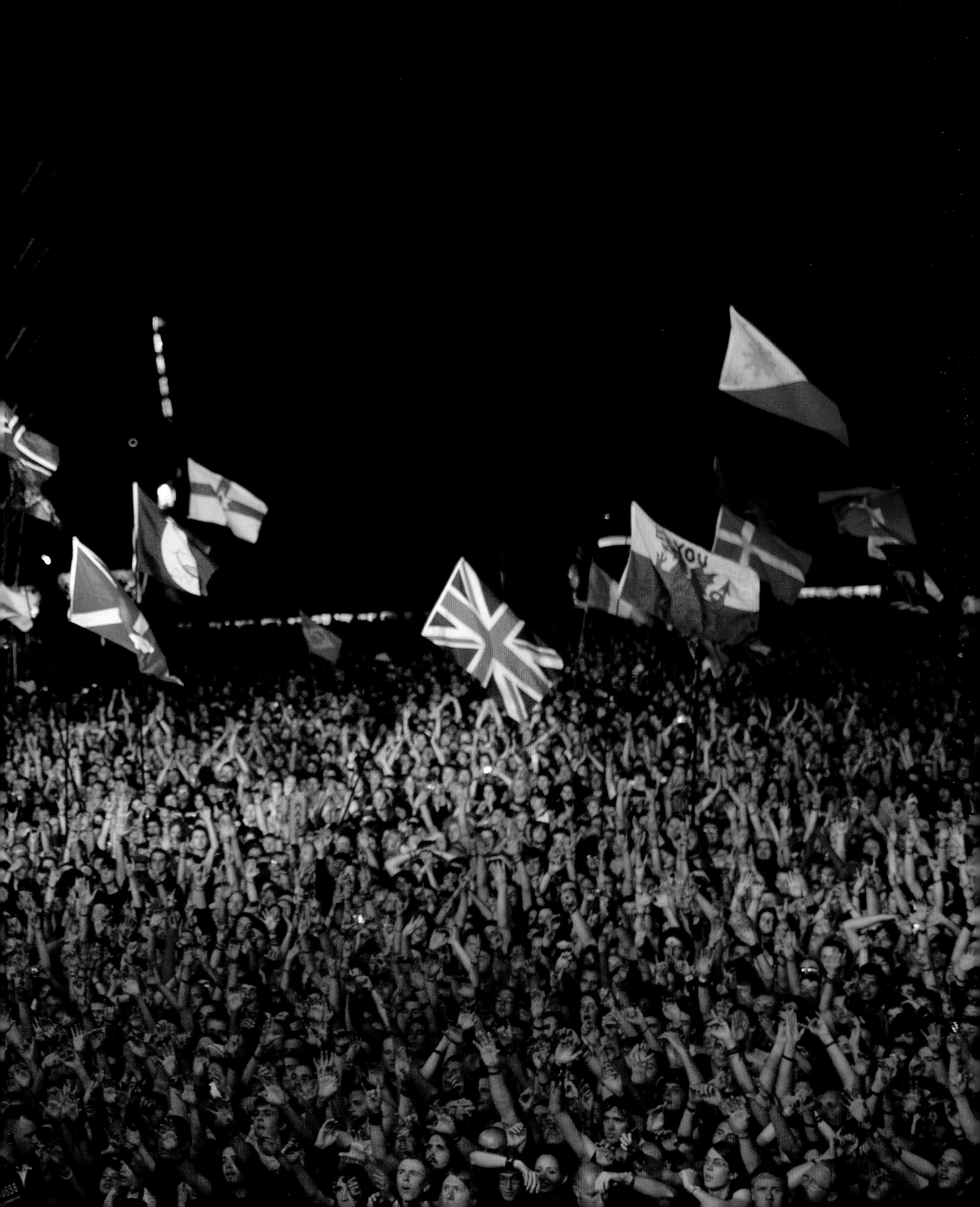

The Final Frontier.
IRON MAIDEN's
15th studio album
is released on 13th
August 2010 to
critical acclaim.
The album reaches
No.1 in over 28
countries.

THE FINAL FRONTIER WORLD TOUR 2011

FEATURING HIGHLIGHTS FROM THE THIRD LEG 'AROUND THE WORLD IN 66 DAYS'

FEBRUARY 2011
11TH MOSCOW, RUSSIA
15TH SINGAPORE
17TH JAKARTA, INDONESIA
20TH BALI, INDONESIA
23RD MELBOURNE, AUSTRALIA
24TH SYDNEY, AUSTRALIA
26TH BRISBANE, AUSTRALIA
27TH SYDNEY, AUSTRALIA

MARCH 2011
4TH MELBOURNE, AUSTRALIA
5TH ADELAIDE, AUSTRALIA
7TH SOUNDWAVE, PERTH, AUSTRALIA
10TH SEOUL, SOUTH KOREA
12TH TOKYO, JAPAN*
13TH TOKYO, JAPAN*
17TH MONTERREY, MEXICO

18TH MEXICO CITY, MEXICO
20TH BOGOTA, COLOMBIA
23RD LIMA, PERU
26TH SAO PAULO, BRAZIL
28TH RIO DE JANEIRO, BRAZIL
30TH BRASILIA, BRAZIL

*CANCELLED DUE TO EARTHQUAKE

APRIL 2011
1ST BELEM, BRAZIL
3RD RECIFE, BRAZIL
5TH CURITIBA, BRAZIL
8TH BUENOS AIRES, ARGENTINA
10TH SANTIAGO, CHILE
14TH SAN JUAN, PUERTO RICO
16TH FT LAUDERDALE, FLORIDA, USA
17TH TAMPA, FLORIDA, USA

The new Final Frontier
ED FORCE ONE is
prepared for the 2011
world tour.

ABOVE: The aircraft is rolled out of the hanger for engine and technical tests.

LEFT: Bruce inspects the aircraft 48 hours before departure.

ABOVE: Minutes before ED FORCE ONE takes to the skies Bruce is alerted to a possible malfunction of the left wing de-icer mechanism. BELOW: The band and crew are forced to stand down while the possible cause is investigated.

Engineers scramble all over the aircraft and locate the problem. Although a minor fault, it has to be fixed. ABOVE: Janick holds the offending part. Contingency plans are put in place to unload the aircraft, then use a freighter to transport the equipment to Moscow and fly the band and crew on an alternative aircraft. Thankfully it doesn't come to this.

The faulty part is quickly replaced and Bruce gets clearance for take off.
ABOVE: Dickie Bell rounds up the crew and ED FORCE ONE takes to the skies.
The 2011 Final Frontier World tour begins.

On arrival in Moscow, TV crews, oblivious to the sub-zero temperatures, greet IRON MAIDEN with enthusiasm.

OPPOSITE PAGE: The following morning Steve Harris stops to sign autographs outside the hotel and ventures into Red Square.

INTRO
FINAL FRONTIER
ELDORADO
2 MINUTES
COMING HOME
DANCE OF DEATH
TROOPER
BLOOD BROTHERS
WICKERMAN
WILD WIND BLOWS
EVIL THAT MEN DO
TALISMAN
FEAR OF THE DARK
IRON MAIDEN
—————————————
NUMBER OF BEAST
HALLOWED
RUNNING FREE

The day before the show IRON MAIDEN arrive at the Olympic Stadium for a soundcheck and production rehearsal.

3pm: ED FORCE ONE covered in frost and ice at Moscow Domodedovo Airport. The temperature has plummeted to a biting -20°C.

The aircraft is sprayed with anti-ice fluid before take-off. All de-icer mechanisms on the aircraft are functioning correctly.

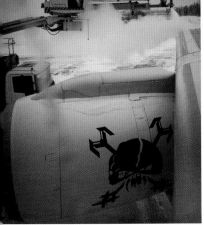

Heading South East via Baku the sun rises over Asia. Ground crew at Singapore airport excitedly welcome IRON MAIDEN. The temperature is +32 degrees, a shift of 52 degrees from Moscow.

Adrian Smith looks out across the skyline of Singapore from the 26th floor of the band's hotel. Meanwhile fans have been gathering since dawn at the Indoor Stadium.

ABOVE: Customs officials board the aircraft on arrival in Jakarta.

ABOVE RIGHT: Airport staff leave their official positions to pose with the group.

RIGHT: Hundreds of fans wait for the band on the other side of the exit doors.

BELOW: IRON MAIDEN are hurried through the lively crowd and into several vehicles.

ABOVE:
Police inspect
the concert site
with sniffer dogs.
No, not drugs,
looking for bombs!

LEFT:
Bruce attends
a busy press
conference for the
waiting Indonesian
media at the hotel.

RIGHT: Outside the venue at Ancol Bay, Muslim IRON MAIDEN fans pray to Allah at a musalla (a mini mosque) before entering the concert. The imam is among those wearing IRON MAIDEN T-shirts.

OPPOSITE TOP: On the outskirts of the concert site, riot police with tear gas and water cannons monitor the crowd waiting to react to the first sign of trouble. There is none.

17TH FEBRUARY 2011. Carnaval Beach, Ancol, Jakarta, Indon

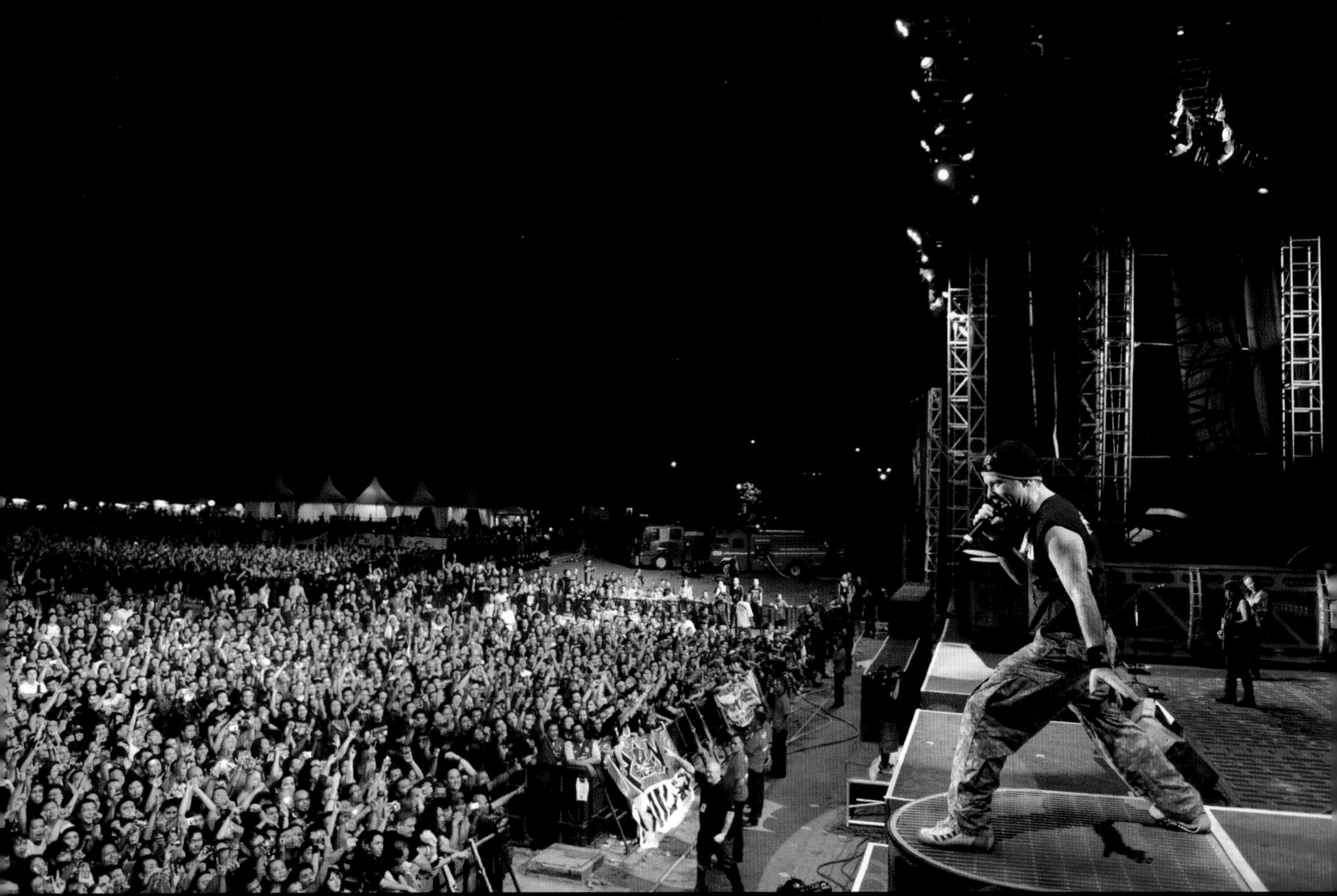

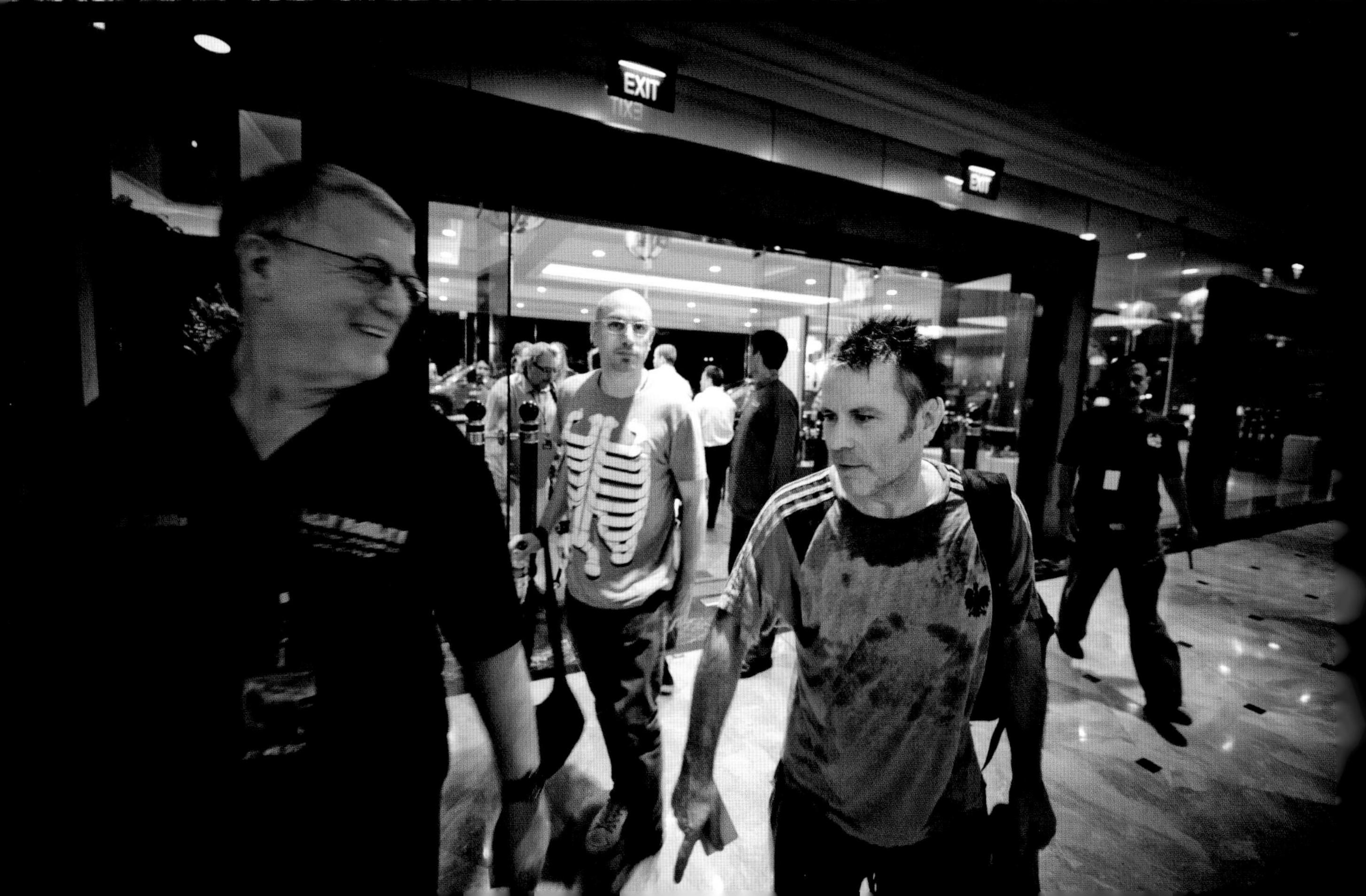

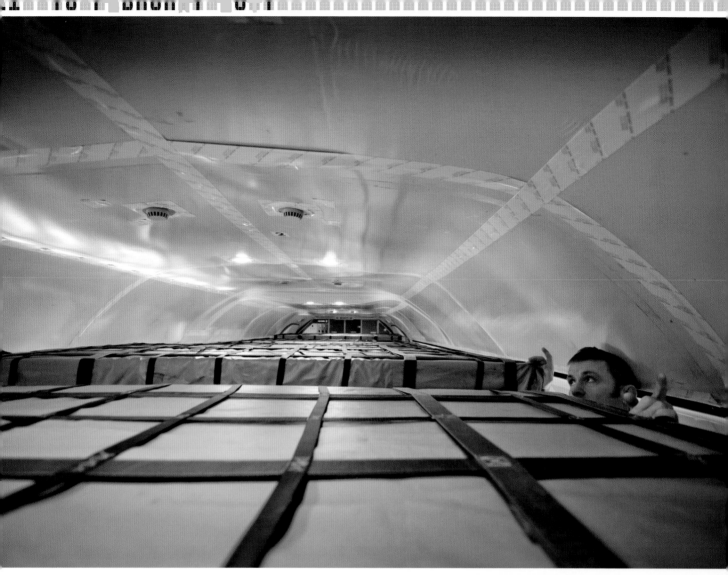

Bruce checks the ... is secure before ...ort flight to Bali.

...T: Military police ... route and assist ...nd's fast getaway ...he airport.

...OM LEFT: Hindu ...n fans follow ... valcade through ...reets of Bali with ...excitement.

...OM RIGHT: ... and Dave are ...d at the hotel ...ecklaces made ...ngipani flowers.

The day before the show, Bruce and Janick with assorted family and crew visit the Ulawatu 'Monkey' Temple to witness the legendary Kecak fire dance. TOP LEFT: A choir of seventy Balinese men chant 'cak.cak.cak' as a story of treachery is played out by Balinese dancers. TOP RIGHT: The climatic finale of the fire dance.

ABOVE LEFT: Bruce and Janick with the Kecak dancers.

The Garuda Wisnu Kencana Cultural Park is one of the most unique settings for an IRON MAIDEN concert. ABOVE: Bruce, wearing a gift (the shirt!) from the Balinese promoter, inspects the stage before a spot of rock climbing.

FAR LEFT: Although 'retired', Dickie Bell has helped with much of the logistics for the tour and has flown ahead to Indonesia to guide the local production crew.

LEFT: The giant park gates are opened to the hordes of eager fans.

23RD FEBRUARY 2011. Hisense Arena, Melbourne, Australia.

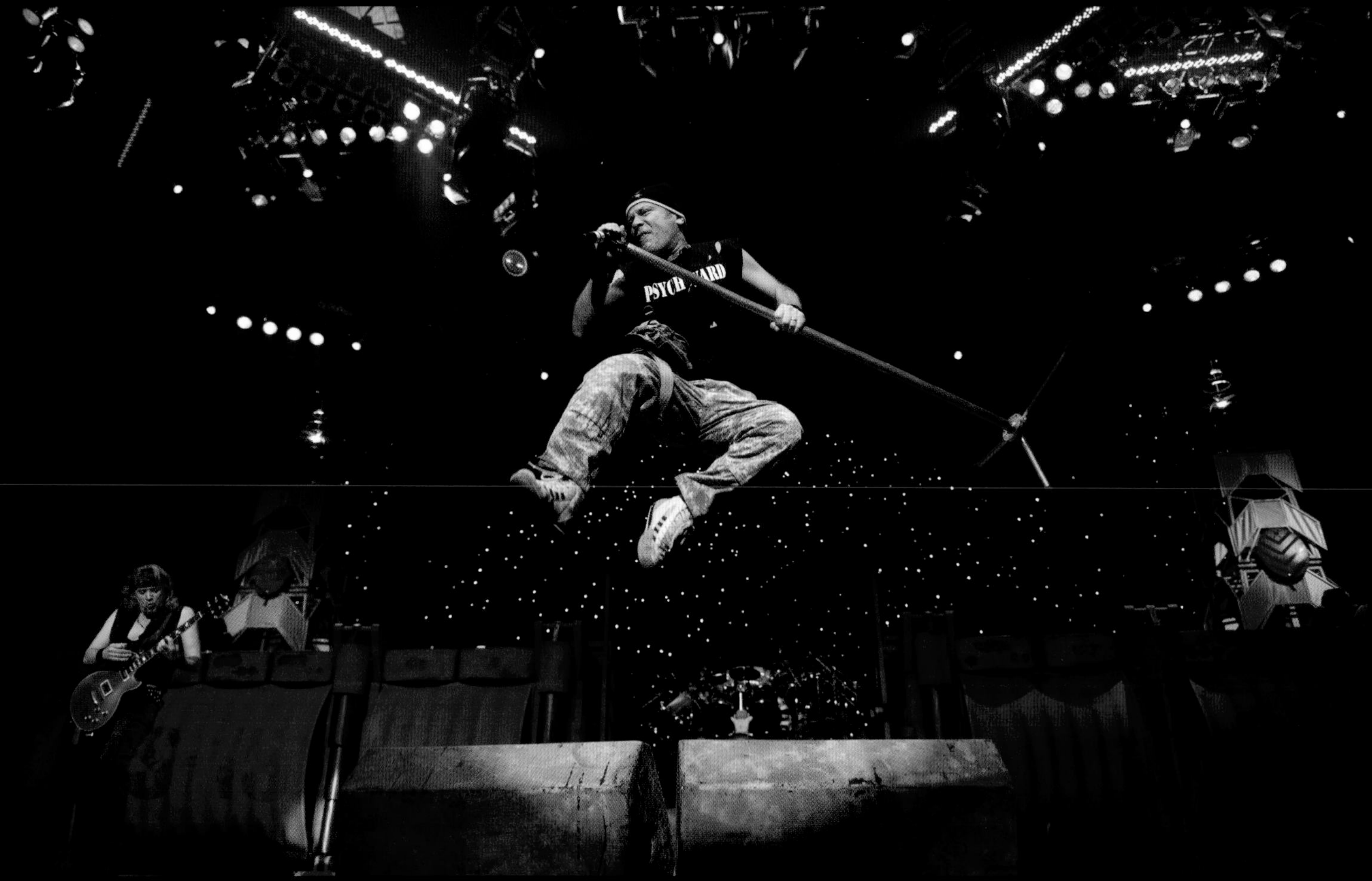

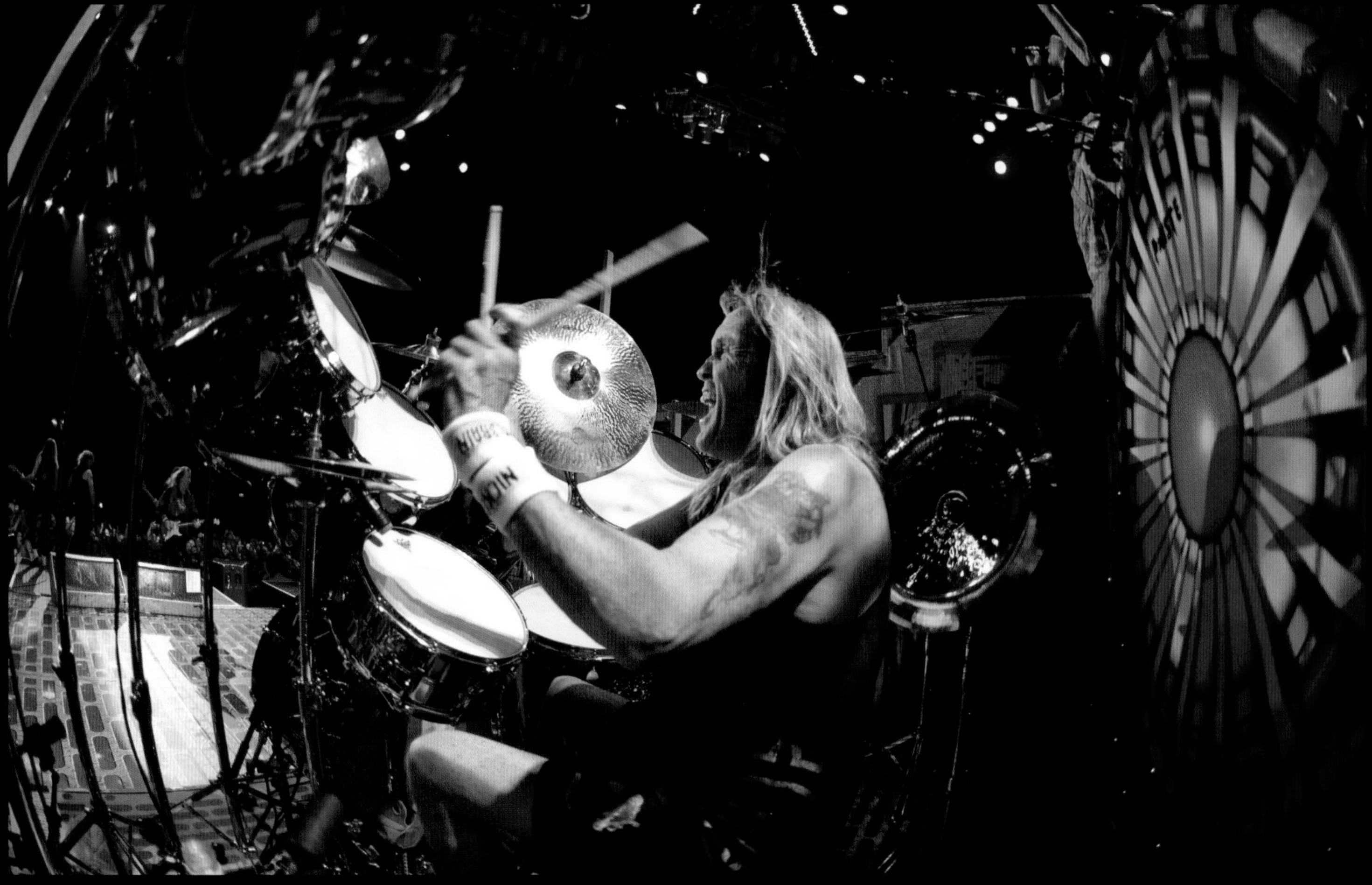

Bruce covers his foot with ice, post show, following a climbing incident a few days earlier in Bali

En route to Sydney, Janick displays a painful 5 inch bruise after landing badly on stage

4TH FEBRUARY 2011. Sydney, Australia.

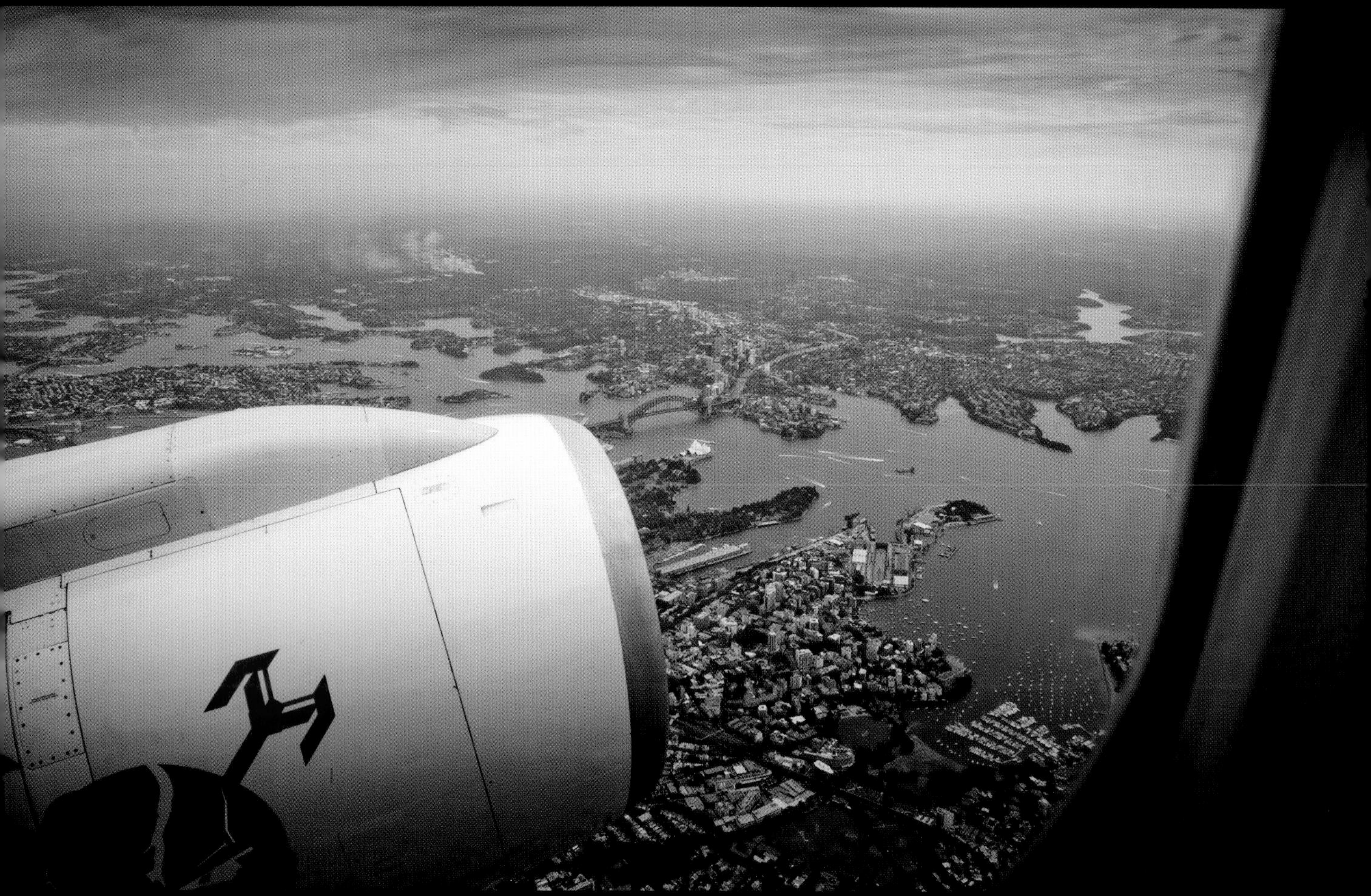

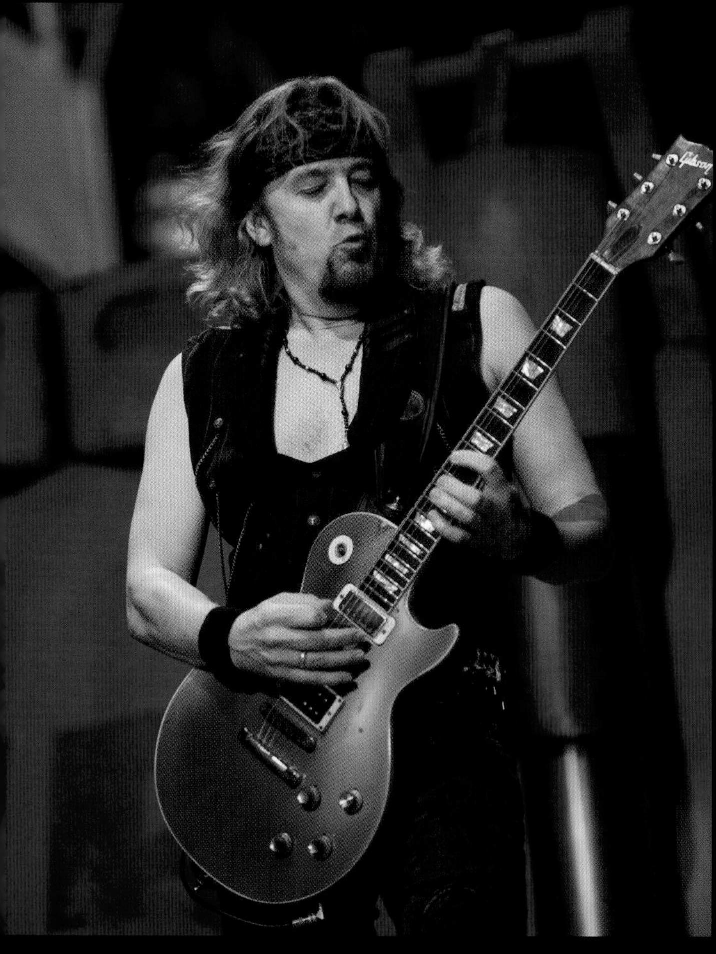

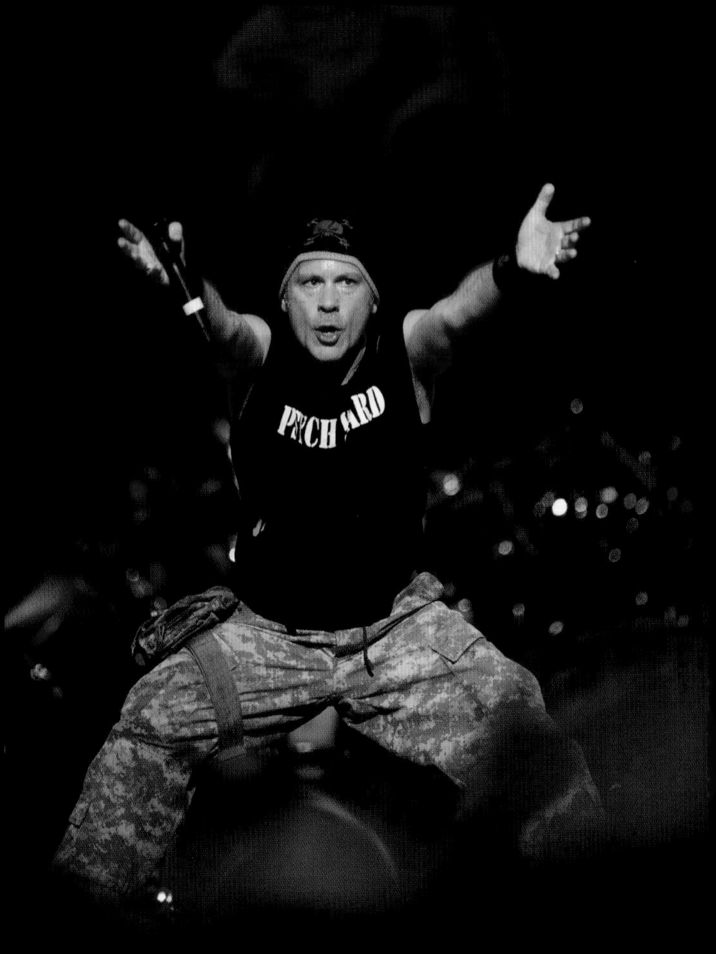

26TH FEBRUARY 2011. Steve Harris at the Lone Pine Koala Sanctuary.

Nicko warms up backstage, Soundwave Festival, Brisbane.

27TH FEBRUARY 2011. Soundwave Festival, Sydney, Australia.

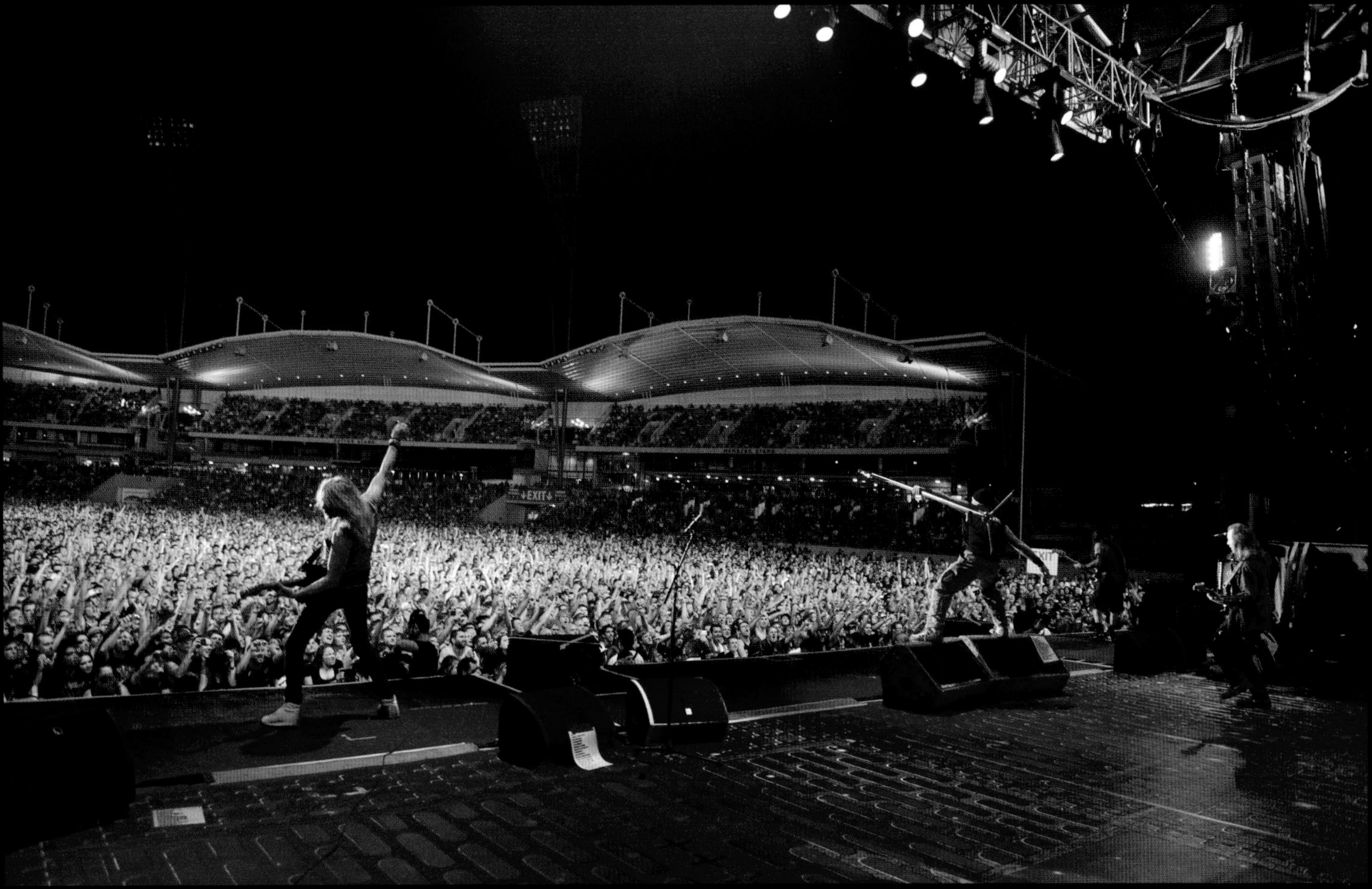

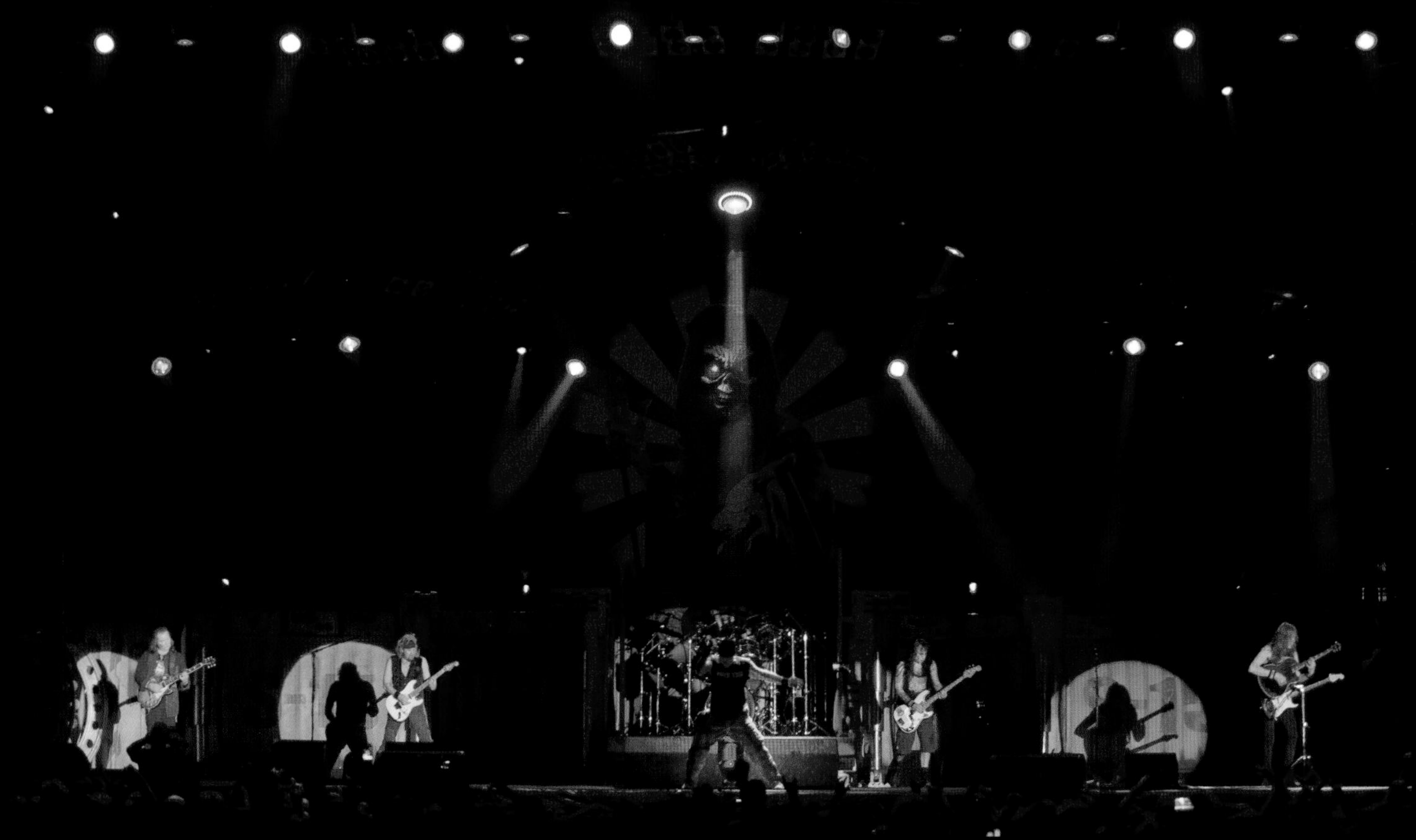

2ND MARCH 2011. Bruce in the cockpit of ED FORCE ONE en route to Melbourne.

Janick at the Melbourne Aquarium.

The band and Killer Krew.

Nicko and Janick visit HMAS *Waller*, one of the largest Diesel-Electric submarines in the world.

Commander Peter Foster gives a guided tour of the ship, giving an intimate insight into life on board.

ABOVE: Nicko clambers down into the sub.

RIGHT: Janick and Nicko on the deck of HMAS *Waller*.

The visit is a morale boosting experience for the crew of the sub.

ABOVE: After exploring the control room, Nicko is shown the torpedo tubes and takes a large gasp of oxygen from an emergency air mask.

9TH MARCH 2011. Janick at the Bongeunsa Temple, Seoul, South Korea.

10TH MARCH 2011. Adrian and Dave make their way through the Olympic Stadium to the stage.

On a crisp clear morning in Seoul, ED FORCE ONE prepares for departure to Tokyo. The band are especially excited to be returning to Japan for two sell out shows. Little does anyone know the calm of Seoul is the quiet before the storm.

10:17
Japanese TV board ED FORCE ONE to film the flight to Tokyo.

10:54
Bruce is in a jovial mood in the cockpit.

12:25
The remaining band party are delayed and the departure time is put back by 35 minutes.

13:00
Flight 666 takes off from Seoul.

14:25
ED FORCE ONE begins its final descent into Tokyo.

14:46:23
Japan has the biggest earthquake in its recorded history, measuring a staggering 9.0. ED FORCE ONE is only 9 minutes away from landing.

14:51
Tokyo airport shuts down and issues a tsunami warning for the entire coast line. Diverted planes criss cross the sky as ED FORCE ONE regains altitude.

14:53
Bruce makes the announcement, 'there has been a massive earthquake below'.

14:59
Flight 666 is diverted to Nagoya.

15:25
ED FORCE ONE lands in Nagoya, 120 miles west of Tokyo.

Everyone stays on board whilst the band and production team discuss what to do next. At this stage the scale of the disaster is not fully known and the band want to do everything they can to play Tokyo. News slowly filters through of the devastation and it dawns on everyone how close ED FORCE ONE was to being on the ground at the time of the quake. The Japanese TV crew, who are still on board, have a translator who assists the production team in securing transport and accommodation in Nagoya.

Everyone's thoughts now turn to those affected by the quake and tsunami as Japanese television plays out the scenes of destruction.

There is little public transport, power supplies are severely affected and there is damage to numerous buildings. The Japanese promoter officially cancels the shows.

ED FORCE ONE sadly departs for Hawaii the following day. The concerned band and crew offer their condolences to the good people of Japan as the tragedy continues to unfold.

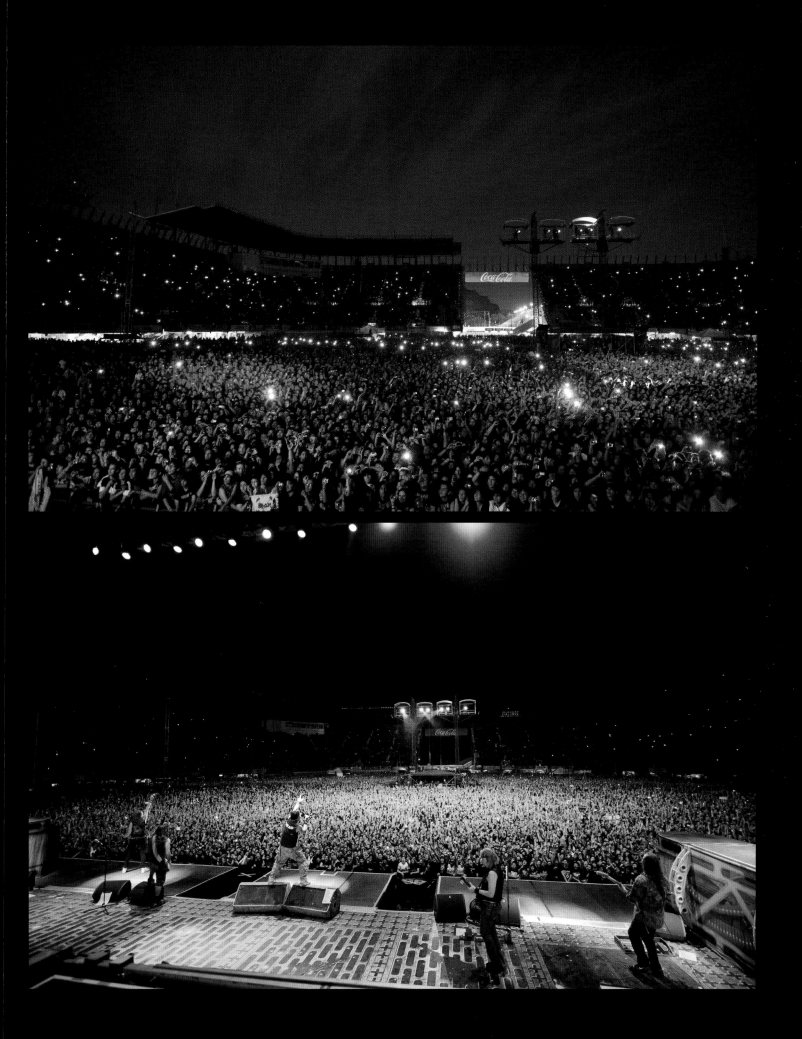

20TH MARCH 2011. Bogota, Colombia.

Tensions run high on the streets of Bogota but the mood inside the concert is one of celebration.

Parque Simon Bolivar, Bogota, Colombia.

The day before the show, Bruce is invited by the Sao Paulo police to the local gun range. In a secret location underground an entire arsenal of weapons is made available for target practice.

NEXT PAGE: As the song 'Iron Maiden' plays out the set, two giant fingers appear either side of the stage, followed by a giant Eddie head snarling at the audience. The surprised fans are the first in the world to see the new 'Big Eddie'.

26TH MARCH 2011. Morumbi Stadium, Sao Paulo, Brazil.

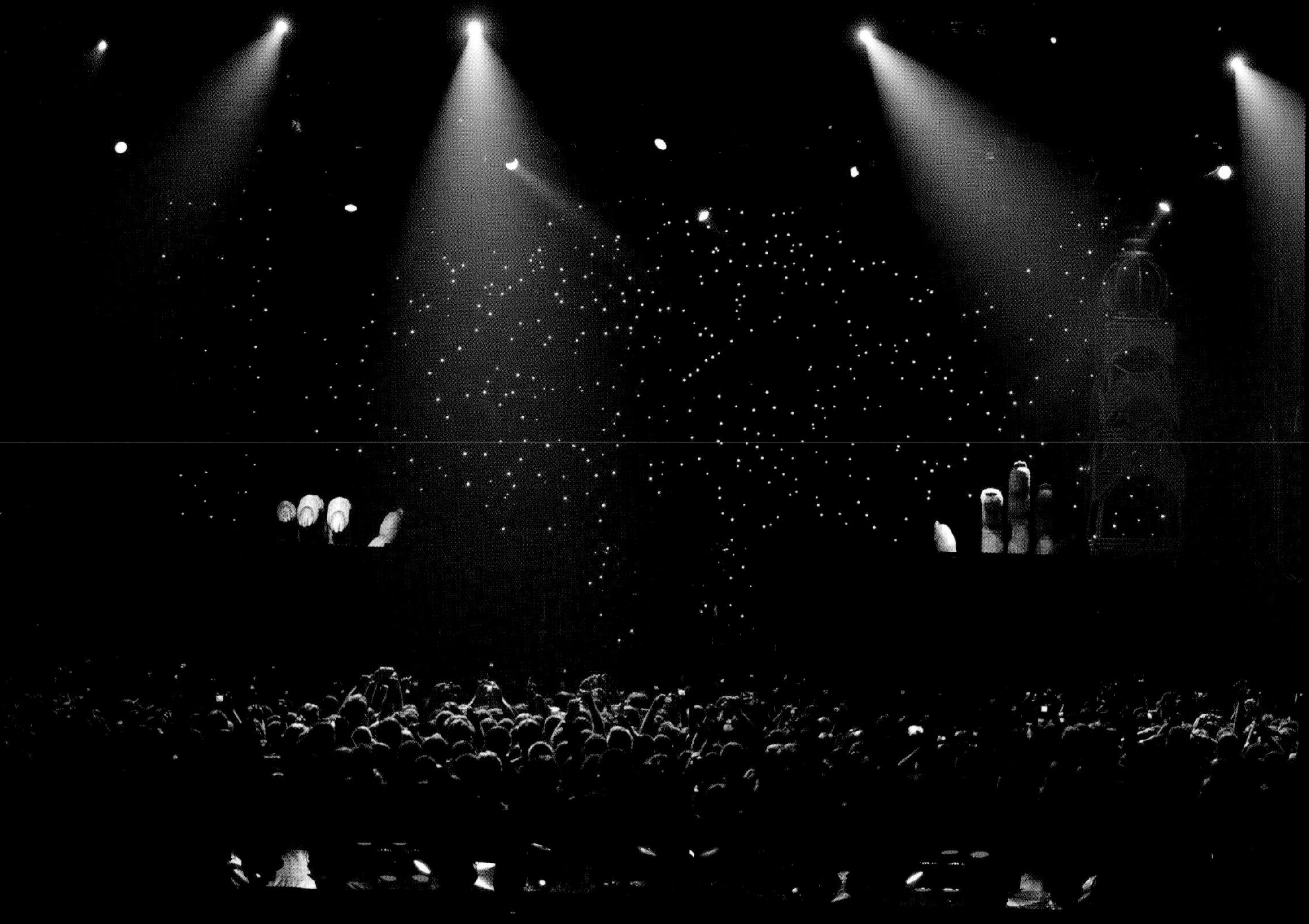

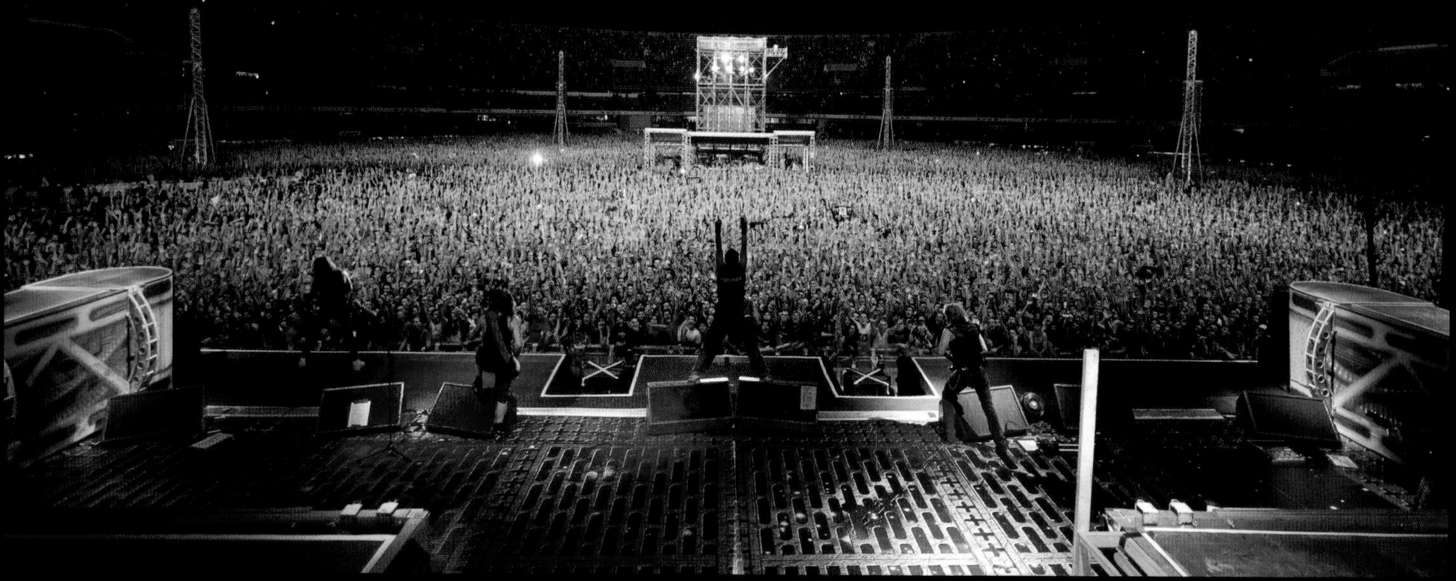

The Killer Krew travel overnight from Sao Paulo by road to build the show in time for the concert that evening – whilst ED FORCE ONE touches down at Rio De Janeiro airport on the day of the show. The band launch on to the stage at 9pm in front of a sold out HSBC Arena.

Seconds into the first song 'The Final Frontier', it is clear there is something very wrong at the front of the audience: the crowd barrier has collapsed, narrowly missing several of IRON MAIDEN's crew in the pit. The band stop playing and Bruce calms the crowd down and instructs everyone to take a step back. The crowd move back and security move in to attempt to fix the barrier. The metal work has splintered and buckled and is beyond repair but fortunately no one is injured. IRON MAIDEN refuse to put the crowd's safety at risk by continuing with the concert and vow to return the following night. With the local promotor to translate, Bruce walks back out on stage and explains the situation to the audience. IRON MAIDEN replace the venue's barrier and the band play to a relieved crowd the next night.

The ED FORCE ONE flight crew are told on approach to Belem that there are massive crowds forming at the airport and security are beginning to voice their concerns. As the excitement gathers in the terminal, military police hastily escort the band directly out of the airport and on to the busy roads of Belem. Flanked by several police outriders, the Maiden cavalcade is soon shadowed by fans in cars and on motorbikes. Approaching the Hilton Hotel, the streets narrow and the sheer size of the crowd celebrating the band's arrival stops the traffic.

The military police already struggling to contain the crowds advise against trying to enter the hotel through the front doors and promptly escort the vehicles to the rear of the hotel. Once in position the police create a human barrier, allowing the band entry through the kitchens. BELOW: Steve is escorted into the hotel by security.

Military police guard ED FORCE ONE, Curitiba, Brazil.

2011 ED FORCE ONE flight crew. Claudine Booth, Ana Belen Ilanes Bravo, Santiago Guerra Arranz, Bruce Dickinson, Kristian Winje, Tom Wilson, Fernando de Freitas, Gloria Vazquez Lopez.

6TH APRIL 2011. Curitiba, Brazil.

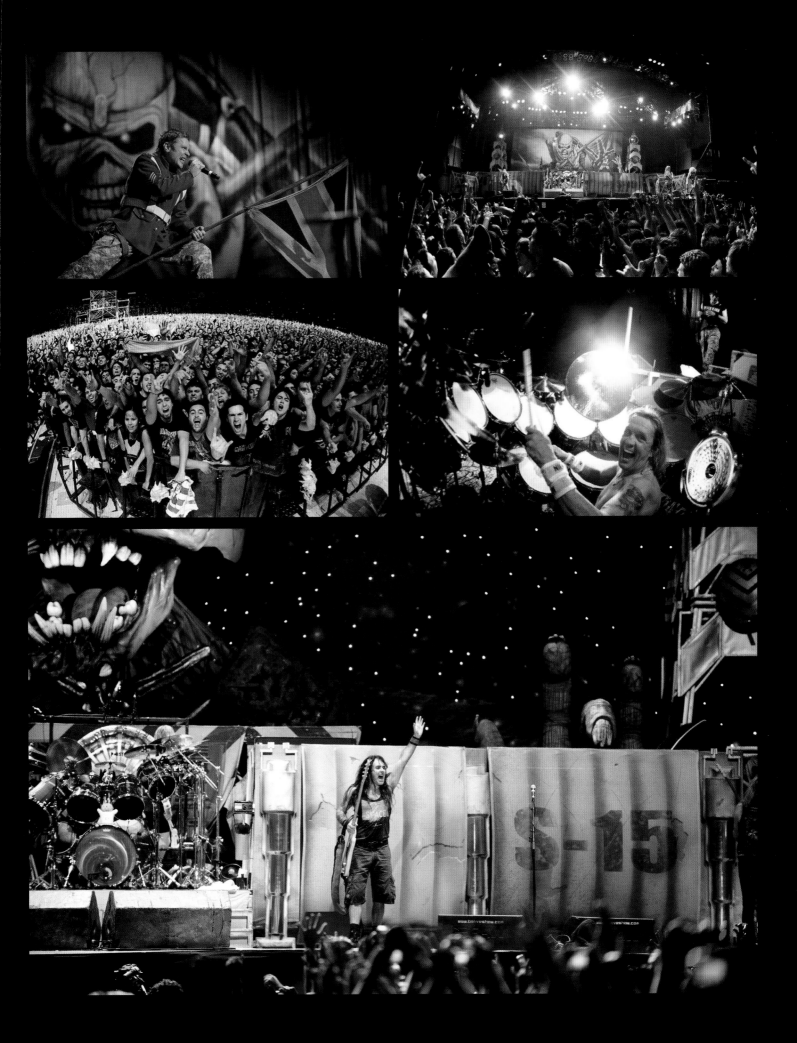

ABOVE: ED FORCE ONE takes off from Buenos Aires.

TOP RIGHT: Dave Murray.

RIGHT: Ground crew at Santiago International Airport greet IRON MAIDEN.

TOP LEFT: Bruce plays the opening bars to 'The Trooper' on a Kazoo as ground transportation takes the band closer to the waiting crowd outside the airport.

ABOVE and LEFT: Bruce Dickinson Kart racing in Santiago.

10TH APRIL 2011. Estadio Nacional, Santiago, Chile.

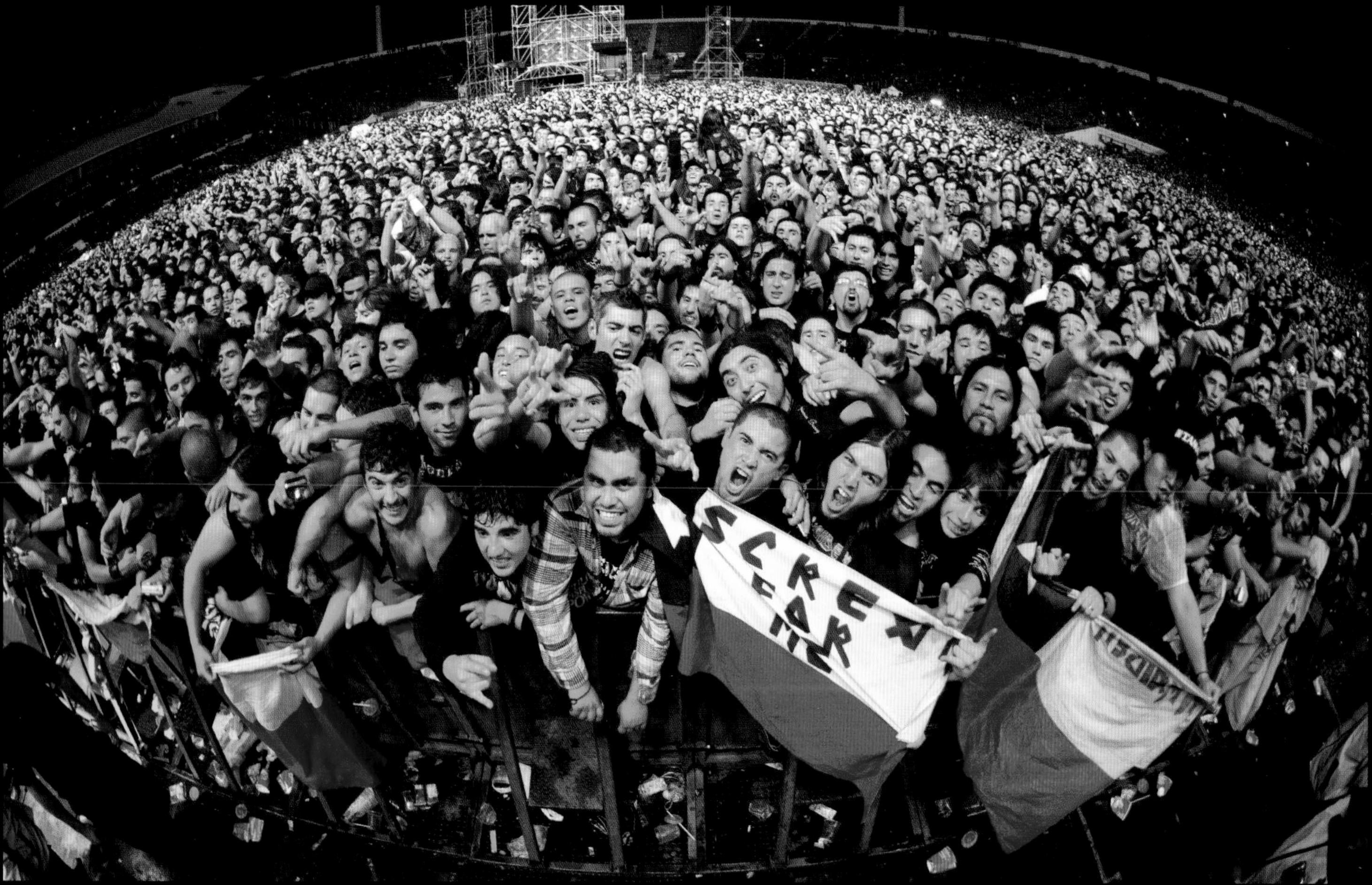

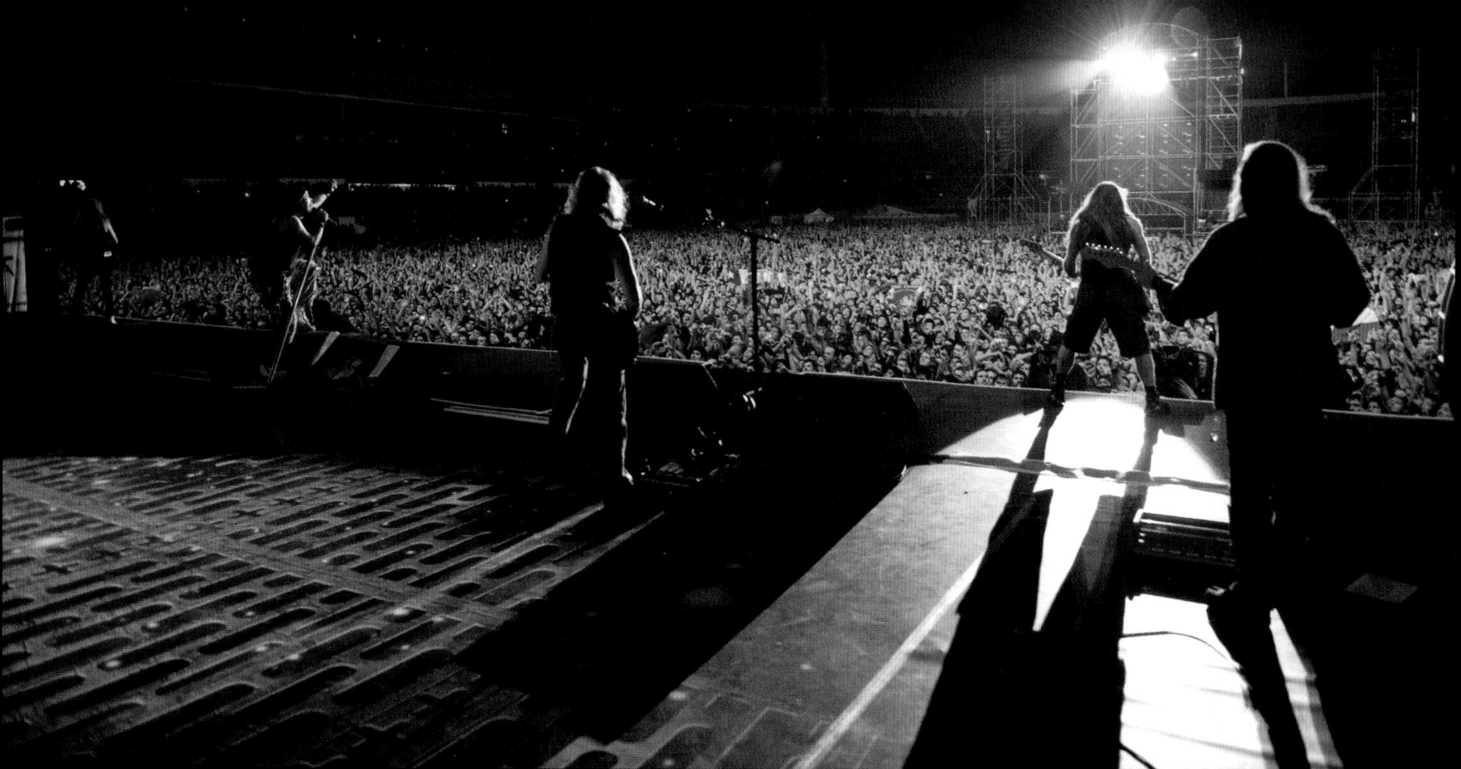

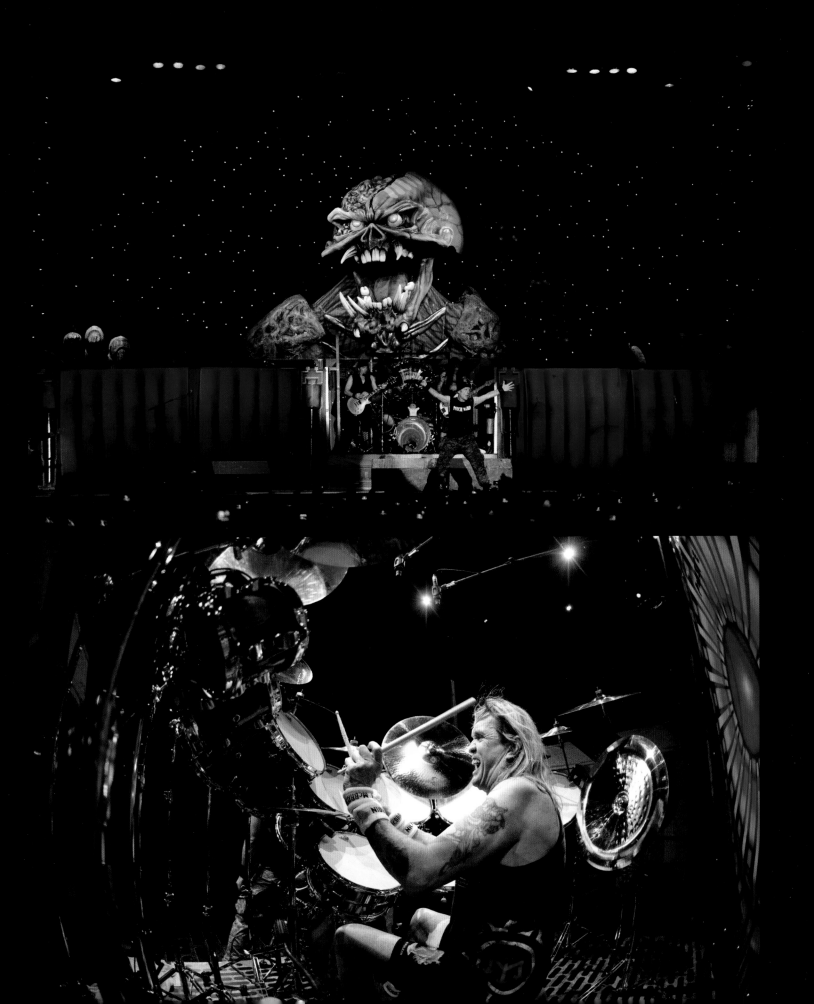

ABOVE: IRON MAIDEN walk on stage for the final show of the Around The World In 66 Days tour.

BELOW: Before introducing the song 'Blood Brothers', Bruce reminds every one that no one is excluded from the Maiden family.

After finishing their Final Frontier tour in London on 6th August 2011, IRON MAIDEN will have played to 2.3 million people, across 5 continents and 37 different countries, having visited a staggering 94 cities on this tour alone.

Bruce flies the final 4574 miles home.

ED FORCE ONE returns to Stansted airport after a gruelling but spectacular 66 day tour.

RIGHT: ED FORCE ONE refuels in Bermuda.

6:45AM: ED FORCE ONE makes its final approach towards Stansted Airport, England.

When I stand before you shining
In the early morning sun
When I feel the engines roar
And I think of what we've done.

Country home far away
As the vapour trails alight
Where I've been tonight
You know I will not stay

(The singer bloke)

6TH AUGUST 2011. O2 Arena, London, England. The Last Show Of The Final Frontier Tour. Over the whole touring period, including both tours, the band have travelled over 200, 000 miles, performing in 127 different cities, visiting 52 countries and playing to over 4 million fans.

IRON MAIDEN WOULD LIKE TO THANK YOU, THE FANS, FOR BEING THERE AND MAKING ALL OF THIS POSSIBLE.

This edition first published in Great Britain in 2011
by Orion Books
an imprint of the Orion Publishing Group Ltd
Orion House, 5 Upper St Martin's Lane,
London WC2H 9EA
An Hachette UK Company

10 9 8 7 6 5 4 3 2 1

'Coming Home' lyrics reproduced courtesy of Universal
Music Publishing International MGB Ltd.

A CIP catalogue record for this book is available
from the British Library.

ISBN: 9781409141365

Printed in Italy

Every effort has been made to fulfil requirements with
regard to reproducing copyright material. The author
and publisher will be glad to rectify any omissions at
the earliest opportunity.

www.orionbooks.co.uk

John McMurtrie would like to thank:

My adorable wife Jo and my superheroes Miles & Archie.

Bruce Dickinson, Steve Harris, Janick Gers,
Dave Murray, Adrian Smith and Nicko McBrain.
Rod Smallwood and Andy Taylor.
Val Janes for all her help and support with this project.
Mary Henry, Pete De Vroome, Aky Najeeb,
Katherine Pedder, Sarah Philp and everyone at
Phantom Management.
Ian Day, Steve Gadd, Dickie Bell, Patrick Ledwith
and all the Iron Maiden Killer Krew.

John Mahon, Fernando de Freitas and all the Astraeus
crew, past and present.
Jeremy Smith at ROCK-IT Cargo.
Jim Eames at ATL .
Everyone at Nikon Worldwide especially Jeremy Gilbert
at Nikon UK for his continued support.
Michael Dover, Rowland White, Jillian Young, Helen Ewing,
Mark Rusher, Mark Stay, Elizabeth Allen and Debbie
Woska at Orion Publishing.
Alex & Emma Smith at Smith & Gilmour.
Roo Ball at Allied Photolabs/Display.
James Isaacs, Alexander Milas, Chris Ingham and
everyone at Metal Hammer Magazine.
Will Luff and Paul Fletcher at EMI.
Chris Ayres.
Matt Munday.
Daniel Lezano.
David Beck at the Flash Centre.
Johnny 'Skywire' Burke.
Dave Pattenden.
Martin Hawkes, Frank 'the shot' Shortt, Sam Dunn,
Scot McFadyen, Kevin Mackenzie and all at Banger Films.
Lauren Harris, Kerry Harris, Richie Faulkner,
Randy Gregg, Tommy McWilliams, Ollie Smith.
Rise to Remain.
Jeannie Aquino and Mike Massimino at NASA Houston.
Monkey and Patten.
The Norse – Hughes, Anstis, Lovett & Bushell.
The McMurtrie family.
Lexar, Adobe Lightroom, Elinchrom and Tamrac.

YOU ALL ROCK!

www.johnmcmurtrie.co.uk
www.ironmaiden.com

DRAWING NUMBER
ATL11630-003

NOTES:

1. PREPARATION OF SURFACES TO BE CARRIED OUT IN ACCORDANCE WITH CHAPTERS 51-21 (METAL COMPONENTS) AND 53-52 (AERODYNAMIC FAIRINGS, NOSE CONE ETC) OF THE AIRCRAFT MAINTENANCE MANUAL.

2. THIS DRAWING DOES NOT COVER THE EXTERNAL MANDATORY MARKINGS, IT DEFINES THE PAINT SCHEME ONLY. MANDATORY MARKINGS TO BE APPLIED IN ACCORDANCE WITH CHAPTER 11 OF THE AIRCRAFT MAINTENANCE MANUAL.

3. LOGOS MUST NOT OBSCURE MANDATORY MARKINGS.

4. WHERE VINYL DECALS ARE USED THE FOLLOWING NOTES ARE TO BE FOLLOWED.

    A) CLEAN AND PREPARE THE AIRCRAFT SURFACES WHERE REQUIRED IN STRICT ACCORDANCE WITH THE CURRENT B757 AIRCRAFT MAINTENANCE MANUAL

    B) CUT AND TRIM DECALS ON INSTALLATION TO SUIT DOORS, WINDOWS AND MOVEABLE SURFACES. POSITION TO GIVE BEST VISUAL PRESENTATION.

    C) ATTACH DECALS IN ACCORDANCE WITH MANUFACTURERS INSTRUCTIONS.

    D) ENSURE THAT RVSM AREA IS CLEAR OF PAINT AND DECALS.

    E) ENSURE THAT PITOT AREA IS CLEAR OF PAINT AND DECALS.

    F) SEAL EDGES OF DECALS BY APPLYING BETWEEN 0.025" AND 0.05" THICKNESS OF CLEAR BMS 10-60 PAINT IN A 1.0" WIDE BAND FALLING 0.5" OVER BOTH THE EDGE OF THE DECAL AND THE AIRCRAFT SKIN.

5. ADJUST LETTER HEIGHT TO SUIT CURVATURE OF AIRCRAFT, LETTERING SHOULD BE AS SEEN ON SHEET 1.

6. DESTINATION LIST TEXT SIZE 2.70 NOM, FONT STYLE 'ARIAL'

7. EXISTING 2 INCH WIDE BAND AROUND DOORS AND ESCAPE HATCHES EXCLUDING DOOR 2 LH AND RH WHERE DOOR BAND IS POSITIONED OUTSIDE DOOR SURROUND AS SHOWN ON SHEET 2 DETAILS C AND D IN COLOUR INDICATED ON COLOUR TABLE.

8. EXISTING 2 INCH WIDE BAND AND ALL PLACARDS TO BE REMOVED FROM DOORS 3 AND 4 AND REPLACED BY 'NO ACCESS TO PASSENGER COMPARTMENT' PLACARD ITEM 10.

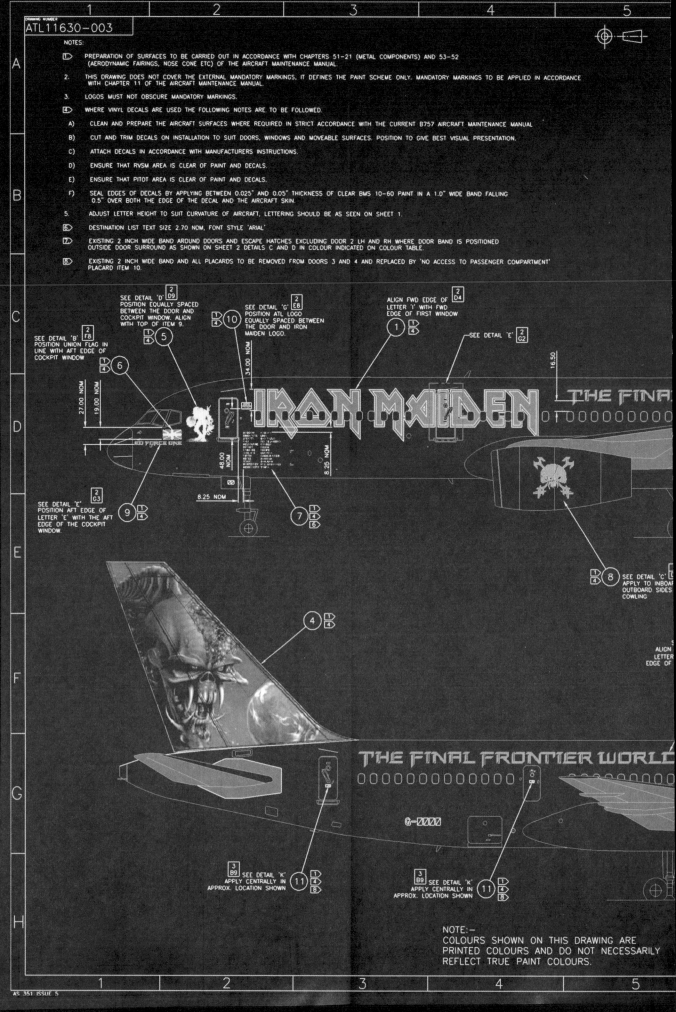

SEE DETAIL 'D'
POSITION EQUALLY SPACED BETWEEN THE DOOR AND COCKPIT WINDOW. ALIGN WITH TOP OF ITEM 9.

SEE DETAIL 'G'
POSITION ATL LOGO EQUALLY SPACED BETWEEN THE DOOR AND IRON MAIDEN LOGO.

ALIGN FWD EDGE OF LETTER 'I' WITH FWD EDGE OF FIRST WINDOW

SEE DETAIL 'E'

SEE DETAIL 'B'
POSITION UNION FLAG IN LINE WITH AFT EDGE OF COCKPIT WINDOW

SEE DETAIL 'E'
POSITION AFT EDGE OF LETTER 'E' WITH THE AFT EDGE OF THE COCKPIT WINDOW.

SEE DETAIL 'C'
APPLY TO INBOARD OUTBOARD SIDES COWLING

THE FINAL FRONTIER WORLD

G-⌀⌀⌀⌀

SEE DETAIL 'K'
APPLY CENTRALLY IN APPROX. LOCATION SHOWN

SEE DETAIL 'K'
APPLY CENTRALLY IN APPROX. LOCATION SHOWN

NOTE:-
COLOURS SHOWN ON THIS DRAWING ARE PRINTED COLOURS AND DO NOT NECESSARILY REFLECT TRUE PAINT COLOURS.